Mediterranean Passages

Mediterranean

The
University of
North Carolina
Press
Chapel Hill

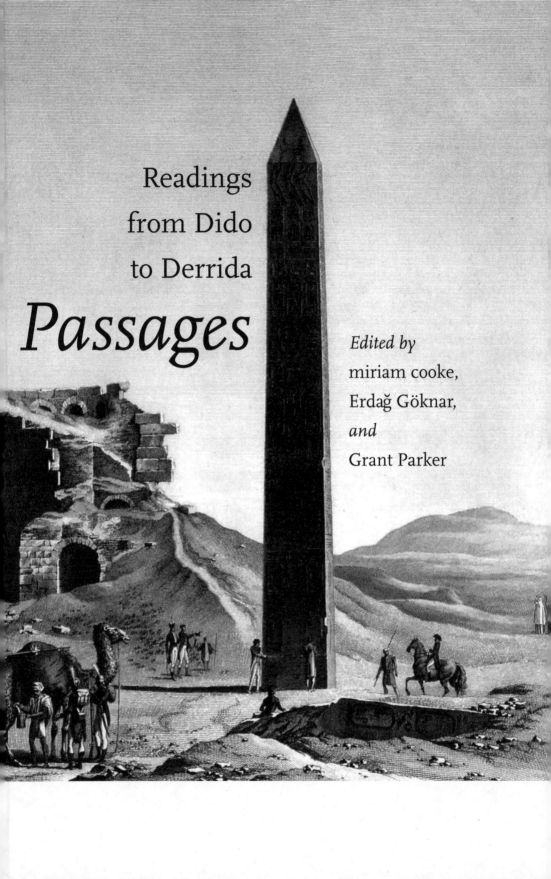

Readings
from Dido
to Derrida

Passages

Edited by
miriam cooke,
Erdağ Göknar,
and
Grant Parker

© 2008 The University of North Carolina Press
All rights reserved
Manufactured in the United States of America
Designed by Kimberly Bryant
Set in Scala and Scala Sans by Tseng Information
Systems, Inc.

*The paper in this book meets the guidelines for permanence
and durability of the Committee on Production Guidelines for
Book Longevity of the Council on Library Resources.*

Library of Congress Cataloging-in-Publication Data
Mediterranean passages : readings from Dido to Derrida /
edited by miriam cooke, Erdağ Göknar, and Grant Parker.
— 1st ed.
p. cm.
Includes bibliographical references and index.
ISBN 978-0-8078-3183-0 (cloth : alk. paper) —
ISBN 978-0-8078-5871-4 (pbk. : alk. paper)
1. Mediterranean Region—History—Sources.
2. Mediterranean Region—Civilization. I. cooke, miriam.
II. Göknar, Erdağ M. III. Parker, Grant Richard, 1967–
DE3.M347 2008
909′.09822—dc22
2008005821

cloth   12 11 10 09 08   5 4 3 2 1
paper   12 11 10 09 08   5 4 3 2 1

The material for the maps in this book originated on the
Interactive Ancient Mediterranean Website (<http://
iam.classics.unc.edu>). It has been used here under the
terms of IAM's fair use policy. © 1998, Interactive Ancient
Mediterranean.

Contents

Thematic Contents

WOMEN

Preface

The present volume is the culmination of years of discussions and debate about the Mediterranean. It has involved many colleagues, at Duke University and beyond, beginning in the late 1990s with the "Oceans Connect" project funded by the Ford Foundation and held under the aegis of Duke University's Center for International Studies.

During regular interdisciplinary meetings, colloquia, and conversations, the Mediterranean Study Group came up with the idea of assembling a sourcebook that would demonstrate our conception of bodies of water as entities that create cultural exchange, and of the Mediterranean as a highly varied yet also integrated space.

Mediterranean Passages assembles texts and images that could provide the basis for an interdisciplinary and chronological curriculum on the Mediterranean world but that can also be used more broadly. It will also appeal to any reader interested in travel writing. Although specific chapters may be used by classicists or medievalists or modernists, we believe that *Mediterranean Passages* will be most useful and most interesting when read as a whole. Our goal has been to challenge the usual divisions between periods and regions rather than reiterate them.

We are deeply grateful for major contributions, both conceptual and substantive, from Julia Clancy-Smith, Javier Krauel, Bruce Lawrence, Michele Longino, and Luk van Rompay who worked so closely with us during earlier stages of the process. They were generous with their time, advice, and knowledge as we experimented with different approaches. Each was deeply involved in the shaping of this book, and each provided one or more selections that allowed us to put together the puzzle of the Mediterranean over time and space. Without their input this book would not have been possible.

We thank Taieb Belghazi, Sadok Boubaker, Jamil Chaker, Randi Deguilhem, and Nabiha Jerad who traveled to Duke University from the Mediterranean to consult with us on the volume as it was taking shape.

Eric Meyers, Walter Mignolo, Aman Nadhiri, Maureen Quilligan, and Francis Newton each provided suggestions, and in some cases actual texts, and we are grateful to them for their input.

Special thanks to Jason Aftosmis, Peter Burian, Diskin Clay, Micah Myers, and Francis Newton for contributing new translations.

We would also like to acknowledge the suggestions, comments, and help of various kinds from Evelyne Accad, Sahar Amer, Carla Antonaccio, Kalman Bland, Giovanna Ceserani, George Christie, Sheila Dillon, Janet Edwards, Elaine Fantham, Kevin Fogg, Banu Gökarıksel, Sherif Hetata, Ranjana Khanna, Tabea Linhard, Adriano Palma, Orhan Pamuk, Olga Richmond, Lou Ruprecht, Nawal El Saadawi, Samia Serageldin, Marcel Tetel, Monika Truemper, Paul Vieille, and the Duke University Mediterranean Study Group.

Many thanks to our students: Ginny Jones, Stephen Schmulenson, Max Fosque, and Khaled Talhouni.

For generous support of the project from the beginning, our thanks to Paul and Eula Hoff and to the Duke University Center for International Studies and especially its director, Rob Sikorski.

The responsibility for the final form of the volume rests with the editors.

Mediterranean Passages

Introduction

The Mediterranean is a sea, a territory, but above all it is a space of mobility linking people and places. Geographical and historical perspectives have generally subordinated water to land. Within a conventional understanding of world regions and area studies, where land defines spatial expanses and their boundaries, a body of water like the Mediterranean might be split into discrete parts. One possibility is continental, so that the Sea connects Africa, Europe, and Asia. A second is peninsular, focusing on the Anatolian, Balkan, Italian, and Iberian peninsulas. A third highlights its multitude of islands, not only the five major ones—Sicily, Sardinia, Cyprus, Corsica, and Crete—but also the many archipelagoes. An alternative land-based approach would accentuate the many nation-states making up the regions around the rim.

The sea-based perspective of this volume highlights connections, confluences, and crossings. Travel and migration, trade routes, the distribution of labor and capital, military conquest, and cultural exchange have produced the Mediterranean as a single but also multiple geographical spaces. Over millennia, ideas, texts, and art have been circulated by pirates, refugees, converts, or slaves. From the Carthaginian queen Dido to the French Algerian philosopher Jacques Derrida, from the Berber conqueror Tariq ibn Ziyad to the American journalist I. F. Stone, *Mediterranean Passages* juxtaposes the voices and experiences of people who have inhabited or crossed the Sea since before 1200 B.C.E.

The Mediterranean has brought the three major monotheistic religions (Judaism, Christianity, and Islam) and the three continents of Africa, Asia, and Europe into contact. Thus the Mediterranean might be viewed as something approximating what literary critic Mary Louise Pratt called a contact zone. Contact zones bring together people and cultures "previously separated by geographic and historical disjunctures" (*Imperial Eyes*, 7). They change centers into margins; they foreground the logs of voyages over the histories of individual places, and, like Odysseus in Constantine Cavafy's poem "Ithaca," they emphasize ports of call over single destinations. Such exchanges and translations forge Mediterranean identities that are at once connected across the Sea and rooted in particular places—identities that are not predicated on single languages and territories or on myths of a timeless nation-state.

Clichés such as Roman universalism, the Grand Tour, or the triad of cereals, grapes, and olives have often been invoked as ways of representing the Mediterranean. By contrast, the focus here is on the networks of exchange that the Sea and its surrounding microclimates have fostered and necessitated. Such exchanges have involved tangible objects as much as ideas and beliefs. Stories of cultural, social, and economic interactions among constituencies reflect a deep history of connections and conversions. They have involved far-flung coastlines and the contexts of subsidiary seas, including the Adriatic, the Aegean, and the Libyan.

Mediterranean Passages includes stories that the grand narratives of history have erased. Women and men have crossed these waters for many, sometimes contradictory, reasons: some travel to pay homage to religious sites and peoples, others for economic gain; some journey for pleasure, others for conquest, and the less fortunate to escape persecution. Whereas Egeria's fourth-century C.E. travels to Jerusalem and other holy places of Christianity were undertaken as a pilgrimage, the twelfth-century Crusaders went there to wrest holy sites from Muslims for Christendom. Military generals Tariq ibn Ziyad and Napoleon Bonaparte traversed the Mediterranean at the beginning of the eighth and the end of the eighteenth century, bringing their own notions of universal civilization. Thinkers like Pythagoras and Ibn Battuta have long traveled to learn from masters in cities across the Sea. Individuals such as Evliya Çelebi in the seventeenth century and Lady Wortley Montagu in the eighteenth prefigured today's Club Med tourist.

Others have traveled under compulsion. Forced out of their homes, exiles hope that some day the keys saved across generations will slip back into their locks. The Jews who escaped Jerusalem after the destruction of the Second Temple in 70 C.E. looked back to 586 B.C.E. and the destruction of the Temple to understand the catastrophe. Both events resonate with the expulsion of the Jews from Granada at the end of the fifteenth century and from Europe in the middle of the twentieth century. Mediterranean migrants today mirror such conditions of exile.

CONCEPTUALIZING THE MEDITERRANEAN

In Plato's *Phaedo*, Socrates imagines human society living "like frogs and ants round a pond" (109B). The point is cosmological, namely to contrast the hugeness of the world with the relative insignificance of human habitation within it. But it is tempting to see in Socrates' phrase an expression of the Mediterranean as a single, coherent region since at least the fifth century B.C.E.

2   Different contexts, scholarly, artistic, and popular, have led to the

use of different designations for this transnational arena. For example, Shlomo Goitein writes that none of the Geniza documents dating back to tenth-century Cairo uses the word "Mediterranean" per se: "It was 'The Sea' par excellence, and as such, of course, it is mentioned in our records countless times" (*Mediterranean Society*, 42). However, the first use of the term in the way we now know it goes back to the seventh-century C.E. *Etymologies* of Isidore of Seville: "It is called *mediterraneus* because it flows through the middle of the earth."

During the second half of the twentieth century, some prominent intellectuals sought new ways to approach trans-Mediterranean connections. Peregrine Horden and Nicholas Purcell, Fernand Braudel, Shlomo Goitein, and the Rencontres d'Averroès scholars produced influential works reassessing the nature of the Sea since antiquity.

The Corrupting Sea is a study of the premodern-era Mediterranean from the second millennium B.C.E. to the later Middle Ages. Distinguishing between history *of* and *in* the Mediterranean, Horden and Purcell make a strong case for the significance of environmental history in making sense of the Mediterranean. Their thesis centers on two contrasting but mutually dependent concepts, namely *fragmentation* of the landscape into microregions and *connectivity* between them. The region's variegated ecology provides the major impulse to interaction and exchange. *The Corrupting Sea* presents ancient ideas about the centrality of the sea to the cultures of those sharing its shores: "In the ancient geographical tradition the sea shapes the land, not the other way about. [. . .] This logical priority of the sea [. . .] resulted principally from the centrality of the sea to communications" (11). Ancient thinking provides points of departure for their work and also for ours.

This conception of the Mediterranean owes much to the influential work of Fernand Braudel. His multivolume study *The Mediterranean and the Mediterranean World in the Age of Philip II* (first published in French in 1949) situated the tumultuous sixteenth century within the long history of the Sea and accented the role of human geography in the unfolding of world history. For Braudel what mattered were not individual events but the processes of the *longue durée*. He gave weight to structures of everyday life, to technology and interreligious exchange rather than to diplomatic and political histories, with their slant toward elites. The environment is not merely the background of human activity, but rather it is something with which humans have a complex and dynamic relationship. Braudel's sixteenth-century Mediterranean, with its focus on economic relations, anticipates the representation of today's Sea, which is again divided between the northern littoral—

3

modern, urban, diverse, rich, and powerful—that is more European than Mediterranean, and the southern coast—traditional, rural, nomadic, homogeneous, and poor—that is more African than Mediterranean.

An equally monumental but contrasting study is Shlomo Goitein's *A Mediterranean Society: The Jewish Communities of the Arab World as Portrayed in the Documents of the Cairo Geniza* (1967–93). Another multivolume history, it recounts the stories of people who lived on and around the Sea during Europe's Middle Ages. Through the extraordinary archive of documents discovered in the *geniza* (sealed depository) of a synagogue in Cairo, Goitein opened up a new history of the period. Merchants' receipts, letters between family members separated by circumstances, and pilgrims' and scholars' reports record centuries of crossings, exchanges, and networks linking people of different religions, cultures, and nations across the Sea. Medieval mariners moved around its waters easily: "A journey from Spain to Egypt or from Marseilles to the Levant was a humdrum experience, about which a seasoned traveler would not waste a word. Commuting regularly between Tunisia or Sicily or even Spain and the eastern shores of the Mediterranean was nothing exceptional. [. . .] The Mediterranean was a *pontos euxeinos*, a friendly, inviting sea" (1:42–43). Lists of traveling scholars from France, Palestine, Spain, and North Africa reveal a history of cosmopolitan exchange in centers of learning like Cairo, Istanbul, Tyre, Aleppo, Venice, and Fez.

In the late 1990s, the Rencontres d'Averroès, a group of Mediterranean scholars in the natural and social sciences, met to contest the persisting notion of a Mediterranean split between the Greco-Latin rationality of the "enlightened" North and the faith-mindedness of the "superstitious" South. They drew inspiration from Averroès, a twelfth-century Andalusian philosopher credited with reviving Aristotelian thought and combining faith with reason in his writings. Algerian historian of science Roshdi Rashed calls Averroès "a representative of this borderless culture that developed around the Mediterranean axis of creativity and exchange" ("Les Sciences," 73). Acknowledging the influence of Aristotle on Muslim philosophers, Rashed calls for a corresponding appreciation of Averroès's influence on Latin, Hebraic, Byzantine, and Arab philosophies: "Here is the universal dimension of this culture of exchanges. Historians [. . .] in Mediterranean cultures should reject all temptations to culture-centrism and linear history . . . remaining attentive to the dialectic between permanence and ruptures" (75, 81). Rashed suggests that the history of cultural connections in the Mediterranean enables a special kind of networked thinking that refuses dichotomies

4

and borders, and he proposes a history that looks at the nineteenth century through the prism of the twelfth to bring all littorals into a single conversation.

The Mediterranean of Braudel, Horden and Purcell, Goitein, and the Rencontres d'Averroès has provided the framework for *Mediterranean Passages*. Culture and trade have long connected the numerous nodes of this liquid continent. Movement, exchanges, contagions, and conflicts turn boundaries into zones of contact.

Few regions have inspired so much artistic production celebrating their beauty and wide appeal. Since antiquity the Mediterranean has attracted visitors to its shores, where at midday everything seems to stop and meridional time takes over. In the twenty-first century, Club Med clients repeat the experiences of earlier sojourners, and extend them. One can now travel to a "Mediterranean" in any of seventy locales as far-flung as Cancún, Japan, and French Polynesia. The creation of such resorts throughout the world turns this Sea into an emblem of luxury and leisure. Club Med began on the island of Mallorca in 1950, and its remarkable and growing popularity hints at the seduction of the Sea and highlights its central place in the imagination of modern tourists. Club Med pleasure has become an exportable commodity available outside of workaday time, a place that promises freedoms unavailable at home. Such idyllic notions obscure other stories of shipwrecks, plagues, conquests, and exiles and also the project to plant a European pleasure palace on the beaches of Gaza (see ill. 30).

Our approach juxtaposes romantic and violent narratives, in which water both connects and *dis*connects places. Take, for example, the massive earthquake of 365 C.E. that changed the topography of two widely separated places: new land emerged out of the waters in southern Crete, while many settlements on the northeastern shore of Libya were destroyed. This catastrophic event revealed a connection between these two places that is typically obscured by hundreds of miles of uninterrupted water. Today, the splendid harbor of Cyrene at Apollonia remains sunk below the surface of the sea, its only traces being two tiny land masses a mile off the shore. The settings of Greek mythology, stretching beyond the Aegean, are further proof of the connections and affiliations more powerful than the waters that separate such far-flung areas.

DOCUMENTING CONNECTIONS

"Ancient Diasporas" (twelfth to third century B.C.E.) begin our encounter with the Mediterranean at the end of the Bronze Age. The arrival of the mysterious Sea Peoples marks a new stage in the history of a connected sea. The term "Diaspora" denotes the Jews' Babylonian exile in the sixth century B.C.E. that resonates with other movements of dispersed populations. By 1200 B.C.E., despite the difficulty and danger of seafaring at that time, men and women had long plied these waters in search of power, or sustenance, or pleasure, or adventure, yet many of their stories have been lost. Looking beyond the familiar sources of Jews, Greeks, and Romans, we have searched for a range of ancient peoples, like the Phoenicians, whose defeat was not only military but also discursive: they are known more from the historical accounts of their enemies than from their own chronicles. Even if there is no real way of righting the imbalance of sources, these documents and their accompanying images allow us to signal the silences.

The second chapter, "*Mare Nostrum*: Our Sea" (third century B.C.E. to seventh century C.E.), highlights the five centuries of Roman domination over "Our Sea" dating from the mid–second century B.C.E. People crisscrossed the Sea with staple and luxury goods under the Roman emporium but only with permission from the Roman state. During the imperial era, Alexandria supplied distant Rome with grain and other staples, and on occasion it also supplied obelisks for display in the city's public spaces. For Egyptian pharaohs, as for Roman emperors and nineteenth-century colonial leaders, obelisks symbolized imperial power. By virtue of its longevity and public visibility, an obelisk exported to Rome (like those later taken to Istanbul, Paris, London, and New York) linked different human histories. Its very relocation impelled one to consider the way in which it was appropriated.

The third chapter, "*Barzakh*: The Waters Between" (eighth to fifteenth centuries), describes liminal states of separation and connection between political and religious communities. Beginning with Tariq ibn Ziyad's conquests into Spain in the eighth century, Islamic states expanded steadily for most of the Middle Ages, culminating in the conquest of Constantinople by the Ottomans in 1453. From the Straits of Gibraltar to the Straits of the Bosphorus, the Sea had come to accommodate a new religion and new centers of power. Islam's encounter with medieval Europe established new borders that sometimes separated nations and at other times formed new centers with their own new margins. One feature of this period was the refinement of Muslim cartography, particularly in the twelfth century. This time span was marked not only by violent border crossings but also by multiple translations, including the transfer of Greek philosophy and science into Arabic under the leadership of the ninth-century Muslim Abbasid caliph Harun al-Rashid in Baghdad. A century or two later these Arabic translations were being rendered into Latin, with North Africans such as Constantine the African bringing a mass of medical knowledge to southern Italy. The Crusades and Muslim responses drew and redrew communal borders. However, even when tensions were at their most severe, people, goods, and ideas continued to travel through the Mediterranean. Pilgrims, merchants, and scholars expected to find in it a network of hospitality.

The "Grand Tours" of Chapter 4 link Columbus's 1492 transatlantic voyage, which some consider to mark the beginning of modernity, with the northern European discovery of a romantic Mediterranean in the 1700s and also with Napoleon Bonaparte's invasion of Egypt at the close of the eighteenth century. In this chapter, writings about voyages of "discovery," battles for hegemony over sea routes, and colonial conquests accompany elite accounts of early tourism: these travelogues come not only from the familiar eighteenth-century Grand Tour but also from less expected sources such as a seventeenth-century Ottoman's tale of adventure. The Grand Tour, a rite of passage for aristocratic young men, focused travel upon classical ruins and artifacts. In the later eighteenth century, a more scholarly approach to the study of antiquities was emerging in German universities. Northern Europeans saw Italy and Greece as the natural homes of classical culture and claimed to be its heirs. In 1798, southerly journeys assumed a new aspect when Napoleon Bonaparte led his forces into Egypt. This short-lived tour fell short of its colonial aims but marked the birth of modern Orientalism. Napoleon modeled his campaign on the earlier conquests by Alexander the Great, for whom in turn the Achaemenid rulers of Persia provided a precedent.

The ambivalent pleasures of the Grand Tour ironically foreshadow the growing violence of "Epic Encounters" between colonialists and local resistance movements that occurred during the nineteenth and early twentieth centuries. This chapter presents a new stage in Mediterranean power relations, documenting variations on the *mission civilisatrice* in relation to inhabitants of the South and East. Early Orientalist representations of the Ottoman Empire begin to appear. The nationalization of the Balkans and countries in the eastern Mediterranean caused the exile or massacre of millions and anticipated the violence that accompanied the birth of other nation-states. The disintegration of the Ottoman Empire after World War I brought national consciousness into play. Anticolonial movements gained momentum in the 1930s and 1940s, at a time when British, French, and Italian colonists began a process of repatriation. National liberation movements, furthermore, spawned other reform ventures, notably women's rights activism. The chapter ends with Jews escaping the Holocaust from northern ports to the eastern Mediterranean.

The "Global Pond" of Chapter 6 sees the establishment of the new Jewish state of Israel and the exile of Palestinians. Amid a revolution in transport and, later, information technology, the world was turning into a global village and the Sea into a "Global Pond." Travel was democratized and globalized, with people and objects moving around at unprecedented speeds. Planes and hydrofoils brought mass tourism to classical and modern sites. At the same time, postindependence crises on the southern and eastern coasts caused mass migrations that would change the face of western Europe. Migrants established ethnic, national, and religious enclaves in port cities like Marseilles and Naples, long-standing multicultural nodes, and in European capitals. Most of these migrants remained linked to their home countries through transnational networks and political allegiances.

The visual essay offers a synchronic reading of the Mediterranean. While the images relate to specific histories, they have been paired to highlight influences from one place to another and from one period to another. Together they invite the reader to think anew about the themes that unify this volume and to resist the temptation to isolate regions, events, and people within specific time frames. Placed at the midpoint of this volume, Janus-faced, they point backward and forward across the millennia. The thematic table of contents provides another organizational framework. The eight themes are not meant to be exhaustive or exclusive but rather to invite the reader to reconsider disparate texts through new juxtapositions.

Mediterranean Passages covers some three thousand years of transactional networks in what Halikarnas Balıkçısı and others have called the sixth continent. This liquid continent is both single and multiple: essentially one, it has often been reconfigured and fragmented by various imperial and national desires.

In the process of compiling *Mediterranean Passages* we have had to make difficult choices. We hope, however, that the texts and images we have selected will inspire travelers and students to imagine connections between the farthest reaches of the Sea. We invite them to look below the concrete of modern cities and the rubble of archaeological sites in order to uncover their interconnectedness and to decipher the extraordinary palimpsest that is the Mediterranean.

8

WORKS CITED

Braudel, Fernand. *The Mediterranean and the Mediterranean World in the Age of Philip II.* 2 vols. Trans. Siân Reynolds. New York: Harper and Row, 1972.

Goitein, Shlomo D. *A Mediterranean Society: The Jewish Communities of the Arab World as Portrayed in the Documents of the Geniza.* 6 vols. Berkeley: University of California Press, 1967–93.

Horden, Peregrine, and Nicholas Purcell. *The Corrupting Sea: A Study of Mediterranean History.* Malden, Ma.: Blackwell, 2000.

Pratt, Mary Louise. *Imperial Eyes: Travel Writing and Transculturation.* New York: Routledge, 1992.

Rashed, Roshdi. "Les Sciences en Méditerranée, une Question Optique." In *Rencontres d'Averroès. La Mediterranée entre la raison et la foi,* edited by Thierry Fabre, 73–82. Marseilles: Babel, 1994.

Ancient Diasporas

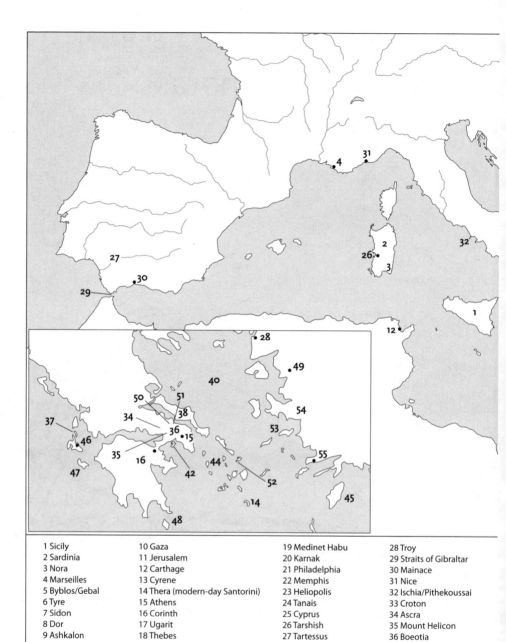

1 Sicily	10 Gaza	19 Medinet Habu	28 Troy
2 Sardinia	11 Jerusalem	20 Karnak	29 Straits of Gibraltar
3 Nora	12 Carthage	21 Philadelphia	30 Mainace
4 Marseilles	13 Cyrene	22 Memphis	31 Nice
5 Byblos/Gebal	14 Thera (modern-day Santorini)	23 Heliopolis	32 Ischia/Pithekoussai
6 Tyre	15 Athens	24 Tanais	33 Croton
7 Sidon	16 Corinth	25 Cyprus	34 Ascra
8 Dor	17 Ugarit	26 Tarshish	35 Mount Helicon
9 Ashkalon	18 Thebes	27 Tartessus	36 Boeotia

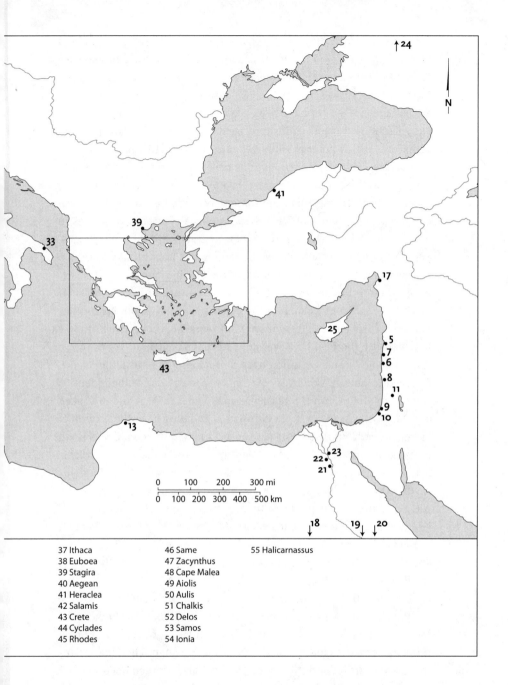

37 Ithaca
38 Euboea
39 Stagira
40 Aegean
41 Heraclea
42 Salamis
43 Crete
44 Cyclades
45 Rhodes

46 Same
47 Zacynthus
48 Cape Malea
49 Aiolis
50 Aulis
51 Chalkis
52 Delos
53 Samos
54 Ionia

55 Halicarnassus

Around 1200 B.C.E. the complex civilizations of Hittites, Egyptians, and Mycenaeans collapsed in the space of only a few decades. Bronze Age cities of the eastern Mediterranean were destroyed, and long-distance exchange was curbed; the use of lavish grave goods in burials declined. Such changes seem to have been accompanied by both military raids and mass migration. The most precise dates emerge from Egyptian inscriptions, which point to violent events between 1232 and 1188 B.C.E. Archaeological finds confirm that the collapse was a process drawn out over the twelfth century B.C.E., when bronze began to replace iron for everyday use. During this time foreigners settled on the eastern seaboard, particularly in northern Syria-Palestine (Canaan), as well as in Sicily and Sardinia. Among these new arrivals were the Phoenicians, known in the Hebrew Bible as Canaanites or Philistines, who in due course would become a major force in the Mediterranean.

What motivated these changes? Egyptian inscriptions of Ramses III mention "Sea Peoples" such as the Peleset and Tjeker, but such information raises as many questions as it answers. This collective term was first used by the French Egyptologist Gaston Maspero (1846–1916). These people came from different areas, including Anatolia, the Aegean and Mediterranean islands. Scholars have speculated as to their identity, suggesting, for example, that the Denyen were the Daunoi, the Shekelesh the Sicels, the Peleset the Philistines, and the Tjeker the Teucroi of Homer's *Iliad*, but there is no consensus on these matters. Greek myth recounts an invasion or "return" of the sons of Herakles, or Dorians. While archaeologists and historians do not agree about whether this myth reflects any historical event or process, it may indicate the movement of bands of people from the north into southern Greece. Amid several theories, ancient and modern, the identity of the Sea Peoples remains uncertain. More certain is that there were widespread political and cultural disruptions and movements of populations at the end of the Bronze Age.

Whatever the exact course of events, the main beneficiaries were the Phoenicians, who established themselves as traders throughout the Mediterranean, based initially in timber-rich areas of the eastern Mediterranean coast, including today's Syria and Lebanon. The Phoenicians themselves left no narrative accounts and only a limited documentary record, of which the Nora stone and Marseilles inscription are significant examples. The consequent difficulty of reconstructing their history, not to mention the modern implications of that history, has led to controversy in recent times concerning cultural origins and racial descent. It is ironic that the Phoenicians, from whom the Greeks acquired their alphabet probably in the eighth century B.C.E., are themselves better known from the often hostile viewpoint of others than from their own writings.

The earlier part of the period covered in this chapter saw the establishment of colonies and trading posts by Phoenicians, far beyond their eastern port cities of Byblos, Sidon, and Tyre. The most famous of these was at Carthage in modern-day Tunisia, which remained a major city throughout antiquity, its origins linked with the mythological queen Dido. By the start of the second century B.C.E., the Carthaginians would lose out to the Romans as main traders of the Mediterranean, following a lengthy series of conflicts, and Carthage itself would be destroyed in 146 B.C.E.

Another group whose documents and histories are reflected here are the Greeks. Like the Phoenicians, they established communities of their own between roughly 750 and 450 B.C.E., particularly in Sicily and southern Italy (called *Magna Graecia*, or "Great Greece"). Much of this westward momentum came from the island of Euboea, whose city-states produced many of the new settlers. The mythical travels of Odysseus point to the connected nature of the Aegean and other parts of the Sea in the late eighth century B.C.E. The foundation decree of Cyrene in modern-day Libya legislated the establishment of a settlement from the volcanic island of Santorini in the seventh century B.C.E.: it was rearticulated three centuries later. When, in the fourth century B.C.E., the philosopher Aristotle theorized about human communities, he recognized that proximity to the Mediterranean brought advantages to his hypothetical city-state (*polis*). But he acknowledged counterarguments that the Sea brought corruption because of the influx of persons and goods.

But commerce and colonization were by no means the only kinds of travel in the early Iron Age Mediterranean. A well-known instance of violent displacement took place in 586 B.C.E. when the Jews were conquered by the Neo-Babylonians under King Nebuchadnezzar and their sacred site, Solomon's Temple at Jerusalem, was destroyed. For decades several thousands of Jews lived as an exiled community in Babylon and other Diaspora centers in Babylonia, Egypt, and Persia. In exile, Jews reflected on their past, and one result of that reflection was the editing of the Bible as it was known at the time, namely the Pentateuch (first five books) and the prophets. In 539, however, the Persian king Cyrus crushed the Neo-Babylonian Empire and allowed the Jews to return to Jerusalem, where they built the Second Temple. This exile proved to be paradigmatic in the formation of Jewish history and identity. It would also produce the definitive, historic experience of Diaspora, a term that invites comparison with other forced movements of people throughout history. The movement of people into and out of Palestine in this period is thus central to the first of the three monotheistic faiths of the Mediterranean.

The loss of Judaean independence under the Persian Empire allowed Greek traders and settlers to establish themselves on the Levantine coast. Among the trading posts (*emporia*) established were Dor, Ashkalon, and Gaza; Tyre remained a strong Phoenician enclave, which is why the prophet Ezekiel condemned it. Attic wares and Greek-style fortifications and construction techniques became a permanent part of regional material culture for centuries to come, an indication of the traffic in goods generating from and circulating among Athens, Corinth, and other city-states.

The Sea Peoples
Letters from Ugarit (ca. 1200 B.C.E.) and Inscriptions of Ramses III (1188 B.C.E.)

The large-scale migrations across the Mediterranean in the late thirteenth and early twelfth centuries B.C.E. are connected with the mysterious "Sea Peoples." Their movement has been linked with the collapse of Bronze Age states, including those of the Hittites and Mycenaeans. It is not clear whether the Sea Peoples themselves were bringers of upheaval or fugitives from it. It is mainly from their victims that the Sea Peoples are known: among the evidence is a cache of Hittite letters from Ugarit and Egyptian inscriptions from Thebes, excerpted below. Before Ugarit was destroyed by the Sea Peoples, for some seven centuries it had been one of the main ports connecting the Bronze Age Levant. Today, its site at Ras Shamra in northern Syria is eight miles inland, a measure of a coastal shift over three millennia. Clay tablets unearthed there in the twentieth century are letters exchanged between regional leaders. In one, the last Hittite king, Suppiluliuma II, writes with alarm about "Shikalayu who live in boats." The tablets indicate that many cities in the eastern Mediterranean, including Ugarit, Ashkalon, and Hazor, suffered destruction over a period of several decades. Byblos and Sidon escaped devastation, presumably because the new arrivals chose to settle there.

The funerary temple of Ramses III (ruled ca. 1195–1164 B.C.E.) at Medinet Habu in Thebes provides a second set of evidence. In an inscription referring to his eighth regnal year, that is 1188 B.C.E., he boasts of checking the westward incursion of a "conspiracy" of various peoples who had already destroyed several states in the eastern Sea. Elaborate reliefs also depict Ramses' battles on land and sea. Their viewpoint is informed by Egyptian concerns and royal self-presentation. Ramses' success seems exaggerated since it was in such circumstances that Egyptian power in the Levant came to an end. When Wenamun traveled to Phoenicia nearly a century later, the treatment he received indicates how much Egypt's power in the eastern Mediterranean had diminished.

[1] LETTER FROM THE SENIOR GOVERNOR OF ALASHIYA TO THE KING OF UGARIT

Thus says Eshuwara, senior prefect of Alashiya: Say to the king of Ugarit: May you and your land too be well!

Concerning the things which the enemy has done to these citizens of your land and your ships: they have committed the transgression(?) against the people of the country. So don't be angry(?) with me.

And now the twenty ships which the enemy hadn't yet launched in the mountainous region haven't stayed put. They set out suddenly and we don't know where they've turned up(?). I've written to you to inform you, so that you can take defensive measures. Be aware!

[2] LETTER FROM THE KING OF ALASHIYA TO AMMURAPI OF UGARIT

Thus says the king: say to Ammurapi, king of Ugarit: May you be well, and may the gods guard you in well-being!

Concerning that which you wrote me: "Enemy ships were observed at sea!"—if it is true that ships have been sighted, then make yourself very strong. Now where are your infantry and chariotry stationed? Aren't they stationed with you? No? Who is sending you after(?) the enemy? Surround your cities with walls. Bring your infantry and chariotry into them. Be on the lookout for the enemy and make yourself very strong.

[3] LETTER FROM THE KING OF UGARIT
TO THE KING OF ALASHIYA

Say to the king of Alashiya, my father: Thus says the king of Ugarit, your son: I fall at the feet of my father. May my father be well! May your palaces, your wives, your infantry, and everything which belongs to the king of Alashiya, my father, be very, very well!

My father, now the ships of the enemy have been coming. They have been setting fire to my cities and have done harm to the land. Doesn't my father know that all my infantry and [chariotry] are stationed in Hatti, and that all of my ships are in the land of Lukka? They haven't arrived back yet, so the land is thus prostrate. May my father be aware of this matter. Now the seven ships of the enemy which have been coming have done harm to us. Now if other ships of the enemy turn up, send me a report somehow(?) so that I will know.

Trans. Gary Beckman, in Sources for the History of Cyprus II: Near Eastern and Aegean Texts from the Third to the First Millennia BC, *ed. A. Bernard Knapp (Altamont, N.Y.: Greece and Cyprus Research Center, 1996), 27.*

INSCRIPTIONS OF RAMSES III

[a] Year 8 under the majesty of (Ramses III) [. . .]

The foreign countries made a conspiracy in their islands. All at once the lands were removed and scattered in the fray. No land could stand before their arms, from Hatti, Kode, Carchemisch, Arzawa, and Alashiya on, being cut off at [*on time*]. A camp [*was set up*] in a place in Amor. They desolated its people, and its land was like that which has never come into being. They were coming forward toward Egypt, while the flame was prepared before them. Their confederation was the Philistines, Tjeker, Shekelesh, Denye(n), and Weshesh, lands united. They laid their hands upon the lands as far as the circuit of the earth, their hearts confident and trusting: "Our plans will succeed!"

Now the heart of this god, the Lord of the Gods, was prepared and ready to ensnare them like birds. . . . I organized my frontier in Djahi, prepared for them: — princes, commanders of garrisons, and *maryanu* [*Asiatic princes*]. I have the river-mouths prepared like a strong wall, with warships, galleys and coasters, (fully) equipped, for they were manned completely from bow and stern with valiant warriors carrying their weapons. The troops consisted of every picked man of Egypt. They were like lions roaring upon the mountain tops. The chariotry consisted of runners, of picked men, of every good and capable chariot-warrior. The horses were quivering in every part of their bodies, prepared to crush the foreign countries under their hoofs. I was the valiant Montu [*god of war*], standing fast at their head, so that they might gaze upon the capturing of my hands. . . .

Those who reached my frontier, their seed is not, their and their soul are finished forever and ever. Those who came forward together on the sea, the full flame was in front of them at the river-mouths, while a stockade of lances surrounded them on the shore. They were dragged in, enclosed, and prostrated on the beach, killed, and made into heaps from tail to head. Their ships and their goods were as if fallen into the water.

I have made the lands turn back from (even) mentioning Egypt; for when they pronounce my name in their land, then they are burned up. Since I say upon the throne of Har-akhti and the Great-of-Magic [*i.e., uraeus serpent, royal symbol*] was fixed upon my head like Re, I have not let foreign countries behold the frontier of Egypt, to boast thereof to the Nine Bows. I have taken away their land, their frontiers being added to mine. Their princes and their tribespeople are mine with praise, for I am on the ways of the plans of the All-Lord, my august, divine father, the Lord of Gods.

[*b*]

The northern countries quivered in their bodies, Philistines, Tjekker . . . They cut off their (own) land and were coming, their soul finished. They were *teher*-warriors on land; another (group) was on the sea. Those who came on [land were overthrown and killed . . .]. Amon-Re was after them, destroying them. Those who entered the river-mouths were like birds ensnared in the net. . . . Their leaders were carried off and slain. They were cast down and pinioned. [. . .]

[*d*] Text on frieze depicting a naval battle, while the pharaoh and his troops fight from the shore [*see ill. 1*]

Now then, the northern countries which were in their island were quivering in their bodies. They penetrated the channels of the river-mouths. Their nostrils have ceased [*to function, so*] their desire is to breathe the breath. His majesty has gone forth like a whirlwind against them, fighting on the battlefield like a runner. The dread of him and the terror of him have entered into their bodies. They are capsized and overwhelmed where they are. Their heart is taken away, their soul is flown away. Their weapons are scattered upon the sea. His arrow pierces whom of them he may have wished, and the fugitive is become one fallen into the water. His majesty is like an enraged lion, attacking his assailant with his arms: plundering on his right hand and powerful on his left hand, like Seth destroying the serpent "Evil of Character." It is Amon-Re who has overthrown for him the lands and has crushed for him ever land under his feet.

Trans. J. A. Wilson in Ancient Near Eastern Texts Relating to the Old Testament, *3rd ed., ed. J. B. Pritchard (Princeton, N.J.: Princeton University Press, 1969), 262–64. Reprinted by permission of the publisher.*

Cedars for Egypt
Wenamun (1080s B.C.E.)

The Sea Peoples feature also in a vivid account of the journey of Wenamun, priest of the Egyptian god Amun at Karnak, which survives on an eleventh-century papyrus now in the Moscow Museum. He was sent to Byblos in Phoenicia to acquire cedar logs for the god's ceremonial Nile barges. Touching on the ports of Tanis, Dor, and Tyre, he experienced various mishaps along the way, making for an almost picaresque tale. The text has the features of a skillful literary narrative, with humor even, yet it refers to historically identifiable persons and places and closely reflects changing east Mediterranean geopolitics in the early eleventh century B.C.E. In the text excerpted here, their king, Beder, initially receives Wenamun hospitably as an emissary; nonetheless, it is clear that Egypt's empire is a thing of the past. The papyrus breaks off tantalizingly before Wenamun's return, but the use of first-person narration has led readers to surmise that he did somehow get back to Egypt.

[. . .] In the third month of the third season they dragged them to the shore of the sea, and the Prince came out and stood by them. And he sent to me, saying: "Come!" Now when I presented myself near him, the shadow of his lotus-blossom fell upon me. And Pen-Amon, a butler who belonged to him, cut me off, saying: "The shadow of Pharaoh—life, prosperity, health!—your lord, has fallen on you!" But he was angry at him, saying: "Let him alone!"

So I presented myself near him, and he answered and said to me: "See, the commission which my fathers would have done for me, and you too should have done! See, the last of your woodwork has arrived and is lying here. Do as I wish, and come to load it in—for aren't they going to give it to you? Don't come to look at the terror of the sea! If you look at the terror of the sea, you will see my own too! Why, I have not done to you what was done to the messengers of Kha-em-Waset, when they spent seventeen years in this land—they died where they were!" And he said to his butler: "Take him and show him their tomb in which they are lying."

But I said to him: "Don't show it to me! As for Kha-em-Waset—they were men whom he sent to you as messengers, and he was a man himself. You do not have one of his messengers here in me, when you say: 'Go and see your companions!' Now, shouldn't you rejoice and have a stela made for yourself and say on it: 'Amon-Re, King of the Gods, sent to me Amon-of-the-Road, his messenger—life, prosperity, health!—and Wen-Amon, his human messenger, after the woodwork for the great and august barque of Amon-Re, King of the Gods. I cut it down. I loaded it in. I provided it with my ships and my crews. I caused them to reach Egypt, in order to ask fifty years of life from Amon for myself, over and above my fate.' And it shall come to pass that, after another time, a messenger may come from the land of Egypt who knows writing, and he may read your name on the stela. And you will receive water in the West, like the gods who are here!"

And he said to me: "This which you have said to me is a great testimony of words!" So I said to him: "As for the many things which you have said to me, if I reach the place where the High Priest of Amon is and he sees how you have carried out this commission, it is your carrying out of this commission which will draw out something for you."

And I went to the shore of the sea, to the place where the timber was lying, and I spied eleven ships belonging to the Tjeker coming in from the sea, in order to say: "Arrest him! Don't let the ship go to the land of Egypt!" Then I sat down and wept. And the letter scribe of the Prince came out to me, and he said to me: "What's the matter with you?" And I said to him: "Haven't you seen the birds go down to Egypt a second time? Look at them—how they travel to the cool pools! But how long shall I be left here! Now don't you see those who are coming again to arrest me?"

So he went and told it to the Prince. And the Prince began to weep because of the words which were said to him, for they were painful. And he sent out to me his letter scribe, and he brought to me two jugs of wine and one ram. And he sent to me Ta-net-Not, an Egyptian singer who was with him, saying: "Sing to him! Don't let his heart take on cares!" And he sent to me, to say: "Eat and drink! Don't let your heart take on cares for tomorrow for you shall hear whatever I have to say." 21

When morning came, he had his assembly summoned, and he stood in their midst, and he said to the Tjeker: "What have you come for?" And they said to him: "We have come after the blasted ships which you are sending to Egypt with our opponents!" But he said to them: "I cannot arrest the messenger of Amon inside my land. Let me send him away, and you go after him to arrest him."

So he loaded me in, and he sent me away from there at the harbor of the sea. And the wind cast me on the land of the Alashiya. And they of the town came out against me to kill me, but I forced my way through them to the place where Heteb, the princess of the town, was. I met her as she was going out of one house of hers and going into another of hers.

So I greeted her, and I said to the people who were standing near her: "Isn't there one of you who understands Egyptian?" And one of them said: "I understand it." So I said to him: "Tell my lady that I have heard, as far away as Thebes, the place where Amon is, that injustice is done in every town but justice is done in the land of Alashiya. Yet injustice is done here every day!" And he said: "Why, what do you mean by saying it?" So I told her: "If the sea is stormy and the wind casts me on the land where you are, you should not let them take me in charge to kill me. For I am a messenger of Amon. Look here—as for me, they will search for me all the time! As to this crew of the Prince of Byblos which they are bent on killing, won't its lord find ten crews of yours, and he also kill them?"

So she had the people summoned, and they stood there. And she said to me: "Spend the night [. . .]"

Trans. J. B. Pritchard in Ancient Near Eastern Texts Relating to the Old Testament, *3rd ed., ed. Pritchard (Princeton, N.J.: Princeton University Press, 1969), 28–29.*

Phoenicians in the West

Nora Stone (9th or early 8th century B.C.E.) and Marseilles Inscription (3rd or early 2nd century B.C.E.)

The island of Sardinia, rich in metal ores, attracted early Phoenician trade. It was within easy reach of their settlements in North Africa and northwest Sicily and soon became a key part of their maritime network. This was particularly true of Nora, a port on the western shore of the Bay of Cagliari. Located near silver and iron deposits, the port had been used in the Bronze Age by Mycenaeans from the Aegean. By the seventh century B.C.E. there is evidence of Phoenician architecture as far afield as Cyprus and southern Spain. Many Phoenician inscriptions have survived, in the script from which Greeks developed their own alphabet. They make it clear that their Semitic language was as widely diffused as their commercial network. But they provide no historical narrative to match that of their neighbors, and in many cases it is hard to assign a date. One of the most famous inscriptions comes from Nora and is dated on palaeographic grounds to the ninth century or somewhat later. It appears to mark the founding of a cult of the god Pummay, whose name was later taken up by Phoenician kings. The western presence of the Phoenicians and their colonies is further illustrated in a cultic inscription found in 1845 at Marseilles, founded originally by Phoenicians. The two stones on which it was inscribed were probably quarried from the area of Carthage. Carefully engraved, they date from the third or early second century B.C.E. A substantial number of similar inscriptions have been found in Carthage. The inscription, the beginning of which is quoted below, details the amount to be paid to the officiating priest, depending on the sacrifice made.

NORA STONE

He fought
with the Sardinians
at Tarshish,
and he drove them out.
Among the Sardinians
he is now at peace,
(and) his army is at peace:
Milkaton son of
Shubna (Shebna), general
of (king) Pummay.

F. M. Cross, "An Interpretation of the Nora Stone," Bulletin of the American Society of Oriental Research 208 (1972): 13–19.

MARSEILLES INSCRIPTION

Temple of Ba'L-[Zaphon]
Tariff of payments set up [by the men in charge of] the payments in the time of [the lords Hilles]ba'l, the suffete [magistrate], the son of Bodtanit,

the son of Bod[eshmun, and Hillesba'l,] the suffete, the son of Bodesh-
mun, the son of Hillesba'l, and their colleagues.

For an ox, as a whole offering or a substitute offering or a complete
whole offering, the priests shall have ten silver (pieces) for each. In the
case of a whole offering, they shall have, over and above this payment,
meat [weighing three hundred]. In the case of a substitute offering, they
shall have neck and shoulder joints, while the person offering the sacrifice shall have the skin, ribs, feet, and the rest of the meat. . . .

Trans. J. B. Pritchard in Ancient Near Eastern Texts Relating to the Old
Testament, *3rd ed., ed. Pritchard (Princeton: Princeton University Press, 1969),
656–57.*

Odysseus's Wanderings
Homer (ca. 700 B.C.E.)

The Greek prince Odysseus, also known as Ulysses, is the hero
of the *Odyssey*, one of two epic poems attributed to Homer, along
with the *Iliad*. Seafaring informs much of the plot of the *Odyssey*,
which recounts Odysseus's decade-long return journey from Troy
to his native island of Ithaca. Though the poems purport to relate
much earlier events around the time of the Trojan War (thirteenth
century B.C.E.), it is the conditions of the Late Dark Age, around 800
B.C.E.—some three generations before their initial compilation—that
they most closely reflect. In the following extract Odysseus recounts
his adventures to his host, King Alcinous at Scheria, land of the
Phaeacians. The story itself is part of the gift exchange of elite guest-
friendship (*xenia*): Alcinous has provided the storm-tossed visitor and
his companions with a lavish banquet before even asking his name or
the nature of his journey. Some of the encounters described, such as
those involving the Laistrygonians and Cyclopes, are hostile and thus
contrast with the conviviality enjoyed by the travelers at Scheria. For
example, later in the work the Cyclops Polyphemus suspects Odysseus
of being a pirate (9.252–55, and compare Thucydides, below). For
many subsequent writers in a Mediterranean context and beyond,
the figure of Odysseus has been the prototype of the traveler, open
to adaptation. Whereas the extract illustrates the folkloric element
of the poem (see also ill. 4), several later writers have focused on the
theme of its later part: his actual return (*nostos*) to Ithaca and his wife,
Penelope, and his difficulties in trying to regain his former social

status there.

Resourceful Odysseus then replied to Alcinous:

"Lord Alcinous, most renowned of men,
it is indeed a truly splendid thing
to listen to a singer such as this,
whose voice is like a god's. For I say
there's nothing gives one more delight
than when joy grips entire groups of men
who sit in proper order in a hall
feasting and listening to a singer,
with tables standing there beside them
laden with bread and meat, as the steward
draws wine out of the mixing bowl, moves round,
and fills the cups. To my mind this seems
the finest thing there is. But your heart
wants to ask about my grievous sorrows,
so I can weep and groan more than before.
What shall I tell you first? Where do I stop?
For the heavenly gods have given me
so much distress. Well, I will make a start
by telling you my name. Once you know that,
if I escape the painful day of death,
then later I can welcome you as guests,
though I live in a palace far away.
I am Odysseus, son of Laertes,
well known to all for my deceptive skills—
my fame extends all the way to heaven.
I live in Ithaca, a land of sunshine.
From far away one sees a mountain there,
thick with whispering trees, Mount Neriton,
and many islands lying around it
close together—Dulichium, Same,
forested Zacynthus. Ithaca itself,
low in the sea and furthest from the mainland,
lies to the west—while those other islands
are a separate group, closer to the Dawn
and rising Sun. It's a rugged island,
but nurtures fine young men. And in my view,
nothing one can see is ever sweeter
than a glimpse of one's own native land.
When Calypso, that lovely goddess, tried

to keep me with her in her hollow caves,
longing for me to be her husband,
or when, in the same way, the cunning witch
Aeaean Circe held me in her home
filled with keen desire I'd marry her,
they never won the heart here in my chest.
That's how true it is there's nothing sweeter
than a man's own country and his parents,
even if he's living in a wealthy home,
but in a foreign land away from those
who gave him life. But come, I'll tell you
of the miserable journey back which Zeus
arranged for me when I returned from Troy.
    "I was carried by the wind from Troy
to Ismarus, land of the Cicones.
I destroyed the city there, killed the men,
seized their wives, and captured lots of treasure,
which we divided up. I took great pains
to see that all men got an equal share.
Then I gave orders we should leave on foot—
and with all speed. But the men were fools.
They didn't listen. They drank too much wine
and on the shoreline slaughtered many sheep,
as well as shambling cows with twisted horns.
Meanwhile the Cicones set off and gathered up
their neighbors, tribesmen living further inland.
There are more of them, and they're braver men,
skilled at fighting enemies from chariots
and also, should the need arise, on foot.
They reached us in the morning, thick as leaves
or flowers growing in season. Then Zeus
brought us disaster—he made that our fate,
so we would suffer many casualties.
They set their ranks and fought by our swift ships.
We threw our bronze-tipped spears at one another.
While the morning lasted and that sacred day
gained strength, we held our ground and beat them back,
for all their greater numbers. But as the sun
moved to the hour when oxen are unyoked,
the Cicones broke through, overpowering

26

Achaeans. Of my well-armed companions,
six from every ship were killed. The rest of us
made our escape, avoiding Death and Fate."

"We sailed away from there, hearts full of grief
at losing loyal companions, though happy
we had eluded death ourselves. But still,
I would not let our curved ships leave the place
until we'd made the ritual call three times
for our poor comrades slaughtered on that plain,
killed by the Cicones. Cloud-gatherer Zeus
then stirred North Wind to rage against our ships—
a violent storm concealing land and sea,
as darkness swept from heaven down on us.
The ships were driven off course, our sails
ripped to shreds by the power of that wind.
We lowered the masts into the holds and then,
fearing for our lives, quickly rowed the ships
toward the land. For two whole days and nights
we lay there, hearts consumed with sorrow
and exhaustion. But when fair-haired Dawn
gave birth to the third day, we raised the masts,
hoisted white sails, and took our place on board.
Wind and helmsman held us on our course,
and I'd have reached my native land unharmed,
but North Wind, sea currents, and the waves
pushed me off course, as I was doubling back
around Malea, driving me past Cythera.

"Nine days fierce winds drove me away from there,
across the fish-filled seas, and on the tenth
we landed where the Lotus-eaters live,
people who feed upon its flowering fruit.
We went ashore and carried water back.
Then my companions quickly had a meal
by our swift ships. We had our food and drink,
and then I sent some of my comrades out
to learn about the men who ate the food
the land grew there. I chose two of my men
and with them sent a third as messenger.
They left at once and met the Lotus-eaters,
who had no thought of killing my companions,

but gave them lotus plants to eat, whose fruit,
sweet as honey, made any man who sampled it
lose his desire to ever journey home
or bring back word to us—they wished to stay,
to remain among the Lotus-eaters,
feeding on the plant, eager to forget
about their homeward voyage. I forced them,
eyes full of tears, into our hollow ships,
dragged them underneath the rowing benches,
and tied them up. Then I issued orders
for my other trusty comrades to embark
and sail away with speed in our fast ships,
in case another man might eat a lotus
and lose all thoughts about his journey back.
They raced on board, went to their places,
and, sitting in good order in their rows,
struck the gray sea with their oar blades.

"We sailed away from there with heavy hearts
and reached the country of the Cyclopes,
a crude and lawless people. They don't grow
any plants by hand or plough the earth,
but put their trust in the immortal gods,
and though they never sow or work the land,
every kind of crop springs up for them—
wheat and barley and rich grape-bearing vines,
and Zeus provides the rain to make them grow.
They live without a council or assembly
or any rule of law, in hollow caves
among the mountain tops. Each one of them
makes laws for his own wives and children,
and they shun all dealings with each other.

"Now, near the country of the Cyclopes,
outside the harbour, there's a fertile island,
covered in trees, some distance from the shore,
but not too far away. Wild goats live there
in countless numbers. They have no need
to stay away from any human trails.
Hunters never venture there, not even those
who endure great hardships in the forest,
as they roam across the mountain peaks.

28

That island has no flocks or plough land—
through all its days it's never once been sown
or tilled or known the work of human beings.
The only life it feeds is bleating goats.
The Cyclopes don't have boats with scarlet prows
or men with skills to build them well-decked ships,
which would enable them to carry out
all sorts of things—like traveling to the towns
of other people, the way men cross the sea
to visit one another in their ships—
or men who might have turned their island
into a well-constructed settlement.
The island is not poor. All things grow there
in season. It has soft, well-watered meadows
by the shore of the gray sea, where grape vines
could flourish all the time, and level farm land,
where they could always reap fine harvests,
year after year—the sub-soil is so rich.
It has a harbor, too, with good anchorage,
no need for any mooring cable there,
or setting anchor stones, or tying up
with cables on the stern. One can beach a ship
and wait until a fair wind starts to blow
and sailors' hearts tell them to go on board.
At the harbor head there is a water spring—
a bright stream flows out underneath a cave.
Around it poplars grow. We sailed in there.
Some god led us in through the murky night—
we couldn't see a thing, and all our ships
were swallowed up in fog. Clouds hid the moon,
so there was no light coming from the sky.
Our eyes could not catch any glimpse of land
or of the long waves rolling in onshore,
until our well-decked ships had reached the beach.
We hauled up our ships, took down all the sails,
went up along the shore, and fell asleep,
remaining there until the light of Dawn."

Homer, Odyssey, *9.1–151, trans. Ian Johnston, <http://books.google.com/
books?hl=enlid=3gj9e/boujyc&printsec=frontcover&dq=Ian+Johnston>*

Travels of a Farmer

Hesiod (ca. 700 B.C.E.)

Hesiod's didactic poem *Works and Days* seems to be broadly
contemporary with the *Iliad* and *Odyssey*. Though written in the
same meter, it differs from the Homeric epics in being directed at
the present rather than the past, and concerned with ordinary rather
than heroic lives. The poem borrows features of Near Eastern wisdom
literature, offering advice of a practical nature that is here linked to
small-scale agriculture. It is addressed to his brother, Perses. Their
father had migrated from Asia Minor to Ascra in Boeotia to escape
poverty; his own disdain for travel emerges explicitly. The poet's
world is that of the peasant, much of whose life is spent negotiating
the frequent scarcity of food and water. The extract below speaks of
the need to spend some time every year traveling, so as to exchange
resources with neighbors. Of particular importance is the timing
of voyages. The picture that emerges is broadly that the fragmented
Mediterranean topography, with its dry conditions and jagged
coastlines, necessitated and facilitated small-scale journeys such as
that prescribed here.

Rouse up your slave to winnow the sacred yield of Demeter
at the time when powerful Orion first shows himself; do it
in a place where there is a good strong wind, on a floor that's
rounded.
Measure it by storing it neatly away in the bins. Then after
you have laid away a good store of livelihood in your house,
put your hired man out of doors, and look for a serving-maid
with no children, as one with young to look after's a nuisance;
and look after your dog with the sharp teeth, do not spare feeding
him,
so the Man Who Sleeps in the Daytime won't be getting at your
goods.
Bring in hay and fodder so that your mules and your oxen
will have enough to eat and go on with. Then, when that is done,
let your helpers refresh their knees, and unyoke your oxen.
Then, when Orion and Seirios are come to the middle
of the sky, and the rosy-fingered Dawn confronts Arcturus,
then, Perses, cut off all your grapes, and bring them home with
you.
30   Show your grapes to the sun for ten days and for ten nights,

cover them with shade for five, and on the sixth day press out
the gifts of bountiful Dionysus into jars. Then after
the Pleiades and the Hyades and the strength of Orion
have set, then remember again to begin your seasonal plowing,
and the full year will go underground, completing the cycle.
　　But if the desire for stormy seagoing seizes upon you:
why, when the Pleiades, running to escape from Orion's
grim bulk, duck themselves under the misty face of the water,
at that time the blasts of the winds are blowing from every

　　　　　　　　　　　　　　　　　　　　　　　　direction,

then is no time to keep your ships on the wine-blue water.
Think of working your land instead, as I keep telling you.
Haul your ship up on the dry land, and make an enclosure
of stones about it, to keep out the force of winds that blow wet,
and pull the plug, so the rains of Zeus will not rot the timbers.
Take all the tackle that's rigged to the ship, and lay it up indoors,
neatly stowing the wings of the ship that goes over the water;
hang the well-wrought steering-oar over the smoke of the fireplace,
and yourself wait for the time to come when a voyage is in season.
Then drag your swift ship down to the sea, and put it in a cargo
that will be suitable for it, so you can bring home a profit,
as did my father, and yours too, O Perses, you great fool,
who used to sail in ships, for he wanted to live like a noble,
and once on a time, leaving Kyme of Aiolis, he came here,
in his black ship, having crossed over a vast amount of water;
and it was not comfort he was fleeing, nor wealth, nor prosperity,
but that evil poverty that Zeus gives men for a present;
and settled here near Helikon in a hole of a village,
Askra, bad in winter, tiresome in summer, and good at no season.
　　As for you, Perses, remember the timely seasons for all work
done, but remember it particularly about seafaring.
Admire a little ship, but put your cargo in a big one.
The bigger the cargo, the bigger will be the profit added
to profit—if only the winds hold off their harsh gales from it.
　　But when, turning your easily blown thoughts toward a

　　　　　　　　　　　　　　　　　　　　　　　　merchant's

life, you wish to escape your debts, and unhappy hunger,
I will show you the measures of the much-thundering sea, I
who am not one who has much knowledge of ships and sea

　　　　　　　　　　　　　　　　　　　　　　　　voyages;

for I never did sail in a ship across the wide water

except across to Euboia from Aulis, where once the Achaians
stayed out the storm and gathered together a great many people
from sacred Hellas to go to Troy, the land of fair women.
There I crossed over to Chalkis for the games held in honor
of gallant Amphidamas, for the sons of this great-hearted
man had set out many chosen prizes. There I can claim,
I won the contest with a song and took off an eared tripod;
and this I set up as an offering to the Muses of Helikon,
where they first had made me a master of melodious singing.
This is all my experience with intricately bolted
ships, but still I can tell you the thought, which is of the aegis-
                                     bearing
Zeus, for the Muses have taught me to sing immortal poetry.
   For fifty days, after the turn of the summer solstice,
when the wearisome season of the hot weather goes to its
                                   conclusion
then is the timely season for men to voyage. You will not
break up your ship, nor will the sea drown its people, unless
Poseidon, the shaker of the earth, of his volition,
or Zeus, the king of the immortals, wishes to destroy it,
for with these rests authority for all outcomes, good or evil.
At that time the breezes can be judged, and the sea is untroubled.
At that time, trusting your swift ship to the winds, can you draw
                                         her
down to the sea at will, and load all your cargo inside her;
but make haste still, for the sake of an earlier homecoming,
and do not wait for the season of new wine and the autumn
rain, and the winter coming on, and the hard-blowing southwind
who comes up behind the heavy rains that Zeus sends in autumn
and upheaves the sea and makes the open water difficult.
   There is one sailing season for men, in spring time.
At that point, when you first make out on the topmost branches
of the fig tree, a leaf as big as the print that a crow makes
when he walks; at that time also the sea is navigable
and this is called the spring sailing season. I for my part
do not like it. There is nothing about it that I find pleasant.
It's snatched. You will find it hard to escape coming to grief. Yet
                                       still
and even so, men in their short-sightedness do undertake it;
for acquisition means life to miserable mortals;
but it is an awful thing to die among the waves. No, rather

I tell you to follow with all your attention, as I instruct you.
Do not adventure your entire livelihood in hollow ships.
Leave the greater part ashore and make the lesser part cargo.
For it is awful to run on disaster in the waves of the open
water, and awful to put an overwhelming load on your wagon
and break the axle, and have all the freight go to nothing.
Observe measures. Timeliness is best in all matters.

Hesiod, Works and Days, *lines 597–694, from Hesiod,* The Works and Days, Theogony, the Shield of Herakles, *trans. Richard Lattimore (Ann Arbor: University of Michigan Press, 1959), 89–101. Reprinted by permission of the publisher.*

Exile and Return

Psalm 137 (586 B.C.E.) and Ezra (after 538 B.C.E.)

This psalm is the most famous lament for Jerusalem and its destruction. Composed in the postexilic era in captivity, it calls upon the Judaean exiles to "remember Zion," symbol of Jerusalem, the place on which the holy Temple stood. In Jewish tradition it is recited on the ninth of Av, the day on which the Temple was destroyed, giving a vivid impression of the trauma suffered by the Jews when they were forcibly removed from their homes and country. Their captors taunt them to "sing . . . the songs of Zion," but the exiles are unable to "sing the Lord's song in a strange land." Verses 5 and 6 offer the familiar oath never to forget Jerusalem. This injunction is heeded in Jewish liturgy by means of sacred orientation, whereby worship in synagogues is directed to the east; the breaking of a glass at Jewish weddings, further, commemorates the fall of the Temple. The psalm concludes with a denunciation of both the Babylonians and their Edomite allies, and a call for retribution, a common theme in laments.

In 538 B.C.E. the Persian king Cyrus issued an edict allowing nations under his control to worship their own gods and rebuild the temples in their homelands. This account was presented as the fulfillment of Jeremiah's prophecy (Jeremiah 29:10). The edict is typical of Persian policies toward conquered peoples, a kind of toleration of limited home rule and a sense of religious freedom. Jeremiah and many other prophets, however, saw in this policy the prospect of one day reestablishing the independence of the Jewish state. The high regard enjoyed by the Persian king is also recognized in the book of Isaiah (44:28 and 45:1).

PSALM 137

By the rivers of Babylon, there we sat down, yea, we wept, when we remembered Zion. We hanged our harps upon the willows in the midst thereof. For there they that carried us away captive required of us a song; and they that wasted us required of us mirth, saying, "Sing us one of the songs of Zion."

How shall we sing the Lord's song in a strange land? If I forget thee, O Jerusalem, let my right hand forget her cunning. If I do not remember thee, let my tongue cleave to the roof of my mouth; if I prefer not Jerusalem above my chief joy.

Remember, O Lord, the children of Edom in the day of Jerusalem; who said, Rase it, rase it, even to the foundation thereof. O daughter of Babylon, who art to be destroyed; happy shall he be, that rewardeth thee as thou hast served us. Happy shall he be, that taketh and dasheth thy little ones against the stones.

From the Hebrew Bible, King James Version.

EZRA

In the first year of King Cyrus of Persia, in order that the word of the Lord by the mouth of Jeremiah might be accomplished, the Lord stirred up the spirit of Cyrus king of Persia so that he sent a herald throughout all his kingdom, and also in a written edict declared:

"Thus says King Cyrus of Persia: The Lord, the God of heaven, has given me all the kingdoms of the earth, and he has charged me to build him a house at Jerusalem in Judah. Any of those among you who are his people—may their God be with them!—are now permitted to go up to Jerusalem in Judah, and rebuild the house of the Lord, the God of Israel—he is the God who is in Jerusalem; and let all survivors, in whatever place they reside, be assisted by the people of their place with silver and gold, with goods and with animals, besides freewill offerings for the house of God in Jerusalem."

The heads of the families of Judah and Benjamin, and the priests and the Levites—everyone whose spirit God had stirred—got ready to go up and rebuild the house of the Lord in Jerusalem. All their neighbors aided them with silver vessels, with gold, with goods, with animals, and with valuable gifts, besides all that was willingly offered. King Cyrus himself brought out the vessels of the house of the Lord that Nebuchadnezzar had carried away from Jerusalem and placed in the house of his

gods. King Cyrus of Persia had them released into the charge of Mithre-
dath the treasurer, who counted them out to Sheshbazzar the prince of
Judah.

Ezra 1, Hebrew Bible, Revised Standard Version.

Lamentation over Tyre
Ezekiel (ca. 563 B.C.E.)

Ezekiel's lamentation over Tyre reveals the central importance of
this maritime city on the Phoenician coast. Having joined Judah in
the revolt against Babylonia, it held out against Nebuchadnezzar for
thirteen years and finally submitted to him without being conquered.
The four oracles concerning Tyre (Ezekiel 26:1–21) underscore what
an important commercial rival Tyre was to the kingdom of Judah.
When the prophet portrays Tyre as a well-built ship in verses 3–9, he
encapsulates the essence of the city's dominance in the commercial
sphere. An island accessible by a narrow causeway, Tyre remained
impregnable to would-be conquerors until Alexander, who after a long
siege captured it in 332 B.C.E. Among the places mentioned, Elishah is
probably Cyprus, and Gebal was later known as Byblos. It is unclear
whether Tarshish is in Sardinia or if it refers to Tartessus in southern
Spain (compare extract from Jonah below); at any rate, the survey of
Tyre's commercial network moves from west to east, including the
Ionians or Greeks ("Javan") and Sheba in southwest Arabia.

The word of the Lord came to me: Now you, son of man, raise a lamentation over Tyre, and say to Tyre, who dwells at the entrance to the sea,
merchant of the peoples on many coastlands, thus says the Lord God:
    O Tyre, you have said, "I am perfect in beauty."
    Your borders are in the heart of the seas; your builders made perfect
your beauty.
    They made all your planks of fir trees from Senir; they took a cedar
from Lebanon to make a mast for you.
    Of oaks of Bashan they made your oars; they made your deck of pines
from the coasts of Cyprus, inlaid with ivory.
    Of fine embroidered linen from Egypt was your sail, serving as your
ensign; blue and purple from the coasts of Eli'shah was your awning.
    The inhabitants of Sidon and Arvad were your rowers; skilled men
of Zemer were in you, they were your pilots.

The elders of Gebal and her skilled men were in you, caulking your seams; all the ships of the sea with their mariners were in you, to barter for your wares.

Persia and Lud and Put were in your army as your men of war; they hung the shield and helmet in you; they gave you splendor.

The men of Arvad and Helech were upon your walls round about, and men of Gamad were in your towers; they hung their shields upon your walls round about; they made perfect your beauty.

Tarshish trafficked with you because of your great wealth of every kind; silver, iron, tin, and lead they exchanged for your wares. Javan, Tubal, and Meshech traded with you; they exchanged the persons of men and vessels of bronze for your merchandise. Beth-togar'mah exchanged for your wares horses, war horses, and mules. The men of Rhodes traded with you; many coastlands were your own special markets, they brought you in payment ivory tusks and ebony. Edom trafficked with you because of your abundant goods; they exchanged for your wares emeralds, purple, embroidered work, fine linen, coral, and agate. Judah and the land of Israel traded with you; they exchanged for your merchandise wheat, olives and early figs, honey, oil, and balm. Damascus trafficked with you for your abundant goods, because of your great wealth of every kind; wine of Helbon, and white wool, and wine from Uzal they exchanged for your wares; wrought iron, cassia, and calamus were bartered for your merchandise. Dedan traded with you in saddlecloths for riding. Arabia and all the princes of Kedar were your favored dealers in lambs, rams, and goats; in these they trafficked with you. The traders of Sheba and Ra'amah traded with you; they exchanged for your wares the best of all kinds of spices, and all precious stones, and gold. Haran, Canneh, Eden, Asshur, and Chilmad traded with you. These traded with you in choice garments, in clothes of blue and embroidered work, and in carpets of colored stuff, bound with cords and made secure; in these they traded with you. The ships of Tarshish traveled for you with your merchandise.

So you were filled and heavily laden in the heart of the seas.

Your rowers have brought you out into the high seas. The east wind has wrecked you in the heart of the seas.

Your riches, your wares, your merchandise, your mariners and your pilots, your caulkers, your dealers in merchandise, and all your men of war who are in you, with all your company that is in your midst, sink into the heart of the seas on the day of your ruin.

At the sound of the cry of your pilots the countryside shakes, and down from their ships come all that handle the oar. The mariners and all the pilots of the sea stand on the shore and wail aloud over you, and cry bitterly. They cast dust on their heads and wallow in ashes; they make themselves bald for you, and gird themselves with sackcloth, and they weep over you in bitterness of soul, with bitter mourning.

In their wailing they raise a lamentation for you, and lament over you: "Who was ever destroyed like Tyre in the midst of the sea?

When your wares came from the seas, you satisfied many peoples; with your abundant wealth and merchandise you enriched the kings of the earth.

Now you are wrecked by the seas, in the depths of the waters; your merchandise and all your crew have sunk with you.

All the inhabitants of the coastlands are appalled at you; and their kings are horribly afraid, their faces are convulsed.

The merchants among the peoples hiss at you; you have come to a dreadful end and shall be no more for ever."

Ezekiel 27, Hebrew Bible, Revised Standard Version.

Delos at the Crossroads
Homeric Hymn to Apollo (6th century B.C.E.)

The island of Delos contains evidence of Aegean civilizations from as early as the third millennium and of its abandonment by the fourteenth century C.E. In Greek myth it was Apollo's birthplace, and it is in this connection that it features in the *Hymn to Apollo*, a poem linked in antiquity with the poet Homer but clearly a later composition. Typically of hymns, it begins by articulating the god's names and attributes, which in this case underline the poet's link with the island. Delos was a center for the cult of Apollo, attracting visitors from all over the Aegean and beyond. Tiny and lacking in drinking water, it was unable to support a population of any magnitude. Yet it was a major entrepôt for seafarers, and its economic role was closely tied to its religious significance (see ill. 8). It is a measure of Delos's cosmopolitanism that it also contained no fewer than twenty sanctuaries to foreign divinities, including Sarapea (shrines honoring the Egyptian god Sarapis) from the third century B.C.E. There is also evidence of Jewish observance dating from the first century B.C.E.

Delos clearly played a major role in trans-Mediterranean traffic. In the tale of Apollo's birth, the poet recounts a dialogue between Apollo's still pregnant mother Leto and the island of Delos, at a time when she was seeking a place in which to give birth. It was in such narratives, sung at festivals, that the island's sacred status was reaffirmed.

> "Delos, would you want to be the abode of my son,
> Phoibos Apollon, and to house him in a lavish temple?
> For it cannot escape you that no other will touch you
> since I think you shall never be rich in oxen or sheep
> and shall produce vintage nor grow an abundance of plants.
> If you have a temple for Apollon who shoots from afar,
> then all men shall gather here and bring
> hecatombs, and the ineffably rich savor of burning fat
> shall always rise, and you shall feed your dwellers
> from the hands of strangers, since your soil is barren."
> So she spoke. Then Delos rejoiced and gave this answer:
> "Leto, most glorious daughter of great Koios,
> I would gladly receive your offspring, the lord
> who shoots from afar; since truly the sound of my name
> is no pleasure to men, thereby I would be greatly honored.
> But, Leto, I shall not hide the fear this word brings me.
> They say that Apollon will be haughty
> and greatly lord it over the immortal gods
> and the mortal men of the barley-bearing earth.
> Thus I dreadfully fear in my heart and soul
> lest, when he first sees the light of the sun,
> scorning an island whose ground is rocky,
> he overturn me with his feet and push me into the deep sea.
> And there a great billow will always flood me
> up to my highest peak, while he arrives at another land,
> where it may please him to establish a temple and wooded groves.
> Then polyps will settle on me and black seals on me
> will make their carefree abodes where there are no people.
> But, goddess, if only you would deign to swear a great oath,
> that here first he would build a beautiful temple
> to be an oracle for men and afterwards [. . .]
> among all men, since today many are his names.
> "Earth be my witness and the wide heaven above
> and the cascading water of the Styx, which is the greatest

and most awful oath among the blessed gods,
that here there shall always be a fragrant altar and temple
for Phoibos and that he shall honor you above all others."

The Homeric Hymns, *2nd ed., translation, introduction, and notes by*
Apostolos N. Athanassakis (Baltimore: Johns Hopkins University Press, 2004), 15–16
(Hymn to Delian Apollo, lines 51–88). Reprinted by permission of the publisher.

Study Tours

Diogenes Laertius (3rd century C.E.) and Herodotus (before 425 B.C.E.)

Pythagoras (ca. 580–ca. 500 B.C.E.) was one of the most celebrated
figures of pre-Socratic philosophy, but he is also one of its most
obscure ones. He came from the Ionian island of Samos; indeed Ionia,
now the west coast of Turkey, was the center of early Greek thought.
Nearby Miletus had produced Thales and Anaximander. Supposedly,
Pythagoras fled political oppression in Samos and headed for Croton
in Calabria, Italy, where he founded a secret religious society. Later
tradition considerably embroiders and fabricates such details. His
biography surviving in the *Lives of the Sophists* by Diogenes Laertius
(third century C.E.), excerpted below, reveals the extent to which he
had taken on legendary proportions by Roman times. This biography
has Pythagoras visiting Egypt in search of special knowledge. Whether
or not these journeys are historically accurate, they certainly were a
common theme found, for example, in the lives of other major Greek
intellectuals, including Solon and Plato.

The earliest surviving Greek history provides further evidence of
eastward ventures in search of knowledge. In the second book of his
Histories, Herodotus of Halicarnassus (ca. 484–425 B.C.E.) provides
a detailed account of Egypt, in the course of wich he mentions his
own journey, his personal observation of natural phenomena, and his
conversations with priests. These topics reflect not only the theme
of the study tour but also Herodotus's claims to truthfulness —
claims that have been challenged from antiquity to the present day.
Herodotus's work is devoted to the Persian Wars (compare Aeschylus
below), from which the Egyptian topics of book two are a lengthy
digression. The tripartite division of continents is a frequent theme of
Greek and later Roman cartography.

PYTHAGORAS

While still a young man, in his eagerness for knowledge, he left his homeland [*of Samos*] and became initiated into all possible mystery religions of Greeks and non-Greeks. And he happened to be in Egypt when Polycrates sent him a letter of introduction to [*pharaoh*] Amasis. He learned the Egyptian language, as we learn from Antiphon in his treatise on men of outstanding virtue, and he associated with Chaldaeans and Magians.

While in Crete he went with Epimenides down into the cave of Ida; while in Egypt he entered sanctuaries and learned the Egyptians' secret lore regarding the gods. Then, returning to Samos and finding it subjected to the tyranny of Polycrates, he sailed off to Croton in Italy. There, once he had laid down the laws for the Italians, he and his disciples were held in high regard. Being some three hundred in number, they governed the state so well that its constitution was in effect an aristocracy. [...]

[*In a later section Diogenes Laertius lists several of Pythagoras's supposed precepts, with some explanations.*] When he said that a man when setting out should not turn his eyes homeward, he taught that those departing this life should not be desirous of living, and not be too much drawn to the pleasures here on earth.

Diogenes Laertius, Lives of the Sophists: Pythagoras, *sections 3 and 18, trans. Grant Parker.*

HERODOTUS

I also heard other things at Memphis in conversation with the priests of Hephaestus. Furthermore, I visited both Thebes and Heliopolis for this purpose, namely because I wanted to know if the priests of these places would concur in their accounts with those at Memphis; for the people of Heliopolis are said to be the most learned of the Egyptians. Those of their accounts which I heard concerning the gods I am not eager to relate, except for their names, because I consider that all men are on an equal footing concerning these matters, and whatever things about them I may record I shall record only because I am forced by the course of the story. But as regards human matters, the priests agreed with one another on the following lines: that the Egyptians were the first of all people on earth to reckon by years, and to divide the year as a whole into twelve parts. They learned this from the stars, they said.

Their reckoning is more astute than that of the Greeks, in my opinion, in that the Greeks add an intercalary month every other year, in order to align the seasons—whereas the Egyptians, reckoning the twelve months at thirty days each, add five days every year over and above the total, and in this way the completed circle of the seasons is aligned with the calendar.

[. . .] [*Later, speaking of Egypt's physical geography Herodotus continues as follows:*] If my assessment of this is correct, the opinion of the Ionians about Egypt is not sound: but if the judgment of the Ionians is right, I declare that neither the Hellenes nor the Ionians themselves know how to reckon since they say that the whole earth is made up of three divisions, Europe, Asia, and Libya [*Africa*]: for they ought to count in addition to these the delta of Egypt, since it belongs neither to Asia nor to Libya; for at least it cannot be the river Nile by this reckoning which divides Asia from Libya, but the Nile is cleft at the point of this Delta so as to flow round it, and the result is that this land would come between Asia and Libya.

Herodotus, Histories, 2.3–4 and 2.16, trans. Grant Parker.

Travels in a Fish
Jonah (5th or 4th century B.C.E.)

The story of Jonah, the most famous among the Hebrew Bible's few accounts of seafaring, presents the Mediterranean as a place of danger, where God's mercy is most keenly sensed. Jonah is an unwilling servant of God—unusual among the prophets—even by the end of this brief prose narrative. Called to preach at the Mesopotamian city of Nineveh, he tries instead to flee. Tarshish, his preferred destination, is probably the Spanish port of Tartessus (also mentioned at Isaiah 23:1–2 and Ezekiel 27:12 and 25), proverbially the farthest point in the opposite direction. The book likely dates to the postexilic period, perhaps the fifth or fourth century B.C.E. Its function was to call Jews to repentance and remind them of their mission to preach to all nations.

Now the word of the Lord came unto Jonah the son of Amittai, saying, "Arise, go to Nineveh, that great city, and cry against it; for their wickedness is come up before me." But Jonah rose up to flee unto Tarshish from the presence of the Lord, and went down to Joppa; and he found a ship going to Tarshish: so he paid the fare thereof, and went down into it, to go with them unto Tarshish from the presence of the Lord.

But the Lord sent out a great wind into the sea, and there was a mighty tempest in the sea, so that the ship was like to be broken. Then the mariners were afraid, and cried every man unto his god, and cast forth the wares that were in the ship into the sea, to lighten it of them. But Jonah was gone down into the sides of the ship; and he lay, and was fast asleep. So the shipmaster came to him, and said unto him, "What meanest thou, O sleeper? arise, call upon thy God, if so be that God will think upon us, that we perish not."

And they said every one to his fellow, "Come, and let us cast lots, that we may know for whose cause this evil is upon us." So they cast lots, and the lot fell upon Jonah. Then said they unto him, "Tell us, we pray thee, for whose cause this evil is upon us; What is thine occupation? and whence comest thou? what is thy country? and of what people art thou?" And he said unto them, "I am an Hebrew; and I fear the Lord, the God of heaven, which hath made the sea and the dry land." Then were the men exceedingly afraid, and said unto him, "Why hast thou done this?" For the men knew that he fled from the presence of the Lord, because he had told them.

Then said they unto him, "What shall we do unto thee, that the sea may be calm unto us?" for the sea wrought, and was tempestuous. And he said unto them, "Take me up, and cast me forth into the sea; so shall the sea be calm unto you: for I know that for my sake this great tempest is upon you." Nevertheless the men rowed hard to bring it to the land; but they could not: for the sea wrought, and was tempestuous against them. Wherefore they cried unto the Lord, and said, "We beseech thee, O Lord, we beseech thee, let us not perish for this man's life, and lay not upon us innocent blood: for thou, O Lord, hast done as it pleased thee." So they took up Jonah, and cast him forth into the sea: and the sea ceased from her raging. Then the men feared the Lord exceedingly, and offered a sacrifice unto the Lord, and made vows.

Now the Lord had prepared a great fish to swallow up Jonah. And Jonah was in the belly of the fish three days and three nights.

Jonah 1, Hebrew Bible, King James Version.

Beyond the Pillars of Hercules

Hanno the Carthaginian (after 480 B.C.E.)

Carthaginian seaborne mobility is attested by a highly unusual document. A brief Greek text, known as the "Periplus [literally 'sailing-around'] of Hanno the Carthaginian," purports to recount, in translation, a westward voyage through the Straits of Gibraltar, proceeding down the Morocco coast. This text, spare in language but rich in details, contains several references to the foundations of settlements on the West African coast. It leaves readers with many questions, including that of how far down the African coast it reaches, perhaps Senegal and Sierra Leone. It is possible but not certain that the current form of the Greek text was compiled between one and two centuries later than the historical Hanno. It presents, at the very least, a Greek view of Carthaginian activity in the western Mediterranean, and serves as a reminder that ancient Mediterranean colonization sometimes stretched beyond the mythical boundary of the Pillars of Hercules, namely the Straits of Gibraltar. Its final section presents humans encountered as animals, suggesting they had trophy value back at Carthage. The translation quoted below was adapted by Ezra Pound as part of his *Canto XL* (1934).

It pleased the Carthaginians that Hanno should voyage outside the Pillars of Hercules, and found cities of the Libyphoenicians. And he set forth with sixty ships of fifty oars, and a multitude of men and women, to the number of thirty thousand, and with wheat and other provisions.

After passing through the Pillars we went on and sailed for two days' journey beyond, where we founded the first city, which we called Thymaterium; it lay in the midst of a great plain. Sailing thence toward the west we came to Solois, a promontory of Libya, bristling with trees. Having set up an altar here to Neptune, we proceeded again, going toward the east for half the day, until we reached a marsh lying no great way from the sea, thickly grown with tall reeds. Here also were elephants and other wild beasts feeding, in great numbers.

Going beyond the marsh a day's journey, we settled cities by the sea, which we called Caricus Murus, Gytta, Acra, Melitta and Arambys. Sailing thence we came to the Lixus, a great river flowing from Libya. By it a wandering people, the Lixitae, were pasturing their flocks; with whom we remained some time, becoming friends. Above these folk lived unfriendly Aethiopians, dwelling in a land full of wild beasts, and

43

shut off by a great mountains, from which they say the Lixus flows, and on the mountains live men of various shapes, cave-dwellers, who, so the Lixitae say, are fleeter of foot than horses.

Taking interpreters from them, we sailed twelve days toward the south along a desert, turning thence toward the east one day's sail. There, within the recess of a bay we found a small island, having a circuit of fifteen stadia; which we settled, and called it Cerne. From our journey we judged it to be situated opposite Carthage; for the voyage from Carthage to the Pillars and thence to Cerne was the same.

Thence, sailing by a great river whose name was Chretes, we came to a lake, which had three islands, larger than Cerne. Running a day's sail beyond these, we came to the end of the lake, above which rose great mountains, peopled by savage men wearing skins of wild beasts, who threw stones at us and prevented us from landing from our ships. Sailing thence, we came to another river, very great and broad, which was full of crocodiles and hippopotami. And then we turned about and went back to Cerne.

Thence we sailed toward the south twelve days, following the shore, which was peopled by Aethiopians who fled from us and would not wait. And their speech the Lixitae who were with us could not understand. But on the last day we came to great wooded mountains. The wood of the trees was fragrant, and of various kinds. Sailing through these mountains for two days, we came to an immense opening of the sea, from either side of which there was level ground inland; from which at night we saw fire leaping up on every side at intervals, now greater, now less.

Having taken in water there, we sailed along the shore for five days, until we came to a great bay, which our interpreters said was called Horn of the West. In it there was a large island, and within the island a lake of the sea, in which there was another island. Landing there during the day, we saw nothing but forests, but by night many burning fires, and we heard the sound of pipes and cymbals, and the noise of drums and a great uproar. Then fear possessed us, and the soothsayers commanded us to leave the island.

And then quickly sailing forth, we passed by a burning country full of fragrance, from which great torrents of fire flowed down to the sea. But the land could not be come at from the heat. And we sailed along with all speed, being stricken with fear. After a journey of four days, we saw land at night covered with flames. And in the midst there was one lofty fire, greater than the rest, which seemed to touch the stars. By day this was seen to be a very high mountain, called Chariot of the Gods. Thence, sailing along by the fiery torrents for three days, we came to a bay, called Horn of the South. In the recess of this bay there was an island, like the former one, having a lake, in which there was another island, full of savage men. There were women, too, in even greater number. They had hairy bodies, and the interpreters called them *Gorillae*. When we pursued them we were unable to take any of the men; for they all escaped, by climbing the steep places and defending themselves with stones; but we took three of the women, who bit and scratched their leaders, and would not follow us. So we killed them and flayed them, and brought their skins to Carthage. For we did not voyage further, provisions failing us.

The Periplus of Hanno, *trans. Wilfred H. Schoff (Philadelphia: Commercial Museum, 1912), 3–5.*

Persians versus Greeks
Aeschylus (472 B.C.E.)

Under Cyrus, its first ruler (ca. 557–530 B.C.E.), the Persian Empire reached a size previously unknown in the Mediterranean or western Asia. Its ambitions in the Aegean brought conflict with the Greeks, who dubbed those encounters the Persian Wars. The Persian threat brought together Greek city-states to an unprecedented degree. It also provided the incentive and framework for one of the earliest Greek historical works, namely Herodotus's *Histories*, and also for the *Persians* by Aeschylus (ca. 525–ca. 456 B.C.E.). Performed at Athens in 472, this tragedy commemorated the Greek victory over the Persians in 480 at the battle of Salamis. The play is set in the Persian court at Susa, near today's Khuzastan on the Persian Gulf. All the characters are Persians and some are sympathetically presented, yet the play— written in Greek for an Athenian audience—gives an Athenian perspective. In effect, it is a celebration of Athens's democratic ideology, using Persian monarchy as a mirror. The following extract consists of a messenger's report to Atossa, mother of the Persian king Xerxes, about the disaster at Salamis. This was one of the final and most decisive encounters between Persians and Greeks; its outcome ended Persia's westward momentum. Nonetheless, the wars would provide Alexander with a pretext for attacking the Persian Empire in around 336 B.C.E., amid claims of revenge.

ATOSSA: Is the city of Athens still not sacked?

MESSENGER: As long as men remain, the ramparts hold.

ATOSSA: But tell me how the fleets first met in battle.
              Who attacked? The Greeks? Or was it my son,
              Full of pride at his vast array of ships?

MESSENGER: The cause of the whole disaster, royal lady,
              Was some malign power or avenging spirit
              That appeared, I cannot say from where.
              A Greek, you see, came from the Athenian fleet
              To tell your son Xerxes that when black night
              Spread her gloom, the Greeks would not remain
              At their posts, but leap upon the rowing benches
              And flee in secret, some this way, some that,
              Trying to save their lives. As soon as Xerxes
              Heard this, knowing nothing of the Greek's deceit
              Or the gods' ill-will, he ordered his captains
              All, when the sun stopped scorching the earth with its
                                        rays
              And gloom overtook the sky's high precinct, to deploy
              Most of the ships in three columns guarding
              The narrow passages out to the pounding sea,
              And other ships to encircle the island of Ajax
              On all sides. And if the Greeks should find
              Some furtive means of escape, the King decreed
              That every one of the captains would lose his head.
              He said all this with heart and spirits high,
              Because he did not know what the gods had planned.
                   Our men, with no unruliness but hearts
              Obedient to their lord, got supper ready,
              And every sailor fastened his oar-thong snugly
              To its pin, fitted well for rowing.
              But when the sun's light died away and night
              Came on, each oar-lord went on board his vessel
              And every soldier skilled at wielding arms.
              From bank to bank of rowers cheerful cries
              Rang out along the length of the ships. They sailed
              Out, each according to the orders given,
              And through the night the lordly captains kept
              Their crews plying a passage to and fro.
                   Night began to depart, and the Greeks were still

Far from making any furtive flight.
Then, when day's white steeds spread her brightness
Over all the earth, a cry chanted
Loud and clear in tones of happy omen
Arose from the Greeks; and from the island's rocks
An echo, high and shrill, returned the cry.
Fear seized all the barbarians as they saw
How wrong they had been, for the Greeks were not in
                                                    flight
As they sang the awesome paean, but rather rushing
Into battle spirited and courageous.
A trumpet's blare fired up the fleet
And instantly, upon command, they pulled
Together, striking the salty deep with a plash
Of oars, and at speed they all hove into view.
First the right wing, in orderly formation,
Made a disciplined advance, and next
The entire fleet was charging out against us,
And at that very moment we could hear
A mighty cry: "You sons of Greece, come on,
Free you fatherland, children, wives; free
The shrines of your ancestral gods and your
Forefathers' tombs. This fight is for your all."
And from our side in answer arose a clamor
In the Persian tongue. The time for delay had passed.
    Suddenly, ship rammed ship with bronze-clad beak.
A Greek ship started the assault, shearing off
The stern of a Phoenician galley. Each captain
Steered his craft against another. At first,
The flood-tide of Persian force held off the foe,
But when the great mass of our fleet was squeezed
Into the narrows and they could not help each other,
They rammed their own themselves with bronzed-
                                                    mouthed beaks
And scattered all the rowing gear. Sensing
Their advantage, the Greek ships circled round
And struck. Hulls toppled over and now the sea
Disappeared from view, so full it was
Of wreckage from the ships and slaughtered men.
    Shores and shoals were buried under corpses

And every ship in the barbarian fleet
Plied its oars to take disordered flight.
But the Greeks kept clubbing and stabbing with broken
oars
And chunks of flotsam, as if our men were tunnies
Or a haul of fish. All the while, shrieks
And groans filled the expanse of the salt sea
Till night's dark eyes cast their pall on the carnage.
I could not give the mass of our disasters
full measure, even if I took ten days
To tell you the story line by line, but be sure
Of this: never on a single day
Did men in such huge numbers meet their death.

Aeschylus, Persians, *lines 348–432, trans. Peter Burian.*

King Minos and Thalassocracy
Thucydides (397 B.C.E.)

In his *Peloponnesian War* Thucydides recounts the lengthy conflict between Athenians and Spartans (431–404 B.C.E.). An Athenian statesman, Thucydides (460/455–ca. 397) briefly took part in this war as a general. However, in 424, after leading a failed naval campaign, he was sent into exile, where he wrote about the war. The introduction (1.1–22) presents the origins of Greek sea power, which he traces back to the mythical king Minos of Crete. The thalassocracy of Minos depended on his ability to send colonists across the Aegean and to quash piracy. For Thucydides, the Trojan War heralded the unification of Hellas. Piracy marked the period before states were formed, and it persisted into Thucydides' time. The greater degree of communication facilitated by sea travel, he says, brought both increased availability of commodities and a military threat to individual city-states.

Indeed, they [*the Hellenic communities*] could not unite for this expedition [*the Trojan War*] till they had gained increased familiarity with the sea. And the first person known to us by tradition as having established a navy is Minos. He made himself master of what is now called the Hellenic sea, and ruled over the Cyclades, into most of which he sent the first colonies, expelling the Carians and appointing his own sons governors; and thus did his best to put down piracy in those waters, a necessary step to secure the revenues for his own use.

For in early times the Hellenes and the barbarians of the coast and islands, as communication by sea became more common, were tempted to turn pirates, under the conduct of their most powerful men; the motives being to serve their own cupidity and to support the needy. They would fall upon a town unprotected by walls, and consisting of a mere collection of villages, and would plunder it; indeed, this came to be the main source of their livelihood, no disgrace being yet attached to such an achievement, but even some glory. An illustration of this is furnished by the honor with which some of the inhabitants of the continent still regard a successful marauder, and by the question we find the old poets everywhere representing the people as asking of voyagers, "Are they pirates?"—as if those who are asked the question would have no idea of disclaiming the imputation, or their interrogators of reproaching them for it. The same rapine prevailed also by land. And even at the present day many of Hellas still follow the old fashion, the Ozolian Locrians for instance, the Aetolians, the Acarnanians, and that region of the continent; and the custom of carrying arms is still kept up among these continentals, from the old piratical habits.

The whole of Hellas used once to carry arms, their habitations being unprotected and their communication with each other unsafe; indeed, to wear arms was as much a part of everyday life with them as with the barbarians. And the fact that the people in these parts of Hellas are still living in the old way points to a time when the same mode of life was once equally common to all. The Athenians were the first to lay aside their weapons, and to adopt an easier and more luxurious mode of life; indeed, it is only lately that their rich old men left off the luxury of wearing undergarments of linen, and fastening a knot of their hair with a tie of golden grasshoppers, a fashion which spread to their Ionian kindred and long prevailed among the old men there. On the contrary, a modest style of dressing, more in conformity with modern ideas, was first adopted by the Lacedaemonians, the rich doing their best to assimilate their way of life to that of the common people. They also set the example of contending naked, publicly stripping and anointing themselves with oil in their gymnastic exercises. Formerly, even in the Olympic contests, the athletes who contended wore belts across their middles; and it is but a few years since that the practice ceased. To this day among some of the barbarians, especially in Asia, when prizes for boxing and wrestling are offered, belts are worn by the combatants. And there are many other points in which a likeness might be shown between the life of the Hellenic world of old and the barbarian of today.

With respect to their towns, later on, at an era of increased facilities of navigation and a greater supply of capital, we find the shores becoming the site of walled towns, and the isthmuses being occupied for the purposes of commerce and defense against a neighbor. But the old towns, on account of the great prevalence of piracy, were built away from the sea, whether on the islands or the continent, and still remain in their old sites. For the pirates used to plunder one another, and indeed all coast populations, whether seafaring or not.

The islanders, too, were great pirates. These islanders were Carians and Phoenicians, by whom most of the islands were colonized, as was proved by the following fact. During the purification of Delos by Athens in this war all the graves in the island were taken up, and it was found that above half their inmates were Carians: they were identified by the fashion of the arms buried with them, and by the method of interment, which was the same as the Carians still follow. But as soon as Minos had formed his navy, communication by sea became easier, as he colonized most of the islands, and thus expelled the malefactors. The coast population now began to apply themselves more closely to the acquisition of wealth, and their life became more settled; some even began to build themselves walls on the strength of their newly acquired riches. For the love of gain would reconcile the weaker to the dominion of the stronger, and the possession of capital enabled the more powerful to reduce the smaller towns to subjection. And it was at a somewhat later stage of this development that they went on the expedition against Troy. . . .

[*Thucydides proceeds to discuss the Trojan War in terms of sea power*]

Even after the Trojan War, Hellas was still engaged in removing and settling, and thus could not attain to the quiet that must precede growth. The late return of the Hellenes from Ilium caused many revolutions, and factions ensued almost everywhere; and it was the citizens thus driven into exile who founded the cities. Sixty years after the capture of Ilium, the modern Boeotians were driven out of Arne by the Thessalians, and settled in the present Boeotia, the former Cadmeis; though there was a division of them there before, some of whom joined the expedition to Ilium. Twenty years later, the Dorians and the Heraclids became masters of Peloponnese; so that much had to be done and many years had to elapse before Hellas could attain to a durable tranquility undisturbed by removals, and could begin to send out colonies, as Athens did to Ionia and most of the islands, and the Peloponnesians to most of Italy and Sicily and some places in the rest of Hellas. All these places were founded subsequently to the war with Troy.

Thucydides, History of the Peloponnesian War, *trans. Richard Crawley (1874; London: Dent, 1910), 3–6, 9 (1.3.4–8, 12).*

Grain Trade Dispute

Attributed to Demosthenes (323 B.C.E.)

Trade in the "Mediterranean triad" of cereals, wine, and olives is attested from both literary and archaeological evidence. One instance is a speech prosecuting a certain Dionysodorus for defaulting on a loan: this is transmitted among the speeches of the Athenian statesman Demosthenes (384–322 B.C.E.) but likely postdating his death. The plaintiff was one Dareius, who had made a loan for a ship to sail from the Peiraeus, Athens's port, to Egypt, and to return laden with grain. Both principal and interest were payable upon the return of the ship, which itself served as security, whereas loss of the ship would absolve the borrowers of any liability. On the other hand, failure to keep their contract would render the borrowers liable to double the amount of the loan. Now Dionysodorus's associate Parmeniscus, while in Egypt, found out that the price of grain at Athens had fallen as a result of imports from Sicily, and he consequently chose to sell the grain at Rhodes instead, where it commanded a higher price. This he did for several months. At issue in the speech is the extent of the borrowers' liability, since they claimed that damage to the ship prevented it from reaching the Peiraeus. The speech reveals the reliance of the classical Greek city-states on grain imported from Egypt, and the depth of their commercial infrastructure.

You see, men of Athens, Dionysodorus here and his partner Parmeniscus came to us last year in early September, saying that they wished to borrow money on the security of their ship on the condition that they sail to Egypt and from Egypt to Rhodes or Athens; and they agreed that the interest be paid to either one of these ports. When we answered, gentlemen of the jury, that we would not lend money on a ship headed to any port other than Athens, they agreed to sail here, and upon this agreement they borrowed from us on the security of their ship three thousand drachmae for the round-trip journey; they signed a contract on these terms. In the agreement Pamphilus here was named the lender; but I, although not mentioned in the contract, had a share in the loan with him. The clerk shall now read you the actual contract.

CONTRACT:

According to this agreement, gentlemen of the jury, Dionysodorus here and his partner Parmeniscus, having got the money from us, sent their ship from Athens to Egypt. Parmeniscus sailed in command of the ship, while Dionysodorus remained here at Athens. Bear in mind now, gentlemen of the jury, that these men were all underlings and accomplices of Cleomenes, who had been ruler in Egypt and who, from the time he became ruler, did no small harm to your city, as well as to the rest of the Greeks. He did this by reselling grain and fixing its price, and he did this with these men by his side. For, while some of them would ship the goods from Egypt, others would sail in charge of the cargoes, and others still would remain here and handle the sale of those shipments. Then, those who remained here would send letters to those abroad advising them of the market prices: if grain was expensive here among you, they would ship it here; but if it was cheap, they would ship it to some other port. It was primarily in this way, gentlemen of the jury, that the price of grain was manipulated, by communications and conspiracies such as these. So, when these men sent their ship from Athens, grain was fairly expensive; and for this reason they did not object to having it written in the contract that they sail to Athens and to no other port. But after this, gentlemen of the jury, when the Sicilian grain-fleet arrived and the prices here were falling, and their ship had already set sail for Egypt, this man here, Dionysodorus, immediately sent a man to Rhodes to tell his partner Parmeniscus what was happening here, knowing for certain that his ship would have to put in at Rhodes.

In the end, when Parmeniscus, this man's partner, had received the letter sent by him and had learned the market price of grain here, he unloaded his ship's grain at Rhodes and sold it there. He did this in contempt of the contract, gentlemen of the jury, and of the penalties which they themselves, of their own accord, had drawn up, in case they should overstep the agreement in any way; in contempt of your laws too, did he do this, laws which require that ship-owners and the merchants onboard sail to the port on which they have agreed, or else be subject to severe penalties.

Pseudo-Demosthenes, Against Dionysodorus, *5–10, trans. Jason Aftosmis.*

Foundation Decree of Cyrene

Anonymous (4th century B.C.E.)

In the 630s B.C.E., the small volcanic island of Santorini (ancient Thera) sent a party to establish settlements in what is now Libya. By 631 it had founded Cyrene, and soon several others close by, dubbing the area Cyrenaica. Greek colonizing activity was centered initially on Sicily and southern Italy, but over time it stretched to the southern coastline, including the Nile Delta, into the Black Sea, and as far west as Mainace in Spain, and Marseilles (Massilia) and Nice (Nikaia) in France. Among the earliest colonies was that on the island of Ischia (Pithekoussai) in the Bay of Naples, from which a brief inscription survives on an eighth-century goblet. The causes of such migrations are not always easy to identify: such factors as overpopulation, crop failure, political disputes, and the desire for trade played a part but cannot account for all cases. Greek colonization was in any case not a uniform phenomenon but initiated by individual city-states over an extended period, roughly from 750 to 580 B.C.E. The following inscription dates from the fourth century B.C.E., involving the rights of new colonists from Thera, but it purportedly quoted the original seventh-century foundation decree. Scholars are divided as to whether this really does reflect the original decree. Either way, it does reassert the link between Thera and Cyrene some three centuries after the foundation. It shows the importance of religion, especially oracles, in the establishment of colonies. The first settlers had to swear an oath by the gods, and its contravention would bring dire consequences—constraints by which the Therans maintained a strong hold over the new colonies. It also shows a degree of coercion among the early settlers.

Let the god stand witness. Let there be good fortune. Damis, son of Bathykles, has declared: in response to the request made by the Therans, as represented by Kleudamas, son of Euthykles, the Therans are to be granted citizenship, in order that the city should prosper and the people of Cyrene be fortunate. This citizenship is in accordance with that ancestral custom which our forefathers established, both those who came from Thera to found Cyrene and those who stayed at Thera; just as when Apollo granted to Battus and those Therans who founded Cyrene that they enjoy good fortune if, when they sent out the colony according to the command of first-founder Apollo, they abided by the agreement that our forefathers themselves once made. With good fortune the people have decided that Therans will continue to have equal citizenship in

Cyrene just as before. And all Therans who reside in Thera are to swear to the same agreement that the others once made, and to be assigned to a tribe and a phratry and nine social groups. This decree is to be inscribed on a marble stele, and that stele placed in the ancestral shrine of Pythian Apollo; the agreement is also to be written on the stele that the colonists made when they sailed to Libya with Battus, from Thera to Cyrene. As for the expense of the stone or the inscription, let those overseeing the accounts provide it from the revenues of Apollo.

THE AGREEMENT OF THE FOUNDERS

The assembly decided: since Apollo has given a spontaneous prophecy to Battus and the Therans to colonize Cyrene, the Therans have resolved to send Battus into Libya as founder and king, and for the Therans to sail as his comrades. They are to sail on fair and equal terms, according to household, and one son is to be chosen [*from each family;*] those in the prime of life [*are to sail*], as well as, from the rest of the Therans, any free man [*who wishes may*] sail. If the settlers establish a colony, any relative sailing to Libya later is to have a share of citizenship and rights and receive a portion of unallocated land. But if they do not establish a colony, and cannot be helped by the Therans, but rather are driven on in trouble for five years, then let them leave that land for Thera without fear to regain their own property and be citizens. But the one who is unwilling to sail when the city sends him, he shall be liable to the death penalty and his property seized. And the one who harbors or protects him—even if it be a father defending his son, or a brother shielding his brother—he will suffer the same penalty as that man not willing to sail.

Both those remaining there and those who were sailing on a colonization expedition agreed on these conditions; and they put curses on those who transgressed the conditions and did not abide by them, whether from among those settling in Libya or remaining in Thera. They—men, women, boys, and girls, all together—made wax figures and burnt them while uttering this curse: The man who does not abide by the agreements, but rather transgresses them, that man is to melt and waste away just as the figures, the man himself, his children and his property alike; but to those who abide by these agreements, both those sailing to Libya and those staying in Thera, let many good things come to them and their offspring.

Foundation decree of Cyrene, trans. Jason Aftosmis.

Where to Found a Polis

Aristotle (before 322 B.C.E.)

The hypothetical founding of a colony is addressed in the *Politics* of Aristotle (384–322 B.C.E.). Born in Stagira in the northwestern Aegean, Aristotle came to Athens to study in Plato's Academy. For a few years he was tutor of the young Macedonian prince Alexander, and it is a matter of debate to what extent Aristotle's teachings would influence Alexander's urban foundations in the course of his Asian campaign (336–323 B.C.E.) (see Plutarch in Chapter 2 below). In his own school, the Lyceum, Aristotle taught philosophy and guided research projects in the natural sciences and political history. A major theme in his ethical treatises is human happiness or flourishing (*eudaimonia*). In the *Politics*, he discusses the features of the ideal polis. Here, he weighs the advantages and disadvantages of proximity to the sea, before concluding that it is beneficial. Aristotle further articulates an idea found in ancient texts going back to Herodotus and Hippocrates that there is an innate connection between the character (*ethos*) of a people and the climate in which they live. This concept, environmental determinism, would be influential in Enlightenment anthropology.

Every one would agree in praising the territory which is most entirely self-sufficing; and that must be the territory which is all-producing, for to have all things and to want nothing is sufficiency. In size and extent it should be such as may enable the inhabitants to live at once temperately and liberally in the enjoyment of leisure. Whether we are right or wrong in laying down this limit we will inquire more precisely hereafter, when we have occasion to consider what is the right use of property and wealth: a matter which is much disputed, because men are inclined to rush into one of two extremes, some into meanness, others into luxury.

It is not difficult to determine the general character of the territory which is required (there are, however, some points on which military authorities should be heard); it should be difficult of access to the enemy, and easy of egress to the inhabitants. Further, we require that the land as well as the inhabitants of whom we were just now speaking should be taken in at a single view, for a country which is easily seen can be easily protected. As to the position of the city, if we could have what we wish, it should be well situated in regard both to sea and land. This then is one principle, that it should be a convenient center for the protection of the whole country: the other is, that it should be suitable for receiving the fruits of the soil, and also for the bringing in of timber and any other products that are easily transported.

Whether a communication with the sea is beneficial to a well-ordered state or not is a question which has often been asked. It is argued that the introduction of strangers brought up under other laws, and the increase of population, will be adverse to good order; the increase arises from their using the sea and having a crowd of merchants coming and going, and is inimical to good government. Apart from these considerations, it would be undoubtedly better, both with a view to safety and to the provision of necessaries, that the city and territory should be connected with the sea; the defenders of a country, if they are to maintain themselves against an enemy, should be easily relieved both by land and by sea; and even if they are not able to attack by sea and land at once, they will have less difficulty in doing mischief to their assailants on one element, if they themselves can use both. Moreover, it is necessary that they should import from abroad what is not found in their own country, and that they should export what they have in excess; for a city ought to be a market, not indeed for others, but for herself.

Those who make themselves a market for the world only do so for the sake of revenue, and if a state ought not to desire profit of this kind it ought not to have such an emporium. Nowadays we often see in countries and cities dockyards and harbors very conveniently placed outside the city, but not too far off; and they are kept in dependence by walls and similar fortifications. Cities thus situated manifestly reap the benefit of intercourse with their ports; and any harm which is likely to accrue may be easily guarded against by the laws, which will pronounce and determine who may hold communication with one another, and who may not.

There can be no doubt that the possession of a moderate naval force is advantageous to a city; the city should be formidable not only to its own citizens but to some of its neighbors, or, if necessary, able to assist them by sea as well as by land. The proper number or magnitude of this naval force is relative to the character of the state; for if her function is to take a leading part in politics, her naval power should be commensurate with the scale of her enterprises. The population of the state need not be much increased, since there is no necessity that the sailors should be citizens: the marines who have the control and command will be freemen, and belong also to the infantry; and wherever there is a dense population of *Perioeci* [*neighbors*] and husbandmen, there will always be sailors more than enough. Of this we see instances at the present day.

The city of Heraclea, for example, although small in comparison with many others, can man a considerable fleet. Such are our conclusions respecting the territory of the state, its harbors, its towns, its relations to the sea, and its maritime power.

Having spoken of the number of the citizens, we will proceed to speak of what should be their character. This is a subject which can be easily understood by any one who casts his eye on the more celebrated states of Hellas, and generally on the distribution of races in the habitable world. Those who live in a cold climate and in Europe are full of spirit, but wanting in intelligence and skill; and therefore they retain comparative freedom, but have no political organization, and are incapable of ruling over others. Whereas the natives of Asia are intelligent and inventive, but they are wanting in spirit, and therefore they are always in a state of subjection and slavery. But the Hellenic race, which is situated between them, is likewise intermediate in character, being high-spirited and also intelligent. Hence it continues free, and is the best-governed of any nation, and, if it could be formed into one state, would be able to rule the world. There are also similar differences in the different tribes of Hellas; for some of them are of a one-sided nature, and are intelligent or courageous only, while in others there is a happy combination of both qualities. And clearly those whom the legislator will most easily lead to virtue may be expected to be both intelligent and courageous. Some say that the guardians should be friendly towards those whom they know, fierce towards those whom they do not know. Now, passion is the quality of the soul which begets friendship and enables us to love; notably the spirit within us is more stirred against our friends and acquaintances than against those who are unknown to us, when we think that we are despised by them; for which reason Archilochus [*the poet*], complaining of his friends, very naturally addresses his soul in these words: "For surely thou art plagued on account of friends."

The Politics of Aristotle, *trans. Benjamin Jowett (Oxford: Clarendon Press, 1885), 215–19 (book 7, 1326b27–1328a5).*

Escorting a Princess
Artemidorus (252 B.C.E.)

The massive military campaign of Alexander the Great of Macedon destroyed the Achaemenid Empire, setting up Greek elites throughout the eastern Mediterranean and western Asia. The two most powerful of the newly reestablished states to emerge in their place were Egypt, ruled by the Ptolemaic dynasty for three centuries, and the Seleucid kingdom of Asia Minor. Though the Hellenistic period saw much competition and even war between the kingdoms, there were also less violent kinds of exchange. Journeys of different kinds are visible in a cache of some two thousand papyrus documents belonging to a certain Zenon, private secretary to Apollonius, who was finance minister of Ptolemy II Philadelphus (r. 281–246 B.C.E.). Preserved in Egypt's dry climate, these letters offer unmatched insights into ancient Egyptian lives. In the following letter Artemidorus, Apollonius's private physician, addresses several requests to Zenon as Artemidorus undertakes a return journey from the Seleucid kingdom. At the time of writing Apollonius was at the port city of Sidon while Zenon, whom we know to have undertaken several journeys on state business, was at Philadelphia in Egypt's Fayum territory. Apollonius had escorted Ptolemy's daughter Berenike to the Seleucid kingdom, where she was to marry King Antiochus II, and Artemidorus was part of the royal entourage. The letter reveals the kinds of commodities that formed part of an important bureaucrat's life, and shows how they could be mobilized at a distance.

Artemidorus to Zenon, greeting. If you are well, that would be a good thing. I also am well and Apollonius is healthy and other matters are in order. As I write this to you, we have just reached Sidon having escorted the princess [*Berenike*] to the frontier, and I assume that we shall be with you shortly. Please do me the favor of taking care of your own health and writing to me if you desire anything done that I can do for you. And please buy me, so that I may have them on arrival, three *metretae* of the best honey and 600 *artabae* of barley for the animals, paying the price from the produce of the sesame and croton [*i.e., castor-oil plant*]; also attend to the house in Philadelphia so that I find it roofed on my arrival. Try to the extent possible to keep an eye on the oxen, pigs, geese and other livestock there, for in this way I shall have a better supply of provisions. Also make sure that the crops are harvested somehow, and if any outlay is needed, do not hesitate to pay what is required. Farewell. Year 33, intercalary Peritius 6. (Addressed) To Zenon. To Philadelphia. (Docketed) Year 33, Phamenoth 6. Artemidorus.

P. Cairo Zen., *59251, from the Zenon Archive, trans. Grant Parker.*

CHAPTER 2

Mare Nostrum

Our Sea

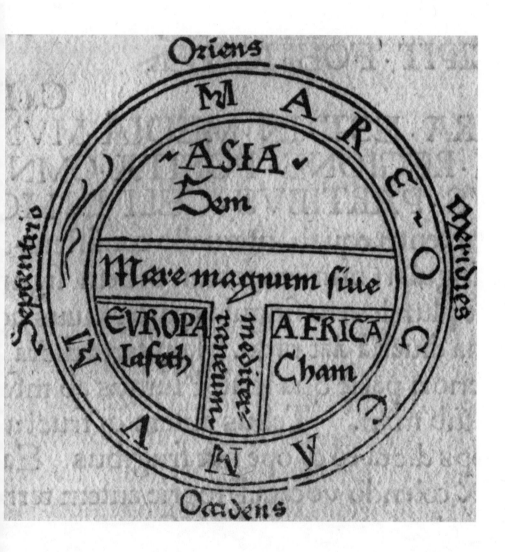

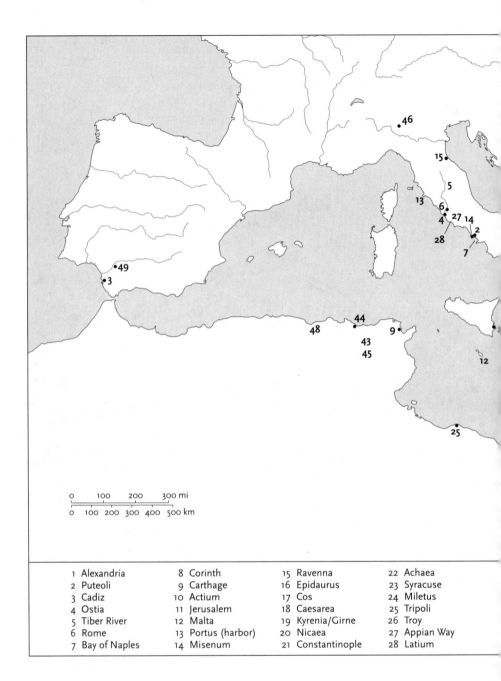

1	Alexandria	8	Corinth	15	Ravenna	22	Achaea
2	Puteoli	9	Carthage	16	Epidaurus	23	Syracuse
3	Cadiz	10	Actium	17	Cos	24	Miletus
4	Ostia	11	Jerusalem	18	Caesarea	25	Tripoli
5	Tiber River	12	Malta	19	Kyrenia/Girne	26	Troy
6	Rome	13	Portus (harbor)	20	Nicaea	27	Appian Way
7	Bay of Naples	14	Misenum	21	Constantinople	28	Latium

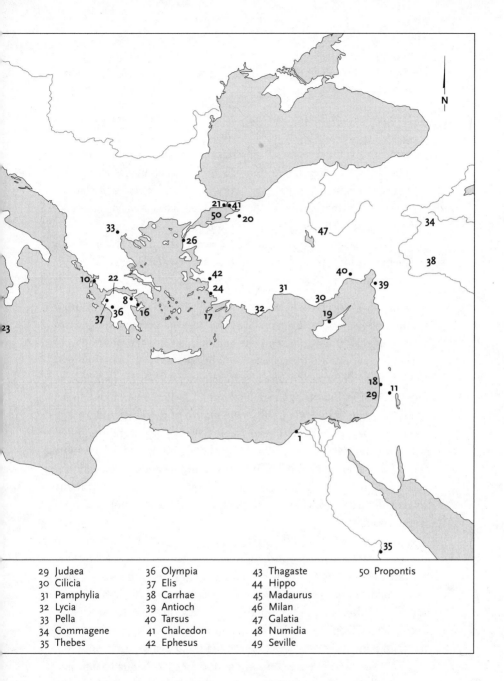

29 Judaea	36 Olympia	43 Thagaste	50 Propontis
30 Cilicia	37 Elis	44 Hippo	
31 Pamphylia	38 Carrhae	45 Madaurus	
32 Lycia	39 Antioch	46 Milan	
33 Pella	40 Tarsus	47 Galatia	
34 Commagene	41 Chalcedon	48 Numidia	
35 Thebes	42 Ephesus	49 Seville	

The Romans' standard term for the Mediterranean was "our sea" (*mare nostrum*)—a measure of both expanding control and growing self-confidence. Thus, the enthusiasm of the Elder Pliny (d. 79 C.E.) for long-distance exchange is telling:

> Two prefects of Egypt, Galerius and Balbillus, made the voyage from the Straits of Sicily to Alexandria within seven and six days, respectively. Fifteen years later Valerius Marianus, a senator of praetorian rank, reached Alexandria from Puteoli in less than nine days, in summertime, on a very slight breeze. To think that commerce brings Cadiz, by the Straits of Gibraltar, within seven days of Ostia, Hither Spain within four days, the province of Narbonese Gaul within three, and Africa, even on a very gentle breeze, within two, as happened to Gaius Flavius, legate of the proconsul Vibius Crispus! (Pliny, *Natural History*, 19.3–4)

Such travel would have been unthinkable without the political unity brought about by the Roman state. The passage serves also as a reminder of the tight embrace of the commercial and the political, and particularly of the extent to which a maritime network linked the metropolis with all corners of the Mediterranean. A river port with some one million inhabitants by the first century C.E., Rome had access to the Mediterranean mainly via Ostia at the mouth of the Tiber and Puteoli (modern Pozzuoli) on the Bay of Naples. Such ports were integrated with an extensive system of roads throughout Italy and increasingly the entire empire. The Appian Way, linking Rome and Brindisi and described by the poet Statius as "queen of long roads," is one of many roads still visible. Milestones are further evidence of land-based communications.

Two victories in the year 146 B.C.E., in the east over Corinth and in the west over Carthage, confirmed Roman hegemony over the Mediterranean. Corinth and Carthage had both been major trading states, their vast economic power confirmed by the diffusion of their distinctive wares. With the conquest of Egypt in 30 B.C.E., in the course of which both queen Cleopatra and her Roman lover Marcus Antonius lost their lives, Romans added the last corner of the Inner Sea to their dominion. The battle of Actium (31 B.C.E.), where the forces of Augustus defeated those of Cleopatra and Antonius, is celebrated in Horace's *Ode*, 1.37. Horace, with both ancients and moderns, would look back on the battle of Actium as the inauguration of the "Roman peace" (*Pax Romana*) under Augustus that fostered the high degree of trans-Mediterranean traffic. One immediate effect of the new political dispensation was the settling of former soldiers in military colonies, with many citizens experiencing the confiscation of their land. The poet Virgil, for one, narrowly escaped this fate, as his first and ninth *Eclogues* indicate.

It is essential to see Roman power also from the point of view of its subjects. Thus the historian Tacitus, a senator and critic of the de facto monarchy that began with Julius Caesar, attributes the following sentence to the British leader Calgacus in a speech exhorting his fellow countrymen to stand firm against Rome: "They give the false name of empire to their plundering, murdering and thieving, and where they make a desert they call it peace" (*Agricola*, 30). By this time Roman power had edged toward northern Europe. The most famous case of regional resistance came in the province of Judaea. Here the Jews revolted during the years 66–70 C.E. This episode is recounted by Josephus, a Jewish aristocrat who initially opposed the Romans but later allied with them. The campaign ended in disaster for the Jews, many of whom fled. The destruction of the Temple in Jerusalem marked the beginning of the Diaspora and continues to be remembered in Jewish tradition as a foundational event. Philo, Josephus's older contemporary, had previously led an embassy to Rome seeking greater recognition for the Jews of Alexandria; his writings (in Greek) reveal a concerted effort to align Jewish belief and Hellenistic philosophy.

Threats to travel came from both environmental and human sources. In the case of the apostle Paul, a prisoner placed on a grain freighter heading from Alexandria to Italy, an unexpected storm brought shipwreck off the island of Malta. At the commercial harbor of Portus some 200 ships were lost during a single storm in 62 C.E., writes Tacitus (*Annals*, 15.18). Piracy was another factor, particularly before the *Pax Romana*. Fictional representations of this are seen in Chariton's *Chaereas and Callirhoe* and other Greek novels. Roman efforts to quell piracy in the eastern Mediterranean, especially Pompey's campaign of 67 B.C.E., met with considerable success. Augustus established a permanent navy at Misenum on the Bay of Naples and Ravenna in the Adriatic; Pliny the Elder commanded the fleet at Misenum until his death caused by an eruption of Mount Vesuvius in 79 C.E.

But travel was not purely a matter of danger: it could also be a source of healing. A favorite destination was the sanctuary of the divinity Asclepius at Epidaurus, to which travelers would come in search of a cure; another of many Asclepius's many shrines was on the island of Cos, which was linked with the supposed father of Greco-Roman medicine, Hippocrates. Irrespective of destination, however, a voyage itself could be beneficial to a patient's health. In his medical treatise, Aulus Cornelius Celsus (ca. 25 B.C.E.–ca. 50 C.E.) recommends a voyage from Italy to Alexandria as treatment for tuberculosis:

> If there is graver illness and true tuberculosis, it is necessary to combat it right away at its inception; for when it has lasted for some time it is not easily defeated. If the patient's strength allows, a long sea voyage is needed, as is a change of air, of such a kind that a denser atmosphere should be sought than that which the patient leaves. For this reason the voyage from Italy to Alexandria is most suitable. Generally the body ought to be able to bear this in the early stages, since this disease arises especially during the most robust part of life, namely, between the ages of eighteen and thirty-five years. If the patient's weak state does not permit this, the most advantageous is for him to be rocked in a ship without going very far. (Celsus, *On Medicine*, 3.22.8)

Since the 1960s, new insights into Roman-period trade have come from underwater archaeology: maritime technology, travel patterns, and commodities are all subject to new data. Even ancient harbors, such as Caesarea and Alexandria, have been investigated in this manner. In some cases wrecks have been reconstructed, as at Girne (ancient Kyrenia) on Cyprus. A frequent type of find has been African "red slip" pottery, used for two-handled pots (amphorae) transporting olive oil or wine. Its diffusion across the Mediterranean points to the broad reach of commercial networks in this period.

One implication of Rome's Mediterranean-wide power in the early centuries C.E. is that it allowed Christianity to spread from its Palestinian origins, partly in journeys like that of the imprisoned Paul. It was under Constantine in the early fourth century C.E., some 150 years before the collapse of the western Roman Empire, that Christianity was officially accepted, and by the late fourth century it was actively promoted by the Roman state. In fact, the ecumenical councils of the church's bishops, beginning in 325 when Constantine convened the Council of Nicaea, provide stark reminders of trans-Mediterranean networks—unified by the universalism of the Catholic Church and at the same time by that of the Roman state.

This chapter ends in the early medieval period. The legal and architectural enterprises of the Byzantine emperor Justinian would have major repercussions in its own time and beyond. Constantinople, the Byzantine capital, claimed direct heirship to Rome, not only in a political and economic sense but also as metropolis of the Christian church. Whereas the Roman Empire in the west fell to Germanic invaders in the late fifth century, the eastern empire centered on Constantinople continued until 1453. On the far side of the Sea, the Iberian Peninsula had become home to the Visigoths, a Germanic people: while migrating westward they had sacked the city of Rome in 410 under the leadership of Alaric. One text from the Visigothic world, whose leaders had converted to Christianity in the fifth century, was the *Etymologies* of Isidore of Seville, an influential codification of classical learning.

A Roman Mediterranean
Polybius (118 B.C.E.)

The *Universal History* by Polybius (ca. 200–ca. 118 B.C.E.) presents a grand narrative of Rome's growing power in the Sea in the third and second centuries B.C.E. In this work, which survives only in part, Polybius aimed to narrate and explain "how, and by a state with what kind of constitution, nearly the entire known world came under the sole rule of the Romans in a space of not quite fifty-three years" (1.1.5). The Roman constitution is at the heart of his analysis of these developments. Rome's ascendancy had much relevance for Polybius's contemporary Greek-speaking readers, for it explained the reduced autonomy of Greek states. Polybius himself spent several years at Rome as a prisoner-of-war. In the course of his incarceration he received the patronage of the powerful statesman Publius Cornelius Scipio Aemilianus (185/4–129 B.C.E.). This excerpt reveals Polybius's idea that Roman power changed Mediterranean history from isolated episodes into an organic whole. In such terms he explains his decision to begin his history with the Second Punic War in 220 B.C.E. The work continues up to the capture of Corinth in 146 B.C.E., which Polybius witnessed as a companion of Scipio. This was the year Carthage was destroyed at the end of the Third Punic War. His travels took him to various parts of the Mediterranean, including an overland journey from Spain to Italy on the same route Hannibal had taken. Polybius's work stands out both for his emphasis on historical process over individual events and for his close experience of them.

My *History* begins in the 140th Olympiad. The events from which it starts are these. In Greece, what is called the Social war: the first waged by Philip, son of Demetrius and father of Perseus, in league with the Achaeans against the Aetolians. In Asia, the war for the possession of Coele-Syria which Antiochus and Ptolemy Philopator carried on against each other. In Italy, Libya, and their neighborhood, the conflict between Rome and Carthage, generally called the Hannibalian war [*218–201 B.C.E.*]. My work thus begins where that of Aratus of Sicyon leaves off. Now up to this time the word's history had been, so to speak, a series of disconnected transactions, as widely separated in their origin and results as in their localities. But from this time forth history becomes a connected whole: the affairs of Italy and Libya are involved with those of Asia and Greece, and the tendency of all is to unity. This is why I have fixed upon this era as the starting-point of my work. For it was their victory over the Carthaginians in this war, and their conviction that thereby the most difficult and most essential step towards universal empire had been taken, which encouraged the Romans for the first time to stretch out their hands upon the rest, and to cross with an army into Greece and Asia.

Now, had the states that were rivals for universal empire been familiarly known to us, no reference perhaps to their previous history would have been necessary, to show the purpose and the forces with which they approached an undertaking of this nature and magnitude. But the fact is that the majority of the Greeks have no knowledge of the previous constitution, power, or achievements either of Rome or Carthage. I therefore concluded that it was necessary to prefix this and the next book to my *History*. I was anxious that no one, when fairly embarked upon my actual narrative, should feel at a loss, and have to ask what were the designs entertained by the Romans, or the forces and means at their disposal, that they entered upon those undertakings, which did in fact lead to their becoming masters of land and sea everywhere in our part of the world. I wished, on the contrary, that these books of mine, and the prefatory sketch which they contained, might make it clear that the resources they started with justified their original idea, and sufficiently explained their final success in grasping universal empire and dominion.

Polybius' Histories, *trans. E. S. Shuckburgh (London: Macmillan, 1889), 2–3 (1.3).*

Sale of Callirhoe

Chariton (probably 1st century B.C.E.)

Piracy and escape abound in the Greek novels, and *Chaereas and Callirhoe* is no exception. It cannot be assigned a date with any precision, and the author's claim to be from Aphrodisias in Asia Minor is suspect. The work is set in Syracuse in the early fifth century B.C.E., likely some four centuries before its composition. Chaereas and Callirhoe, the beautiful young hero and heroine, marry at the beginning of the novel, but jealous rivals engineer a quarrel between them. Chaereas unintentionally kicks Callirhoe to death after hearing malicious accusations of infidelity. In the extract Callirhoe has been mistakenly buried alive before being found by pirates engaged in tomb-robbing. Eager to capitalize on their treasure, they sail first to Athens and then Miletus in Asia Minor, where they sell her as a high-value slave. In the meantime her grief-stricken husband searches for her far and wide. After many twists and turns in the plot, they are finally reunited and can return to Syracuse, where they live happily ever after.

While Callirhoe lamented her many troubles trapped inside the tomb, Theron [*pirate leader*] and his men, waiting until the dead of night, approached the tomb without a sound, gently stroking the sea with their oars. Theron was the first man ashore, and he assigned the men their task. Four of his men he sent to keep watch: if anyone came near, they were to try to kill him or, failing that, give warning of his approach. Theron himself went to the tomb with four other men. The remaining seven—for there were sixteen in all—he ordered to stay at the boat and keep the oars poised like wings, so that, in the event of an emergency, they could swiftly pick up the men on shore and sail away. Theron and his henchmen started opening the tomb using crowbars and, as it began to burst open, the noise grew louder. Still inside the tomb, Callirhoe felt every emotion at once: fear, joy, pain, wonder, hope, and disbelief.

"What sound is this, and from where does it come?" she wondered. "Perhaps some god has come for pitiful me; gods do come to those who are dying. Or is it not just a noise but the voice of those beneath the earth, a voice summoning me to them? No—it's more likely grave-robbers. This, this too is heaped onto my misfortunes; wealth is no help to a corpse!" Such were Callirhoe's thoughts when one of the bandits peered into the tomb and crept forward slightly. Wishing to be set free, Callirhoe fell down at his feet at once, but the robber was terrified; he leapt back and called to his friends. "Let's get out of here!" his voice trembled. "There's some kind of spirit guarding what's inside, and he won't let us in!"

Theron mocked this man, calling him cowardly and more lifeless than the corpse. He then demanded that someone else enter, but when no one would dare, Theron himself went in, sword thrust before him. When Callirhoe saw the iron's edge flash, she feared she would be killed and lay down in the corner. From there she pleaded softly: "Pity me, whoever you are, pity me, for neither my husband nor my parents pitied me. Do not kill the girl you've now rescued!"

With this Theron just grew bolder and, clever as he was, realized what must have taken place. He stood there pensively, weighing his options. At first he planned to kill the girl, thinking she'd interfere with his entire venture, but soon he realized how profitable she could be. And so he had a change of heart. "Why not make her a part of the plunder too?" he said to himself. "There is a good bit of silver, and quite a lot of gold, but her beauty is more valuable than all of these things." Taking her by the hand, he led her out and called out to his henchman: "Look! Here's the ghost that scared you off! Look after her—I want to return her to her parents. Let's get the rest of the treasure inside, since not even a corpse guards it now."

After they had filled up the boat with the plunder, Theron asked the guard to take the girl aside while they deliberated over what to do with her. Several opinions were expressed, each in conflict with the other. "My friends, we came for something else," began the first man, "but Fortune has granted us something better. So let's profit from it! We can do this without much risk. I say we leave the treasure here on land and return her to her husband and father. We tell them that we weighed anchor near the tomb, just as fishermen would. But when we heard a voice coming from the tomb, we pried it open out of compassion, to save the girl trapped inside. We'll make her swear to testify to all this, and she'll be happy to repay this to the kindly men who saved her life. Imagine how happy we'll make all of Sicily, and how great the rewards we'll get! Besides, we'll be doing something that men think is just, and something the gods think holy."

Before Theron could finished speaking, another man took issue: "Fine timing, you fool—now you ask us to be philosophers? Has robbing graves made us honest men? Are we going to show her mercy when her own husband showed no mercy in killing her? She has done us no harm, I realize, but she will do us the greatest harm. First of all, if we give her back to her relatives, it's not clear how they'll react to the situation; and they cannot but suspect our real reason for being present at the tomb. Besides, even if the girl's relatives forego charges against us, the magistrates and the people still won't release grave-robbers in possession of plunder. Perhaps someone will say that the more profitable thing is to sell the girl; her beauty will bring a good price. Yet this brings with it some danger: gold has no voice, and silver will not say where we got it. It's possible that we make up some story about them, but as for property that has eyes and ears and a tongue, who can keep it hidden? Nor is her beauty the human sort that will go unnoticed. Are we going to say that she is a slave? Who's going to believe that, once they've had a look at her? So let us kill her right here, and not bring with us our own prosecutor."

Although many agreed with this course of action, Theron did not approve. "The one of you courts danger," he began, "and the other ruins our profit. I, however, will sell the girl rather than kill her. While she's up for sale, she'll stay quiet out of fear; once she's been sold, let her go on and accuse us—we'll be long gone! It's not like we lead a life that's free from peril. So let's get on board and sail! It's already nearly daylight."

With this they put to sea, and their ship glided on magnificently. Neither wind nor wave opposed them, since they had no particular course; every wind was a favoring, stern wind. All the while Theron was trying to reassure Callirhoe, seeking to deceive her with complicated explanations. Callirhoe did not fail to recognize her plight and the corrupt sense in which he had "rescued" her, yet she pretended not to understand; she feigned belief, afraid that they would kill her if she showed her anger. Professing that she could not stand the sea, she covered her head in a veil and wept: "Father, in this sea you once beat three hundred Athenian ships at sea. But now a small boat has snatched up your daughter, and you are no help. I am being taken to a foreign land to be a slave, even though I am well-born. Perhaps it will be some Athenian master who purchases this daughter of Hermocrates! How much better to lie dead, a corpse, in the tomb; at least Chaereas would have been buried with me. But, as it is now, both in life and in death we are separated."

While Callirhoe lamented her many troubles, the bandits sailed on, passing by towns and small islands. Their merchandise was not such as suits poor men; they were looking for men of wealth. They anchored just opposite Attica, in the shelter of a headland where there was a spring, plentiful and pure, and a lovely meadow. Here they took Callirhoe on shore for a bath and respite from the sea, in order to preserve the girl's valuable beauty. Once the robbers were alone, they discussed where they should sail. "Athens isn't far off," suggested one man, "and it's a large and prosperous city. We'll find a lot of traders, and a lot of rich people. Within Athens alone you can see as many towns as you see men in a marketplace."

So they all agreed to sail to Athens, but Theron did not care for the officiousness of the city. "Are you the only ones who haven't heard how meddlesome the Athenians are?" he asked. "They are a gossipy people, and litigious too. In the harbor there are hundreds of informers who will interrogate us as to who we are and where we got our goods; injurious suspicions will overrun their ill-disposed minds. The court of the Areopagus is there, and the magistrates are even more troublesome than tyrants. We should be even more afraid of the Athenians than the Syracusans. No, Ionia is the place for us; that's where the wealth is royal, flowing in from all of vast Asia. There the people live luxuriously and aren't as meddlesome. Besides, I expect I'll see some people there that I know."

With this, they drew water and got provisions from merchant ships nearby, and then sailed straight for Miletus. Two days later they moored about ten miles from town in a well-situated natural harbor.

Chariton, Chaereas and Callirhoe, 1.9–11, trans. Jason Aftosmis.

Cleopatra's Death

Horace (31 B.C.E.)

Cleopatra VII (69–30 B.C.E.) was the last major ruler of Egypt's Ptolemaic dynasty. With the conquest of her kingdom the Romans added the last corner of the Mediterranean to their empire. The decisive naval battle took place on September 2, 31 B.C.E., off the coast of Actium, when the forces of Octavian, who later took the title of Augustus, defeated the combined navy of Cleopatra and her Roman lover Marcus Antonius. This defeat gave Octavian unchallenged monarchy that, by the time of his death in 14 C.E., had become entrenched as the Julio-Claudian dynasty. In this poem Horace celebrates Octavian's victory, which was led in his absence by his lieutenant, Marcus Vipsanius Agrippa (ca. 63–12 B.C.E.). He focuses on Cleopatra, though without naming her, presenting her association with Antonius as a source of shame. Horace (65–8 B.C.E.) was born to a modest family but rose to prominence through his writing, gaining the attention and patronage of Augustus's aide, Maecenas. Many of his poems, particularly *Odes*, 3.1–6, reflect the values and agendas of the Augustan regime. While it is likely that this poem was written in the aftermath of the battle of Actium, Horace's first three books of *Odes* were not published until 23 B.C.E.

Now is the time to drink, to shake
the earth with uninhibited feet,
and deck our deities' couches
with Salian banquets, friends.

It would have been wrong to fetch the Caecuban
sooner from family stores, while a queen
contrived the Capitol's mad
destruction and death for the empire,

she and her tainted crew of infested
heroes. Intoxicated by mellow
fortune, she lost control
of her hopes. But a single ship

surviving the flames diminished her madness,
and Caesar restored realistic fear
to a mind Egyptian wine
had addled. On oars from Italy

he pressed her flight like a hawk pursuing
a gentle dove or a hunter chasing
a rabbit through snowy Thessalian
fields, to put the deadly

monster in chains. Intent on a nobler
death, she neither swooned at the sight
of a sword nor repaired to hidden
shores with her speedy fleet.

She dared to pay her fallen palace
a peaceful visit and braved the touch
of serpents' scales that her body
might drink their fatal venom.

Her death was defiance: she thereby refused
to be taken away dethroned in Liburnian
galleys and mocked in a triumph,
being no submissive woman.

Horace's Odes and Epodes, trans. David Mulroy (Ann Arbor: University of
Michigan Press, 1994), 96–97 (Odes, 1.37). Reprinted by permission of the publisher.

Dido and Aeneas

Virgil (before 19 B.C.E.)

The Trojan prince Aeneas and his companions are shipwrecked off
Carthage in their westward flight from Troy. Initially attacked, they
receive a hospitable reception from Queen Dido—partly, as Dido
tells the Trojans, because she sympathizes with their plight as exiles.
Aeneas does not immediately join in the meeting, observing from
under cover of the clouds. The love affair that ensues between Dido
and Aeneas sours when Aeneas, reminded by the gods of his mission
to found Rome, suddenly departs. With this story Virgil sought to
explain the rivalry between Carthage and Rome manifested in the
Punic Wars. At this point of the *Aeneid*, the common ground between
Romans and Carthaginians is emphasized: both are colonies founded
by exiles from the eastern Mediterranean. Like Horace, Virgil (70–
19 B.C.E.) received the patronage of Maecenas, and was thus close to
Augustus. His final and major work, the *Aeneid*, tells of the founding
of Rome by Aeneas, a Trojan prince fleeing the destruction of his city
at the hands of the Greeks. In this respect the poem complements
Homer's *Iliad* and *Odyssey*, and its conception is deeply informed by
the Greek epics. In turn, Virgil soon became the Latin Homer, the
Aeneid achieving classic status in Virgil's own lifetime. Much of the
Aeneid celebrates Augustus's accession as the arrival of peace, but
the poem also contains a pessimistic note, reminding readers of the
human cost of Rome's founding.

They entered, received permission to speak in her presence
and Ilioneus, the eldest, began with quiet emotion.
"My queen, Jupiter gave you power to settle
a new city and check the pride of people with justice.
We are miserable Trojans, driven by all of the sea-winds.
We beg you: stop your men from burning our ships: it's

unspeakable.

Spare a decent people. Look on our cause with some kindness.
We haven't approached you with swords to plunder the House-

> Gods

of Libya, to drag stolen goods to the beaches.
Swagger and brute force are not for us losers.
There *is* a place, the Greeks call it Hesperia,
an ancient land with rich soil and powerful armies:
Oenotrians lived there once but now they say that a younger
people have named it Italy, after their leader.
We set that course
but Orion suddenly surged and stormed on the water,
heaved us at blind shoals and drove us completely
apart with blustering southwinds and massed waves, impassable
sea-cliffs. Some of us reached your beaches by swimming.
Who are these men, your people? What barbarous country
allows them to act so? To keep us from welcoming beachsand,
to goad us to fight or stop us from standing our ground here —
if human kind and dying weapons are sneered at,
remember the Gods remember the law and the outlaw.
Our prince was Aeneas. No one's justice was higher,
no one was more conscientious or stronger with weapons in

> wartime.

If Fates rescued the man, if he still savors this higher
air, not lying yet with Underworld shadow,
we fear nothing. And first competing in kindness
won't harm you. There's also Sicilian land to return to,
Trojan farms and towns of well-known Acestes.
Let us haul our wind-rattled ships from the water,
shape new oars and refit our hulls with your timber.
If Gods restore our kind, our friends and a heading
for Italy, gladly we'll make for Latium's country.
If not — if you're not safe, you best father of Trojans,
if Libyan waters hold you, the hope of Iulus demolished —
at least we'll head for Sicilian straits where we came from.
Homes are ready there. We'll look for kingly Acestes."
When Ilioneus finished, all of the Trojans
voiced their approval.

With downcast looks Dido spoke to them briefly.
"Release fear from your hearts, Trojans. Banish anxiety.
Our life is hard here. The kingdom's youth has compelled me

to mass defenses and post watches at outlying borders.
The house of Aeneas! Who's not heard of the city
of Troy, your brave men in that great war and its firestorms?
Our own Phoenician hearts have not been so blunted:
your Sun-God's horse-team is not that far from our Tyrian city.
Whether you choose broad Hesperia, the farmland of Saturn,
or sail for the country of King Acestes and Eryx,
I will help. I'll send you in safety; our wealth will assist you.
And what if you wish to remain as our equals in Carthage?
The city I'm building is yours. Draw out your vessels.
I'll treat you without bias, Trojan and Tyrian.
If only Aeneas himself, your leader, were present,
nudged by the same Southwind! In fact I'll order reliable
troops to search the shore and Libyan outposts,
to see if he's thrown by surf into bush, or lost in some village."

Her words inspirited both lordly Aeneas
and steady Achates. Both for a long time had been eager
to break from the mist. Achates first encouraged Aeneas:
"You, the son of a Goddess, what are your thoughts now?
You see they are all safe: our friends and ships have been rescued.
Except for one—we saw him ourselves in the maelstrom,
sucked down—the rest confirms the word of your mother."
He'd hardly spoken when suddenly all the surrounding
mist parted itself and cleared away in a crosswind.
Aeneas stood there, a clear glow on his godlike
shoulder and face. Venus herself had exhaled on
her son's hair a splendor, a youthfully ruddy
light on his face, on his eyes a luster and gladness,
the way a craftsman's hand might add splendor to ivory
or set in yellow gold Parian marble or silver.
Abruptly he spoke to the queen and everyone present,
saying openly, "Here I am, the person you're seeking,
Aeneas of Troy, snatched from Libyan water.
And you, the only person to pity our struggle,
the curse on Troy, to share your home and your city
with us, remnants exhausted by Greeks on land and by every
mischance at sea, utterly beggared! To properly thank you,
Dido, is not in our power: all that's left of the Trojan
people throughout the world is everywhere scattered.
Gods must bring the reward you deserve, if a Power

regards reverence, if justice continues to matter,
and men's knowledge of right. What glad generation
gave you birth, what great parents conceived you?
While rivers flowed to the sea, while shadow in mountain
coombs wander and skies nourish the starlight,
your name, honor and praise will continue to live on,
whatever land calls me." He finished and held out
hands to his friends Ilioneus, Serestus,
then to the others, rugged Gyan and rugged Cloanthes.

Dido of Sidon was struck first by the face of Aeneas,
then by the man's hard losses. She answered,
"The son of a Goddess! What great danger and downfall
have chased you? What Power leads you to primitive coast-lines?
You're truly Aeneas? The one whom kindly Venus delivered
to Troy's Anchises close to the flowing Phrygian Simois?
And yes, I recall a Teucer coming to Sidon,
expelled from his father's land. He looked for a younger
kingdom with help from Belus, my Father, when Belus
exploited the wealth of Cyprus and held it under his power.
From that time on I knew of the fall of your Trojan
city, the names of Pelasgian rulers, and your name.
Your enemy Teucer gave you Trojans exceptional credit
and claimed he branched himself from an old family of Trojans.
Come, then, all of you men—enter our household.
A similar luck drove me as well through a number
of hardships, picking this land at last for our settling.
I know of pain. I've learned to alleviate sadness."

The Aeneid of Virgil, *trans. Edward McCrorie (Ann Arbor: University of Michigan Press, 1995), 30–34 (1.520–630). Reprinted by permission of the publisher.*

Translating the Law
Philo (mid-1st century C.E.)

The syncretistic world of Alexandria under Roman rule
emerges from the massive output of Philo of Alexandria, younger
contemporary of the historian Flavius Josephus. Born to a powerful
priestly family of Alexandria, he wrote commentaries on the
Pentateuch as well as other works. In 39/40 C.E. he led a delegation
to the emperor Gaius (Caligula) at Rome, protesting the persecution

of Jews in general and in particular the introduction of statues of Roman emperors into synagogues. This event provides the only fixed date in his biography. Allegorical interpretation is a major part of his exegetical method: through it, he attempted to combine Jewish with Greek thought. He was deeply influenced by Stoic philosophy, which would also have an impact on Augustine and other Christians. In the *Life of Moses* he offers a summary of Jewish law, presumably for a more general audience than that of his biblical commentaries. He emphasizes the respect accorded the Jews by other nations (2.17–24), offering the following account of the process whereby the Pentateuch was translated into Greek. The same story is told, at greater length and with different details, in the *Letter of Aristeas* (probably third century B.C.E.). The generous patronage of Ptolemy II Philadelphus had made Alexandria into a center of learning and the arts, with much of this activity centering on the Museum and the Library. Among the city's cosmopolitan population was a substantial group of Jews.

And that beauty and dignity of the legislation of Moses is honored not among the Jews only, but also by all other nations, is plain, both from what has been already said and from what I am about to state. In olden time the laws were written in the Chaldaean language [*i.e., Hebrew in this instance*], and for a long time they remained in the same condition as at first, not changing their language as long as their beauty had not made them known to other nations; but when, from the daily and uninterrupted respect shown to them by those to whom they had been given, and from their ceaseless observance of their ordinances, other nations also obtained an understanding of them, their reputation spread over all lands; for what was really good, even though it may through envy be overshadowed for a short time, still in time shines again through the intrinsic excellence of its nature. Some persons, thinking it a scandalous thing that these laws should only be known among one half portion of the human race, namely, among the barbarians, and that the Greek nation should be wholly and entirely ignorant of them, turned their attention to their translation. And since this undertaking was an important one, tending to the general advantage, not only of private persons, but also of rulers, of whom the number was not great, it was entrusted to kings and to the most illustrious of all kings. [. . .]

[*He goes on to praise the beneficence of Ptolemy II Philadelphus.*]

He, then, being a sovereign of this character, and having conceived a great admiration for and love of the legislation of Moses, conceived the idea of having our laws translated into the Greek language; and immediately he sent out ambassadors to the high-priest and king of Judea, for they were the same person. And having explained his wishes, and having requested him to pick him out a number of men, of perfect fitness for the task, who should translate the law, the high-priest, as was natural, being greatly pleased, and thinking that the king had only felt the inclination to undertake a work of such a character from having been influenced by the providence of God, considered, and with great care selected the most respectable of the Hebrews whom he had about him, who in addition to their knowledge of their national scriptures, had also been well instructed in Grecian literature, and cheerfully sent them. And when they arrived at the king's court they were hospitably received by the king; and while they feasted, they in return feasted their entertainer with witty and virtuous conversation; for he made experiment of the wisdom of each individual among them, putting to them a succession of new and extraordinary questions; and they, since the time did not allow of their being prolix in their answers, replied with great propriety and fidelity as if they were delivering apophthegms which they had already prepared. So when they had won his approval, they immediately began to fulfill the objects for which that honorable embassy had been sent; and considering among themselves how important the affair was, to translate laws which had been divinely given by direct inspiration, since they were not able either to take away anything, or to add anything, or to alter anything, but were bound to preserve the original form and character of the whole composition, they looked out for the most completely purified place of all the spots on the outside of the city. For the places within the walls, as being filled with all kinds of animals, were held in suspicion by them by reason of the diseases and deaths of some, and the accursed actions of those who were in health. The island of Pharos lies in front of Alexandria, the neck of which runs out like a sort of tongue towards the city, being surrounded with water of no great depth, but chiefly with shoals and shallow water, so that the great noise and roaring from the beating of the waves is kept at a considerable distance, and so mitigated. They judged this place to be the most suitable of all the spots in the neighborhood for them to enjoy quiet and tranquility in, so that they might associate with the laws alone in their minds; and there they remained, and having taken the sacred scriptures, they lifted up them and their hands also to heaven, entreating of God that they might not fail in their object. And he assented to their prayers, that the greater part, or indeed the universal race of mankind might be benefited, by using these philosophical and entirely beautiful commandments for the correction of their lives.

Therefore, being settled in a secret place, and nothing even being present with them except the elements of nature, the earth, the water, the air, and the heaven, concerning the creation of which they were going in the first place to explain the sacred account; for the account of the creation of the world is the beginning of the law; they, like men inspired, prophesied, not one saying one thing and another another, but every one of them employed the self-same nouns and verbs, as if some unseen prompter had suggested all their language to them. And yet who is there who does not know that every language, and the Greek language above all others, is rich in a variety of words, and that it is possible to vary a sentence and to paraphrase the same idea, so as to set it forth in a great variety of manners, adapting many different forms of expression to it at different times. But this, they say, did not happen at all in the case of this translation of the law, but that, in every case, exactly corresponding Greek words were employed to translate literally the appropriate Chaldaic words, being adapted with exceeding propriety to the matters which were to be explained; for just as I suppose the things which are proved in geometry and logic do not admit any variety of explanation, but the proposition which was set forth from the beginning remains unaltered, in like manner I conceive did these men find words precisely and literally corresponding to the things, which words were alone, or in the greatest possible degree, destined to explain with clearness and force the matters which it was desired to reveal. And there is a very evident proof of this; for if Chaldaeans were to learn the Greek language, and if Greeks were to learn Chaldaean, and if each were to meet with those scriptures in both languages, namely, the Chaldaic and the translated version, they would admire and reverence them both as sisters, or rather as one and the same both in their facts and in their language; considering these translators not mere interpreters but hierophants and prophets to whom it had been granted it their honest and guileless minds to go along with the most pure spirit of Moses.

The Works of Philo, trans. C. D. Yonge (1854; Peabody, Mass.: Hendrickson, 1993), 79–82 (Life of Moses, 2.25–28 and 31–40). Reprinted by permission of the publisher.

Shipwreck at Malta

Acts of the Apostles (later 1st century C.E.)

Antiquity's most famous description of a shipwreck is found in the Acts of the Apostles. This is the key narrative of the early Christian community, spanning the time from Jesus's resurrection to Paul's arrival in Rome, "proclaiming the kingdom and God and teaching about the Lord Jesus Christ with all boldness and without hindrance" (28:31). Paul, preaching the good news in Jerusalem, has fallen foul of the authorities, and is sent to Caesarea to be tried by Antonius Felix, Roman procurator of Judaea in the years 52–58 c.e. There he also appears before the Jewish client king, Herod Agrippa II. Paul's insistence on being tried as a Roman citizen causes him to be sent to the city of Rome. Though undertaken for legal reasons in the first instance, this voyage becomes in effect another of the missionary journeys that dominate the book of Acts. It began after the Day of Atonement (27:9), namely in the winter, outside the sailing season. The shore they reach at the end of the chapter turns out to be the island of Malta, where to this day Paul's visit is widely memorialized. Previously a Phoenician and Carthaginian settlement, it was acquired by Rome in 218 b.c.e. and made part of the province of Sicily.

And when it was decided that we should sail for Italy, they delivered Paul and some other prisoners to a centurion of the Augustan Cohort, named Julius. And embarking in a ship of Adramyttium, which was about to sail to the ports along the coast of Asia, we put to sea, accompanied by Aristarchus, a Macedonian from Thessalonica. The next day we put in at Sidon; and Julius treated Paul kindly, and gave him leave to go to his friends and be cared for. And putting to sea from there we sailed under the lee of Cyprus, because the winds were against us. And when we had sailed across the sea which is off Cilicia and Pamphylia, we came to Myra in Lycia. There the centurion found a ship of Alexandria sailing for Italy, and put us on board. We sailed slowly for a number of days, and arrived with difficulty off Cnidus, and as the wind did not allow us to go on, we sailed under the lee of Crete off Salmone. Coasting along it with difficulty, we came to a place called Fair Havens, near which was the city of Lasea.

As much time had been lost, and the voyage was already dangerous because the fast had already gone by, Paul advised them, saying, "Sirs, I perceive that the voyage will be with injury and much loss, not only of the cargo and the ship, but also of our lives." But the centurion paid more attention to the captain and to the owner of the ship than to what Paul said. And because the harbor was not suitable to winter in, the majority advised to put to sea from there, on the chance that somehow they could reach Phoenix, a harbor of Crete, looking northeast and southeast, and winter there.

And when the south wind blew gently, supposing that they had obtained their purpose, they weighed anchor and sailed along Crete, close inshore. But soon a tempestuous wind, called the northeaster, struck down from the land; and when the ship was caught and could not face the wind, we gave way to it and were driven. And running under the lee of a small island called Cauda, we managed with difficulty to secure the boat; after hoisting it up, they took measures to undergird the ship; then, fearing that they should run on the Syrtis, they lowered the gear, and so were driven. As we were violently storm-tossed, they began next day to throw the cargo overboard; and the third day they cast out with their own hands the tackle of the ship. And when neither sun nor stars appeared for many a day, and no small tempest lay on us, all hope of our being saved was at last abandoned.

As they had been long without food, Paul then came forward among them and said, "Men, you should have listened to me, and should not have set sail from Crete and incurred this injury and loss. I now bid you take heart; for there will be no loss of life among you, but only of the ship. For this very night there stood by me an angel of the God to whom I belong and whom I worship, and he said, 'Do not be afraid, Paul; you must stand before Caesar; and lo, God has granted you all those who sail with you.' So take heart, men, for I have faith in God that it will be exactly as I have been told. But we shall have to run on some island."

When the fourteenth night had come, as we were drifting across the sea of Adria, about midnight the sailors suspected that they were nearing land. So they sounded and found twenty fathoms; a little farther on they sounded again and found fifteen fathoms. And fearing that we might run on the rocks, they let out four anchors from the stern, and prayed for day to come. And as the sailors were seeking to escape from the ship, and had lowered the boat into the sea, under pretense of laying out anchors from the bow, Paul said to the centurion and the soldiers, "Unless these men stay in the ship, you cannot be saved." Then the soldiers cut away the ropes of the boat, and let it go.

As day was about to dawn, Paul urged them all to take some food, saying, "Today is the fourteenth day that you have continued in suspense and without food, having taken nothing. Therefore I urge you to take some food; it will give you strength, since not a hair is to perish from the head of any of you." And when he had said this, he took bread, and giving thanks to God in the presence of all he broke it and began to eat. Then they all were encouraged and ate some food themselves. (We were in all two hundred and seventy-six persons in the ship.) And when they had eaten enough, they lightened the ship, throwing out the wheat into the sea.

Now when it was day, they did not recognize the land, but they noticed a bay with a beach, on which they planned if possible to bring the ship ashore. So they cast off the anchors and left them in the sea, at the same time loosening the ropes that tied the rudders; then hoisting the foresail to the wind they made for the beach. But striking a shoal they ran the vessel aground; the bow stuck and remained immovable, and the stern was broken up by the surf. The soldiers' plan was to kill the prisoners, lest any should swim away and escape; but the centurion, wishing to save Paul, kept them from carrying out their purpose. He ordered those who could swim to throw themselves overboard first and make for the land, and the rest on planks or on pieces of the ship. And so it was that all escaped to land.

Acts 27, Christian Bible, Revised Standard Version.

Alexander's Civilizing Mission
Plutarch (later 1st/early 2nd century C.E.)

Alexander's campaign started in 336 in his native Pella, moving eastward into the mighty Persian Empire after an initial stop in Troy, where he paid homage to the mythical Achilles. By the time he died of fever in 323 B.C.E. at Babylon, he had conquered the Persian Empire and established an even more expansive realm of his own. But after his death no one could hold together this conquered land, which was divided into a number of successor states headed by Greek-speakers. The area thus demarcated, stretching from the western Aegean to Afghanistan, would be known in the modern times as the Hellenistic world. Macedonian conquest emerges in Plutarch's essay, *On the Fortune or Virtue of Alexander*, to take one example, as a kind of "mission civilisatrice" that foreshadows modern colonial ideologies. One of the main parts of this Hellenistic world was Egypt, where ancient pharaonic rule had been replaced first by Persians and now by Greeks and Macedonians. Among many cities founded in the course of the expedition was Alexandria (331 B.C.E.), which would soon become a cosmopolitan political and cultural capital. Unlike the pharaohs' old capital of Memphis, Alexandria was located on the Mediterranean in the Nile Delta, and thus became also a major conduit of trade. Throughout antiquity, Alexandria would remain one of the main cities of the Mediterranean, a status it would retain until the rise of Cairo after the Islamic invasions of the seventh century. Among Plutarch's output are also biographies of eminent Greeks and Romans known as the *Parallel Lives*, in which he emphasizes ethical themes, loosely in keeping with the Stoic philosophy. He pairs the biography of Alexander with that of the Roman statesman Pompey (106–48 B.C.E.).

When a small chest, which seemed very valuable to those in charge of the treasure and baggage taken from Darius, was brought to Alexander, he asked his friends what the most fitting thing to keep in it was. After they suggested many different things, he said that he was going to put the *Iliad* in there for safekeeping. Several credible sources attest to these events. And if what the Alexandrians, who attribute this story to Heraclides, say is true, Homer was apparently neither a lazy nor an unhelpful companion on campaign.

They say that when he had conquered Egypt, Alexander wanted to settle a large and populous Greek city, and to name it after himself. Therefore, he intended to measure out and mark off a site according to the advice of his city planners. However, one night while he was asleep, he had a marvelous vision, in which an aged man with gray hair seemed to stand before him and recite these verses:

> There is an island in the relentlessly beating sea
> off the coast of Egypt. They call it Pharos. [Odyssey, 4.354–55]

Alexander awoke straightaway and went to Pharos, which is situated just above the Canobic mouth of the Nile. It was still an island then; now, however, a causeway connects it to the mainland. The site was very suitable: it is a strip of land, similar to a wide isthmus, separating a sizable harbor and the sea, which terminates there in another large harbor. When Alexander surveyed the spot, he said that Homer was both amazing in many other respects and a wise city planner. Then he ordered his planners to outline the boundaries of the city on the site. Lacking chalk, they took barley and drew a round figure on the black soil of the plain. Within the outline of the figure they added straight lines starting from the edges, in order to narrow the breadth uniformly into the shape of a military cloak.

As the king was delighting in his design, suddenly birds of infinite number, type, and size came from the river and the harbor, swooping down like clouds upon the site, and ate all the barley. Alexander was distraught at the omen. However, the seers exhorted him to be in good spirits, for the city he was founding would be bountiful and a nurse to people of all sorts. Therefore, Alexander ordered the workers to proceed. He himself set out for the shrine of Ammon.

Plutarch, Life of Alexander, 26, trans. Micah Myers.

Touring Egypt
Julia Balbilla (130 C.E.)

Julia Balbilla, member of the royal family of Commagene on the upper Euphrates, joined the emperor Hadrian (ruled 117–38) and his wife, Sabina, on a visit to the so-called Colossi of Memnon near Thebes. Their visit took place on November 19, 130 C.E. All this we know from four Greek poems she composed to mark the event and which she had inscribed on one of the colossi. The poems referring to her noble ancestry (poem 2), are the only surviving source of information about her. The reference to Hadrian in the first of the poems (lines 9–12) suggests that the emperor commissioned them, whereas a misspelling of her name in the title of the first poem makes it likely that someone else performed the task of inscribing them. The statue was originally dedicated to the Egyptian pharaoh Amenophis III, one of a pair located outside his temple. But the Greeks and Romans associated it with Memnon, mythical king of Ethiopia, who fought at Troy in defense of his uncle Priam before being killed by Achilles. The poems describe successive visits over two or more days, complete with Memnon's response. They are, however, not recorded in chronological order: that honoring Hadrian is placed first, though it recounts his second visit. More than a hundred Greek and Latin inscriptions were carved into the statue, emphasizing its status as an ancient tourist attraction, no less than it would later be for Shelley in "Ozymandias." Central to its ancient fame was its reputation of "singing" at dawn, a phenomenon caused by heat-induced movement amidst the cracked stone, the damage having resulted from human intervention and possibly an earthquake. In this case the term "graffiti" would miss the sophistication of the poems, whose literary character is underpinned by stylistic features as well as historical and mythical references. Among the other inscriptions are poems by several other women, testimony to the literacy and mobility of some aristocratic women of the empire.

(1) WHEN THE REVERED HADRIAN HEARD MEMNON
BY JULIA BALBILLA

Memnon the Egyptian, I learnt, when warmed by the rays of the
sun,
Speaks from Theban stone.
When he saw Hadrian, the king of all, before the rays of the sun
He greeted him—as far as he was able.
But when the Titan driving through the heavens with his steeds of
white
Brought into shadow the second measure of hours,
Like ringing bronze Memnon again sent out his voice
Sharp-toned; he sent out his greeting and for a third time a mighty
roar.
The Emperor Hadrian then himself bid welcome to
Memnon and left on stone for generations to come
This inscription recounting all that he saw and all that he heard.
It was clear to all that the gods love him.

(2) WHEN WITH THE REVERED SABINA
I STOOD BEFORE MEMNON

Memnon, son of Aurora and holy Tithon,
Seated before Thebes, city of Zeus,
Or Amenoth, Egyptian king, as learned
Priests recount from ancient stories,
Greetings, and singing, welcome her kindly,
The august wife of the Emperor Hadrian.
A barbarian man cut off your tongue and ears,
Impious Cambyses; but he paid the penalty,
With a wretched death struck by the same word point
With which pitiless he slew the divine Apis.
But I do not believe that this statue of yours will perish,
I saved your immortal spirit forever with my mind.
For my parents were noble, and my grandfathers,
The wise Balbillus and Antiochus the king,
Balbillus the father of our royal mother,
And Antiochus the king, father of my father.
From their race I too was given noble blood,
And these verses are mine, Balbilla, the pious.

(3) WHEN ON THE FIRST DAY
WE DID NOT HEAR MEMNON

Yesterday Memnon met his wife in silence,
So the beautiful Sabina would come back again.
For you enjoy the beloved beauty of our queen.
But when she returns, send out your divine roar,
Lest the king grow angry with you. Too long without fear
You hold up his august wedded wife.
And Memnon trembling at the mighty power of Hadrian
Suddenly sang, which she heard and enjoyed.

(4)

I, Balbilla, heard, when he sang from the stone,
The divine voice of Memnon or Phamenoth.
I had come here with my beloved queen Sabina;
The sun was holding its course for the first hour.
In the fifteenth year of Emperor Hadrian,
When Hathyr was in his twenty-fourth day.
On the twenty-fifth day of the month of Hathyr.

From Women Writers of Ancient Greece and Rome: An Anthology, *trans. I. M. Plant (Norman: University of Oklahoma Press, 2004), 152–53. Reprinted by permission of the publisher.*

Carthaginian Ascendancy
Appian (first half of 2nd century C.E.)

Seaborne settlers from Tyre founded the city of Carthage (Qart Hadasht or "new city")—an event dated by ancient writers to the year 814 B.C.E. The deeply indented Bay of Tunis offers some of the best port facilities of the North African coast. Virtually impregnable from either land or sea, the site also provided access to the fertile agrarian hinterland. The city's central location soon gave it a commanding role in trans-Mediterranean commerce. Here people exchanged olive oil and wine (detectable now from the clay vessels that contained them), iron from Spanish mines, wood, grain, and bright red and pink corals brought up from the sea floor by divers and fishermen. The earliest account of the establishment of Carthage is found in the writings of

Timaeus, a Greek historian from Sicily (ca. 350–ca. 260 B.C.E.). The passage below is by Appian, a Greek historian born in Alexandria in the late first century C.E. (d. 160s). He looks back on a period, particularly the third and second centuries B.C.E., when Carthage curbed the spread of Roman power. Appian's work, which shows marked admiration for Rome, is arranged ethnographically, covering particular groups in the order of their subjugation.

The Phoenicians settled Carthage, in Africa, fifty years before the capture of Troy. Its founders were either Zorus and Carchedon, or, as the Romans and the Carthaginians themselves think, Dido, a Tyrian woman, whose husband had been slain clandestinely by Pygmalion, the ruler of Tyre. The murder being revealed to her in a dream, she embarked for Africa with her property and a number of men who desired to escape from the tyranny of Pygmalion, and arrived at that part of Africa where Carthage now stands. Being repelled by the inhabitants, they asked for as much land for a dwelling place as they could encompass with an ox-hide. The Africans laughed at this frivolity of the Phoenicians and were ashamed to deny so small a request. Besides, they could not imagine how a town could be built in so narrow a space, and wishing to unravel the mystery they agreed to give it, and confirmed the promise by an oath. The Phoenicians, cutting the hide round and round in one very narrow strip, enclosed the place where the citadel of Carthage now stands, which from this affair was called Byrsa ("hide").

Proceeding from this start and getting the upper hand of their neighbors, as they were more adroit, and engaging in traffic by sea, like the Phoenicians, they built a city around Byrsa. Gradually acquiring strength they mastered Africa and the greater part of the Mediterranean, carried war into Sicily and Sardinia and the other islands of that sea, and also into Spain. They sent out numerous colonies. They became a match for the Greeks in power, and next to the Persians in wealth. But about 700 years after the foundation of the city the Romans took Sicily and Sardinia away from them, and in a second war Spain also. Then, assailing each the other's territory with immense armies, the Carthaginians, under Hannibal, ravaged Italy for sixteen years in succession, but the Romans, under the leadership of Cornelius Scipio the elder, carried the war into Africa, crushed the Carthaginian power, took their ships and their elephants, and required them to pay tribute for a time. A second treaty was now made between the Romans and the Carthaginians which lasted fifty years, until, upon an infraction of it, the third and last war broke out between them, in which the Romans under Scipio the younger razed Carthage to the ground and forbade the rebuilding of it. But another city was built subsequently by their own people, very near the former one, for convenience in governing Africa. Of these matters the Sicilian part is shown in my Sicilian history, the Spanish in the Spanish history, and what Hannibal did in his Italian campaigns in the Hannibalic history. This book will deal with the operations in Africa from the earliest period.

The Roman History of Appian of Alexandria, *trans. Horace White, 2 vols. (New York: Macmillan, 1899), 1:146–47 (Punic Wars, 1–2).*

Olympic Origins
Pausanias (ca. 150 C.E.)

The lengthy *Description of Greece* written by Pausanias purports to describe "everything Greek" but in fact is restricted to what had become the Roman province of Achaea. It focuses on monuments of the archaic and classical periods of the Greek world, with much attention to their mythic or historical origins. In narrowing his scope in this way, Pausanias reflects the archaizing spirit of many Greeks living under the Roman Empire. As with other writers and rhetoricians of the Second Sophistic movement, his enthusiasm for classical Greek pasts was a response to the reality of Roman political power. The Pausanias that emerges from the *Description* may be considered an early tourist attuned to the sacred and to history. Both elements are apparent in the extract on Olympia, where the Olympic Games were held at the sanctuary of Zeus. This was one of the four panhellenic festivals, bringing together athletes and spectators from all over the Aegean. The god was honored by contests and religious rituals. The four-year cycle of games was central to Greek time-reckoning, so that years were counted in four-year increments or "Olympiads" from the supposed first games in 776 B.C.E. Their polytheist nature caused their abolition in 393 C.E. by the Christian emperor Theodosius I (379–95). Until that time the sanctuary was subject to many and various building projects, including not only the temples of Hera and Zeus but also dwellings for priests and pilgrims.

Along the road to Olympia, before crossing the Alpheius River, there is a steep mountain with high cliffs outside of Scillus, called Typaeum. At Elis it is the law that women who are discovered at the games, or even having crossed the Alpheius on the days it is forbidden, are thrown down from this mountain. They say that no woman has ever been caught, save one, called Callipateira by some, Pherenice by others. After her husband died, this woman put on a costume to make herself look in every way like an athletic trainer, and brought her son to Olympia to compete. [. . .]

Regarding the origins of Olympic games, the historians at Elis say that when Cronus was the first king in heaven, the people of that age, who were called the golden race, built a temple for him at Olympia. Later, when Zeus was born, Rhea put her child under the guardianship of the Idaean Dactyls — who are also called the Curetes. The Dactyls, who were named Heracles, Paeonaeus, Epimedes, Iasius, and Idas, came to Olympia from Ida in Crete. For sport, the eldest of them, Heracles, organized a footrace for his brothers, and crowned the winner among them with the branch of a wild olive tree. There was so much wild olive that they slept on beds made from the still green leaves. According to tradition, Heracles brought the wild olive to Greece from the land of the Hyperboreans, who live beyond the North Wind.

Olen the Lycian in his hymn to Achaeia was the first to write that Achaeia came to Delos from the Hyperboreans. Later Melanopus of Cyme in his ode to Opis and Hecaerge sang that these two had come to Delos from the Hyperboreans before Achaeia. Aristeas of Proconnesus also mentioned the Hyperboreans. He perhaps learned about them from the Issedones, for he says in his epic that the Hyperboreans came to those people. At any rate, it is believed that Heracles of Ida was the first to organize games and to use the name Olympia. Further, he ordained that the games be held every fifth year [i.e., every fourth, counting inclusively], because he and his brothers were five in number.

Some say that Zeus wrestled Cronus for power at Olympia, while others believe that he held games there after he overthrew Cronus. It is also said that among the victors was Apollo, who both outran Hermes and beat Ares at wrestling. They say it is for this reason that the Pythian flute-song is played at the jumping competition during the pentathlon [i.e., sprinting, wrestling, long jump, javelin, and discus], since this flute-song is sacred to Apollo, and he won Olympic victories. [. . .]

Under the current ordering of the games, sacrifices are made to the god for the pentathlon and the chariot race after the other events. This system was instituted after the seventy-seventh Olympiad. Previously, both the competitions for men and for horses were held on the same day. However, at these particular games, the competitors in the pancration [i.e., mixed martial arts] were not called in on time, and ended up being delayed until after nightfall. The chariot races and the pentathlon in particular were the cause of the delay. The Athenian Callias was the victor in this pancration. However, after that Olympiad, they scheduled the pentathlon and the chariot races later so that they no longer interfered with the pancration.

Pausanias, Description of Greece: Elis, 1.6.7–8, 1.7.6–10, 1.9.3, trans. Micah Myers.

Women in the Holy Land
Eusebius of Caesarea (339) and Egeria (384)

Constantine was the first Roman emperor to convert to Christianity. His reign (306–37) witnessed what we might call the invention of Christian space, established in part by his mother, Helena. In the years 327–28, aged nearly eighty, she visited Palestine, which was soon to become known as the "Holy Land." Her itinerary was largely shaped by the life of Christ, which she sought to honor. At the tomb where Jesus lay following the crucifixion she founded the Church of the Holy Sepulcher, one of Christianity's holiest sites. The major description of this journey can be found in Eusebius's *Life of Constantine* (3.42–47). Eusebius of Caesarea (ca. 260–339) is best known for his *Ecclesiastical History*, which subsumes all of human history under God's providence. His narration of Helena's journey dwells on its religious aspects, hence it has been viewed as a pilgrimage; it might, however, have had political elements as well. Later sources amplify Helena's role in the discovery of relics from the True Cross.

Some fifty years later, another Christian woman called Egeria (or perhaps Aetheria) visited the eastern Mediterranean. Her report, reinforcing this notion of a Holy Land, has several unusual features: it offers a detailed account of Christian liturgy at Jerusalem; it is a Latin work composed by a woman for other women; diverging from the classical language of Cicero, it documents the emergence of vernacular (Romance) languages. Composed around 380–84 in Constantinople, it is addressed to her "sisters," presumably pious laywomen or nuns in her native land of Spain or Gaul. The sole surviving manuscript is incomplete, leaving many questions about work and author unanswered, not least her social and institutional status. The following extract gives a taste of her travels among various sites in Palestine and the Sinai Peninsula, all of them seen through the lens of the Bible, particularly the historical books of the Hebrew Bible. The hospitality she receives at various monasteries indicates an already well established network of Christians.

HELENA

Helena then decided to offer her piety to God, the Lord, for the sake of both her son, the great emperor Constantine, and his sons, her grandchildren, the divinely favored Caesars. Thinking it necessary to render her thanksgivings through prayers, the elderly woman went with youthful eagerness to learn about that wondrous land, and out of imperial considerations to visit the nations of the east, the people, and their communities. She offered proper adoration to the footsteps of the Savior in accordance with the prophetic word: "Let us adore in that place, where his feet stood" [*Psalm 132:7*]. And in that moment she bequeathed the fruits of her own piety to her descendants.

Eusebius, Life of Constantine, 3.42, *trans. Micah Myers.*

EGERIA

Next, after the two days which I had spent at Carrhae, the bishop brought us to the well where holy Jacob had drawn water for the flocks of holy Rachel. This well is six miles from Carrhae. Nearby, in honor of the well a very large and beautiful holy church has been built. When we had come to the well, the bishop said a prayer, read a description of the place from Genesis, and recited an appropriate psalm. Then the bishop said another prayer, and blessed us. We also saw an enormous stone, which is on display even today, lying to the side of the well. This is the stone which holy Jacob had moved off of the well.

No one lives by the well except the clergy of the church there and the monks, who have a monastery nearby. The holy bishop described to us the monks' truly exceptional way of living. After I prayed in the church, along with the bishop I visited the holy monks in their monastery cells, giving thanks to God and to the monks themselves. For they consented to receive me willingly into their cells, wherever I went, and they said the sort of things that are appropriate for monks to say. In addition, they saw fit to give gifts to me and to everyone who was with me. It is the custom among monks to give such things to those whom they receive willingly into their monastery cells.

The well itself is on a large plain; along our route the holy bishop showed me a large settlement perhaps five hundred paces away. Now this settlement, the bishop said, is called Fadana, because it was once the farm of Laban the Syrian. He showed me the shrine of Laban, who was the father-in-law of Jacob. He also showed me the place where Rachel stole her father's idols. When, in the name of the Lord, we had seen everything, we bid farewell to the holy bishop and to the monks, who had deigned to accompany us all the way to the village. Then we went back by the same course and rest stops by which we had come from Antioch.

When I had returned to Antioch, I stayed there afterward for seven days until those things which were necessary for my trip were ready. Then I set out from Antioch. Journeying via several rest stops, I came to the province called Cilicia, whose main city is Tarsus. In fact, I had already been in Tarsus when I went to Jerusalem. However, in the region of Isauria, at the third rest stop from Tarsus, is the shrine to the martyr Saint Thecla. It was wonderful to travel there, especially since it was so close.

Thus, setting out from Tarsus I came to a certain city on the sea by the name of Pompeiopolis. From there, crossing into Isauria, I stayed in a city called Coricus. On the third day I came to the city named Seleucia in Isauria. When I had arrived there, I met a bishop, a truly holy man, who formerly had been a monk. In this same city I also saw quite a beautiful church.

Since from there to the shrine of Saint Thecla, which is located on a level hill outside the city, is perhaps fifteen hundred paces, I found it preferable to go there to stay overnight. There is nothing around the holy church besides innumerable monastic cells for men and women.

I found a woman there who was a great friend of mine, a holy deaconess named Marthana. Everyone in the east could attest to her upright way of living. I had met her in Jerusalem, where she had journeyed in order to pray. She was in charge of the cells of Apotactitae, or nuns. When she had seen me, what joy there was for her and for me—could I even describe it in writing? But, to return to my narrative, there are many monastic cells there on the hill itself and in the middle of the giant wall that encloses the church. The church houses the shrine of the martyr, which is quite beautiful. The wall was built to protect the church from the Isauri, who are very wicked, and frequently engage in banditry, so that they could not raid the monastery established there.

Therefore, when in the name of the Lord I had come to this place, a prayer was made to the martyr's shrine, and in addition the entire acts of Saint Thecla were read. I gave infinite thanks to Christ our Lord, who saw fit that I, who am unworthy and undeserving, should have my every desire fulfilled.

I spent two days there also seeing the holy monks, or Apotactiti—women and men—who were there. After I had prayed and taken communion, I returned to Tarsus and to my journey. At Tarsus I rested. On the third day I set out on my journey in the name of the Lord. And on that same day I came to a rest stop where I stayed, called Mansocrenae, which is below Mount Taurus.

From there on the next day I journeyed below Mount Taurus and traveled by a familiar route through several provinces, namely Cappadocia, Galatia, and Bithynia. Next I arrived in Chalcedon, where I spent the night. Nearby there is a very famous shrine to the martyr Saint Euphemia, which I already knew from an earlier visit.

And then on the next day I crossed the sea, arriving at Constantinople, and gave thanks to Christ our Lord, because he saw fit to bestow such grace upon me, though I am unworthy and undeserving. That is, that he had granted not only the will to go, but also the opportunity to travel to those places I desired, and to return once more to Constantinople.

When I had come to that city, through several churches of the Apostles and also through several shrines for martyrs, of which there are many there, I did not cease to give thanks to our Lord Jesus, who had deigned to bestow his mercy upon me.

From this place, my dear ladies, while I send these words to you who care for me, it is already my intention to travel in the name of Christ our Lord to Asia, to Ephesus, for the sake of praying at the martyr shrine of the holy and blessed apostle John. However, if after this I am still living, and I am able to visit any other places in addition, if God will have seen fit to bestow this, I will return your affection. Or, certainly, if anything else comes to mind, I will communicate it in letters. You, ladies, are so dear to me. May it be granted that you remember me, whether I am alive or dead.

Egeria, Pilgrimage, 21–23, *trans. Micah Myers.*

Painful Departures
Augustine (400 and 422–23)

The *Confessions* of Augustine (354–430 C.E.) are unusual among ancient texts for their autobiographical content, and even unprecedented in the intensity of their introspection. Composed in the closing years of the fourth century, it looked back on the first thirty-three years of his life, plotting the stages in his conversion to Christianity. It tells of his youth in Thagaste in modern Algeria, as well as his education there and in the other North African cities of Madaurus and Carthage. His intellectual prowess was soon evident, paving the way for a stellar career as a teacher of rhetoric in North Africa, and later Rome (384–86), before he became public orator at the imperial capital of Milan. His stay in Milan was crucial in his gradual conversion to Christianity. Augustine's later decades were spent busily fulfilling his duties as bishop of Hippo in modern Tunisia, but he still found time to write major theological works, including *City of God* (413–26). In the first passage below, the thirty-year-old Augustine bids farewell to his mother Monica at Carthage, as he sets off for Italy to further his career. Such a move would have been typical for an ambitious, talented young man from Rome's provinces.

The young Augustine's willing departure from Carthage contrasts with the involuntary sale of poor tenant farmers (*coloni*) on the same North African coast. A letter sent to his friend Alypius, bishop of Thagaste, conveys information about the slave trade being conducted in his own see. He seeks help in curbing the activities of traders from Galatia in Asia Minor, spurred by horror at the violence and illegalities of their action. Unfree labor was widely practiced in the Roman Empire, including by Christians. In this case its victims would be shipped to Italy and other parts of the Mediterranean. This letter is one of twenty-nine previously unpublished letters of Augustine that came to light in 1975. Dating to the final decades of his life, they vividly show the challenges he faced as bishop of Hippo.

CONFESSIONS

You dealt with me in such a way that I was persuaded to head for Rome and to teach there what I had been teaching at Carthage. How I was so persuaded I shall not neglect to confess to you, because your deepest recesses and your ever-present mercy toward us must be contemplated and proclaimed. I wished to head for Rome not because of the promise of higher compensation and greater prestige among those friends who were urging it—even though at the time those factors also influenced my thinking—but this was the main and virtually only reason, namely that I heard that young men there studied with greater dedication and are controlled by a stricter application of discipline, so that they do not rush into a classroom which is not their own teacher's, and are not even allowed in unless given permission.

By contrast, in Carthage there was disgraceful and extreme disorderliness among schoolchildren: they burst in rudely and with nearly mad demeanor disrupt the good order that each teacher had established for his pupils' sake. They did many offensive things with remarkable impudence, things that would be punishable by law if they were not sanctioned by custom. This custom showed them to be more base, in that they now acted as if allowed to do things that by your eternal law shall never be allowed, and thought that they are acting with impunity, though they were being punished by that very blindness and suffered incomparably worse than what they actually did. And so when teaching I was forced to endure those ways which when studying I did not want to make my own. Therefore it pleased me to go where those in the know said such behavior did not take place. However, "You, . . . my refuge and my portion in the land of the living" [*Psalm 141:6*]—at Carthage you nudged me to exchange an earthly dwelling for the salvation of my soul, that I might be torn from it; at Rome you offered me allurements so I could be drawn there through men who loved a life-in-death, some pursuing foolish activities and others promising fruitless ones: for the sake of correcting my steps you secretly used both their perversity and mine. For they who disrupted my quiet were blinded with a shameful blindness, and those who invited me elsewhere were merely tasting the earth. I, who here despised true misery, there sought specious happiness.

But you knew why I had to go here and go there, Lord, and you did not make it clear to me or to my mother, who lamented my departure vociferously and followed me right up to the sea shore. But I tricked her while she was holding on to me forcefully, so that she could either call me back or depart with me: I pretended that I could not abandon a friend of mine until he could sail with a favorable wind. And thus I lied to my mother, to such a mother, and I escaped. You have forgiven me even this, mercifully kept me, full of foul wrongdoings, from the water of the sea for the water of your grace. By which, once I was cleansed, the rivers flowing from my mother's eyes would be dried, eyes with which on my behalf she daily wet the ground under her face while praying to you. In light of her refusal to return without me, with difficulty I persuaded her to stay that night at a shrine of Saint Cyprian, very close to our ship. But that night I set off secretly, while she remained amid entreaties and weeping. And what was she seeking, oh Lord, with such tears, except that you should not allow me to sail? But you, taking care from on high and grasping the essence of her wish, did not grant what she then sought, namely that you make me what she always wanted. The wind gusted and filled our sails and removed from our view the shore where in the morning she would go wild with grief, filling your ears with tirades and weeping. These you disregarded, although you were removing me from my own desires for the sake of fulfilling those very desires. Thus her earthly longing was being lashed by the deserving cudgel of grief. For she loved to have me with her in the manner of a mother, but much more than others, and she did not know what joy you were preparing for her by my absence. She did not know and therefore wept and wailed and exhibited in those torments the legacy of Eve. And yet, after accusing me of deceit and cruelty, she turned again to you with prayers on my behalf. She went her usual way—and I to Rome.

Augustine, Confessions, 5.8, trans. Grant Parker.

LETTER ON THE SLAVE-TRADE

And another thing: In North Africa there is such a profusion of those commonly known as "slave-traders" that to a large extent they are draining it of human beings, by moving those bought—nearly all of them free persons—to overseas provinces. Only small numbers are found to be sold by their parents—not persons whom they purchase [as indentured laborers] up to the age of twenty-five in keeping with Roman law, but ones whom they in fact purchase as slaves and sell overseas as slaves; only very rarely are true slaves sold by their masters. From this rabble, the throng of fraudulent and pillaging traders has grown so great that, ululating with terrifying, warlike, savage appearance, they are able to invade thinly populated and rural locations and violently to kidnap persons whom they can sell to those traders. [. . .]

It is not possible to say adequately how many have sunken to the same evil enterprise through unbelievable blindness of greed and unthinkable spread of this disease, as it were. Who can believe, for one thing, that a woman was found, among us at Hippo in fact, who, under the pretext of buying wood, is in the habit of inveigling, confining, beating, and then selling women of Gidda? Who would believe that a tenant farmer of our church, seemingly an upstanding man, should have sold his wife, the very mother of his own children, not for any blame on her part, but stirred up purely by the agitation of this disease? A certain young man of about twenty years, a prudent bookkeeper and clerk for our monastery, was ensnared and sold; only with difficulty was he able to be freed by the church.

If I wanted to list all the crimes that we alone have come across, I would not be able to do so. Take one case from which you can infer everything that is going on throughout North Africa and all its coasts. Around four months before the time of writing, people were being assembled by Galatian traders (who are especially keen in taking part in these activities) from all over and particularly from Numidia, in order to be transported from the coast of Hippo. At hand there was one of the faithful, who, knowing our practice as regards charitable acts of this kind, made the situation known to the church. Right away, around 120 persons were freed by our people, in my own absence, partly from the ship onto which they had already been loaded, and partly from the place where they were being hidden with a view to loading. Among these, scarcely five or six were found to have been sold by their parents; as for the rest, hardly anyone could hold back tears in hearing stories of how they came to the Galatians via kidnappers and thieves.

Augustine, Letter, 10*.2, 6–7, trans. Grant Parker.

Law and Holy Wisdom
Justinian (ca. 530) and Procopius (mid-6th century)

The lengthy reign of Justinian (527–65) marked a particular phase of Byzantine, or east Roman, civilization. His ambitious program of "restoration of the empire" involved reconquering parts of the western Roman Empire that had succumbed to Germanic groups. However, much of this was short-lived, and over time, conflict in the east with the Sasanian Empire led to a gradual weakening of Byzantium. Among Justinian's enterprises was a codification of all Roman law, and this led to the compilation of the *Corpus of Civil Law* in 528–33 under the jurist Tribonian. The *Codex of Justinian* is one part of this body of legal writing. In the passage quoted below Justinian applies to Palestine a law governing other provinces: that *coloni* be legally restricted to their place of residence. In terms of the Roman Empire's colonate system, laborers were thus restricted to particular locations, in ways that foreshadowed medieval serfdom, yet they could not be bought and sold in the manner of chattel slaves.

Justinian's major accomplishment in architecture was the construction of the massive Church of Hagia Sophia ("Holy Wisdom"), dedicated in 537, at a prominent location overlooking the Bosphorus.

The historian Procopius of Caesarea (ca. 500–ca. 565) lionizes the emperor as ruler and religious leader in his treatise *On Buildings*, though he is hostile in his presumably later *Secret History*.

Justinian's two enterprises reflected here were both destined to have lengthy lives up to the present: Roman jurisprudence thus systematized would become the base for many subsequent systems of civil law, and the Hagia Sophia (which served as a mosque from 1453 and a museum since 1935) remains one of the Mediterranean's most imposing, distinctive buildings.

JUSTINIAN

Since throughout other provinces which lie under the control of our serene majesty, a law has been passed by the fathers which detains the *coloni* by a certain law of all time, so that they are not allowed to depart from those places, the fruits of which support them, nor to desert those lands which they once took up for cultivation, and since this is not allowed to the landholders in Palestine, we ordain, that even throughout Palestine no *colonus* shall altogether of his own right boast himself a freeman or wanderer, but according to the example of other provinces he shall be attached to the lord of the land so that he may not be able to depart without suffering penalties; moreover, we further decree that full authority of recalling him may be given to the lord of the estate.

Codex of Justinian, *11.51.1, trans. Grant Parker.*

PROCOPIUS

The emperor Justinian, disregarding all matters of cost, keenly set construction work in motion, assembling artisans from all over the world. Anthemius of Tralles, in the craft known as building most adept not only among his contemporaries but also when compared with those lived long before him, served the emperor's zest, overseeing the tasks of the different artisans, and preparing plans for future construction. In collaboration with him was another master-builder known as Isidorus, from Miletus, adept and well suited to work for the emperor. [. . .]

And so the church has become a spectacle of the greatest beauty, extraordinary to those who see it but completely unimaginable to those who know it purely by reputation. For it soars up to a heavenly height, and as if detaching itself from surrounding buildings it stands tall and looks down on the rest of the city, adorning it because the church is part of it, but also glorying in its own beauty because, though part of the city and dominating it, it towers above the city at such a height that the entire city is viewed from there as from a watchtower. Its breadth and length have both been so meticulously proportioned that it can rightly be said to be hugely tall and unusually broad. It revels in its inexpressible beauty. For it proudly reveals its mass and the harmony of its proportions, having neither excess nor fault: it is both more pompous than the usual sort of buildings and much more noble than those which are merely large. [. . .]

Whenever someone enters into the church to pray, he understands immediately that it is not by any human power or craft but by the influence of God that this work has been so perfectly consummated. The devotee's mind is uplifted toward God and treads on air, thinking that God loves to dwell especially in this place that he has chosen. And this does not happen only to the one seeing it for the first time, rather one experiences the same thing continually, on each visit, just as if the vision were constantly coming into being. No one has ever grown tired of this spectacle; those who are in the church rejoice in the things they see, and those who have left it take proud pleasure in conversations about it. Further, as to the treasures of this church—the gold, the silver, and the works in precious stone that Emperor Justinian dedicated here—it would be impossible to give an accurate count. But with a single example I shall let those reading this to draw an inference. For that part of the church that is especially sacred, and which only priests may enter—this they call the sacrificial chamber—that part is inlaid with forty-thousand pounds of silver.

Procopius, On Buildings, 1.1.23–24, 27–29, 61–65, trans. Jason Aftosmis.

T-O Map

Isidore of Seville (early 7th century)

The *Etymologies* by Isidore of Seville (ca. 560–636) are a vast compendium of classical knowledge in excerpted form, within a Christian frame. Produced in Visigothic Spain, it would be enormously influential on cultures of learning in the western Middle Ages, and particularly on the T-O form of medieval cartography. His discussion of geography includes the first use of the term "Mediterranean" in its modern sense. The fame of the *Etymologies* goes a long way toward explaining the later use of the term.

Concerning the Mediterranean Sea. The Great Sea that flows from the circumambient Ocean in the west and verges into the south and then heads north. It is called "great" because it is larger than other seas. And it is called "mediterranean" because it flows through the middle of the earth as far as the east, separating Europe, Africa, and Asia. The bay of its first part, which flows around the Spanish peninsula, is called Iberian and Balearic. Then comes the Gallic, which washes the province of Narbonne. Next is the Ligurian, which is in immediate proximity to Genoa. After this is the Tyrrhenian, touching on Italy, which Greeks call the Ionian and the Italians call the Lower Sea. Then comes the Sicilian Sea, which extends from Sicily right up to Crete. Then the Cretan, which goes up to Pamphylia and Egypt. Then the Hellespont, turning toward the north, is drawn out in great bays alongside Greek lands and Illyricum into straights of seven stades. Once Xerxes had constructed a bridge for his ships, he crossed into Greece: Abydos is located there. Divided there in open waters it becomes channeled again and makes the Propontis. But next it is squeezed into a width of fifty paces and becomes the Thracian Bosphorus, across which Darius moved his forces. From there the Black Sea is very full from the back of Sea of Azov. From the multitude of tributary rivers, this sea is sweeter than others, and cloudy and smaller. Pontus is so called because it is accessible; and for that reason, apart from seals, tuna-fish, and dolphins it does not sustain larger animal life. Just as the earth, since it is one thing, is called by various names at different locations, so this great sea is differently named for its various adjacent regions. For the Iberian and Asian seas are named from provinces, but the Balearic, Sicilian, Cretan, Cyprian, Aegean, and Carpathian from islands.

Isidore, Etymologies, 13.16.1–5, trans. Grant Parker.

CHAPTER 3

Barzakh
The Waters Between

ATLANTIC
OCEAN

SPAIN

Usturqa (Astorga)

Arbuna
(Narbonne)

Marseilles

TUSCANY

Venice

Florence

Corsica

Rome

Tudela

Tuaitula (Toledo)

Marida (Merida)

AL-ANDALUS

Valencia

Sardinia

Amalfi

Córdoba (Qurtuba)

Ishbiliyya (Seville)

Granada

Lipari

Cartagena (Carteya)

Palermo

Algeciras

Gibraltar

Trapani

Sicily

Tanja (Tangiers)

Ceuta

Straits of Gibraltar

Carthage

Tunis

Susa

Fez

MOROCCO

MAGHRIB

NORTH AFRICA

Tripoli

Aix-la-Chapelle

0   100   200   300 mi

0   100 200 300 400 500 km

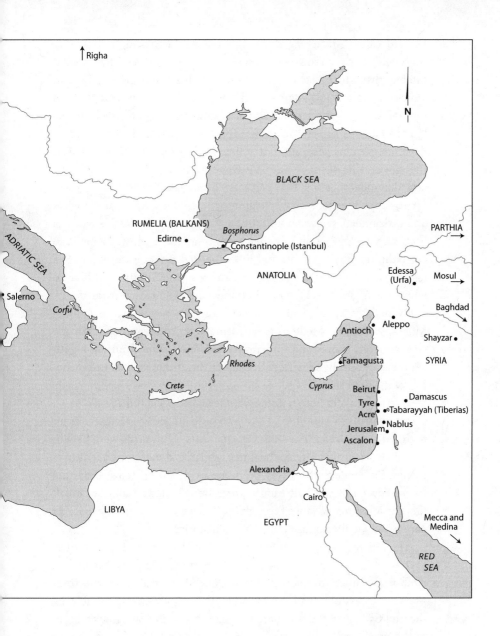

↑ Righa

ADRIATIC SEA

BLACK SEA

RUMELIA (BALKANS)

Bosphorus

Edirne •

• Constantinople (Istanbul)

ANATOLIA

PARTHIA →

Edessa
(Urfa) •

Mosul →

Baghdad ↘

Salerno •

Corfu

N

Aleppo •

Antioch •

Shayzar •

SYRIA

Rhodes

Famagusta •

Cyprus

Crete

Beirut •

Damascus •

Tyre •

• Tabarayyah (Tiberias)

Acre •

• Nablus

Jerusalem •

Ascalon •

Alexandria •

Cairo •

LIBYA

EGYPT

Mecca and
Medina ↘

RED
SEA

Edward Lane's *Arabic-English Lexicon* defines *Barzakh* as "a thing that intervenes between any two things; the interval between the present life and that which is to come; what is between the beginning of faith which is the acknowledgment, or confession, of God, and the end thereof, which is the removal of what is hurtful from the road." In the Qur'an *Barzakh* appears as an isthmus that "separates two things. It is never an extreme separation; it is like the line that separates between the sun and its shadow, and like God's saying: He let forth the two seas that meet together, between them a *barzakh* they do not overpass" (55:19–20). By extension *barzakh* designates the water that connects and disconnects sea water and the fresh waters of rivers; this water is both salty and sweet and neither. With time, the term was applied to the isthmus that separates and links the Red Sea and the White Sea (as the Mediterranean was known) and also the Straits of Gibraltar, where the Atlantic and the Mediterranean meet and are separated.

By analogy, *Barzakh* aptly characterizes this period that introduces Muslims into the Mediterranean. Umayyad Arabs appropriated the southwestern shores and transformed *Mare Nostrum* from the eighth century onward. By the fifteenth century the Ottomans had taken control of the eastern half of the Sea.

In 711, a Muslim Berber military leader called Tariq Ibn Ziyad crossed a narrow strip of water linking Morocco to Spain and the Mediterranean to the Atlantic Ocean. The straits he crossed with his army were the Pillars of Hercules that Hanno the Carthaginian had mentioned centuries earlier. He landed on a rocky promontory that until today bears his name: *Jabal Tariq*, or "the Mountain of Tariq," known today as Gibraltar. The Muslims' advance through Spain toward the north inextricably connected Mediterranean and Muslim histories.

The Muslim conquest of Spain punctuated a process begun farther to the east, in Arabia. After the death of the Prophet Muhammad in 632, Arab armies under the banner of Islam fanned out in all directions from Mecca. Successfully challenging and looting empires next to Arabia, by the mid-650s they had conquered Afghanistan in the east, Iraq and Iran to the north and, to the west, Egypt, Libya, and ultimately the North African littoral. Fighting both Berbers and Byzantines, they reached the Atlantic Ocean in the 680s. No military conquest of this magnitude had occurred since the expansion of the Roman Empire more than seven hundred years earlier. It made Arab militaries the major controlling force in the Mediterranean. While both Muslim and Christian historians considered the Muslim crossing into Spain to be an axial event, for the Christians it was a story of barbarism that required a reconquest, and for the Arabs it was a continuation of the conquest of Egypt, an extension of the favor God bestowed upon Muslims.

In Spain, the Christians retreated to mountain enclaves in the Pyrenees and Asturian and Cantabrian mountains, where they resisted the Muslims as they had the Visigoths before them. Meanwhile, the Muslims established the Arab province of al-Andalus, where they fostered cooperation among adherents of the three monotheisms. The Muslims established in Spain the center of a multicultural, multilingual empire attracting Christians and Jews from all over the Mediterranean.

Around 800, three major powers dominated the Mediterranean world. Byzantium under the empress Irene was ruled from Constantinople. The kingdom of the Franks under Charlemagne reached out from the banks of the Rhine to Caesar's Gaul, Rome, and northern Europe. The Abbasid Empire under Harun al-Rashid in Baghdad ruled the southern Mediterranean shores into Spain. Despite official rivalry between their empires, the one embodying Western Christianity and the other famed for its role in saving the works of classical Greek authors through translation into Arabic, Charlemagne and Harun had cordial relations. The cultural and intellectual revival characterizing Charlemagne's reign was known as the Carolingian Renaissance. The Carolingians claimed to be direct heirs to the Roman Empire that had crumbled three hundred years earlier. Scholars from Italy, Spain, Northumbria, and Gaul participated in a wide educational network, and monasteries played an important role in the study and copying of ancient texts. Western involvement in the eastern Mediterranean began in the Holy Land, where the Carolingians built churches and settlements. The Abbasid Empire was also known for its cultural and intellectual vitality; the labor of Arabic-speaking scholars in translating, adapting, and elaborating works of Greek science and philosophy has been credited with saving precious works that would have otherwise been lost. These Arabic works were then rendered into Latin by scholars like the eleventh-century Constantine the African and later integrated into the conceptual frameworks of medieval Europe. There was a thirst among the people of the northern rim for the knowledge and luxury items of the Muslim Mediterranean.

This vibrant interchange of cultures on the eve of the Crusades is the backdrop against which Christian challenges to Muslim hegemony in many parts of the Sea need to be seen. The Norman conquest of Sicily in 1090, and the Catholics' project to reoccupy Spanish cities and lands lost to Muslims in the eighth century launched a competition between new and old powers. Christians challenged the Seljuk Turks, who controlled most of the eastern Muslim world. In 1095 Pope Urban II launched the First Crusade, linking the liberation of Jerusalem to the eradication of Muslim rule elsewhere in the Sea. A popular crusade of the dispossessed was the response to the pope's appeal. Though few reached Constantinople, en route they savagely attacked Jews in the city of Mainz. When a later "official" Crusader group took Jerusalem in 1099, once again it was Jews and Eastern Christians along with Muslims who became victims. The risk perceived by Jews dwelling in the Holy Land is graphically portrayed in a letter by Karaite Jews.

The Crusaders' capture of Jerusalem intensified the rivalry between the Vatican and Byzantium. In response to the loss of Jerusalem and perhaps taking advantage of the division among Christian leaders, Muslim armies mobilized, and during the next two centuries Crusaders (or "Franks") and Muslims (or "Saracens" and "Turks") met on many occasions.

Despite the heterogeneity of Mediterranean communities, the notion of Muslim-Christian warfare came to be inscribed in the history of the Mediterranean. The grand Crusades narrative tells of a conflict between two universal truths that required territory seized and held by a religious leader to fulfill the divine mandate. But there are other local stories that reveal the complexity of individual encounters that we read, for example, in a humorous text from the Syrian Usamah ibn Munqidh, a Muslim "gentleman" who interacted with Frankish counterparts. Commenting on their barbaric behavior, he notes the civilizing influence of time spent with Muslims. Generally obscured, then as today, has been a tradition of respect and civility, even between enemies, that characterizes Saladin, the Muslim Kurdish ruler based in Egypt, and Richard the Lionhearted, as can be read in Ambroise's epic poem.

While the Crusades frayed the fabric of Mediterranean society, they also brought far-flung communities into unprecedented contact and created new networks. The restless traveling of Benjamin of Tudela, Ibn Jubayr, and Ibn Battuta is symptomatic of the major changes and power shifts taking place in the Mediterranean.

While rulers were fighting for control of the Sea, Jews, Christians, Muslims, and others created their own philosophical and psychological worlds that sometimes clashed and at other times interacted. Although they never met, two men born in Córdoba, the Muslim Ibn Rushd (Averroës, 1126–98) and the Jew Moses ben Maimon (Maimonides, 1135–1204), were spiritual and philosophical kin through their engagement with the Aristotelian tradition rethought in Arabic. Averroës's controversial commentaries were translated from Arabic into

Latin and became popular among the intellectuals in Paris, and Maimonides' works in Arabic and in Hebrew had a profound impact on later Jewish tradition. The growing tensions in Spain at the end of the twelfth century drove Averroës and Maimonides to North Africa. Averroës died in Marrakech and Maimonides in Egypt, where he had become a leader of the Jewish community and Saladin's physician.

Not only philosophers and scholars but also pilgrims and travelers like Benjamin of Tudela and Ibn Jubayr in the twelfth and Ibn Battuta in the fourteenth century trusted they would be welcomed wherever they sailed. The writings of these three men provide a window onto the lands of their destination and also onto their homelands. Like all who travel for sacred or profane knowledge (pilgrims and scholars) and also for pleasure ("tourists"), foreigners wrote about the unknown land in ways that often reflected their homeland. A crucial characteristic of these travel accounts was how familiar the foreign remained and how cosmopolitan these travelers were. In contrast to his treks through Southeast Asia or even sub-Saharan Africa, all of Ibn Battuta's stops around the Mediterranean engaged him in a constant dialogue with his Moroccan homeland.

A different seascape emerges from the northern coast in the fourteenth century. Among his many adventurous tales, Giovanni Boccaccio writes of lovers lost and found between Sicily and Tunisia. Dante Alighieri's *Purgatory* takes readers on a trip through the region that divides heaven from hell. The meaning of *Purgatory* echoes the *barzakh* but with a Christian difference: purgatory is a place of purging that excludes outsiders. *Barzakh*, on the other hand, describes a liminal state that connects this world with the hereafter, faith with its absence, and even two or more conflicting religions.

Barzakh also refers to a water passage linking the Mediterranean to another sea. In this case, it is the Bosphorus that connects the White Sea and the Black Sea, also linking and separating Asia and Europe. In the final selections in this chapter we read of the connection between Byzantium and the new Ottoman capital in Constantinople. At the close of the fifteenth century, Islam was receding from the Iberian Peninsula and becoming established in the Balkans. The long Byzantine-Ottoman transition introduced an unlikely cooperation between these empires. Like the Arabs in Spain, the Ottomans established a system whereby different confessional communities could live together. Calling himself Caesar of Roman lands, Mehmet II established Muslim rule in the northeastern Mediterranean that would continue into the early twentieth century.

Ornament of the World

Ibn 'Abd al-Hakam (ca. 850)

In 711 the Berber general Tariq ibn Ziyad led an army of Muslims from Tangiers across the Pillars of Hercules to the southern tip of Spain. They swept through the south and were only restrained in the north. They remained in parts of Spain for almost eight centuries. Muslim-dominated southern Spain was called al-Andalus, and it has become legendary for the intercommunal conviviality, or *convivencia*, it fostered. Jews, Christians, and Muslims lived together as People of the Book, common descendants of Abraham, and they produced a rich culture called Andalusian. The following extract comes from *Futuh Misr wa al-Maghrib wa al-Andalus* (Victories over Egypt, the Magreb, and al-Andalus) by Ibn 'Abd al-Hakam (d. 871). He compiled his history of the conquest of Spain from oral accounts and the earliest Arabic narrative by Ibn Habib (d. 852) and elaborated it in the style of *A Thousand and One Nights*.

The encounter between Tariq and Ludhiq [*Roderick*] took place in the Wadi Lakka [*Lago de la Janda*] in Shudhuna [*Sidonia*]. Allah put Roderick to flight. He was heavily encumbered with armor, and threw himself into the Wadi Lago; he was never seen again.

It is said that the Visigoth kings had a palace at Tuaitula [*Toledo*] in which was a sepulchre containing the Four Evangelists, on whom they swore their [*coronation*] oaths. The palace was greatly revered, and was never opened. When a king died, his name was inscribed there. When Roderick came to the throne, he put the crown on his head himself, which gave great offence to the Christians; then he opened the palace and the sepulchre, despite the attempts of the Christians to prevent him. Inside they found effigies of the Arabs, bows slung over their shoulders and turbans on their heads. At the bottom of the plinths it was written: "When this palace is opened and these images are brought out, a people in their likeness will come to al-Andalus and conquer it."

Tariq entered al-Andalus in Ramadan 92 [*began June 22, 711*]. His reason for coming was as follows: One of the Spanish merchants called Yul-yan [*Julian*] used to come and go frequently between al-Andalus and the land of the Berbers [*North Africa*]. Tanja [*Tangiers*] was [*one of the places he regularly visited*]. The people of Tangiers were Christian. . . . He used to bring back from there fine horses and falcons for Roderick. The merchant's wife died, and he was left with his beautiful daughter. Roderick ordered him to proceed to al-'Udwa [*North Africa*], but Julian excused himself on the grounds that his wife had died and he had no-one with whom he could leave his daughter. He ordered her to be brought to the palace. When Roderick saw her, she pleased him greatly, and he took her. On his return, her father learned of this, and said to Roderick, "I have left behind horses and falcons such as you have never seen here before." Roderick authorized him to go there and gave him money. Julian went to Tariq b. Ziyad and excited his interest in al-Andalus, describing its fine points and the weakness of its inhabitants, and their lack of courage. Tariq b. Ziyad wrote to Musa b. Nusair with this information, and was ordered to invade al-Andalus. Tariq mustered the troops.

Once he was on board with his men, he couldn't keep his eyes open and in his sleep he saw the Prophet (God bless him and grant him salvation) surrounded by the Muhajirun and the Ansar girded with their swords and with their bows slung over their shoulders. The Prophet (on whom be peace) passed in front of Tariq and said to him, "Pursue your business!" Tariq saw the Prophet and his companions in his sleep until they entered al-Andalus. He took this as a good omen, and encouraged his men with the good news.

So Tariq crossed over to the coast of al-Andalus and the first place he conquered was the town of Qartajanna [*Carteya, or Torre de Cartagena*] in the district of al-Jazira [*Algeciras*]. [. . .] He pushed on to Astija [*Ecija*] and Qurtuba [*Córdoba*], then to Toledo and the pass known as the Pass of Tariq, through which he entered Jilliqiyya [*Galicia*]. He overran Galicia, ending up in Usturqa [*Astorga*].

When Musa b. Nusair heard how successful he had been, he became envious of him, and set off with a large force. [. . .] When he came to the coast of North Africa, he left the point from which Tariq b. Ziyad had entered and went [*instead*] to a place known as Marsa Musa [*the anchorage of Musa near Ceuta*]. He avoided the route followed by Tariq and took the Sidonia coast. He arrived one year after Tariq, and proceeded via Sidonia to Ishbiliyya [*Seville*], which he conquered. From there, he went to Laqant [*Fuente de Cantos*], to a place called Musa's Pass at the edge of Fuente de Cantos, [*and from there*] to Marida [*Merida*]. Some scholars say that the people of Merida surrendered on terms and were not taken by storm. Musa advanced into Galicia through the pass named after him, and overran the territory he entered, and appeared before Tariq in Astorga.

When Tariq crossed over, the troops from Cordova went to meet him, and were scornful because they saw the small number of his followers. They fought a severe battle and were defeated; Tariq didn't cease slaughtering them until they reached Cordova. Roderick heard this and advanced from Toledo. They met at a place called Sidonia, on a river called today the Wadi Umm Hakim, and fought a hard battle. Almighty God killed Roderick and his men. Mughith al-Rumi, the slave of al-Walid b. 'Abd al-Malik [*Umayyad caliph, 705–15*], was Tariq's cavalry commander and he marched to Cordova; Tariq went to Toledo. He entered it, and asked after the Table, which was the only thing that concerned him. The People of the Book [*the Jews and Christians*] assert that this was the table of Solomon son of David. . . .

[*Tariq*] conquered al-Andalus on behalf of Musa b. Nusair, and took from it the Table of Solomon son of David (on whom be peace), and the crown. Tariq was told that the Table was in a fortress called Firas, two days' journey from Toledo, commanded by the son of Roderick's sister. Tariq sent him and his family a safe conduct; the prince came down [*from the castle*] and Tariq carried out his promise towards him. Tariq said "Hand over the Table to me," which he did; it had gold decoration and precious stones such as he had never seen. Tariq removed one of its legs together with its ornamentation of gold and jewels, and made a replacement leg for it. The Table was valued at 200,000 dinars because of its precious stones. Tariq took all the jewels, armor, gold, silver, and plate he found there, and besides that acquired wealth such as had not been seen before. He collected it all up and went to Cordova, where he made his base. He then wrote to Musa b. Nusair informing him of all the conquest of Spain and of all the booty that he had acquired. [. . .]

It is also said that it was Musa, after his arrival in al-Andalus, who sent Tariq to Toledo, which is halfway between Cordova and Arbuna (Narbonne). Narbonne marks the furthest extent of al-Andalus and the limit of where the writ of 'Umar b. 'Abd al-'Aziz [*Umayyad caliph, 717–20*] was effective, before the polytheists overran it. It is still in their hands today. [*It is also said that*] it was only here that Tariq acquired the Table. Roderick was in possession of 2,000 miles of coast over and above that. [*From these wide domains*] the Muslims won great booty in gold and silver. 'Abd al-Malik b. Maslama told me, on the authority of al-Laith b. Sa'd, "The carpets there were found [*to be*] woven with rods of gold, which formed a string of gold, pearls, rubies and emeralds. When the Berbers found one, and were unable to carry it away, they took an axe to it and cut it down the middle. Two of them took half each for themselves [*and went off*] together with a large crowd, while the troops were preoccupied with other things."

[*The same authorities relate that*] when al-Andalus was conquered, someone came to Musa b. Nusair and said to him, "Send someone with me and I will show you a [*buried*] treasure." Musa sent people with him and the man said to them, "dig here." They did so, and emeralds and rubies such as they had never seen before poured out all over them. When they saw it they were overawed, and he said, "Musa b. Nusair will never believe us." They sent someone to get him and he saw it for himself. [*The same sources*] relate that when Musa b. Nusair conquered al-Andalus he wrote to [*the caliph*] 'Abd al-Malik: "It's not a conquest, so much as the Day of Judgement."

From Charles Melville and Ahmad Ubaydli, eds., Christians and Moors in Spain, *3 vols. (Warminster, Wiltshire: Aris and Phillips, 1992), 3:3–9. Reprinted by permission of Oxbow Books.*

Charlemagne and Harun
Einhard and the Monk of St. Gall (ca. 800)

To the north of the Sea, Charlemagne was king of the Franks (r. 768–814) and founder of one of medieval Europe's largest empires. His court at Aix-la-Chapelle was the center of the Carolingian Renaissance. His empire became the Holy Roman Empire, and it was his example that Napoleon I had in mind when he tried to assume his succession in 1804. To the east, Harun al-Rashid (r. 786–809), the fifth caliph of the Abbasid dynasty, ruled a splendid court in Baghdad, later immortalized in *A Thousand and One Nights*. He had diplomatic relations with Charlemagne. Einhard and the Monk of St. Gall write about the well-documented embassy and exotic gift exchange in 801 between the two emperors. The authors wanted to show that the newly crowned Charlemagne was widely recognized and enjoyed the personal esteem of Harun al-Rashid, who is referred to as Persian. Clearly unaware of the sophistication of the Baghdadi envoys, the Monk of St. Gall writes that Harun's emissaries were overawed by the luxury of Charlemagne's palace and cathedral. Yet it is clear that Harun's lavish presents were unprecedented in western Europe, and they may have had an influence on Carolingian culture.

EINHARD'S *LIFE OF CHARLEMAGNE*

With Aaron [*Harun*], the King of the Persians, who ruled over all the East, with the exception of India, he entertained so harmonious a friendship that the Persian King valued his favour before the friendship of all the kings and princes of the world, and held that it alone deserved to be cultivated with presents and titles. When, therefore, the ambassadors of Charles, whom he had sent with offerings to the most holy sepulcher of our Lord and Saviour and to the place of His resurrection, came to the Persian King and proclaimed the kindly feelings of their master, he not only granted them all they asked but also allowed that sacred place of our salvation to be reckoned as part of the possessions of the Frankish King. He further sent ambassadors of his own along with those of Charles upon the return journey, and forwarded immense presents to Charles—robes and spices, and the other rich products of the East—and a few years earlier he had sent him at his request an elephant, which was then the only one he had.

The Emperors of Constantinople, Nicephorus, Michael, and Leo, too, made overtures of friendship and alliance with him, and sent many ambassadors. At first, Charles was regarded with much suspicion by them, because he had taken the imperial title, and thus seemed to aim at taking from them their empire; but in the end a very definite treaty was made between them, and every occasion of quarrel on either side thereby avoided. For the Romans and the Greeks always suspected the Frankish power; hence there is a well-known Greek proverb: "the Frank is a good friend but a bad neighbor." [. . .]

He was most devout in relieving the poor and in those free gifts which the Greeks call alms. For he gave it his attention not only in his own country and in his own kingdom, but he also used to send money across the sea to Syria, to Egypt, to Jerusalem, Alexandria, and Carthage—in compassion for the poverty of any Christians whose miserable condition in those countries came to his ears. It was for this reason chiefly that he cultivated the friendship of kings beyond the sea, hoping thereby to win for the Christians living beneath their sway some succour and relief.

THE MONK OF ST. GALL'S LIFE OF CHARLEMAGNE

About the same time also envoys of the Persians were sent to him. They knew not where Frankland lay; but because of the fame of Rome, over which they knew that Charles had rule, they thought it a great thing when they were able to reach the coast of Italy. They explained the reason of their journey to the Bishops of Campania and Tuscany, of Emilia and Liguria, of Burgundy and Gaul and to the abbots and counts of those regions; but by all they were either deceitfully handled or else actually driven off; so that a whole year had gone round before, weary and footsore with their long journey, they reached Aix at last and saw Charles, the most renowned of kings by reason of his virtues. They arrived in the last week of Lent, and, on their arrival being made known to the emperor, he postponed their presentation until Easter Eve. Then when that incomparable monarch was dressed in incomparable magnificence for the chief of the festivals, he ordered the introduction of the envoys of that race that had once held the whole world in awe. But they were so terrified at the sight of the most magnificent Charles that one might think they had never seen king or emperor before. He received them however most kindly, and granted them this privilege—that they might go wherever they had a mind to, even as one of his own children, and examine everything and ask what questions and make what enquiries they chose. They jumped with joy at this favour, and valued the privilege of clinging close to Charles, of gazing upon him, of admiring him, more than all the wealth of the east.

They went up into the ambulatory that runs round the nave of the cathedral and looked down upon the clergy and the nobles; then they returned to the emperor, and, by reason of the greatness of their joy, they could not refrain from laughing aloud; and they clapped their hands and said: "We have seen only men of clay before: here are men of gold." Then they went to the nobles, one by one, and gazed with wonder upon arms and clothes that were strange to them; and then came back to the emperor, whom they regarded with wonder still greater. They passed that night and the next Sunday continuously in church; and, upon the most holy day itself, they were invited by the most munificent Charles to a splendid banquet, along with the nobles of Frankland and Europe. There they were so struck with amazement at the strangeness of everything that they had hardly eaten anything at the end of the banquet. [. . .]

These same Persian envoys brought the emperor elephant, monkeys, balsam, nard, unguents of various kinds, spices, scents and many kinds of drugs: in such profusion that it seemed as if the east had been left bare that the west might be filled. They came by-and-by to stand on very familiar terms with the emperor; and one day, when they were in a specially merry mood and a little heated with strong beer, they spoke in jest as follows: "Sir emperor, your power is indeed great; but much less than the report of it which is spread through all the kingdoms of the east." [. . .]

[*The envoys tell the emperor about the ill treatment they had undergone in*

Italy, whereupon the emperor punished all those that had shown inhospitable behavior toward the Persians.]

Soon after the unwearied emperor sent to the emperor of the Persians horses and mules from Spain: Frisian robes, white, grey, red and blue; which in Persia, he was told, were rarely seen and highly prized. Dogs too he sent him of remarkable swiftness and fierceness, such as the King of Persia had desired, for the hunting and the catching of lions and tigers. The King of Persia cast a careless eye over the other presents, but asked the envoys what wild beasts or animals these dogs were accustomed to fight with. . . . [*In a test, the dogs successfully pursue a lion; the envoys follow at a distance.*] The German dogs caught the Persian lion, and the envoys slew him with swords of northern metal, which had already been tempered in the blood of the Saxons.

At this sight Haroun, the bravest inheritor of that name, understood the superior might of Charles from very small indications, and thus broke out in his praise: — Now I know that what I heard of my brother Charles is true: how that by the frequent practice of hunting, and by the unwearied training of body and mind, he has acquired the habit of subduing all that is beneath the heavens. How can I make worthy recompense for the honours which he has bestowed upon me? If I give him the land which was promised to Abraham and shown to Joshua, it is so far away that he could not defend it. I fear that the provinces which lie upon the frontiers of the Frankish kingdom would revolt from his empire. But in this way I will try to show my gratitude for his generosity. I will give that land into his power; and I will rule over it as his representative. Whenever he likes or whenever there is a good opportunity he shall send me envoys; and he will find me a faithful manager of the revenue of that province.

Thus was brought to pass what the poet spoke of as an impossibility: —

The Parthian's eyes the Arar's stream shall greet
And Tigris' waves shall lave the German's feet:

for through the energy of the most vigorous Charles it was found not merely possible but quite easy for his envoys to go and return; and the messengers of Haroun, whether young or old, passed easily from Parthia into Germany and returned from Germany to Parthia.

Early Lives of Charlemagne, by Einhard and the Monk of St. Gall, *ed. A. J. Grant (London: Chatto & Windus, 1922),* 28–29, 42–43, 116–24.

Arabic Medicine in Europe
Constantine the African (ca. 1080)

The translations and adaptations from Arabic of Constantine
the African (ca. 1020–1100) were vital in the transmission of
Greek and Arabic medicine to Europe. What had been known of
ancient medicine through translations before Constantine was a
fraction of the medical information which he brought to light. A
number of his works were included in the *Articella*, a collection of
medical texts which remained a standard basis of the curriculum
in medical teaching over all of Europe until the sixteenth century.
The excerpts below present two versions of Constantine's life and
his arrival in Salerno, the premier medical school of Europe: the
first is the *Chronicle of Monte Cassino*, a brief account probably by
Leo Marsicanus, a contemporary of Constantine's, or his successor,
Guido; the second is a fragment by Magister Matthaeus. According
to these sources, Constantine arrived in Salerno from Tunis with
his rich background in the medical science of the Islamic world
sometime between 1060 and 1075. There he won the support of
Abbot John of the Curia, then of the Norman rulers Robert Guiscard
and Prince Richard of Capua. Richard endowed Constantine with
the church of Saint Agatha in Aversa (an early "genius grant" for a
medical researcher) that he turned over to Monte Cassino when he
became a monk there. Of some twenty-five works that Constantine
adapted into Latin, the most ambitious was the *Pantegni*, a Greek title,
meaning "The Complete Art." It was the first comprehensive vision of
philosophical and therapeutic medicine in the medieval west. The first
extract and sections of the second are taken from a work originally
composed before 978. In the third extract, Stephen of Antioch's later,
more literal translation of the penultimate sentence reads: ". . . to
visit patients whoever they may be, and hospitals . . ." Constantine
had omitted ʿAli ibn al-ʿAbbas's mention of hospitals, since they were
present in Islamic society but not known in the west.

[1] CHRONICLE OF MONTE CASSINO
[PROBABLY EARLY TWELFTH CENTURY]

In the time of this abbot [*Desiderius, abbot, 1058–87*], Constantine
the African, coming to this place [*Monte Cassino*] and donning the habit
of the holy religious life, with deepest devotion presented in this holy

place the church of St. Agatha in Aversa, which had been granted to him by Prince Richard [*of Capua*]. It seems altogether necessary to hand down to the memory of future generations a written account of his nature and his greatness. He then, departing from Carthage, where he was born, made his way to Babylonia [*Fustat, or Old Cairo*], where he received a thorough education in grammar, dialectic, geometry, arithmetic, mathematics, [*and*] astronomy, as well as in the physic [*healing art*] of the Chaldaeans, Arabs, Persians, Saracens, Egyptians, and Indians. Now when he had completed thirty-nine years in learning studies of this kind, he returned to Africa. When the Africans saw that he was so deeply learned in the fields of study of all nations, they conceived the idea of killing him. Learning this, Constantine secretly embarked on a ship and came to Salerno, and for some time remained hidden there under the guise of a poor man. Thereafter, he was recognized by the brother of the king of the Babylonians, who had come there at the time, and [*Constantine*] was treated with great honor by Duke Robert [*Guiscard, the Norman conqueror of Salerno in the year 1077*]. Then, leaving there, Constantine came to this place [*Monte Cassino*], and became a monk, as I have said. And, established in this monastery, he translated out of the languages of diverse peoples a great quantity of books. Among them were these in particular: the *Pantegni*, which he divided into twelve books, in which he set forth what a doctor ought to know; [*and*] the *Practica*, in which he expounded the means by which a doctor preserves health and cures sickness; the *Book of Degrees*; the *Diet of Food*; the *Book of Fevers*, which he translated from Arabic; the *Book on Urine*; *On the Inner Organs*; the *Viaticum*, which he divided into seven parts, namely, *On Diseases Arising in the Head, On Facial Disease, On Instruments [of respiration], On Infirmities of the Stomach and Intestines, On Affliction of the Liver, Kidneys, Bladder, and Spleen; On All Things that Arise Without, on the Skin*; the *Exposition of the Aphorismus*; the *Book of the Tegni*; *Of the Megategni*; *Of the Microtegni*; the *Antidotarium*; the *Dispute of Plato and Hippocrates on the Sentences*; *On Simple Medicine*; *On Gynaecology*; *On Pulses*; *On Experiments*; *Glosses on Herbs and Spices*; *On Eyes*.

[2] LATE-TWELFTH-CENTURY FRAGMENT BY MAGISTER MATTHAEUS, TEACHER AT SALERNO, PRESERVED IN A MANUSCRIPT AT ERFURT

But it must be remarked that it was not Constantine but Isaac who composed this work [*Isaac Iudaeus*, Liber diaetarum universalium], and

Constantine translated it. But since we have nowhere related how the aforesaid Constantine came here and translated the books, I have considered it for this reason appropriate to speak of it here. Now Constantine was a Saracen, and a merchant, for he came here [*Salerno*] for the sake of trade, and brought considerable trading goods with him. As he was by chance making his way through the public square, he climbed up to the Curia of St. Peter, where was an excellent physician [*John*], the brother of the Prince [*Gisulf II, the last Lombard prince of Salerno*], who was called "abbot of the Curia." Therefore Constantine, observing him as he was passing judgment upon urine specimens, and being completely unacquainted with our language, gave a payment to the Saracen servants, to translate for him the judgments that he [*the abbot*] rendered. He [*Abbot John*], learning through the interpreters that the man himself [*Constantine*] had considerable competence in medicine, asked him through his interpreters about the color and consistency of the urine; and in all respects he answered well regarding the urine specimens. He [*Constantine*] asked him through the Saracens whether many books on medicine were available in Latin. He answered that there were not, and that he himself had gained it [*medical knowledge*] only by dint of concentrated interest and practice. Constantine therefore, returning to Africa, for three straight years diligently directed his attention to medical science; and at last, taking many books, returned here. When he had reached Cape Palinurus, a seastorm broke out, and a great quantity of water came into the boat and destroyed a certain part of the *Pantegni*, namely the "Practica." But when he had come here and learned the Roman Latin tongue, and, making himself a Christian, he offered himself as a monk at St. Benedict of Monte Cassino. And those books he translated into our language. But of the "Practica" of the *Pantegni* he translated only three books, for it had been destroyed by the water. Stephanon, however, a certain Pisan, went to those parts and, learning that language, translated it in its entirety, what is now known as the "Practica" of the *Pantegni* of Stephanon as well. But Constantine, in place of it [*the missing part*], published the *Books of the Simples of Medicine* and the *Book of Degrees*; and for Archbishop Alfanus he independently created the *Book of the Stomach*, which proved of the greatest usefulness to him. Archbishop Alfanus wished to imburse him his costs for completing the "Practica" of the *Pantegni*.

[3] CONSTANTINE'S TRANSLATION OF "OATH OF HIPPOCRATES: WHAT CHARACTER STUDENTS SHOULD POSSESS," FROM 'ALI IBN 'ABBAS AL-MAGUSI'S *KITAB KAMIL AS-SINA'A AT-TIBBIYA* [THE COMPLETE BOOK OF THE MEDICAL ART] (CHAPTER 2)

It is fitting that one who wishes to assume the physician's gown should honor his teacher, should praise him, and should serve him as he would his own parents. For honor should be shown one's parents, as being those from whom one's very being is derived. A teacher is to be honored, as being one by whom all that is rough and shapeless is given form. Now whatsoever one a teacher has undertaken to instruct, let him see to it that the student is worthy of himself. And thereafter let that one himself teach ones also who are worthy, and that without fee, and without contract [*of apprenticeship*], and without any reward of future service; and let him deem it right not to admit to this field of learning those who are unworthy. Moreover, let him devote his effort to restoring the health of the patient; and let him not do this in hope of money, nor should he give more consideration to the rich than to the poor, nor more to nobles than to the low-born. He should not himself teach [*the art of*] harmful potion, nor give consent to those who teach [*it*], lest some private citizen, hearing [*about it*], on the basis of his authority should concoct a potion that caused death. Nor should he teach how to bring about abortion. And when he visits a patient, he should not set his heart upon the patient's wife, or give [*amorous*] thought to his maidservant or his daughter. For these are the things that blind the heart of a man. And he ought to be the sole possessor of [*the secrets of*] an illness that is entrusted to him, for at times a patient reveals to his doctor that which he would blush to confess to his parents. Let him shun lechery; let him avoid the pleasures of the world, and drunkenness as well. For these [*indulgences*] unbalance the mind, and they promote weakness in the body. Let him have a passion for constant attention to caring for the health of the body, and let him not grow weary of reading, so that, if at any time he should lose his books, memory might come to his aid. Nor let him think it beneath him to visit patients whoever they may be, so that he may ever grow stronger in practice. Let him be devout, humble, gentle, lovable, [*and given to*] seeking the help of aid that comes from God.

Trans. Francis Newton.

Refugee Dispatch
Karaite Jews from Ascalon (1100)

The senders of this letter were Jews from Ascalon who had taken refuge from the Crusaders in Egypt, probably in Alexandria. From there they organized the support of those Jews who had fallen into the hands of the Franks and converted to Christianity during the capture of Jerusalem in 1099. The document thus subverts the grand Crusader narrative and also sheds light on the cultures of conversion. The letter was sent shortly after Passover 1100 to another Jewish congregation in Egypt, probably in al-Fustat (Cairo), with a view to raising money for the rescue operation. The general situation of warfare was aggravated by the outbreak of the plague. Of special interest is the reference to the books owned by the community of Jerusalem: "two hundred and thirty Bible codices, a hundred other volumes, and eight Torah Scrolls." These had been bought back from the Franks and were temporarily kept in Ascalon.

News still reaches us continuously that of those who were redeemed from the Franks and remained in Ascalon some are in danger of dying from want of food, clothing, and from exhaustion. Others remained in captivity, of whom some were killed with all manner of torture out of sheer lust to murder before the eyes of others who were spared. We did not hear of a single man of Israel in such danger without exerting ourselves to do all that was in our power to save him.

God the exalted has granted opportunities for relief and deliverance to individual refugees, of which the first and most perfect instance—after the compassion of Heaven—was the presence in Ascalon of the honorable elder Abu'l-Fadl Sahl, son of Yushua', son of Sha'ya—may God preserve him—who has dealings with the government—may God bestow upon it glorious victories—whose influence is great in Alexandria, where his word is very much heeded. He arranged matters wisely to overcome this emergency; but it would require a lengthy discourse to explain how he did it. He could not ransom some people and leave others.

In the end, all those who could be bought from them [*the Franks*] were liberated, and only a few whom they kept remained in their hands, including a boy of about eight years of age, and a man known as Abū Sa'd, the son of the Tustarī's wife. It is reported that the Franks urged the latter to embrace the Christian faith of his own free will and promised to treat him well, but he said to them, how could a Kohen become a Christian and be left in peace by those [*the Jews*] who had already disbursed a large sum on his behalf. Until this day, these captives remain in their [*Franks'*] hand, as well as those who were taken to Antioch, but they are few; and not counting those who abjured their faith because they lost patience, as it was not possible to ransom them, and because they despaired of being permitted to go free.

We were not informed, praise be to God, the exalted, that the accursed ones who are called Ashkenaz violated or raped women, as others do.

Now, among those who have reached safety are some who escaped on the second and third days following the battle and left with the governor who was granted safe conduct, and others who, after having been caught by the Franks, remained in their hands for some time and escaped in the end; these are but a few. The majority consists of those who were bought free.

To our sorrow, some of them ended their lives in all kinds of suffering and affliction. The privations that they had to endure caused some of them to leave for this country [*Egypt*] without provisions or protection against the cold, and they died on the way. Others perished at sea; and still others, after having arrived here safely, became exposed to a "change of air"; they came at the height of the plague, and a number of them died. We had, at that time, reported the arrival of each group.

But when the aforementioned honored elder arrived, he brought a group of them, that is, most of those who had reached Ascalon; he passed the Sabbath and celebrated Passover with them on the way in the manner required by such circumstances. He contracted a private loan for the sum needed to pay the camel drivers and for their maintenance on the way, as well as for the caravan guards and other expenses, after having already spent other sums of money, which he did not charge to the community.

All this is in addition to the money that was borrowed and spent in order to buy back two hundred and thirty Bible codices, a hundred other volumes, and eight Torah Scrolls. All these are communal property and are now in Ascalon.

The community, after having disbursed on different occasions about 500 dinars for the actual ransom of the individuals, for maintenance of some of them and for the ransom, as mentioned above, of the communal property, remained indebted for the sum of 200 and some odd dinars. This is in addition to what has been spent on behalf of those who have been arriving from the beginning until now, on medical potions and treatment, maintenance and, insofar as possible, clothing. If it could be calculated how much this has cost over such a long period, the sum would indeed be huge.

Had the accepted practice been followed, that is, of selling three Jewish captives for a hundred (dinars), the whole available sum would have been spent for the ransom of only a few. However, the grace of the Lord, may his name be glorified, has been bestowed upon these wretched people, who may, indeed, cry out as it is written: "You let them devour us like sheep, and scattered us among the nations. You have sold your people for a trifle, demanding no high price for them." Indeed, all the money we have spent to meet this emergency, from the beginning until now, is but insignificant and negligible with respect to its magnitude and the intensity of the sorrow it has entailed.

[. . .]

Gird now your loins together with us in this matter, and it will be accounted for you as a mark of merit in the future, as it has been in the past . . . for we have no one in these parts to whom we could write as we are writing to you. It is proper that we should turn to you and take the liberty of causing you some inconvenience.

The main sections of this letter should be read out to your community, after you have announced that everyone was obliged to attend. The benefit will thus be complete and general, both to those who pay and to those who receive payment. For it is unlikely that there should not be among the people persons who had made a vow; there may be others who owe a sum to the communal chest, the use of which has not been defined; such should, then, be invited to earmark their contribution; others might volunteer a gift without strings. Or there may be those who intend to make a contribution to one cause rather than to another. In this manner, you will achieve your purpose, extricate strength from the weak, and deal with us in your accustomed generosity and excellent manner . . . and you will deserve, through this charitable act, to acquire both worlds.

S. D. Goitein, The Individual: Portrait of a Mediterranean Personality of the High Middle Ages as Reflected in the Cairo Geniza, vol. 3 of A Mediterranean Society (Berkeley: University of California Press, 1988), 374–79. Reprinted by permission of the publisher.

Aristotle in Andalus

Maimonides (1165) and Averroës (1190)

Maimonides, known as "Rambam" for Rabbi Moses ben Maimon (1135–1204), was a native of Córdoba. He was forced to flee Spain when he was young because of the strife between Jewish and Muslim communities. A doctor, rabbi, religious scholar, mathematician, and astronomer, he came to be considered the greatest intellectual figure of medieval Judaism. He eventually settled in Cairo (1165), where he won fame for his medical skill, and became court physician to Sultan Saladin, the ruler who defeated the Christians in the Third Crusade. His writings include a code of Jewish law, the Mishnee Torah (in Hebrew), and a classic work of religious philosophy, the *Guide for the Perplexed* (in Arabic, 1190). Influenced by the teachings of Aristotle, it called for a more rational approach to Judaism and sought to reconcile science, philosophy, and religion. The following letter was written to his pupil R. Joseph Ibn Aknin (son of R. Yehuda) and explains the motivation for the writing of the *Guide*.

Abu al-Walid Muhammad Ibn Ahmad Ibn Rushd, or Averroës (1126–98), came from a Córdoba family of Maliki legal scholars. It was Ibn Tufayl, the vizier of Yusuf al-Mansur, who introduced Averroës to the court. In 1170 Averroës was made judge of Seville. He wrote commentaries on Aristotle and a medical encyclopedia. With the wave of fanaticism that swept Andalus at the end of the twelfth century, his controversial writings were censured and some destroyed. He left Córdoba for Morocco, where he died in 1198. In the following selection Averroës again focuses on the inbetween, the *barzakh*, of existence and the world.

MAIMONIDES

In the name of God, Lord of the Universe
To R. Joseph (may God protect him!), son of R. Yehuda (may his repose be in Paradise!):

My dear pupil, ever since you resolved to come to me, from a distant country, and to study under my direction, I thought highly of your thirst for knowledge, and your fondness for speculative pursuits, which found expression in your poems. I refer to the time when I received your writings in prose and verse from Alexandria. I was then not yet able to test your powers of apprehension, and I thought that your desire might possibly exceed your capacity. But when you had gone with me through a course of astronomy, after having completed the [other] elementary studies which are indispensable for the understanding of that science, I was still more gratified by the acuteness and the quickness of your apprehension. Observing your great fondness for mathematics, I let you study them more deeply, for I felt sure of your ultimate success. Afterwards, when I took you through a course of logic, I found that my expectations of you were confirmed, and I considered you fit to receive from me an exposition of the esoteric ideas contained in the prophetic books, that you might understand them as they are understood by men of culture. When I commenced by way of hints, I noticed that you desired additional explanation, urging me to expound some metaphysical problems; to teach you the system of the Mutakallemin; to tell you whether their arguments were based on logical proof; and if not, what their method was. I perceived that you had acquired some knowledge in those matters from others, and that you were perplexed and bewildered; yet you sought to find out a solution to your difficulty. I urged you to desist from this pursuit, and enjoined you to continue your studies systematically; for my object was that the truth should present itself in connected order, and that you should not hit upon it by mere chance. Whilst you studied with me I never refused to explain difficult verses in the Bible or passages in rabbinical literature which we happened to meet. When, by the will of God, we parted, and you went your way, our discussion aroused in me a resolution which had long been dormant. Your absence has prompted me to compose this treatise for you and for those who are like you, however few they may be. I have divided it into chapters, each of which shall be sent to you as soon as it is completed. Farewell!

Moses Maimonides, The Guide for the Perplexed, *trans. M. Friedländer (London: Hebrew Literature Society, 1881), 1.*

AVERROËS

Concerning the question whether the world is pre-eternal or came into existence, the disagreement between the Ash'arite theologians and the ancient philosophers is in my view almost resolvable into a disagreement about naming, especially in the case of certain of the ancients. For they agree that there are three classes of beings: two extremes and one intermediate between the extremes. They agree also about naming the extremes; but they disagree about the intermediate class.

[1] One extreme is a being which is brought into existence from something other than itself and by something, i.e. by an efficient cause and from some matter; and it, i.e. its existence, is preceded by time. This is the status of bodies whose generation is apprehended by sense, e.g., the generation of water, air, earth, animals, plants, and so on. All alike, ancients and Ash'arites, agree in naming this class of beings "originated." [2] The opposite extreme to this is a being which is not made from or by anything and not preceded by time; and here too all members of both schools agree in naming it "pre-eternal." This being is apprehended by demonstration; it is God, Blessed and Exalted, Who is the Maker, Giver of being and Sustainer of the universe; may He be praised and His Power exalted!

[3] The class of being which is between these two extremes is that which is not made from anything and not preceded by time, but which is brought into existence by something, i.e. by an agent. This is the world as a whole. Now they all agree on the presence of these three characters in the world. For the theologians hold that it is finite (this is the doctrine of Plato and his followers), while Aristotle and his school hold that it is infinite, as is the case with future time.

Thus it is clear that [3] this last being bears a resemblance both to [1] the being which is really generated and to [2] the pre-eternal Being. So those who are more impressed with its resemblance to the pre-eternal than its resemblance to the originated name it "pre-eternal," while those who are more impressed with its resemblance to the originated name it "originated." But in truth it is neither really originated nor really pre-eternal, since the really originated is necessarily perishable and the really pre-eternal has no cause. Some — Plato and his followers — name it "originated and coeval with time," because time according to them is finite in the past.

Thus the doctrines about the world are not so very far apart from each other that some of them should be called irreligious and others not. For this to happen, opinions must be divergent in the extreme, i.e. contraries such as the theologians suppose to exist on this question; i.e. [they hold] that the names "pre-eternity" and "coming into existence" as applied to the world as a whole are contraries. But it is now clear from what we have said that this is not the case.

Averroës, "The Decisive Treatise: Determining the Nature of the Connection between Religion and Philosophy," in On the Harmony of Religion and Philosophy, trans. George F. Hourani (London: Luzac, 1976), 1.

Jewish and Muslim Networks

Benjamin of Tudela (1173) and Ibn Jubayr (1183)

Two travelers from Spain crossed the Mediterranean on the eve of the Third Crusade. Whereas one was preoccupied by the daily challenges of his journey, the other was obsessed by the millennial struggle pitting Islam against Christianity. Nothing is known of Benjamin apart from a few general comments in the preface to his work. His travelogue consists of summary descriptions, lists of place names, distances, and basic information on major cities, especially concerning their Jewish communities. The travelogue, which is excerpted below, reads like a guide for Jewish travelers and businessmen, helping them to find hospitality with coreligionists all over the Mediterranean. Although he occasionally mentions hardships imposed on the Jews, he does not express antagonism toward Islam or Christianity and scarcely comments on the general political situation. By identifying monuments and sites, Benjamin constructs Jewish space shared with Muslims and Christians but in which Jews are excluded from political power.

On the other hand, Christian hostility to Muslims is pervasive in the report of Abu al-Husayn Muhammad Bin Ahmad Bin Jubayr, a native of Valencia and secretary to the governor of Granada. Under the rule of the North African Almohads little remained of the openness toward other religions that had earlier characterized Andalusian Islam. After arriving in Alexandria by boat, Ibn Jubayr and his travel companion join the pilgrim caravan to Mecca and Medina. After the Hajj, the two men visited Kufa, Baghdad, and Mosul in today's Iraq. They next went to Aleppo, Damascus, and Acre, whence they sailed to southern Italy, Sicily, Sardinia, and back to Spain. Just four years after he passed through this region and mourned for it, his prayers for a Muslim restoration would be fulfilled when Saladin recaptured Jerusalem in 1187.

BENJAMIN OF TUDELA

From there it is three parasangs to Jerusalem, which is a small city, fortified by three walls. It is full of people whom the Mohammedans call Jacobites, Syrians, Greeks, Gregorians, and Franks, and of people of all tongues.

It contains a dyeing-house, for which the Jews pay a small rent annually to the king, on condition that besides the Jews no other dyers be allowed in Jerusalem. There are about 200 Jews who dwell under the Tower of David in one corner of the city.

The lower portion of the wall of the Tower of David, to the extent of about ten cubits, is part of the ancient foundation set up by our ancestors, the remaining portion having been built by the Mohammedans. There is no structure in the whole city stronger than the Tower of David.

The city also contains two buildings, from one of which—the hospital—there issue forth 400 knights; and therein all the sick who come thither are lodged and cared for in life and in death. The other building is called the Temple of Solomon; it is the palace built by Solomon the king of Israel.

Three hundred knights are quartered there, and issue therefrom every day for military exercise, besides those who come from the land of the Franks and the other parts of Christendom, having taken upon themselves to serve there a year or two until their vow is fulfilled.

In Jerusalem is the great church called the Sepulcher, and here is the burial-place of Jesus, unto which Christians make pilgrimages. Jerusalem has four gates—the gate of Abraham, the gate of David, the gate of Zion, and the gate of Gushpat, which is the gate of Jehoshaphat, facing our ancient Temple, now called Templum Domini [*Dome of the Rock*]. Upon the site of the sanctuary Omar ben al Khataab erected an edifice with a very large and magnificent cupola, into which the Gentiles do not bring any image or effigy, but they merely come there to pray. In front of this place is the western wall, which is one of the walls of the Holy of Holies. This is called the Gate of Mercy, and thither come all the Jews to pray before the wall of the court of the Temple.

In Jerusalem, attached to the palace which belonged to Solomon, are the stables built by him, forming a very substantial structure, composed of large stones, and the like of it is not to be seen anywhere in the world.

There is also visible up to this day the pool used by the priests before offering their sacrifices, and the Jews coming thither write their names upon the wall.

The Gate of Jehoshaphat leads to the valley of Jehoshaphat, which is the gathering place of nations. Here is a pillar called Absalom's Hand, and the sepulcher of King Uzziah. In the neighborhood is also a great spring, called the Waters of Siloam, connected with the brook of Kidron. Over the spring is a large structure dating from the time of our ancestors, but little water is found, and the people of Jerusalem for the most part drink the rainwater, which they collect in cisterns in their houses.

From the valley of Jehoshaphat one ascends the Mount of Olives; it is the valley which separates Jerusalem from the Mount of Olives. From the Mount of Olives one sees the Sea of Sodom, and at a distance of two parasangs from the Sea of Sodom is the Pillar of Salt into which Lot's wife was turned; the sheep lick it continually, but afterward it regains its original shape. The whole land of the plain and valley of Shittim as far as Mount Nebo are visible from here.

In front of Jerusalem is Mount Zion, on which there is no building, except a place of worship belonging to the Christians. Facing Jerusalem for a distance of three miles are the cemeteries belonging to the Israelites, who in the days of old buried their dead in caves, and upon each sepulcher is a dated inscription, but the Christians destroy the sepulchers, employing the stones thereof in building their houses. These sepulchers reach as far as Zelzah in the territory of Benjamin.

Around Jerusalem are high mountains. On Mount Zion are the sepulchers of the House of David, and the sepulchers of the kings that ruled after him. The exact place cannot be identified, inasmuch as fifteen years ago a wall of the church of Mount Zion fell in. The Patriarch commanded the overseer to take stones of the old walls and restore therewith the church. He did so, and hired workmen at fixed wages; and there were twenty men who brought stones from the base of the wall of Zion. Among these men there were two who were sworn friends. On a certain day the one entertained the other; after their meal they returned to work, when the overseer said to them, "Why have you tarried today?" They answered, "Why do you complain? When our fellow workmen go to their meal we will do our work." When the dinner time arrived, and the other workmen had gone to their meal, they examined the stones, and raised a certain stone which formed the entrance to a cave. Thereupon they said one to the other, "Let us go in and see if any money is to be found there." They entered the cave, and reached a large chamber resting upon pillars of marble overlaid with silver and gold. In front was a table of gold and a scepter and crown. This was the sepulcher of King David. On the left thereof in like fashion was the sepulcher of King Solomon; then followed the sepulchers of all the kings of Judah that were buried there. Closed coffers were also there, the contents of which no man knows. The two men essayed to enter the chamber, when a fierce wind came forth from the entrance of the cave and smote them, and they fell to the ground like dead men, and there they lay until evening. And there came forth a wind like a man's voice, crying out: "Arise and go forth from this place!" So the men rushed forth in terror, and they came unto the Patriarch, and related these things to him. Thereupon the Patriarch sent for Rabbi Abraham el Constantini, the pious recluse, who was one of the mourners of Jerusalem, and to him he related all these things according to the report of the two men who had come forth. Then Rabbi Abraham replied, "These are the sepulchers of the House of David; they belong to the kings of Judah, and on the morrow let us enter, I and you and these men, and find out what is there." And on the morrow they sent for the two men, and found each of them lying on his bed in terror, and the men said: "We will not enter there, for the Lord doth not desire to show it to any man." Then the Patriarch gave orders that the place should be closed up and hidden from the sight of man unto this day. These things were told to me by the said Rabbi Abraham.

The Itinerary of Benjamin of Tudela: Critical Text, Translation and Commentary, *ed. M. N. Adler (London: Frowde, 1907), 22–25.*

IBN JUBAYR (ABU AL-HUSAYN MUHAMMAD BIN AHMAD BIN JUBAYR AL-KANANI AL-ANDALUSI AL-BALANSI)

On that Monday, we stayed in a small village some three and a half miles from Acre. Its headman is a Muslim, appointed by the Franks to oversee the Muslim workers in it. He was extremely hospitable to all members of the caravan, bringing young and old into a large room in his house, giving them all kinds of foods, and overwhelming them with kindness. We were amongst the guests, and spent the night there. On the morning of Tuesday the tenth of the month, which was September 18th, we came to the city of Acre—may God destroy it. We were taken to the customshouse, which is a caravansaray. In front of the door are stone benches covered with carpets. Here the Christian scribes of the Customs sit with their ebony inkstands ornamented with gold, writing Arabic, which they speak.

[. . .]

We rented from a Christian woman a house facing the sea, and prayed God Almighty to save us and ensure our safety.

A note on the city of Acre: May God exterminate [*the Christians in*] it and restore it [*to the Muslims*].

Acre is the capital of the Frankish cities in Syria, the docking place of "ships reared aloft in the sea like mountains" [*Qur'an 55:24*], and a port for all ships. In its greatness it resembles Constantinople. It brings together ships and caravans, and it is the meetingplace of Muslim and Christian merchants from all horizons. Its roads and streets are so crowded that it is hard to walk. It burns fiercely with unbelief and tyranny, and boils with pigs [*Christians*] and crosses. It stinks and is filled with refuse and excrement. The Franks seized it from Muslim hands in the first decade of the sixth hijri century, and Islam wept bitterly for it: it was one of its griefs. Its mosques became churches and its minarets bell towers. But God kept pure one part of the principal mosque, which remained in the hands of the Muslims, as a small mosque where strangers could pray. Near its mihrab is the tomb of the prophet Salih—God's prayers and peace on him and all the prophets. God protected this part from desecration by the unbelievers through the blessing of this holy tomb. To the east of town is the spring called the Spring of the Cattle, from which God brought forth the cattle for Adam—may God bless and preserve him. One descends to this spring down steep steps. Over it is a mosque of which there remains only the mihrab; to the east the Franks have built their mihrab; Muslims and infidels meet there, each for prayer.

[. . .]

On Saturday the 28th of Jumada, October 6th, we embarked on a large ship, taking God's gifts to the Muslims of water and provisions. The Muslims found places far from the Franks. Some Christians called Bulgarians came aboard. A very large number had been on the pilgrimage to Jerusalem, more than two thousand. May God soon relieve us of their company and bring us to safety; He alone should be worshipped. Submitting to the will of the Almighty, we awaited a favorable wind and the loading of the ship.

Rihlat al-katib al-adib Abu al-Husayn Muhammad Bin Ahmad Bin Jubayr al-Kanani al-Andalusi al-Balansi, ed. W. Wright and M. J. de Goeje (Leiden: Brill, 1907), 302–3, 310. Trans. miriam cooke.

Perplexed among Crusaders
Usamah ibn Munqidh (1185)

Usamah ibn Munqidh was born in Shayzar (northern Syria) in 1095, three months before Pope Urban II inaugurated the Crusades. From a noble Arab family, he grew up fighting the Crusaders, but he also engaged them as an emissary. He knew some Frankish leaders and had Frankish knights whom he counted as friends. His autobiography provides insight into how each side fostered mutually exclusive stereotypes that seemed to support religious hostility as natural. Yet he also shows how these same stereotypes often came from persons who held a grudging respect for and a practical engagement with each other. Note how he approves of the behavior of Christians who have spent time with Muslims and have learned from them how to act in a more civilized fashion. He probably dictated his Book of Instructive Example when he was ninety years old.

AN APPRECIATION OF THE FRANKISH CHARACTER

Their lack of sense

Mysterious are the works of the Creator, the author of all things! When one comes to recount cases regarding the Franks, he cannot but glorify Allah (exalted is he!) and sanctify him, for he sees them as animals possessing the virtues of courage and fighting, but nothing else; just as animals have only the virtues of strength and carrying loads. I shall now give some instances of their doings and their curious mentality.

In the army of King Fulk, son of Fulk, was a Frankish reverend knight who had just arrived from their land in order to make the holy pilgrimage and kept such constant company with me that he began to call me "my brother." Between us were mutual bonds of amity and friendship. When he resolved to return by sea to his homeland, he said to me: "My brother, I am leaving for my country and I want thee to send with me thy son (my son, who was then fourteen years old, was at that time in my company) to our country, where he can see the knights and learn wisdom and chivalry. When he returns, he will be like a wise man."

Thus there fell upon my ears words which would never come out of the head of a sensible man; for even if my son were to be taken captive, his captivity could not bring him a worse misfortune than carrying him into the lands of the Franks. However, I said to the man: "By thy life, this has exactly been my idea. But the only thing that prevented me from carrying it out was the fact that his grandmother, my mother, is so fond of him and did not this time let him come out with me until she exacted an oath from me to the effect that I would return him to her."

Thereupon he asked, "Is thy mother still alive?" "Yes," I replied. "Well," said he, "disobey her not."

Their curious medication

A case illustrating their curious medicine is the following:

The lord of al-Munaytirah wrote to my uncle asking him to dispatch a physician to treat certain sick persons among his people. My uncle sent him a Christian physician named Thabit. Thabit was absent but ten days when he returned. So we said to him, "How quickly hast thou healed thy patients!"

He said: "They brought before me a knight in whose leg an abscess had grown; and a woman afflicted with imbecility. To the knight I applied a small poultice until the abscess opened and became well; and the woman I put on a diet and made her humor wet. Then a Frankish physician came to them and said, 'This man knows nothing about treating them.' He then said to the knight, 'Which wouldst thou prefer, living with one leg or dying with two?' The latter replied, 'Living with one leg.' The physician said, 'Bring me a strong knight and a sharp ax.' A knight came with the ax. And I was standing by. Then the physician laid the leg of the patient on a block of wood and bade the knight strike his leg with the ax and chop it off at one blow. Accordingly he struck it—while I was looking on—one blow, but the leg was not severed. He dealt another blow, upon which the marrow of the leg flowed out and the patient died on the spot. He then examined the woman and said, 'This is a woman in whose head there is a devil which has possessed her. Shave off her hair.' Accordingly they shaved it off and the woman began once more to eat their ordinary diet—garlic and mustard. Her imbecility took a turn for the worse. The physician then said, 'The devil has penetrated through her head.' He therefore took a razor, made a deep cruciform incision on it, peeled off the skin at the middle of the incision until the bone of the skull was exposed and rubbed it with salt. The woman also expired instantly. Thereupon I asked them whether my services were needed any longer, and when they replied in the negative I returned home, having learned of their medicine what I knew not before."

I have, however, witnessed a case of their medicine which was quite different from that.

The king of the Franks had for treasurer a knight named Bernard, who (may Allah's curse be upon him!) was one of the most accursed and wicked among the Franks. A horse kicked him in the leg, which was subsequently infected and which opened in fourteen different places. Every time one of these cuts would close in one place, another would open in another place. All this happened while I was praying for his perdition. Then came to him a Frankish physician and removed from the leg all the ointments which were on it and began to wash it with very strong vinegar. By this treatment all the cuts were healed and the man became well again. He was up again like a devil.

Another case illustrating their curious medicine is the following:

In Shayzar we had an artisan named Abu-al-Fath, who had a boy whose neck was afflicted with scrofula. Every time a part of it would close, another part would open. This man happened to go to Antioch on business of his, accompanied by his son. A Frank noticed the boy and asked his father about him. Abu-al-Fath replied, "This is my son." The Frank said to him, "Wilt thou swear by thy religion that if I prescribe to thee a medicine which will cure the boy, thou wilt charge nobody fees for prescribing it thyself? In that case, I shall prescribe to thee a medicine which will cure the boy." The man took the oath and the Frank said:

Take uncrushed leaves of glasswort, burn them, then soak the ashes in olive oil and sharp vinegar. Treat the scrofula with them until the spot on which it is growing is eaten up. Then take burnt lead, soak it in ghee butter and treat him with it. That will cure him.

The father treated the boy accordingly, and the boy was cured. The sores closed and the boy returned to his normal condition of health.

I have myself treated with this medicine many who were afflicted with such disease, and the treatment was successful in removing the cause of the complaint.

Newly arrived Franks are especially rough: one insists that Usamah should pray eastward

Everyone who is a fresh emigrant from the Frankish lands is ruder in character than those who have become acclimatized and have held long association with the Moslems. Here is an illustration of their rude character. Whenever I visited Jerusalem I always encountered the Aqsa Mosque, beside which stood a small mosque which the Franks had converted into a church. When I used to enter the Aqsa Mosque, which was occupied by the Templars, who were my friends, the Templars would evacuate the little adjoining mosque so that I might pray in it. One day I entered the mosque, repeated the first formula, "Allah is great," and stood up in the act of praying, upon which one of the Franks rushed on me, got hold of me and turned my face eastward saying, "This is the way thou shouldst pray!" A group of Templars hastened to him, seized him and repelled him from me. I resumed my prayer, the same man, while the others were otherwise busy, rushed once more on me and turned my face eastward, saying, "This is the way thou shouldst pray!" The Templars again came in to him and expelled him. They apologized to me, saying, "This is a stranger who has only recently arrived from the land of the Franks and he has never before seen anyone praying except eastward." Thereupon I said to myself, "I have had enough prayer." So I went out and have ever been surprised at the conduct of this devil of a man, at the change in the color of his face, his trembling and his sentiment at the sight of one praying towards the qiblah.

Another wants to show to a Moslem God as a child

I saw one of the Franks come to al-Amir Mu'in al-Din (may Allah's mercy rest upon his soul!) when he was in the Dome of the Rock and say to him, "Dost thou want to see God as a child?" Mu'in al-Din said, "Yes." The Frank walked ahead of us until he showed us the picture of Mary with Christ (may peace be upon him!) as an infant in her lap. He then said, "This is God as a child." But Allah is exalted far above what the infidels say about him!

Franks lack jealousy in sex affairs

The Franks are void of all zeal and jealousy. One of them may be walking along with his wife. He meets another man who takes the wife by the hand and steps aside to converse with her while the husband is standing on one side waiting for his wife to conclude the conversation. If she lingers too long for him, he leaves her alone with the conversant and goes away.

Here is an illustration which I myself witnessed:

When I used to visit Nablus, I always took lodging with a man named Mu'izz, whose home was a lodging house for the Moslems. The house had windows which opened to the road, and there stood opposite to it on the other side of the road a house belonging to a Frank who sold wine for the merchants. He would take some wine in a bottle and go around announcing it by shouting, "So and so, the merchant, has just opened a cask full of this wine. He who wants to buy some of it will find it in such and such a place." The Frank's pay for the announcement made would be the wine in that bottle. One day this Frank went home and found a man with his wife in the same bed. He asked him, "What could have made thee enter into my wife's room?" The man replied, "I was tired, so I went in to rest." "But how," asked he, "didst thou get into my bed?" The other replied, "I found a bed that was spread, so I slept in it."

"But," said he, "my wife was sleeping together with thee!"

The other replied, "Well the bed is hers. How could I therefore have prevented her from using her own bed?"

"By the truth of my religion," said the husband, "if thou shouldst do it again, thou and I would have a quarrel." Such was for the Frank the entire expression of his disapproval and the limit of his jealousy.

Another illustration:

We had with us a bath-keeper named Salim, originally an inhabitant of al-Ma'arrah, who had charge of the bath of my father (may Allah's mercy rest upon his soul!). This man related the following story:

I once opened a bath in al-Ma'arrah in order to earn my living. To this bath there came a Frankish knight. The Franks disapprove of girding a cover around one's waist while in the bath. So this Frank stretched out his arm and pulled off my cover from my waist and threw it away. He looked and saw that I had recently shaved off my pubes. So he shouted, "Salim!" as I drew near him he stretched his hand over my pubes and said, "Salim, good! By the truth of my religion, do the same for me." Saying this, he lay on his back and I found that in that place the hair was like his beard. So I shaved it off. Then he passed his hand over the place and, finding it smooth, he said, "Salim, by the truth of my religion, do the same to madame [al-dama]" (al-dama in their language means the lady), referring to his wife. He then said to a servant of his, "Tell madame to come here." Accordingly the servant went and brought her and made her enter the bath. She also lay on her back. The knight repeated, "Do what thou hast done to me." So I shaved all that hair while her husband was sitting looking at me. At last he thanked me and handed me the pay for my service.

Consider now this great contradiction! They have neither jealousy nor zeal but they have great courage, although courage is nothing but the product of zeal and of ambition to be above ill repute.

Here is a story analogous to the one related above:

I entered the public bath in Sur [Tyre] and took my place in a secluded part. One of my servants thereupon said to me, "There is with us in the bath a woman." When I went out, I sat on one of the stone benches and behold! The woman who was in the bath had come out all dressed and was standing with her father just opposite me. But I could not be sure that she was a woman. So I said to one of my companions, "By Allah, see if this is a woman," by which I meant that he should ask about her. But he went, as I was looking at him, lifted the end of her robe and looked carefully at her. Thereupon her father turned toward me and said, "This is my daughter. Her mother is dead and she has nobody to wash her hair. So I took her in with me to the bath and washed her head." I replied, "Thou hast well done! This is something for which thou shalt be rewarded [*by Allah*]!"

Another curious case of medication

A curious case relating to their medicine is the following, which was related to me by William of Bures, the lord of Tabarayyah [Tiberias], who was one of the principal chiefs among the Franks. It happened that William had accompanied al-Amir Mu'in al-Din (may Allah's mercy rest upon his soul!) from 'Akka to Tabarayyah when I was in his company too. On the way William related to us the following story in these words:

We had in our country a highly esteemed knight who was taken ill and was on the point of death. We thereupon came to one of our great priests and said to him, "Come with us and examine so and so, the knight." "I will," he replied, and walked along with us while we were assured in ourselves that if he would only lay his hand on him the patient would recover. When the priest saw the patient, he said, "Bring me some wax." We fetched him a little wax, which he softened and shaped like the knuckles of fingers, and he stuck one in each nostril. The knight died on the spot. We said to him, "He is dead." "Yes," he replied, "he was suffering great pain, so I closed up his nose that he might die and get relief."

Let this go and let us resume the discussion regarding Harim.

A funny race between two aged women

We shall now leave the discussion of their treatment to the orifices of the body to something else.

I found myself in Tabarayyah at the time the Franks were celebrating one of their feasts. The cavaliers went out to exercise with lances. With them went out two decrepit, aged women whom they stationed at one end of the race course. At that other end of the field they left a pig which they had scalded and laid on a rock. They then made the two aged women run a race while each one of them was accompanied by a detachment of horsemen urging her on. At every step they took, the women would fall down and rise again, while the spectators would laugh. Finally one of them got ahead of the other and won that pig for a prize.

Their judicial trials: A duel

I attended one day a duel in Nablus between two Franks. The reason for this was that certain Moslem thieves took by surprise one of the villages of Nablus. One of the peasants of that village was charged with having acted as guide for the thieves when they fell upon the village. So he fled away. The king sent and arrested his children. The peasant thereupon came back to the king and said, "Let justice be done in my case. I challenge to a duel the man who claimed that I guided the thieves to the village." The king then said to the tenant who held the village in fief, "Bring forth someone to fight the duel with him." The tenant went to his village, where a blacksmith lived, took hold of him and ordered him to fight the duel. The tenant became thus sure of the safety of his own peasants, none of whom would be killed and his estate ruined.

I saw this blacksmith. He was a physically strong young man, but his heart failed him. He would walk a few steps and then sit down and ask for a drink. The one who had made the challenge was an old man, but he was strong in spirit and he would rub the nail of his thumb against that of the forefinger in defiance, as if he was not worrying over the duel. Then came the viscount, i.e., the seignior of the town, and gave each one of the two contestants a cudgel and a shield and arranged the people in a circle around them.

The two met. The old man would press the blacksmith backward until he would get him as far as the circle, then he would come back to the middle of the arena. They went on exchanging blows until they looked like pillars smeared with blood. The contest was prolonged and the viscount began to urge them to hurry, saying, "Hurry on." The fact that the smith was given to the use of the hammer proved now of great advantage to him. The old man was worn out and the smith gave him a blow which made him fall. His cudgel fell under his back. The smith knelt down over him and tried to stick his fingers into the eyes of his adversary, but could not do it because of the great quantity of blood flowing out. Then he rose up and hit his head with the cudgel until he killed him. They then fastened a rope around the neck of the dead person, dragged him away and hanged him. The lord who brought the smith now came, gave the smith his own mantle, made him mount the horse behind him and rode off with him. This case illustrates the kind of jurisprudence and legal decisions the Franks have—may Allah's curse be upon them!

Ordeal by water

I once went in the company of al-Amir Mu'in al-Din (may Allah's mercy rest upon his soul!) to Jerusalem. We stopped at Nablus. There a blind man, a Moslem, who was still young and was well dressed, presented himself before al-Amir carrying fruits for him and asked permission to be admitted into his service at Damascus. The amir consented. I inquired about this man and was informed that his mother had been married to a Frank whom she had killed. Her son used to practice ruses against the Frankish pilgrims and cooperate with his mother in assassinating them. They finally brought charges against him and tried his case according to the Frankish way of procedure.

They installed a huge cask and filled it with water. Across it they set a board of wood. They then bound the arms of the man charged with the act, tied a rope around his shoulders and dropped him into the cask, their idea being that in case he was innocent, he would sink in the water and they would then lift him up with the rope so that he might not die in the water; and in case he was guilty, he would not sink in the water. This man did his best to sink when they dropped him into the water, but he could not do it. So he had to submit to their sentence against him—may Allah's curse be upon them! They pierced his eyeballs with red-hot awls.

Later this same man arrived in Damascus. Al-Amir Mu'in al-Din (may Allah's mercy rest upon his soul!) assigned him a stipend large enough to meet all his needs and said to a slave of his, "Conduct him to Burhan al-Din al-Halkhi (may Allah's mercy rest upon his soul!) and ask him on my behalf to order somebody to teach this man the Koran and something of Moslem jurisprudence." Hearing that, the blind man remarked, "May triumph and victory be thine! But this was never my thought." "What didst thou think I was going to do for thee?" asked Mu'in al-Din. The blind man replied, "I thought you wouldst give me a horse, a mule and a suit of armor and make me a knight." Mu'in al-Din then said, "I never thought that a blind man could become a knight."

A Frank domesticated in Syria abstains from eating pork

Among the Franks are those who have become acclimatized and have associated long with the Moslems. These are much better than the recent comers from the Frankish lands. But they constitute the exception and cannot be treated as a rule.

Here is an illustration. I dispatched one of my men to Antioch on business. There was in Antioch at that time al-Ra'is Theodoros Sophianos, to whom I was bound by mutual ties of amity. His influence in Antioch was supreme. One day he said to my man, "I am invited by a friend of mine who is a Frank. Thou shouldst come with me so that thou mayest see their fashions." My man related the story in the following words:

I went along with him and we came to the home of a knight who belonged to the old category of knights who came with the early expeditions of the Franks. He had been by that time stricken off the register and exempted from service, and possessed in Antioch an estate on the income of which he lived. The knight presented an excellent table, with food extraordinarily clean and delicious. Seeing me abstaining from food, he said, "Eat, be of good cheer! I never eat Frankish dishes, but I have Egyptian women cooks and never eat except their cooking. Besides, pork never enters my home." I ate, but guardedly, and after that we departed.

As I was passing in the market place, a Frankish woman all of a sudden hung to my clothes and began to mutter words in their language, and I could not understand what she was saying. This made me immediately the center of a big crowd of Franks. I was convinced that death was at hand. But all of a sudden that same knight approached. On seeing me, he came and said to that woman, "What is the matter between thee and this Moslem?" She replied, "This is he who has killed my brother Hurso." This Hurso was a knight in Afamiyah who was killed by someone of the army of Hamah. The Christian knight shouted at her, saying, "This is a bourgeois [*merchant*] who neither fights nor attends a fight." He also yelled at people who had assembled, and they all dispersed. Then he took me by the hand and went away. Thus the effect of that meal was my deliverance from certain death.

Usamah Ibn-Munqidh, An Arab-Syrian Gentleman and Warrior in the Period of the Crusades, trans. *Philip K. Hitti (1929; New York: Columbia University Press, 2000), 161–70. Reprinted by permission of the publisher.*

Richard and Saladin
Ambroise (1220)

On August 16, 1190, King Richard I of England and his assembled forces set out from Marseilles on the arduous journey to the Levant with the general objective of aiding the Latin kingdom of Jerusalem against the Muslims. Salah al-Din Yusuf ibn Ayyub, or Saladin,

the first Muslim leader to overshadow his Christian adversaries in European accounts, had recently seized a number of Crusader cities and fortresses. Richard I's specific objective was to recapture Jerusalem lost to the Christians three years earlier. In so doing, the English king opened a new chapter in the ongoing epic of the Crusades and introduced England as a major participant. During his lifetime Saladin won praise from Latin chroniclers, and throughout the Middle Ages he figured as the preeminent example of the virtuous Muslim in European literature. Indeed, one of the distinguishing features of the Third Crusade was the equal distribution of ability in the respective leaders on both sides; the reputations of both Richard I and Saladin were enhanced universally. The following excerpt is taken from Ambroise, a little-known panegyrist who traveled with the English king's forces. He narrates an encounter between the forces of Richard I and a large Muslim warship off the coast of Acre that foreshadows the fortunes of the Crusaders under the leadership of Richard I.

[THEY] SET SAIL FOR SYRIA

At Famagusta he took ship
And gave the order to equip
His galleys. And himself took place
In one of great strength, size, and pace.
No harbor under heaven would not
Be terrified and sore distraught
At ships of war so marvelous
And men at arms so valorous.
Behold, the galleys leave the port,
All fit and of the finest sort,
The king, as usual, light and gay,
Fit as a feather, led the way;
And swift as any stag that sped,
Across the sea he journeyed.
Then he saw Margat, on the bord
Of the true country of the Lord,
And then Tortosa he saw next,
Built by a sea storm-tossed and vexed,
And he passed swiftly on his way
Tripoli, Botron, and Infré,
And after that saw Gibelet
With its tower on the castle set.

A GREAT SHIP OF THE SARACENS

Near Beirut, close by Sidon's shore,
Toward the king a ship there bore
Filled with the men of Saladin.
It was equipped by Saphadin,
Manned by the best Turks, chosen from
The finest in all pagandom.
They could not get to Acre, and so
Outside they sailed them to and fro
Till they might safely make the port.
But the king set him out to thwart
Their plan and swiftly on did drive
His galley, till he did arrive
At where they were; he saw their craft
Was broad and high and of great draft,
Masted with three tall masts: 'twas not
A vessel that in haste was wrought.
And by the pagans it had been
Covered, one side, with felt of green;
With yellow felt, as he descried,
Was covered o'er the other side.
And all the ship was in such way
Bedecked, as if 'twere work of fay.
And it was filled with armament
Beyond all count or measurement:
And one man spread abroad the bruit
(Who had been present at Beirut
When this ship took aboard this same
Cargo, to be unshipped in shame),
Of seeing arms laden in store,
An hundred camel-loads and more,
Bow, spear, cross-bow and arbalist
(Hand, wheel, or twisted, as ye list),
And eight hundred well chosen Turks
Sent by the devil for his works,
And more of victuals and supplies
Than one could number or surmise;
Likewise in phials there was Greek
Fire kept, of which men much did speak;

And in the ship were stowed away
Two hundred serpents foul and gray
('Tis written thus, and by him told
Who helped to stow them in the hold)
Which they planned to set free upon
Our host, and spread confusion.

AROUSES THE SUSPICION OF THE ENGLISH

Our galley close to them did steer
So that to touch them it was near;
Our galley-men then gave them greeting,
Being unaware whom they were meeting,
And asked them whence it was they came
And what might be their seigneur's name.
They had a French interpreter,
And they made answer that they were
Englishmen on their way to Tyre.
A wind from Arsur did them spire
Which drove them from the galley's side:
A galley-man who closely spied
The ship and crew, and noted how
With eagerness they fain would row
Away, said to the king: "'Tis plain,
Fair Sire, may I be hanged or slain
If yon craft is not Turk." Whereat
The king said: "Art thou sure of that?"
"Indeed, Sire, most assuredly.
Do but dispatch now hastily
Another galley in pursuit
And order it not to salute
Their men. Then see what they will do
And if their faith be false or true."
The king gave order: and the galiot
Sped toward them, but it hailed them not.

WHO ATTACK THE SHIP

Having for our men little use
Their arrows they began to loose
From arbalist and Damask bow.
The king and his men fell on the foe
With swift attack and vigorous,
When that he saw them shoot at us;
And they defended themselves well:
Bowstrings were twanged, and arrows fell
Thicker than hail, and the mêlée
On either side was under way.
Their ship fared slowly, with small breeze.
Our men came alongside with ease
And often, but they dared not board
It, nor could crush the pagan horde.
A solemn oath the king swore, then
And there, to hang the galley men
If they should weaken or if they
Allowed the Turks to get away.
Then like a tempest on they drove;
And headfirst in the water dove
Beneath the ship; on either side
They swam back, and they deftly tied
The ropes that to the helm were bound
Of the pagan ship, so to confound
The infidels, to make them steer
Awry, and cause their craft to veer.
And thereupon they climbed on board
And straight into the ship they poured.
The foe were not left-handed; they
Fell on our men, to cut and slay.
Those of our folk who were adept
In these things vigorously leapt
Into the ship, while theirs slashed arm
And leg, and did us grievous harm.

Our men did battle of such sort
That they drove them into the port;
The pagans, who exceedingly
Feared death, fought back desperately:
In squads upon the deck they mounted,
Squads carefully arranged and counted:
Fresh soldiers to the battle swarmed,
In bold array, perfectly armed.
And so they fought, and both sides smote
Great blows within the pagan boat.
The Saracens made an attack
So strong they drove our seamen back
But these in their own galleys drew
Together, and assailed anew.
The king told them to ram into
The ship until they stove it through;
And so they rammed, and so hard drove
That it at several points was stove.
It foundered through the holes thus wrought,
Ending this battle fiercely fought.
So giving way, the Saracens
Leapt in the sea by tens and tens.
Each of our men slew all he could:
There had ye seen great blows and good
Dealt by King Richard with a will
Fierce to destroy them and to kill
However, there were thirty-five
Of them that he retained alive.
Of whom some were good engineers,
Skilled in machines, and some emirs:
The rest were drowned: such end was made
Of Persian, Turk, and renegade.
Had the ship come to Acre, 'tis plain
The town would never have been ta'en,
So much defense it would have brought,
But God, who aids His own, so wrought,
And England's king, good, valorous
In warfare, and adventurous.

TO THE GREAT DISTRESS OF SALADIN

The Saracens atop the hill
Had seen this thing which served them ill,
And, filled with fury and chagrin,
Sent word of it to Saladin.
And when that Saladin had heard
It, thrice in wrath he tore his beard,
Then like a man distraught, said he:
"God! now is Acre lost to me,
My men, too, whom I thought secure.
Ye bring me woe hard to endure!"
The pagan army made such wail—
Those who beheld it tell the tale—
That the Turks did cut off their hair
In sorrow, and their clothes did tear,
Because within this ship were lost
Their lords and those they cherished most.

THE FLEET SAILS ON TO ACRE

The king, when he this ship of might
And its crew had captured in the fight,
To move him on to Acre yearned;
Thither with joy his course he turned,
His galleys all in fair array,
Who o'er the ship had won the day.
And when he with the fleet set forth
God sent them good wind from the north;
So before Tyre that night they spent,
Both king and soldiers most content;
The noble king Coeur de Lion,
At morning saw Scandalion,
Then passed Casal Imbert, then clear
Before him he saw Acre appear,
And the flower of all the world he found
Camped there, and drawn up all around;
He saw the mountains and the vales,
The open plains and hills and dales
Clothed with pavilions and with tents,
And men filled with malevolence

Toward Christendom, to do it wrong,
And they were in a mighty throng;
He saw the tents of Saladin
And of his brother, Saphadin;
The pagans were so near, almost
They pressed upon our Christian host.
Quahadin, on the other hand,
The seneschal of paganland,
Guarded the seacoast and the shore
And on our host waged constant war
Always alert to make attack,
To harry us and force us back.

Ambroise, The Crusade of Richard Lion-Heart, *trans. Merton Jerome Hubert (New York: Columbia University Press, 1941), 108–16. Reprinted by permission of the publisher.*

Purgatory
Dante Alighieri (1315–18)

Dante Alighieri (1265–1321) was born in Florence to a wealthy family. His most famous work is the *Divine Comedy*, a work in a hundred cantos, divided into three books of thirty-three cantos each, with a single introductory canto. He wrote the Purgatory, the second part of the *Divine Comedy*, between 1315 and 1318. Influences from the Traditions of the Prophet Muhammad, Islamic philosophy, and mysticism have been found. One of his main sources is the *Kitab al-Mi'raj* (translated into Latin in 1246 as *Il Libro Della Scala*), concerning the Prophet's ascension to Heaven through seven levels. Dante had before him a ready-made pattern of spiritual search based on Islamic writings of the afterlife. The seven levels of *Purgatory* culminate with the poet climbing to the top of the mountain.

For better waters, now, the little bark
of my poetic powers hoists its sails,
and leaves behind that cruelest of seas.

And I shall sing about that second realm
where man's soul does purify itself
and become worthy to ascend to Heaven.

Here let death's poetry arise to life,
O Muses sacrosanct whose liege I am!
And let Calliope rise up and play

her sweet accompaniment in the same strain
that pierced the wretched magpies with the truth
of unforgivable presumptuousness.

The tender tint of orient sapphire,
suffusing the still reaches of the sky,
as far as the horizon deeply clear,

renewed my eyes' delight, now that I found
myself free of the deathly atmosphere
that had weighed heavy on my eyes and heart.

The lovely planet kindling love in man
made all the eastern sky smile with her light,
veiling the Fish that shimmered in her train.

Then to my right I turned to contemplate
the other pole, and there saw those four stars
the first man saw, and no man after him.

The heavens seemed to revel in their flames.
O widowed Northern Hemisphere, deprived
forever of the vision of their light!

And when I looked away from those four stars,
turning a little toward the other pole,
where no sign of the Wain was visible,

I saw near me an ancient man, alone,
whose face commanded all the reverence
that any son could offer to his sire.

Long-flowing was his beard and streaked with white,
as was his hair, which in two tresses fell
to rest upon his chest on either side.

The rays of light from those four sacred stars
struck with such radiance upon his face,
it was as if the sun were shining there.

"Who are you two who challenged the blind stream
and have escaped from the eternal prison?"
he said, moving his venerable locks.

"Who guided you? What served you as a lamp
to light your way out of the heavy night
that keeps the pit of Hell forever black?

Are all the laws of God's Abyss destroyed?
Have new decisions now been made in Heaven
So that, though damned, you come up to my cliff?"

Dante Alighieri's Divine Comedy, *trans. and comm. Mark Musa, 6 vols. (Bloomington: Indiana University Press, 1996), 3:3–5 (Purgatory 1.1–48). Reprinted by permission of the publisher.*

The Reunited Lovers

Giovanni Boccaccio (ca. 1350)

An early Renaissance poet, Boccaccio (1313–75) composed the Decameron between 1349 and 1351 and revised it in 1370. A series of burlesque stories, practical jokes, accounts of hypocritical clergy, and misadventures of traveling merchants that borrow from *A Thousand and One Nights*, the Decameron was thought to have been written during an outbreak of the Black Death, as the plague in Florence was called. Known for its realistic depiction of characters, it tells the fictional story of ten young people who escape the city and tell stories to distract themselves. During the ten days of their asylum, each tells one story a day. Hence, the Decameron contains a hundred different tales. Muslim-Christian rivalry in the Sea frames some of the stories. The following selection is taken from the fifth day and tells a love story between a poor young man, who turns to piracy to win the woman of his dreams, and his beloved. Fortune sends both across the Sea from Christian Sicily to Muslim Tunisia.

FIFTH DAY: NOVEL TWO

Gostanza loves Martuccio Gomito, and hearing that he is dead, gives way to despair, and hies her alone aboard a boat, which is wafted by the wind to Susa. She finds him alive in Tunis, and makes herself known to him, who, having by his counsel gained high place in the king's favour, marries her, and returns with her wealthy to Lipari.

147

Pamfilo's story being ended, the queen, after commending it not a little, called for one to follow from Emilia; who thus began:—

"Meet and right it is that one should rejoice when events so fall out that passion meets with its due reward: and as love merits in the long run rather joy than suffering, far gladlier obey I the queen's than I did the king's behest, and address myself to our present theme. You are to know then, dainty ladies, that not far from Sicily there is an islet called Lipari, in which, no great while ago, there dwelt a damsel, Gostanza by name, fair as fair could be, and of one of the most honourable families in the island. And one Martuccio Gomito, who was also of the island, a young man most gallant and courteous, and worthy for his condition, became enamoured of Gostanza; who in like manner grew so afire for him that she was ever ill at ease, except she saw him. Martuccio, craving her to wife, asked her of her father, who make answer that, Martuccio being poor, he was not minded to give her to him. Mortified to be thus rejected by reason of poverty, Martuccio took an oath in presence of some of his friends and kinsfolk that Lipari should know him no more, until he was wealthy. So away he sailed, and took to scouring the seas as a rover on the coast of Barbary, preying upon all whose force matched not his own. In which way of life he found Fortune favourable enough, had he but known how to rest and be thankful: but 'twas not enough that he and his comrades in no long time waxed very wealthy; their covetousness was inordinate, and, while they sought to gratify it, they chanced in an encounter with certain Saracen ships to be taken after a long defence, and despoiled, and, most part of them, thrown into the sea by their captors, who, after sinking his ship, took Martuccio with them to Tunis, and clapped him in prison, and there kept him a long time in a very sad plight.

"Meanwhile, not by one or two, but by divers and not a few persons, tidings reached Lipari that all that were with Martuccio aboard his bark had perished in the sea. The damsel, whose grief on Martuccio's departure had known no bounds, now hearing that he was dead with the rest, wept a great while, and made up her mind to have done with life; but, lacking the resolution to lay violent hands upon herself, she bethought her how she might devote herself to death by some novel expedient. So one night she stole out of her father's house, and hied her to the port, and there by chance she found, lying a little apart from the other craft, a fishing boat, which, as the owners had but just quitted her, was still equipped with mast and sails and oars. Aboard which boat she forthwith got, and being, like most of the women of the island, not altogether without nautical skill, she rowed some distance out to sea, and then hoisted sail, and cast away oars and tiller, and let the boat drift, deeming that a boat without lading or steersman would certainly be either capsized by the wind or dashed against some rock and broken in pieces, so that escape she could not, even if she would, but must perforce drown. And so, her head wrapped in a mantle, she stretched herself weeping on the floor of the boat. But it fell out quite otherwise than she had conjectured: for, the wind being from the north, and very equable, with next to no sea, the boat kept an even keel, and next day about vespers bore her to land hard by a city called Susa, full a hundred miles beyond Tunis. To the damsel 'twas all one whether she was at sea or ashore, for, since she had been aboard, she had never once raised, nor, come what might, meant she ever to raise, her head.

Now it so chanced, that, when the boat grounded, there was on the shore a poor woman that was in the employ of some fishermen, whose nets she was just taking out of the sunlight. Seeing the boat under full fail, she marveled how it should be suffered to drive ashore, and conjectured that the fishermen on board were asleep. So to the boat she hied her, and finding therein only the damsel fast asleep, she called her many times, and at length awakened her; and perceiving by her dress that she was a Christian, she asked her in Latin how it was that she was come thither all alone in the boat. Hearing the Latin speech, the damsel wondered whether the wind had not shifted, and carried her back to Lipari: so up she started, gazed about her, and finding herself ashore and the aspect of the country strange, asked the good woman where she was. To which the good woman made answer: — "My daughter, thou art hard by Susa in Barbary." Whereupon the damsel, sorrowful that God had not seen fit to accord her the boon of death, apprehensive of dishonour, and at her wits' end, sat herself down at the foot of her boat, and burst into tears. Which the good woman saw not without pity, and persuaded her to come with her into her hut, and there by coaxing drew from her how she was come thither; and knowing that she could not but be fasting, she set before her her own coarse bread and some fish and water, and prevailed upon her to eat a little. Gostanza thereupon asked her, who she was that thus spoke Latin; whereto she answered that her name was Carapresa, and that she was from Trapani, where she had served some Christian fishermen. To the damsel, sad indeed though she was, this same Carapresa, began to take hope, she knew not why, and to grow somewhat less fain of death: wherefore without disclosing who or whence she was, she earnestly besought the good woman for the love of God to have pity on her youth, and advise her how best to avoid insult. Whereupon Carapresa, good woman that she was, left her in her

149

hut, while with all speed she picked up her nets; and on her return she wrapped her in her own mantle, and led her to Susa. Arrived there, she said to her:—"Gostanza, I shall bring thee to the house of an excellent Saracen lady, for whom I frequently do bits of work, as she has occasion: she is an old lady and compassionate: I will commend thee to her care as best I may, and I doubt not she will right gladly receive thee, and entreat thee as her daughter: and thou wilt serve her, and, while thou art with her, do all thou canst to gain her favour, until such time as God may send thee better fortune;" and as she said, so she did.

The old lady listened, and then, gazing steadfastly in the damsel's face, shed tears, and taking her hand, kissed her forehead, and led her into the house, where she and some other women dwelt quite by themselves, doing divers kinds of handiwork in silk and palm leaves and leather. Wherein the damsel in a few days acquired some skill, and thenceforth wrought together with them; and rose wondrous high in their favour and good graces of all the ladies, who soon taught her their language.

Now while the damsel, mourned at home as lost and dead, dwelt thus at Susa, it so befell that, Mariabdela being then King of Tunis, a young chieftain of Granada, of great power, and backed by mighty allies, gave out that the realm of Tunis belonged to him, and having gathered a vast army, made a descent upon Tunis with intent to expel the King from the realm. Martuccio Gomito, who knew the language of Barbary well, heard the tidings in prison, and learning that the King of Tunis was mustering a mighty host for the defence of his kingdom, said to one of the warders that were in charge of him and his comrades:—"If I might have speech with the King, I am confident that the advice that I should give him would secure him the victory." The warder repeated these words to his chief, who forthwith carried them to the King. Wherefore by the King's command Martuccio was brought before him, and being asked by him what the advice, of which he had spoken, might be, answered on this wise:—"Sire, if in old days, when I was wont to visit this country of yours, I duly observed the manner in which you order your battle, methinks you place your main reliance upon archers; and therefore, if you could contrive that your enemy's supply of arrows should give out and your own continue plentiful, I apprehend that you should win the battle." "Ay indeed," replied the King, "I make no doubt that, could I but accomplish that, I should conquer." "Nay but, Sire," returned Martuccio, "you may do it, if you will. Listen, and I will tell you how. You must fit the bows of your archers with strings much finer than those that are in common use, and match them with arrows, the notches of which will not admit any but these fine strings; and this you must do so secretly that your enemy may not know it, else he will find means to be even with you. Which counsel I give you for the following reason: — When your and your enemy's archers have expended all their arrows, you wot that the enemy will fall to picking up the arrows that your men have shot during the battle, and your men will do the like by the enemy's arrows; but the enemy will not be able to make use of your men's arrows, by reason that their fine notches will not suffice to admit the stout strings, whereas your men will be in the contrary case in regard of the enemy's arrows, for the fine string will very well receive the large-notched arrow, and so your men will have an abundant supply of arrows, while the enemy will be at a loss for them."

The King, who lacked not sagacity, appreciated Martuccio's advice, and gave full effect to it; whereby he came out of the war a conqueror, and Martuccio, being raised to the chief place in his favour, waxed rich and powerful. Which matters being bruited throughout the country, it came to the ears of Gostanza that Martuccio Gomito, whom she had long supposed to be dead, was alive; whereby her love for him, some embers of which still lurked in her heart, burst forth again in sudden flame, and gathered strength, and revived her dead hope. Wherefore she frankly told all her case to the good lady with whom she dwelt, saying that she would fain go to Tunis, that her eyes might have assurance of that which the report received by her ears had made them yearn to see. The lady fell heartily in the girl's desire, and, as if she had been her mother, embarked with her for Tunis, where on their arrival they were honourably received in the house of one of her kinswomen. Carapresa, who had attended her, being sent to discover what she might touching Martuccio, brought back word that he was alive, and high in honour and place. The gentlewoman was minded that none but herself should apprise Martuccio of the arrival of his Gostanza: wherefore she hied her one day to Martuccio, and said: — "Martuccio, there is come to my house a servant of thine from Lipari, who would fain speak with thee here privily, and for that he would not have me trust another, I am come hither myself to deliver his message." Martuccio thanked her, and forthwith hied him with her to her house: where no sooner did the girl see him that she all but died for joy, and carried away by her feelings, fell upon his neck with open arms and embraced him, and, what with sorrow of his past woes and her present happiness, said never a word, but softly wept. Martuccio regarded her for a while in silent wonder; then, heaving a sigh, he said: — "Thou livest then, my Gostanza? Long since I heard that thou wast lost; nor was aught known of thee at home." Which said, he tenderly and with tears embraced her. Gostanza told him all her adventures, and how honourably she had been entreated by the gentlewoman with whom she had dwelt. And so long time they conversed, and then Martuccio parted from her, and hied him back to his lord the King, and told him all, to wit, his own adventures and those of the girl, adding that with his leave he was minded to marry her according to our law. Which matters the King found passing strange; and having called the girl to him, and learned from her that 'twas even as Martuccio had said: "Well indeed," quoth he, "hast thou won thy husband." Then caused he gifts most ample and excellent to be brought forth, part of which he gave to Gostanza, and part to Martuccio, leaving them entirely to their own devices in regard of one another. Then Martuccio, in terms most honourable, bade farewell to the old lady with whom Gostanza had dwelt, thanking her for the service she had rendered to Gostanza, and giving her presents suited to her condition, and commending her to God, while Gostanza shed many a tear: after which, by leave of the King, they went aboard a light bark, taking with them Carapresa, and, sped by a prosperous breeze, arrived at Lipari, where they were received with such cheer as 'twere vain to attempt to describe. There were Martuccio and Gostanza wedded with all pomp and splendour; and there long time in easeful peace they had joyance of their love.

Giovanni Boccaccio, The Decameron, trans. J. M. Rigg (London: Routledge, 1905), 12–17.

Between East and West
Ibn Battuta (1355)

Muhammad Ibn 'Abdallah Ibn Battuta (1304–77) is often cited as history's most widely traveled person because of the span of his journey across both time and distance. After performing the Hajj in 1326, he went as far as southern Russia, China, and Java before returning to his homeland in Morocco thirty years later. The sultan of Fez at that time then commissioned Ibn Juzayy, a local belle-lettrist, to write down Ibn Battuta's story, which became the compilation known as the *Rihla*, or "Journey." The rihla had by this time become an established genre of travel literature, so formulaic that it was used by travelers as a template into which they fitted people, places, and monuments they had visited. This selection that is taken from an early stage in Ibn Battuta's travels typifies his account of a place: he tells of his own arrival and experience in Alexandria, followed by an account of the outstanding local attractions and people, and a few anecdotes that he hears from others.

After that, on the 1st of First Jumada [*April 5, 1326*], we arrived at the city of al-Iskandariya [*Alexandria*], may God protect her! She is a well-guarded frontier citadel and a friendly and hospitable region, remarkable in appearance and solid of construction, furnished with all that one could wish for in the way of embellishment and embattlement, and of memorable edifices both secular and religious. Noble are her dwellings, graceful her qualities and to imposing size her buildings unite architectural perfection. She is a unique pearl of glowing opalescence, and a secluded maiden arrayed in her bridal adornments, glorious in her surpassing beauty, uniting in herself the excellences that are shared out [*by other cities between themselves*] through her mediating situation between the East and the West. Every fresh marvel has there its unveiling, every novelty finds its way thither. Men have already described it and descanted at length; they have compiled volumes on its marvelous features, and exceeded all bounds; but for one who would acquire a detailed knowledge of this subject it is enough [*to read*] what Abu ʿUbaid [*al-Bakri*] has written in The Book of Ways.

Its gates and harbor. The city of Alexandria has four gates: the gate of the Lote-tree, and it is to it that the Maghrib road leads; the gate of Rashid [*Rosetta*]; the Sea-gate; and the Green gate. This gate is open only on Fridays, and the people go out through it to visit the tombs. It has also the magnificent port, and among all the ports in the world I have seen none equal to it, except the ports of Kawlam [*Quilon*] and Qaliqut [*Calicut*] in India, the port of the infidels [*Genoese*] at Sudaq in the land of the Turks, and the port of Zaitun in China, all of which will be mentioned later.

The lighthouse. I went to see the lighthouse on this journey and found one of its faces in ruins. One would describe it as a square building soaring into the air. Its door is high above the level of the ground, and opposite its door and of the same height is another building; wooden planks are laid from one to the other, and on these one crosses to the doorway. When they are removed there is no means of approach to it. Inside the door there is a place for the guardian of the lighthouse to sit in, and within the lighthouse itself there are many chambers. The breadth of the passage in its interior is nine spans [*a little less than seven feet*]; and the breadth of the wall ten spans [*ca. seven and a half feet*]; the breadth of the lighthouse on each of its four faces is 140 spans [*ca. 105 feet*]. It is situated on a high mound and lies at a distance of one farsakh [*three miles*] from the city on a long tongue of land, encompassed on three sides by the sea up to the point where the sea is immediately adjacent to the city wall, so that the lighthouse cannot be reached by land except from the city. On this peninsula connected with the lighthouse is the cemetery of Alexandria. I visited the lighthouse [*again*] on my return to the Maghrib in the year 750 [1349], and I found that it had fallen into so ruinous a condition that it was impossible to enter it or to climb up to the doorway. Al-Malik al-Nasir (God's mercy on him) had started to build a similar lighthouse alongside it, which he was prevented by death from completing.

[. . .]

Some of the learned men of Alexandria. One of these was the qadi of the city, 'Imad al-Din al-Kindi, a master of the arts of speech, who used to wear a turban of extraordinary size. Never either in the eastern nor in the western lands have I seen a more voluminous headgear than this. I saw him one day sitting in the forepart of a prayer-niche, and his turban was not far short of filling it up completely.

Another was Fakhr al-Din b. al-Righi, who also was one of the qadis at Alexandria, and a worthy and learned man.

Anecdote. It is related that the grandfather of the qadi Fakhr al-Din al-Righi belonged to the town of Righa, and after devoting himself to the pursuit of learning he set out to go to the Hijaz. He reached Alexandria in the evening, having but little in his hand; and being unwilling to enter the town until he should hear some good omen, he remained seated close to the gate until everybody had gone in, and the hour for closing the gate had arrived. There was no one left there but himself, and the keeper of the gate, annoyed at his lingering, said to him sarcastically, "Come in, O qadi." "Qadi, if God will" he replied and entered into one of the colleges, where he studied assiduously and followed the "way" of the virtuous. His name and fame spread abroad, and he acquired such a reputation for asceticism and piety that at length the reports about him reached the [*ears of the*] king of Egypt. It happened that the qadi of Alexandria died, and in it at that time were a great multitude of learned jurists and theologians, all of whom aspired to the appointment, while he alone amongst them had no ambitions in this direction. Thereupon the sultan sent him the "investiture," that is to say, the diploma of appointment as a qadi. When the courier delivered this to him, he ordered his servant to make public proclamation that any person who had a dispute should present himself for its investigation, and he held sittings for the settling of cases between the inhabitants. The jurists and others met in the house of one of their number, whose claim to the qadi-ship, they had thought, could not be passed over, and discussed the possibility of inducing the sultan to reconsider al-Righi's appointment and of addressing a remonstrance to him to the effect that the population were dissatisfied with al-Righi. There was present at this meeting, however, an astrologer, a man of great perspicacity, who said to them: "Do not do that, for I have cast a horoscope of his appointment and taken pains to assure myself of it, and it has appeared to me that he will hold judicial office for forty years." So they gave up their idea of having his case reconsidered, and his fortunes were as the astrologer had foreseen, and he was noted during the tenure of the qadi-ship for even justice and purity of character.

[. . .]

Anecdote. The following incident occurred in the city of Alexandria in the year 27 [1327], and we received the report of it at Mecca (God ennoble her!).

A quarrel broke out between the Muslims and the Christian traders. The chief of police in Alexandria was a man called al-Karaki, and he adopted a policy of protecting the Europeans. He gave orders to the Muslims to assemble between the two outer walls protecting the gate of the city, and he shut them out of the city as a penalty for their action. The population disapproved of this and thought it monstrous; they broke down the gate and made a riotous assault on the governor's dwelling. He protected himself against them and fought with them from the roof, at the same time dispatching pigeons with the news to al-Malik al-Nasir. The sultan sent an amir named al-Jamali and followed him up by another amir known as Tughan, a stony-hearted tyrant and suspect in his religion—it was said that he used to worship the sun. These two entered Alexandria, arrested the notables among the civil population and the principal merchants of the city, such as the family of al-Kubak and others, and took large sums of money from them. 'Imad al-Din the qadi had an iron shackle to which his hands were attached put on his neck. Subsequently the two amirs put to death thirty-six of the men of the city, and had each man cut in two and the bodies placed on crosses in two rows. This was done on a Friday; the population, going out as usual after the [*midday*] prayer to visit the cemetery, found their executed fellow-citizens hanging there, and were greatly distressed and their sorrows redoubled.

The Travels of Ibn Battuta, 3 vols., *trans. H. A. R. Gibb (Cambridge: Hakluyt Society, 1958), 1:18–28.*

Two Romes

Manuel Chrysoloras (1411)

When Chrysoloras (ca. 1350–1415) first left Constantinople for Italy in 1394–95, it was on a diplomatic mission on behalf of the Byzantine emperor Manuel II Palaiologos (r. 1391–1425): its aim was to gain support against the Ottoman state. Through letters he continued his close connection with the Byzantine court and accompanied the emperor on extensive travels in France and England with the same goal in mind. It was, however, as a teacher of Greek that Chrysoloras made his mark, becoming a professor at Florence in 1397 and teaching later at Pavia, Bologna, Venice, and Rome. His influence on Italian humanists was profound. His efforts as a translator brought Homer and Plato within reach of western Europe and did much to spark and nourish the revival of interest in ancient Greek texts and thought. Chrysoloras's letter to Manuel II's co-regent and son, John, is an extended comparison of the older Rome with the newer. The author is especially interested in the sacred topography of the two cities and admires the extent of long-distance Christian pilgrimage received by the older Rome. In the following extract Chrysoloras expresses awe at ancient triumphal processions but spares a thought for their victims, while drawing moral lessons about the vicissitudes of fortune that seem to foreshadow the eventual fall of the Byzantine Empire in 1453.

Often I wander through the streets over which the triumphal arches stand and turn my thoughts to the conquered princes who were forced down these very streets, and to the other captives, often Armenians, Persians, or other distant peoples. I think also of the generals triumphing over them, what elation they must have felt, but also the feelings of the conquered people. I visualize the Roman crowd gathered on each side of the street, people watching from the tops of buildings, the sound of instruments, the noise, the cheers and applause; I think of the joy of the Romans in their victory, over such distant enemies in fact, but also at the pain on the part of the captives and their families back home in light of defeat and of such a triumphal procession. I think what a great difference between victors and vanquished there seemed to be then, how miserable and wretched the one group, how elated and fortunate the other seemed to themselves and others. But today all of that has been leveled, everything lies in dust: one hardly knows the fate of a Pompey or a Lucullus any better than that of Mithridates or Tigranes.

The very houses, columns, and edifices have fallen to dust: all that remains of them is that the earth is slightly higher at the place where their rubble collapsed. One can see many of the monuments of those successful, blessed conquerors, their trophies and garlands, now fallen into excrement and mud; in the case of other statues the limbs have been removed and strewn everywhere; others burnt to limestone or whitewash or simply used as building material for other structures. The few more fortunate stones—even when they have lost, as Aristotle says, what Protarchos called the "luck of stones" [*to be used in a temple*]—have become stepping-stones for mounting horses, building foundations, or hayboxes for donkeys and oxen.

Manuel Crisolora: Le due Rome, *ed. Francesca Nutti (Bologna: Patron, 2001), 84–86. Trans. Grant Parker.*

A Muslim Caesar
Tursun Beg (1488)

Mehmed II, known as Fatih, or "the Conqueror" (r. 1451–81), recognized the importance of controlling the sea routes to Constantinople before laying siege to the city. To this end he built a formidable fortress known as "Boğaz-Kesen," or "Straits-Cutter," on the Bosphorus in 1452 opposite a smaller one built by his great-grandfather. During the siege of Istanbul, Mehmed's fleet could not enter the Golden Horn inlet due to the boom the Byzantines had laid across the entrance. To circumvent this he built a road of greased logs and rolled his ships across land to strategic advantage in the Golden Horn. This stopped the flow of supplies from Genoan ships and demoralized the Byzantine defenders, who were forced to disperse their forces. The Blachernae walls in the northwest part of the city had been partially damaged by the great cannon designed by the Ottomans for the siege. Crusaders in 1204 had broken through these very walls. The siege ended with conquest on May 29, 1453, when Mehmed was twenty-one. Control of Constantinople enabled Ottoman rule over the Balkans and eastern Mediterranean and was a key event marking the end of the Middle Ages and the start of the Renaissance. In addition to the titles of King, Khan, and Sultan, Mehmed now added Roman Caesar, thus connecting his Muslim rule to great imperial precedents and making it the imperial capital. The first building Mehmed visited in the city was the Hagia Sophia, which he converted to a mosque.

THE CONSTRUCTION OF THE FORTRESS OF BOĞAZ-KESEN

Mehmed was possessed with the idea of conquering Istanbul and constantly insisted on the necessity of taking the city without delay. Senior statesmen spoke of the strength of the fortifications and of the bad consequences that would arise from a prolonged siege of the city, but Mehmed would not listen and immediately began preparations for the siege. With this intention he ordered the building of a fortress on the Bosphorus.

It was intolerable that Istanbul, surrounded by the lands of Islam, should survive under a Christian ruler, the so-called *Kayser-i Rum*, especially since he gave protection within the city walls to pretenders to the Ottoman throne and constantly tried to stir up conflict in the Ottoman territories. In the spring of 856 (1452) Sultan Mehmed came to the spot where the fortress was to be built.

A small castle with twenty portals opening onto the sea was built below Rumeli-Hisari close to the shore and at each opening a cannon was placed. Across the water below the fortress of Yenice-kale a similar small castle was built and the cannons emplaced. In this way the straits were effectively blocked so that unauthorized passage between the Mediterranean and the Black Sea was now impossible. The Sultan gave up all thoughts of relaxation, and through his efforts the work at Rumeli-Hisari was completed in a short time.

THE CONQUEST OF ISTANBUL

After the construction of Rumeli-Hisari had been completed, the Sultan set out for his capital, Edirne. Before the army set out for Edirne, a scuffle took place between some shepherds and a group of Ottoman soldiers. The people inside the city, mistaking the scuffle for the beginning of hostilities, shut the gates of the city and prepared themselves for battle. Some of the Sultan's commanders who happened to be on leave in the city at that time remained within the walls. The Prince treated them well and returned them with an envoy to apologize to the Sultan but Mehmed was not amenable and expressed his hostility by voicing the challenge: "Either surrender the city or stand ready to do battle." He then returned to Edirne.

In the spring of 857 (1453), he left Edirne with the intention of capturing Istanbul. He ordered the large cannons to be dragged by the *yayas*. The master *nakkabs*, stoneborers from the mines in Rumeli, joined the army while the naval forces waited in Gelibolu. The Sultan proceeded by land and the navy by sea. According to custom, the day that camp was to be made near Istanbul the army was ordered by regiment into rows. He ranged at the center of the army around his own person the white-capped Janissary archers, the Turkish and European crossbowmen, and the musketeers and cannoneers. The red-capped *'azebs* were placed on his right and left, joined at the rear by the cavalry. Thus organized, the army marched in formation on Istanbul.

On the other side, the Byzantine emperor had received reinforcements from Christian rulers in Europe. He sent these armoured, mounted knights in front of the gates to meet the approaching army of the Sultan. The Muslim forces pushed them back within the walls, and finally the Sultan arrived on the scene at the outer walls. According to Ottoman practice, the Sultan pitched his large tent at the middle of the ranks. The Janissaries set up their tents in the form of a circle surrounding the Sultan's. The *Beğlerbeği* of Anatolia, Ishak Beg, formerly one of the viziers of Sultan Murad, took up his place on the right wing with the Anatolian forces, while the *Beğlerbeği* of Rumeli, Dayi Karaca Beg, uncle of Prince 'Alaeddin, was on the left. Trenches were dug for emplacing the cannon, and catapults were set up in several places. They set up barricades and vaulted bunkers and showed the miners their places. Hostilities immediately broke out in front of the gates.

One difficulty, however, was the fact that the Golden Horn was closed off. Sultan Mehmed ordered that some of the smaller ships and galleys should be dragged over the hill behind Galata into the Golden Horn. Thus forced to guard the sector of the walls on the Golden Horn as well, the enemy forces would necessarily be spread out. So, as ordered, the ships and galleys were decked out with banners of every color and dragged overland to the Golden Horn. By lashing the boats together a secure bridge was formed over which the soldiers could cross, and the fortress was surrounded on three sides.

Meanwhile, the cannons and catapults continued to bombard the walls. The shock of the balls shook and rent the walls. Fighting continued every day from sunrise to sunset, but the defenders placed their trust in the firmness of the fortifications even after several towers were completely destroyed by cannon fire. At this stage, two coques filled with arms and reinforcements arrived from Europe. At that point the soldiers and naval troops of the Sultan were busily making preparations for the dragging of the ships over to the Golden Horn. With the aid of a favorable wind, the coques began to approach very quickly. The admiral Balta-oğlu Süleyman Beg sent against them all the ships he could gather, and a great battle took place in which the Ottomans were defeated. The Greeks opened up the barrier across the Golden Horn and let in the coques.

After this naval defeat the Muslims were distressed and lost hope, but in fact the arrival of the coques turned out to be a helping factor in the Ottoman's final victory. By that time, the walls facing the Janissaries and the Sultan's soldiers had been destroyed and paths prepared to the trenches. The Greeks feared that the fortress would be taken from this direction and wished to be responsible themselves for its defense. However, the European troops who had come as reinforcements demanded that the defense of this area be given to them, otherwise threatening to withdraw their support. Fearing that they would indeed desert the cause if he did not give in, the Emperor granted their wish. This, in turn, caused discontent among the Greeks in the city, and the forces defending the city fell into disunity.

The Sultan proclaimed a general assault and gave the troops permission to take booty into the city. At night the soldiers reached the walls from the trenches and, against the defenders on the walls, attempted to climb up under the protection of their shields. At daybreak the Sultan approached on horseback and the attack on the fortress began in earnest. The cannons began to fire, then the battle cry was sounded and the general assault was underway. The attackers proceeded to rain arrows on the defenders. In the breaches which had been opened by the cannon fire, soldiers fought breast to breast and sword to sword. The enemy threw Greek fire on the attackers. As the battle proceeded in this fashion, in the section where the cannons had opened breaches in the walls, the European troops met the Ottoman troops in front of the smaller outer walls. The enemy commander arrived at this place and, while he was struggling with an Ottoman soldier on top of the tower, another soldier pierced his belly from below. When they saw that their commander had been wounded, the enemy troops were overcome. They tried to escape by fleeing into the inner fortresses, but the defenders had barred the gate. Left trapped between the walls, they were all put to the sword. The Ottoman troops immediately stormed the inner walls and pushed back the defenders. The rest of the army then began to spread out into the city by means of the breach in the wall while the enemy troops fled before them.

While the Sultan's standing army, the *kapu kulu*, was achieving this victory, the Anatolian, Rumelian, and navy troops continued to fight unaware of the new developments. The Byzantine Emperor and his retinue were reduced to panic when they saw the Janissaries so close behind them, and they too began to flee. Some of them shut themselves in a tower while others perished charging their horses desperately against the Ottoman troops. Still others were taken prisoner.

At that juncture the Emperor was stealthily fleeing towards the Golden Horn with the intention of escaping in one of the ships. He was met on the way by a group of 'azebs. This group of 'azebs had entered the city with a band of Janissaries, and later, becoming separated from them, had wandered into a side street where they met the Emperor with his retinue. A desperate battle ensued. The Emperor's horse slipped as he was attacking a wounded 'azeb, whereupon the 'azeb pulled himself together and cut off the Emperor's head. When they saw this, the rest of the enemy troops lost hope and the 'azebs managed to kill or capture most of them. A great quantity of money and precious stones in the possession of the Emperor's personal retinue was also seized.

After having completely overcome the enemy, the soldiers began to plunder the city. They enslaved boys and girls and took silver and good vessels, precious stones, and all sorts of valuable goods and fabrics from the imperial palace and the houses of the rich. In this fashion many people were delivered from poverty and made rich. Every tent was filled with handsome boys and beautiful girls.

Then the gates of the fortress were opened and Sultan Mehmed toured the city with a group of commanders and religious dignitaries in this retinue. He visited the great buildings and bazaars and particularly expressed his desire to see Hagia Sofia. Over the years this church had deteriorated so that at this time only its dome was left standing.
[. . .]

When the Sultan returned to his headquarters from this tour, a council was held. There the prominent Byzantines were brought into his presence. He ordered some of them executed while others were spared for practical purposes. He appointed Karistiran Süleyman Beg governor of Istanbul and entrusted to him the work of reconstructing the city.

Tursun Beg, History of Mehmed the Conqueror, *trans. Halil İnalcık and Rhoads Murphey (Minneapolis: Bibliotheca Islamica, 1978), 33–37.*

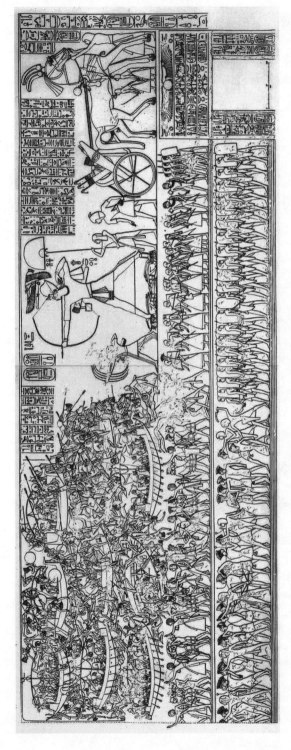

ILL. 1. Ramses III's temple at Medinet Habu, Thebes, commemorating victory over the "Sea People" (early twelfth century B.C.E.). The king, with bow and arrow, is the prominent figure to the right, whereas groups of the enemy are distinctive by their attire and headdress. Courtesy of the Oriental Institute of the University of Chicago.

163

ILL. 2. Etruscan funerary painting from the Tomb of Hunting and Fishing, Tarquinia (sixth century B.C.E.). The Etruscans left only a small documentary record, but a vast array of painting. In the eighth through sixth centuries B.C.E. the Etruscans exercised considerable sea power, which involved commercial and cultural links with the Greek world of the Aegean. In the three centuries preceding its conquest by Rome in 261 B.C.E., Tarquinia was one of their major centers. SEF / Art Resource, N.Y.

ILL. 3. Painting from the Tomb of the Diver, Poseidonia, on Italy's Amalfi
Coast. This detail is a decoration inside the lid of a sarcophagus (fifth century
B.C.E.). Such tombs were usually decorated with scenes from the underworld.
Poseidonia, known from spectacular archaeological remains rather than ancient
texts, throve as a Greek colony in the sixth and fifth centuries. On the site are
some of the best-preserved Doric temples in Magna Graecia. In 273 B.C.E. it
became the Roman colony of Paestum. Erich Lessing / Art Resource, N.Y.

ILL. 4. Attic red-figure stamnos (wide-mouth jar), name vase of the Siren Painter (c. 500–480 B.C.E.), depicting a scene from Homer's *Odyssey*. Here Odysseus has been lashed to the mast of his ship so that he might be unaffected by the alluring song of the sirens (depicted as half woman, half bird). This vase is an example of Attic red-figure, a revolutionary technique invented by vase painters in Athens around 530 B.C.E. In the fifth century, such vases were produced in the thousands and many were exported to Italy, where they were highly prized as burial offerings. This particular example, now in the British Museum (E 440), comes from a tomb in the Etruscan cemetery at Vulci, about fifty miles northwest of Rome. Bridgeman-Giraudon / Art Resource, N.Y.

ILL. 5. Underwater excavations off Bozburun (southwest Turkey) in 1995–98 have revealed a major shipwreck of Byzantine date, ninth or tenth century C.E. Some 500 amphorae have been retrieved from this site, along with remains of the ship itself. Institute of Nautical Archaeology.

ILL. 6. Cleopatra, queen of Egypt: On the wall of her temple at Denderah
(35 B.C.E.), Cleopatra presented herself as the Egyptian goddess Isis (far left).
Standing in front of her is her son and co-ruler from 45 B.C.E. onward, Caesarion.
He was supposedly the son of Julius Caesar, with whom she had a relationship
in 48–47 B.C.E. Historical evidence indicates that she was an effective ruler
domestically, but as Horace's *Ode* indicates, she was most remembered
(and vilified) for her relationship with Marcus Antonius. Erich Lessing /
Art Resource, N.Y.

ILL. 7. Arch of Titus, Rome (constructed 81 C.E.): detail from an interior panel relief inside the arch. The procession depicted here celebrates the Roman victory over the Jews in the revolt of 66–73 C.E. Among the trophies displayed is the menorah, an important Jewish symbol. In processions of this kind the triumphant general would follow the displayed trophies. The fullest account of the revolt is by Flavius Josephus (*Jewish Wars*, 7.121–58), who was himself at the forefront of conflict. Coinciding as it did with a rising of Batavians on the lower Rhine frontier (69–70), this was one of the most determined acts of resistance to Roman power. Most famously, the palace-fortress of Masada withstood a siege until 73 C.E., whereupon most of its 390 inhabitants took their lives rather than capitulate. Alinari / Art Resource, N.Y.

ILL. 8. The market at Delos. View from the theater to the northwest, showing the Agora (marketplace) of the Competaliasts and Hermaists and the Sacred (main) harbor in the background. Apart from its religious importance (see "Delos at the Crossroads" in Chapter 1), Delos was one of the ancient Mediterranean's major slave markets. Photograph by Monika Truemper.

ILL. 9. Facade of the library at Ephesus, built in honor of Tiberius Julius Celsus, governor of the Province of Asia in the early second century C.E. Vanni / Art Resource, N.Y.

ILL. 10. Court of the Lions in the Alhambra Palace of Granada, Spain.
Photograph by Mayassa Bint Hamad al-Thani.

ILL. 11. The Hagia Sophia (Aya Sofya, or "Holy Wisdom"), dedicated by Justinian in 537 C.E., lies at the confluence of the Bosphorus and the Golden Horn. It was converted into a mosque in 1453 and a museum in 1935. The interior marble columns were taken from the Temple of Artemis at Ephesus. <www.sacred-destinations.com>

ILL. 12. T-O, or wheel, map of Isidore recreates the Christian picture of the world in the T-O shape. The habitable lands, divided between the three sons of Noah (Shem: Asia; Ham: Africa; Japheth: Europe), are held within the O of Ocean Sea (*Mare Oceanum*) and divided by the T of flowing waters, with the Mediterranean (*Mare magnum sive mediterraneum*) separating Europe from Africa. East (*Oriens*) is on the top. Isidore's discussion of geography includes the first use of the term "Mediterranean" in its modern sense. The Newberry Library, Chicago, Ill.

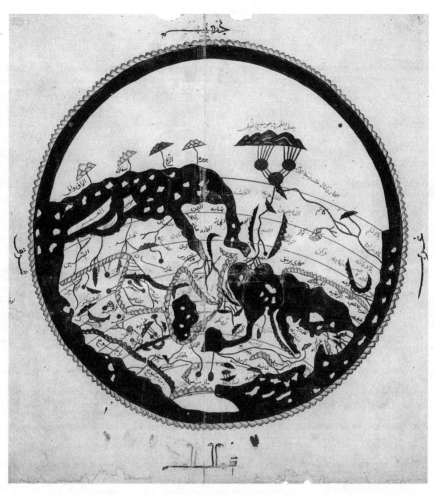

ILL. 13. Idrisi's world map (1154). Whereas maps of the Latin west were oriented
toward Jerusalem, with the east at the top, Arab maps placed the south at
the top, with Mecca, the direction of Muslims' five daily prayers and site of
the annual pilgrimage, as the main meridian. Foremost among Arab map
makers was the Andalusian geographer al-Idrisi (1099?–after 1154). In Sicily,
under the patronage of the Norman king Roger II, he made maps "for the
diversion of those who would travel the world." Borrowing from Ptolemy's
teachings on climate, which accorded each climate its own color, he painted the
Mediterranean, the "fourth climate" in his categorization, green, blue for the sea,
yellow for the desert, and red for the sunrises and sunsets.

ILL. 14. Game of chess between a Crusader and a Muslim, thirteenth century, from a Spanish manuscript on chess by Alfonso X "the Wise" (1221–84), king of Castile and León. The Muslims brought chess to Spain in the tenth century.
HIP / Art Resource, N.Y.

ILL. 15. The ancient deity Isis, originating in Egypt, was taken into Christian tradition and spread throughout the Mediterranean. This illustration is part of a fifteenth-century French manuscript of Giovanni Boccaccio's work on exemplary historical women. The New York Public Library / Art Resource, N.Y.

ILL. 16. Portrait of Abbasid caliph Harun al-Rashid (r. 785–809), depicted as a youth in Indian miniature by Behzad in the seventeenth century. He was a scholar and poet who gave great importance to literature, music, and translation of Greek philosophy and science. He maintained diplomatic relations with Charlemagne. Snark / Art Resource, N.Y.

ILL. 17. Portrait of a scribe
by Gentile Bellini (1429–
1507), who was invited by
Mehmed the Conqueror to
Istanbul, where he spent a
year. This painting is believed
to be a depiction of Cem
Sultan, contender for the
Ottoman throne. Isabella
Stewart Gardner Museum,
Boston.

ILL. 18. Map of Venice by Piri Reis (1465–1554), an Ottoman admiral and
cartographer. He was renowned for the maps and charts collected in his *Kitab-i
Bahriye* (Book of Sea Navigation), which documented Aegean and Mediterranean
ports. Piri Reis began writing his book in 1511, producing his first world map in
1513, based on some twenty older maps and charts he had collected. Bildarchiv
Preussischer Kulturbesitz / Art Resource, N.Y.

ILL. 19. The Ottoman fleet under Barbarossa blockading the port of Marseilles, early sixteenth century. Barbarossa was the name Europeans used for the Ottoman admiral Hayreddin (1466–1546). Originally from Lesbos, he and his brother, Oruç, had established themselves as successful privateers by 1512. He offered allegiance to the Ottoman sultan and in return received military aid that enabled him to capture Algiers in 1529. Appointed admiral in chief (Kapudan Pasha) of the Ottoman Empire (1533) by Süleyman the Magnificent, he went on to conquer Tunisia. Bridgeman-Giraudon / Art Resource, N.Y.

ILL. 20. *Battle of Lepanto*, 1572, by Paolo Veronese (1528–88). Painted within
a few months of the five-hour battle, it depicts the enormous number of ships
involved and the sacralizing of the Christian victory over the Ottomans. St. Peter
implores the Virgin Mary to intercede, and an angel hurls burning arrows on the
Ottoman ships. Alinari / Art Resource, N.Y.

Esclaue Chrestien, François a Alger en Barbarie
La Barbarie est presque remplie de Pirates et Corsaires, dont
la pluspart sont Chrestiens Reniez, qui trafiquent des pau-
ures Captifs, et les vendent comme les chevaux; preferant a la
Religion Turque le prix quils en recoivent. Ils sont plus ou
moins malheureux, suiuant l'humeur des Maistres qui les
achettent. Celui cy est un Gentilhomme François, tres
qualifie, qui souffrit er uellement pendant 15 ans,
de trois diuers maistres mais a la fin il fut vendu
a un autre Maistre plus raisonable, qui l'emploia
a filer, et faire des draps de Coton, dont ils font des
chemises, et des habits Il fut pris aux Isles d'Yeres
en l'annee 1670 et Ra chepte en 1685. Il a fait
faire son Portrait ar nsi que vous le voyez

Se vend A Paris chez F. Jollain l'aine Rue St Jaque a la Ville de Cologne

ILL. 21. French Christian slave in Algiers during fifteen years in captivity, 1670–85. The caption describes Barbary as being filled with pirates, most of whom are Christian.

183

ILL. 22. *Les Bain Turques*, 1862. Jean-Auguste Dominique Ingres's "keyhole" representation was inspired by Lady Montagu's 1717 account of a visit to the Turkish baths in Edirne. Réunion des Musées Nationaux / Art Resource, N.Y.

ILL. 23. *Luxe, calme et volupté*, 1904, by Henri Matisse (1869–1954). Matisse took his title from Charles Baudelaire's 1857 poem "L'invitation au voyage," in which the poet invites his beloved to travel to a place of luxury, calm, and voluptuousness. In his painting, Matisse depicts women sunbathing in St. Tropez. Erich Lessing / Art Resource, N.Y. © 2008 Succession H. Matisse / Artrists Rights Society (ARS), N.Y.

ILL. 24. Delacroix's *Women of Algiers in Their Apartments*. The Orientalist canvases of French romantic painter Eugene Delacroix (1798–1863) are important cultural representations of French imperial power and its "civilizing mission." Delacroix's vision of Algerian women is one of fantasy, as is indicated by his exclamation, "It is beautiful! It is straight out of Homer!" Erich Lessing / Art Resource, N.Y.

ILL. 25. Picasso's cubist homage to Delacroix's *Women of Algiers* made a century later. Scala / Art Resource, N.Y. © 2008 Estate of Pablo Picasso / Artists Rights Society (ARS), N.Y.

ILL. 26. Among the many antiquities depicted in the encyclopedia *Description de l'Égypte*, the obelisk in Alexandria is one of the most distinctive. It was one of two transported northward: one to London in 1877 and the other to New York in 1891. Each is known as Cleopatra's Needle. Réunion des Musées Nationaux / Art Resource, N.Y.

ILL. 27. Freud's study, his antiquities arranged like an audience. This room
contained more than two thousand Egyptian, Greek, Roman, Near Eastern,
and Asian objects. Getty Images.

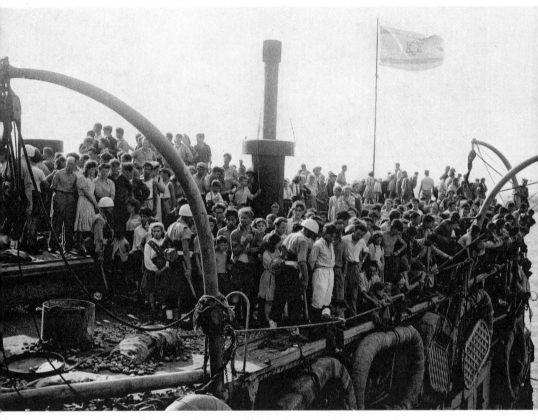

ILL. 28. The ship *Exodus* bringing Jewish refugees from fascist Europe to British Mandate Palestine on July 18, 1947. Getty Images.

ILL. 29. A Palestinian family walks along the shore at the planned site of a Club Med for Gaza. Getty Images.

ILL. 30. Harbor at Pula, Croatia, with Roman amphitheater in the background. At the time the photograph was taken, sometime before 1933, Pula was part of the kingdom of Italy. Courtesy Bryn Mawr College.

ILL. 31. *Dhakirat al-bahr* (Sea Memory) by Lihidheb Mohsen, a Tunisian artist who combs the beaches for objets trouvés that have washed ashore. Many objects come from boats carrying would-be migrants to Europe. Photograph by Lihidheb Mohsen.

ILL. 32. Mohamed Ali el Drougi at work restoring a mosaic (third century C.E.) depicting a resting gladiator. The mosaic, found at Wadi Lebda in Libya, is currently on display in the ancient site of Leptis Magna. Mosaics proliferated in Roman North Africa, particularly in homes of the wealthy, and today play a large role in tourism. © Gilles Mermet / Art Resource, N.Y.

CHAPTER 4

Grand Tours

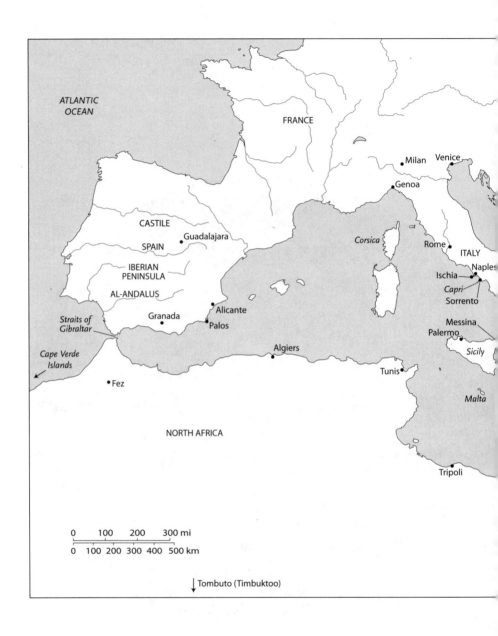

ATLANTIC
OCEAN

FRANCE

Milan Venice
Genoa

CASTILE
Guadalajara

Corsica Rome
SPAIN
ITALY
IBERIAN
PENINSULA
Ischia Naples
AL-ANDALUS
Capri
Sorrento

Granada Alicante
Palos
Messina
Straits of
Gibraltar Palermo
Sicily
Cape Verde
Islands
Algiers Malta
Fez Tunis

NORTH AFRICA

Tripoli

0   100   200   300 mi

0   100 200 300 400 500 km

Tombuto (Timbuktoo)

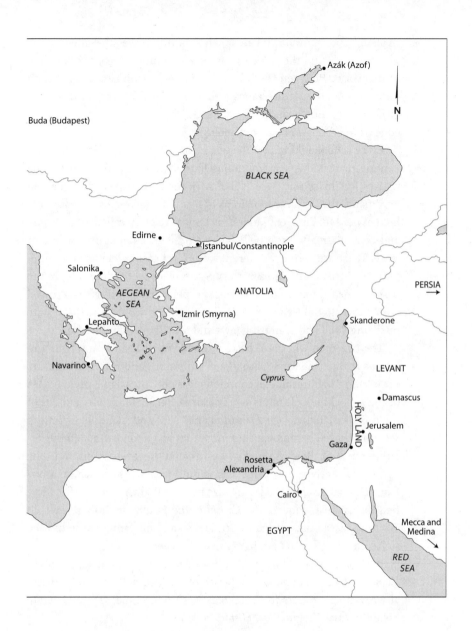

In all directions unknown lands with their untold wealth waited for the Europeans to find them; this was the age of discoveries, the doubling of the world. Between the fifteenth and eighteenth centuries, "grand tours" around the Mediterranean led to the rise of slavery, the discovery of new trade routes, and, ultimately, the fostering of scientific knowledge from ethnography to archaeology.

Every schoolchild knows the year 1492. For western Europeans and Americans it is the year Columbus found America and converted the natives to Christianity. For North Africans it is the year Isabella and Ferdinand, the Catholic monarchs of Spain, took Granada, the last toehold of the Muslims (or "Moors," as they were often called at the time), and soon thereafter compelled non-Christian citizens to convert or leave. These are two very different stories, yet each celebrates the ambitions of Christianity. In each story Spain plays the leading role. In the first instance, it financed the Genoese captain and his ships that crossed the Atlantic to the New World; in the second, it was the Christian state purifying itself and scattering Jews and Muslims around the Sea.

The two men who have become emblems of Spain's universal ambitions at the time were Christopher Columbus and Hasan al-Wazzan. Projecting a Mediterranean consciousness onto the islands and peoples of the Americas, Columbus's daily journal recounts the vicissitudes of the miscalculated voyage. Columbus had followed Claudius Ptolemy's recently revived second-century maps that had underestimated the circumference of the earth and overestimated the size of Asia and thus made a westerly route to the East sound feasible. Meanwhile, a boy from Granada called Hasan al-Wazzan (also known as Leo Africanus) fled the Spanish Inquisition. Crossing the Straits of Gibraltar, which Tariq ibn Ziyad had forded in 711, Hasan and his family brought back to Africa a culture and a religion that had been transformed by almost eight hundred years of interaction with Spaniards, French, and Italians. Captured by Sicilian pirates on behalf of the Medici Pope Leo X, Hasan al-Wazzan spent years in Castel Sant'Angelo in Rome, where he wrote his influential *Geographical History of Africa*.

It was not only Christians who were taking Muslims captive; the reverse was also true. Piracy had long been part of life in the Mediterranean, and it played an important role in the Ottomans' bid to control the Mediterranean. Fear of capture by the enemy developed into an anxiety of becoming Other or "turning Turk." The most famous of all pirates was Khayr al-Din Barbarossa, a Greek sea rover from the island of Mytilene and convert to Islam who was subsequently appointed admiral of the Ottoman navy. Taking Algiers, he made it a major port whose positioning along the fluid borders between the Christian and Muslim worlds earned it the title "The Bulwark of Islam." Alliances with corsairs like Barbarossa helped to secure Ottoman outposts in the western Mediterranean. The 1571 Treaty of the Holy League divided the Sea along a contested line from southern Greece to Cap Bon in today's Tunisia. On October 7th the Ottomans engaged the navy of the Holy League, an alliance of the Hapsburgs, the Vatican, and Venice, in a short but bloody battle in the Greek port city of Lepanto. The Spanish novelist Cervantes fought in the war, and his "Captive's Tale" narrates his experience in Muslim captivity.

Increasingly interconnected during the sixteenth century, the world was no longer seen to be multicentered. The rich variety of local maps, some of which were navigational charts and others cosmological representations, were replaced by world maps drawn around the same axis. The late-fourteenth-century translation into Latin of Ptolemy's *Geography* was vital in this process. Presenting a geocentric conception of the world as a whole, Ptolemy's text provided the coordinates for mapmakers to outline shores, rivers, and mountains with precision. It was thus more useful for navigation than the schematic T-O map of medieval Christianity. Ptolemy also established the convention for placing the north at the top of maps and the east to the right and universalized the expressions for latitude and longitude, thus providing a template for world maps that persists today.

With universal dominion becoming conceivable, the Spanish and Portuguese competed to rule this newly unified world. Their "pure blood" entitled them to this claim of superiority. To resolve their disputes, the pope promulgated the Treaty of Tordesillas of 1494 that divided the world into Spanish and Portuguese domains. A north-south line west of the Cape Verde Islands became the meridian. Lands west of the line, except Brazil, belonged to Spain, and everything east was to be under Portuguese control. The treaty justified massive land appropriation on the basis of racial superiority and shaped an ideology that was to hold sway for centuries to come.

Where difference had before been determined by beliefs, race became the determining factor. With the establishment of the Atlantic trade circuit by the end of the sixteenth century, America became part of the Mediterranean imaginary. This new frontier to be conquered and exploited required an unprecedentedly large labor force. The generally military exchange of captive slaves that had been part of Mediterranean politics until then was supplemented by another kind of slavery, indentured labor. European settlers in the New World needed free workers and they looked to the East. Their ambitions entailed a major redistribution of populations primarily from West Africa to the Americas.

The recentering of the world can be read in the poetry of the Italian Ludovico Ariosto, who represented the New World through the lens of Africa. This was the height of the Renaissance, when Shakespeare was writing his plays. He, too, introduced Africa to a European audience in the person of Othello, and at the turn of the seventeenth century he produced his famous Mediterranean play about a merchant of Venice who loses his vessels to the Sea and almost loses his life to the Jew Shylock.

Although the Holy League had won at Lepanto, there was no sense at the time of the portentousness of the event, because it was a mere year after their defeat that Muslims bested Christian forces in Cyprus. The Ottoman Grand Vizier at the time quipped, "By defeating our navy at Lepanto you have cut off our beards, but by taking Cyprus we have cut off your arms. Beards grow back, arms do not." Such was the pattern of victory and defeat that marked Muslim-Christian relations during this period. But the Christian front was not united, since the French were not part of the League. Intent on increasing their trade and political power in the region, they cultivated relations with the Ottomans, sometimes through the mediation of mothers of rulers, as can be read in a communication between Catherine de Médici and Nurbanu Sultan.

The Hapsburgs worried about the Ottoman threat and doubted the French commitment to a united Christendom. Indeed, when the Ottomans lay siege to Vienna in 1683, the French were slow to help. And when Napoleon Bonaparte invaded Egypt a century later he would remind the Egyptians of the French opposition to the Holy League in its wars against the Ottomans, saying: "Did we not destroy the Pope, who said that war should be waged against the Mussulmans?"

The French had become intoxicated with the Orient, and many traveled there, bringing back new fashions and new tastes to "La France Turbanisée." Thus began the proverbial Grand Tour that brought wealthy young men and women from northern Europe to the Mediterranean, where they encountered the wonders of "their" civilization. To take an interesting example, William Beckford, writing copious letters home to describe the marvels he encountered, seems to foreshadow the emergence of modern tourism. In *Mythologies* (1957), literary critic Roland Barthes's characterization of the twentieth-century *Guide Bleu* and its anachronistic focus on "Art as the fundamental value of culture" evokes the dubious motivations for the Grand Tour of the eighteenth century: "To select only monuments suppresses at one stroke the reality of the land and that of its people, it accounts for nothing of the present, that is, nothing historical, and as a consequence, the monuments themselves become indecipherable, therefore senseless." For some, they are senseless in their indecipherability, for others they serve to create a new story of universal civilization.

Although her travels to Constantinople at the beginning of the eighteenth century were not undertaken for pleasure or as part of the Grand Tour, the English Lady Mary Wortley Montagu was not only enchanted with monuments, but she was also fascinated by the people. Her descriptions of the people she met and her experiences in the women's baths provide us with a kind of early ethnography that contrasts her restrictions with Muslim women's surprising freedoms. Meanwhile, the Ottomans were establishing their first embassies in Europe. In his account of his encounter with Parisian culture, Yirmisekez Mehmet Çelebi mirrors contemporary Lady Montagu's fascination with the Other.

The German poet Johann Wolfgang Goethe also traveled to the region, and he, too, became infatuated with the exotic Mediterranean. His *Italian Journey* was written only two years before the outbreak of the French Revolution and twelve years before Napoleon Bonaparte led the French military, along with scientists, painters, draftsmen, and engravers, across the Mediterranean to invade Egypt. Local Arab reaction to Napoleon's Egyptian campaign was immediate. Historian 'Abd al-Rahman al-Jabarti kept meticulous notes on the arrival of the French and the mobilization of local resistance. Mocking the transparent hypocrisy of Napoleon's Proclamation, he drew attention to local realities that were disregarded by outsiders who were focused on classical fantasies, religious ideals, and imperial gain.

This *mission civilisatrice*, which recalled the rhetoric and modus operandi of the Spanish in the New World, introduced France and then England into West Asia and North Africa and launched the era of European colonization in most of the Muslim Mediterranean. At the same time, it gave birth to new fields of knowledge, including especially archaeology, which became the battleground for struggles over identity and justifications for massive expropriation of land and properties.

The grand tours of this chapter begin and end violently with the Spanish bringing civilization to the indigenous population of America at the end of the fifteenth century and the French beginning to force their culture and values onto North Africans at the end of the eighteenth. Placed between such bookends the sophisticated Grand Tour of the great monuments of Greek and Roman antiquity takes on a different hue; the acquiring of a hands-on classical education can be seen to be part of a bourgeois project to appropriate the past and to project it into a future in which European norms and values would rule supreme around the world.

The Westerly Route to the East
Christopher Columbus (1492)

Even as Muslims and Jews were fleeing the Catholic monarchs in an easterly direction, Christopher Columbus (1451–1506) traveled west on behalf of the same kings. Written for his royal patrons, his journal of his travels is a mine of information about the islands, the indigenous people, and the urgent pursuit of gold. Ironically, the journal itself provides proof that this was no discovery of a "land without people." Rather, it documents meetings with local communities and confesses to the desire to exploit and convert the "natives." It presents a scenario of docile men and women who are friendly and generous. Above all, they are without religion and some "would very readily become Christians, as they have a good understanding." Hints of the violence to come can be read in Columbus's advice about how to rule these godless people. In a letter to his patrons, the Catholic monarchs Isabella and Ferdinand, he suggests how they might administer their colonies and thus link Spain with the Americas in what was to become a major economic network that stretched across the world from Mexico to China. Columbus had prepared for his journey by reading numerous travel treatises, including Marco Polo's *Travels* and Ptolemy's *Geography* (second century C.E.), whose twenty-seven maps were translated into Arabic in the ninth century and into Latin at the beginning of the fifteenth century. It is an often overlooked point that Columbus took the logic of the Inquisition to the Americas.

In the name of our Lord Jesus Christ.

Because, O most Christian, and very high, very excellent, and puis-sant Princess, King and Queen of the Spains and of the islands of the Sea, our Lords, in this present year of 1492, after your Highnesses had given an end to the war with the Moors who reigned in Europe, and had finished it in the very great city of Granada, where in this present year, on the second day of the month of January, by force of arms, I saw the royal banners of your Highnesses placed on the towers of Alhambra, which is the fortress of that city, and I saw the Moorish King come forth from the gates of the city and kiss the royal hands of your Highnesses, and of the Prince my Lord, and presently in that same month, acting on the information that I had given to your Highnesses touching the lands of India, and respecting a Prince who is called *Gran Can*, which means in our language King of Kings, how he and his ancestors had sent to Rome many times to ask for learned men of our holy faith to teach him, and how the Holy Father had never complied, insomuch that many people believing in idolatries were lost by receiving doctrine of perdition: your Highnesses, as Catholic Christians and Princes who love the holy Christian faith, and the propagation of it, and who are enemies to the sect of Mahomat and to all idolatries and heresies, resolved to send me, Cristobal Colon, to the said parts of India to see the said princess, and the cities and lands, and their disposition, with a view that they might be converted to our holy faith; and ordered that I should not go by land to the eastward, as had been customary, but that I should go by way of the west, whither up to this day, we do not know for certain that any one has gone.

Thus, after having turned out all the Jews from all your kingdoms and lordships, in the same month of January, your Highnesses gave orders to me that with a sufficient fleet I should go to the said parts of India, and for this they made great concessions to me, and ennobled me, so that henceforward I should be called Don, and should be Chief Admiral of the Ocean Sea, perpetual Viceroy and Governor of all the islands and continents that I should discover and gain, and that I might hereafter discover and gain in the Ocean Sea, and that my eldest son should succeed, and so on from generation to generation for ever.

I left the city of Granada on the 12th day of May, in the same year of 1492, being Saturday, and came to the town of Palos, which is a seaport; where I equipped three vessels well suited for such service; and departed from that port, well supplied with provisions and with many sailors, on the 3rd day of August of the same year, being Friday, half an hour before sunrise, taking the route to the islands of Canaria, belonging to your Highnesses, which are in the said Ocean Sea, that I might thence take my departure for navigation until I should arrive at the Indies, and give the letters of your Highnesses to those princes, so as to comply with my orders. As part of my duty I thought it well to write an account of all the voyage very punctually, noting from day to day all that I should do and see, and that should happen, as will be seen further on.

[. . .]   *Sunday, September 9th*

This day the Admiral made 19 leagues, and he arranged to reckon less than the number run, because if the voyage was of long duration, the people would not be so terrified and disheartened. In the night, he made 120 miles, at the rate of 12 miles an hour, which are 30 leagues. The sailors steered badly, letting the ship fall off to N.E., and even more, respecting which the Admiral complained many times.

[. . .]   *Sunday, September 23rd*

They shaped a course N.W., and at times more northerly; occasionally they were on their course, which was west, and they made about 22 leagues. They saw a dove and a booby, another river-bird, and some white birds. There was a great deal of weed, and they found crabs in it. The sea being smooth and calm, the crew began to murmur, saying that here there was no great sea, and that the wind would never blow so that they could return to Spain. Afterwards the sea rose very much, without wind, which astonished them. The Admiral here says: "Thus the high sea was very necessary to me, such as had not appeared but in the time of the Jews when they went out of Egypt and murmured against Moses, who delivered them out of captivity."

[. . .]   *Tuesday, September 25th*

[. . .] At sunset Martin Alonso went up on the poop of his ship, and with much joy called to the Admiral, claiming the reward as he had sighted land. When the Admiral heard this positively declared, he says that he gave thanks to the Lord on his knees, while Martin Alonso said the *Gloria in excelsis* with his people. The Admiral's crew did the same. Those of the *Niña* all went up on the mast and into the rigging, and declared that it was land.

[. . .]   *Wednesday, September 26th*

The Admiral continued on the west course until after noon. Then he altered course to S.W., until he made out that what had been said to be land was only clouds. Day and night they made 31 leagues, counting 24 for the people. The sea was like a river, the air pleasant and very mild.

[. . .]   *Monday, October 8th*

The course was W.S.W., and 11½ or 12 leagues were made good in the day and night; and at times it appears that they went at the rate of 15 miles an hour during the night (if the handwriting is not deceptive). The sea was like the river at Seville. "Thanks be to God," says the Admiral, "the air is very soft like the April at Seville; and it is a pleasure to be here, so balmy are the breezes." The weed seemed to be very fresh. There were many land-birds, and they took one that was flying to the S.W. Terns, ducks, and a booby were also seen.

[. . .]   *Wednesday, October 10th*

[. . .] Here the people could endure no longer. They complained of the length of the voyage. But the Admiral cheered them up in the best way he could, giving them good hopes of the advantages they might gain from it. He added that, however much they might complain, he had to go to the Indies, and that he would go on until he found them, with the help of our Lord.

[. . .]   *Thursday, October 11th*

[. . .] At two hours after midnight the land was sighted at a distance of two leagues. They shortened sail, and lay by under the mainsail without the bonnet. The vessels were hove to, waiting for daylight; and on Friday they arrived at a small island of the Lucayos, called, in the language of the Indians, *Guanahani*. Presently, they saw naked people. The Admiral went on shore in the armed boat, and Marin Alonso Pinzon, and Vicente Yañez, his brother, who was captain of the Niña. The Admiral took the royal standard, and the captains went with two banners of the green cross, which the Admiral took in all the ships as a sign, with an F and a Y and a crown over each letter, one on one side of the cross and the other on the other. Having landed, they saw trees very green and much water, and fruits of diverse kinds. The Admiral called to the two captains, and to the others who leaped on shore, and to Rodrigo Escovedo, secretary of the whole fleet, and to Rodrigo Sanchez of Segovia, and said that they should bear faithful testimony that he, in presence of all, had taken, as he now took, possession of the said island for the King and for the Queen, his lords making the declarations that are required, as is more largely set forth in the testimonies which were then made in writing.

Presently many inhabitants of the island assembled. What follows is in the actual words of the Admiral in his book of the first navigation and discovery of the Indies. "I," he says, "that we might form great friendship, for I knew that they were a people who could be more easily freed and converted to our holy faith by love than by force, gave to some of them red caps, and glass beads to put round their necks, and many other things of little value, which gave them great pleasure, and made them so much our friends that it was a marvel to see. They afterwards came to the ship's boats where we were, swimming and bringing us parrots, cotton threads in skeins, darts, and many other things; and we exchanged them for other things that we gave them, such as glass beads and small bells. In fine, they took all, and gave what they had with good will. It appeared to me to be a race of people very poor in everything. They go as naked as when their mothers bore them, and so do the women, although I did not see more than one young girl. All I saw were youths, none more than thirty years of age. They are all very well made, with very handsome bodies, and very good countenances. Their hair is short and coarse, almost like the hairs of a horse's tail. They wear the hairs brought down to the eyebrows, except a few locks behind, which they wear long and never cut. They paint themselves black, and they are the colour of the Canarians, neither black nor white. Some paint themselves white, others red, and others of what colour they find. Some paint their faces, others the whole body, some only round the eyes, others only on the nose. They neither carry nor know anything of arms, for I showed them swords, and they took them by the blade and cut themselves through ignorance. [. . .] They should be good servants and intelligent, for I observed that they quickly took in what was said to them, and I believe that they would easily be made Christians, as it appeared to me that they had no religion. I, our Lord being pleased, will take hence, at the time of my departure, six natives for your Highnesses, that they may learn to speak."

[. . .]   *Saturday, October 13th*

As soon as dawn broke many of these people came to the beach, all youths, as I have said, and all of good stature, a very handsome people. [. . .] I was attentive, and took trouble to ascertain if there was gold. I saw that some of them had a small piece fastened in a hole they have in the nose, and by signs I was able to make out that to the south, or going from the island to the south, there was a king who had great cups full, and who possessed a great quantity.

[. . .]   *Sunday, October 14th*

[. . .] One old man came into the boat, and others cried out, in loud voices, to all the men and women, to come and see the men who had come from heaven, and to bring them to eat and drink. Many came, including women, each bringing something, giving thanks to God, throwing themselves on the ground and shouting to us to come on shore. [. . .] I saw a piece of land which appeared like an island, although it is not one, and on it there were six houses. It might be converted into an island in two days, though I do not see that it would be necessary, for these people are very simple as regards the use of arms, as your Highnesses will see from the seven that I caused to be taken, to bring home and learn our language and return; unless your Highnesses should order them all to be brought to Castille, or to be kept as captives on the same island; for with fifty men they can all be subjugated and made to do what is required of them.

[. . .]   *Tuesday, October 16th*

I sailed from the island of Santa Maria de la Concepcion at about noon, to go to Fernandina island, which appeared very large to the westward, and I navigated all that day with light winds. [. . .] This island is very large, and I have determined to sail round it, because, so far as I can understand, there is a mine in or near it. [. . .] Now, as I am writing this, I made sail with the wind at the south, to sail round the island, and to navigate until I find *Samaot*, which is the island of the city where there is gold, as all the natives say who are on board, and as those of San Salvador and Santa Maria told us. [. . .] They do not know any religion, and I believe they could easily be converted to Christianity for they are very intelligent.

[. . .]   *Friday, October 19th*

[. . .] Before we had sailed for three hours we saw an island to the east, for which we steered, and all three vessels arrived at the north point before noon. Here there is an islet, and a reef of rocks to seaward of it, besides one between the islet and the large island. The men of San Salvador, whom I bring with me, called it *Saomete*, and I gave it the name of *Isabella*. The wind was north, and the said islet bore from the island of Fernandina, whence I had taken my departure, east and west. Afterwards we ran along the coast of the island, westward from the islet, and found its length to be 12 leagues as far as a cape, which I named *Cabo Hermoso*, at the western end. [. . .] To-morrow, before I leave this place, I shall go on shore to see what there is at this cape. There are no people, but there are villages in the interior, where, the Indians I bring with me say, there is a king who has much gold. . . . For my desire is to see and discover as much as I can before returning to your Highnesses, our Lord willing, in April. It is true that in the event of finding places where there is gold or spices in quantity I should stop until I had collected as much as I could. I, therefore, proceed in the hope of coming across such places.

The Journal of Christopher Columbus (During His First Voyage, 1492–93), and Documents Relating to the Voyages of John Cabot and Gaspar Corte Real, trans. Clements R. Markham (London: Hakluyt Society, 1893), 15–17, 22, 27, 29, 30, 34, 36–38, 39, 41, 45–46, 51–53.

An Ottoman Prince on Rhodes

William Caoursin and Hoja Effendi (1496)

Cem Sultan (1459–95), the son of Mehmed the Conqueror and brother of Sultan Bayezid, lived in grand style with an Ottoman entourage as a celebrity captive in France and Italy between 1482 and 1494. His older brother Beyazit had defeated Cem in the race to take the throne after Mehmed's death in 1481. Cem fled first to Egypt and then later to Rhodes, where he was hosted by Pierre d'Aubusson, a member of the Knights of St. John, who had gained widespread fame in Europe for successfully defending Rhodes against Sultan Mehmed II's fleet in 1480. Cem went as a guest, but the Knights betrayed him and he became a prisoner. Afterward, Cem was sent to France. Sultan Bayezid requested that Cem be kept in France and agreed to pay 40,000 in gold each year for his brother's expenses. Pope Innocent VIII intended to organize a new crusade using Cem as a spearhead, but the European monarchs resisted. The pope also proposed that Cem convert to Christianity, but he refused. Whenever Bayezid intended to launch a military campaign in the Balkans, however, the pope reacted by threatening to release the pretender to the Ottoman throne. One of Cem's companions, probably a certain Haydar, left a memoir that may well be the earliest narrative by an Ottoman visitor to Christian Europe. His brief notes on places and people in France and Italy show that the prince stayed in Nice for four months. Part of his entertainment consisted of going to balls, where he, like many later Muslim travelers, was shocked by strange European customs. The life of Cem Sultan and his passionate love affair with Philippine de Sassenage has been a source of inspiration for such authors as Victor Hugo and Lamartine. The following excerpt describes Cem's last night in Rhodes with Pierre d'Aubusson before he sailed for France. About the authors very little is known.

Let all the world know that King Zizim [*Cem Sultan*], of the Race of the Ottomans, Son of the invincible Mahomet, King of Kings, and Soveraign Emperour of Greece and Asia, is infinitely beholding to the thrice generous, and thrice illustrious, the Lord Peter D'Aubusson, Grand Master of Rhodes. Let all the world also know that for the kind Offices he hath shewn me in the most perilous adventures of my life, and to testifie my acknowledgement as far as the present condition of my fortune will give me leave, I promise solemnly to God and our Great Prophet, that if I ever recover either absolutely or in part, the Imperial Crown of my Father, I promise, I say, and swear to hold a perpetual friendship, and inviolable peace with the Grand Master and his successours according to the Articles following.

In the first place I engage my self, my children, and the children of my children to have an eternal kindness for the order of St. John of Jerusalem, so that neither I, nor my children shall do them any injury either by Sea or Land. That we will be so far from stopping the Vessels or disturbing the commerce of the Merchants of Rhodes, or of any other Islands appertaining to the Order, that our ports shall be free to them in all the Provinces under our obedience, as if they themselves were our subjects; or rather we will entertain them as our friends, permitting them to buy, sell, or transport what merchandize they please, without paying any custom, or duty.

Besides this, I consent that the Grand Master shall every year take out of my Territories three hundred Christians of both sexes, and at what age he pleases, to put into the Islands of the order, or to do with them what he thinkes best. And in some measure to make satisfaction for the expences which the Grand Master has bin at, and every day so liberally allows for my sake, I oblige my self to pay in ready mony a hundred and fifty thousand Crowns in Gold. Lastly, I promise upon oath to restore him all the Isles, all the Lands, and all the Fortresses which the Ottoman Emperours have taken from the order. And for a testimony that this is my will, I have sign'd with my hand, and seald with my seal this present Act given at Rhodes in the palace of the French Apartiment the fift of the month Regeb, the year of the Hegira, 887. The 31. Of August in the Year of grace, 1482.

[*Narrative account switches to the third person.*]

The third of September which was the day that the Prince took shipping, he was attended to the Sea with the same Pomp, and the same ceremonie, with which he was receiv'd. He took his leave of the principle Knights, after a most obliging manner, wherin there appear'd nothing of Barbarism. He also laid aside all his haughtiness, when he gave the Grand Master his last farewell: For it is reported the he threw himself at his feet, and kiss'd his hand with a profound respect. The Grand Master tenderly embrac'd him, and wept for some time over him either through compassion, or through some secret dictate that he should never see him again. The Knight de Blanchefort, who was return'd to Rhodes since the raising of the Siege, & the Knight de Rochechenard had order to conduct the Sultan into France, not to mention the Knights who were nam'd to accompany him, and to serve him as a convoy; but they enter'd all together with Zizim into the great ship of the order, and set saile the same day with a favourable wind. The Grand Master, who had already given advice to the Pope of the arrival of the Ottoman Prince, gave him also notice of his departure by this opportunity, and sent him word in particular, that Zizim of his own accord had made choice of France for the security of his Life: that he had good ground for his fears; in regard that for the forty dayes that he had stay'd in Rhodes he was certainly enformd that the Grand Signiour [*Sultan Beyazit II*] had us'd all his endeavours either to take or murder him.

William Caoursin and Rhodgia Afendy [Hoja Effendi], The History of the Turkish War with the Rhodians, Venetians, Egyptians, Persians and Other Nations (London: Whitwood, 1683).

Papal Prisoner
Leo Africanus (1526)

The Reconquista and then the Inquisition of the Catholic monarchs imposed a single language and a single religion on Spain, a land that had for centuries been marked by inclusive, if fraught, polities. Jews and Muslims who had long lived in the Iberian Peninsula, pursuing their own faiths while accommodating those of their neighbors, were forced to convert or to flee. The family of Hasan al-Wazzan (ca. 1485–1550)—also known as Leo Africanus or John Leo A More—moved into what has come to be called the Andalusian section of Fez, a powerful city that had been a center of learning and commerce since the ninth century. They found a wild city and a region in political turmoil with the Spaniards (who pursued the fleeing Grenadines across the waters), Portuguese, and local rulers vying for control. Hasan al-Wazzan grew up in a privileged household, and he traveled widely. In Cairo he was delighted by the different world he encountered. Two years later in Timbuktu he found a city of luxury and learning with "a princely palace built by a most excellent workeman of Granada." Clearly, a network of artists and craftsmen linked Muslim Africa with Spain. The splendor of the court contrasted with the misery of the slave market that would soon become part of what has come to be called the "Black Atlantic" network. Hasan was destined to become a prisoner of Pope Leo X, and he was held in Castel Sant'Angelo until he converted to Catholicism, assumed his patron's name, Leo, with the sobriquet Africanus, and wrote his *Geographical History of Africa* in both Arabic and Italian. It remained for centuries the major reference for cartographers and anyone who wanted to write about the "Dark Continent." Muslim, Christian, Spanish, Moroccan, and Italian, Leo the Medici is an emblem of Mediterranean exchanges and identities at the outset of the early modern era.

OF THE INNS OF FEZ

In this city are almost two hundred inns, the greatest whereof are in the principal part of the city near unto the chief temple. Every one of these inns are three stories high, and contain an hundred and twenty or more chambers apiece. Likewise each one hath a fountain together with sinks and waterpipes, which make avoidance of all the filth. Never, to my remembrance, did I see greater buildings, except it were the Spanish college at Bologna, or the palace of the Cardinal *di San Giorgio* at Rome: of which inns all the chamber-doors have walks or galleries before them. And albeit the inns of this city are very fair and large, yet they afford most beggarly entertainment to strangers: for there are neither beds nor couches for a man to lie upon, unless it be a coarse blanket and mat. And if you will have any victuals, you must go to the shambles your self, and buy such meat for your host to dress, as your stomach stands to. In these inns certain poor widows of Fez, which have neither wealth nor friends to succour them, are relieved: sometimes one, and sometimes two of them together are allowed a chamber; for which courtesy they play both the chamberlains and cooks of the inn. The inn-keepers of Fez being all of one family called Elcheua, go appareled like women, and shave their beards, and are so delighted to imitate women, that they will not only counterfeit their speech, but will sometimes also sit down and spin. Each one of these hath his concubine, whom he accompanieth as if she were his own lawful wife; albeit the said concubines are not only ill-favored in countenance, but notorious for their bad life and behavior. They buy and sell wine freely, that no man controls them for it. None resort hither but most lewd and wicked people to the end they may more boldly commit villainy. The inn-keepers have a consul over them, and they pay tribute unto the governor of the city. And when the king hath occasion to send forth an army, then they, as being most meet for the purpose, are constrained largely to victual the camp. Had not the straight law of history enforced me to make relation of the foresaid particulars as they stand, I would much rather have smothered such matters in silence, as tend so extremely to the disgrace of Fez; which being reformed, there is not any city in all Africa, for the honesty and good demeanor of the citizens, comparable thereunto. For the very company of these inn-keepers is so odious and detestable in the sight of all honest men, learned men, and merchants, that they will in no wise vouchsafe to speak unto them. And they are firmly enjoined not to enter into the temple, into the burse, nor into any bath. Neither yet are they permitted to resort unto those inns which are next unto the great temple, and wherein merchants are usually entertained. All men in a manner are in utter detestation of these wretches: but because the king's army hath some use of them, they are borne withal, whether citizens will or no. [. . .]

A DESCRIPTION OF THE HUGE AND ADMIRABLE CITY OF CAIRO

Cairo is commonly reputed to be one of the greatest and most famous cities in the whole world. But leaving the common reports and opinions thereof, I will exactly describe the form and estate wherein it now standeth. And that I may begin with the Etymology or derivation of the name, Cairo is an Arabian word, corruptly pronounced by the people of Europe: for the true Arabian word is El Chahira, which signifieth an enforcing or imperious mistress. This city built in ancient times by one *Gehoar Chetib* a Dalmatian slave (as I have before signified in the beginning of my discourse) containeth within the walls not above eight thousand families, being inhabited by noblemen, gentlemen, and merchants that sell wares brought from all other places. The famous temple of Cairo commonly called Gemih Hashare, that is to say, the glorious temple, was built also by the foresaid slave, whom we affirmed to be the founder of the city, and whose surname was *Hashare*, that is to say, famous, being given him by the Mahumetan patriarch that was his prince. This city standeth upon a most beautiful plain, near unto a certain mountain called Mucatun, about two miles distant from Nilus, and is environed with stately walls, and fortified with iron gates: the principal of which gates is called Babe Nansre, that is, gate of victory, which standeth eastward towards the desert of the Red Sea; and the gate called Beb Zuaila being next unto the old city and to Nilus; and also Bebel Futuh, that is to say, the gate of triumph, standing towards the lake and the fields. And albeit Cairo aboundeth everywhere with all kind of merchants and artificers, yet that is the principal street of the whole city which stretcheth from the gate of Nansre to the gate of Zuaila; for in it are built most stately and admirable palaces and colleges, and most sumptuous temples, among which is the temple of Gemith Elhechim the third schismatic Caliph of Cairo. Other temples there are of a marvelous bigness, which to describe in particular, I think it superfluous. Here are many bathstoves also very artificially built. Next of all is the street called Beinel Casrain, containing to the number of three-score cooks or victualers shops, furnished with vessels of tin: there are certain other shops also, wherein are to be sold delicate waters or drinks made of all kinds of fruits, being for noblemen to drink of, and these waters they keep most charily in fine vessels, partly of glass, and partly of tin; next unto these are shops where divers confections of honey and sugar, unlike unto the confections of Europe, are to be sold: then follow the fruiterers shops, who bring outlandish fruits out of Syria, to wit, quinces, pomegranates, and other fruits which grow not in Egypt: next unto them are the shops of such as sell eggs, cheese, and pancakes fried with oil. And next of all there is a street of the principal artificers shops. [. . .]

OF THE KINGDOM OF TOMBUTO [*TIMBUKTU*]

This name was in our times (as some think) imposed upon this kingdom from the name of a certain town so called, which (they say) king *Mense Suleiman* founded in the year of the Hegeira 610, and it is situate within twelve miles of a certain branch of Niger, all the houses whereof are now changed into cottages built of chalk, and covered with thatch. Howbeit there is a most stately temple to be seen, the walls whereof are made of stone and lime; and a princely palace also built by a most excellent workman of Granada. Here are many shops of artificers, and merchants, and especially of such as weave linen and cotton cloth. And hither do the Barbarie-merchants bring cloth of Europe. All the women of this region except maidservants go with their faces covered, and sell all necessary victuals. The inhabitants, and especially strangers there residing, are exceeding rich, insomuch that the king that now is married both his daughters unto two rich merchants. Here are many wells, containing most sweet water; and so often as the river Niger overfloweth, they conveigh the water thereof by certain sluces into the town. Corn, cattle, milk, and butter this region yieldeth in great abundance: but salt is very scarce here; for it is brought hither by land from Tegaza, which is five hundred miles distant. When I my self was here, I saw one camel's load of salt sold for 80 ducats. The rich king of Tombuto hath many plates and scepters of gold, some whereof weigh 1300 pounds: and he keeps a magnificent and well furnished court. When he travelleth any whither he rideth upon a camel, which is led by some of his noblemen; and so he doth likewise when he goeth to warfare, and all his soldiers ride upon horses. Whosoever will speak unto this king must first fall down before his feet, and then taking up earth must sprinkle it upon his own head and shoulders: which custom is ordinarily observed by them that never saluted the king before, or come as ambassadors from other princes. He hath always three thousand horsemen, and a great number of footmen that shoot poisoned arrows, attending upon him. They have often skirmishes with those that refuse to pay tribute, and so many as they take, they sell unto the merchants of Tombuto. Here are very few horses bred, and the merchants and courtiers keep certain little nags which they use to travel upon: but their best horses are brought out of Barbarie. And the king so soon as he heareth that any merchants are come to town with horses, he commandeth a certain number to be brought before him, and choosing the best horse for himself, he payeth a most liberal price for him. He so deadly hateth all Jews, that he will not admit any into his city: and whatsoever Barbarie merchants he understandeth have any dealings with the Jews, he presently causeth their goods to be confiscate. Here are great store of doctors, judges, priests, and other learned men, that are bountifully maintained at the king's cost and charges. And hither are brought divers manuscripts or written books out of Barbarie, which are sold for more money than any other merchandise. The coin of Tombuto is of gold without any stamp or superscription: but in matters of small value they use certain shells brought hither out of the kingdom of Persia, four hundred of which shells are worth a ducat: and six pieces of their golden coin with two third parts weigh an ounce. The inhabitants are people of a gentle and cheerful dispotition, and spend a great part of the night in singing and dancing through all the streets of the city: they keep great store of men and women-slaves, and their town is much in danger of fire: at my second being there half the town almost was burnt in five hours' space.

A Geographical Historie of Africa, Written in Arabicke and Italian by John Leo a More, Borne in Granada, and Brought up in Barbarie, trans. John Pory (London: George Bishop, 1600), 128–35, 298–99, 287–88. (The spellings have been standardized.)

New Argonauts

Ludovico Ariosto (1532)

In *Orlando Furioso*, an Italian version of the *Chanson de Roland*, the epic and lyric poet Ludovico Ariosto (1474–1533) represents America through the lens of Africa. He anticipates the Portuguese circumnavigation of Africa; "the line whence blazing Phoebus burns" invokes the imperial adventure Columbus launched forty years earlier. In 1481 the Portuguese had built a slave fort at Elmina on the Gold Coast, using Italian designs and traders, that extended a millennial inter-Mediterranean trade in slaves which included Russians, Germans, Nubians, Greeks, and Slavs. In 1518 Charles had reversed his grandmother Isabella's reluctance to have Africans exported to the Americas, and he authorized the export of African slaves there. This is the turning point in the history of slavery, changing the system from a military to an economic and racial one. Genoese bankers had to use Portuguese ships because no Spanish ships could go to Africa after the pope had given trade on that continent to the Portuguese in the Treaty of Tordesillas of 1494. In the early decades of the sixteenth century, German merchants, Genoese bankers, and Italians were all involved in the trade. European slavery was not at this time race-based. In addition, slaves were free to marry and were full members of the church, and there was even a reverse slave trade, whereby a slave born in the New World but brought back to Spain could be manumitted.

BOOK 15

Far in the west, when years their course have roll'd
I see new Argonauts their sails unfold,
And many a Tiphys ocean's depth explore,
To open wondrous ways untry'd before.

Some coasting round the shelves of Afric, trace
Th' extended country of the sable race,
To pass the line whence blazing Phoebus burns,
And to your realms from Capricorn returns;

At length the Cape's extremest point they gain
That seems to part from ours the western main:
Each clime they view, and search, with ceaseless toils,
The Persian, Indian, and Arabian isles,
Some pass the pillars rais'd on either strand,

The well-known labour of Alcides' hand,
And like the circling sun, with sails unfurl'd
Explore new lands in some remoter world
Behold the sacred Cross uprais'd, behold
On the green turf th' imperial staff unroll'd
Lo some to guard their infant navy run,
Some haste to seize the land their toils have won,
A thousand chased by ten forsake the fields:

To Aragon the furthest India yields.
The chiefs of Charles (The fifth that bears the name)
Where'er they pass, behold them crown'd with fame!

*Ludovico Arioso, Orlando Furioso, vol. 3, trans. John Hoole (printed by the
translator, 1783), 173–74.*

A Sultanate of Women
Catherine de Médici (ca. 1575)

The period from about 1550 to 1687 was characterized by the
dominance of powerful women at the Ottoman court. These women
were usually foreign *hasekis*, or "favorites," who often became queen
mothers, or *valide sultans*. The period was ushered in by haseki
Hürrem Sultan (of Polish/Ukranian descent and known as "Roxalana"
in Europe) during Süleyman the Magnificent's rule and ended with
Turhan Hatice (of Russian origin, queen mother, 1651–83) during the
reign of Mehmed IV. These "women of the harem" communicated
at the highest diplomatic, and even political, levels in the court's
relations with other Mediterranean states: The Venetian-born
Nurbanu Sultan (née Cecilia Venier-Baffo), who had entered the royal
harem after being captured by Ottoman corsairs in 1537 and became
queen mother of Murad III, corresponded with Catherine de Médici,
queen mother and regent for the French king Henry III. Likewise,
the Albanian-born Safiye Sultan (née Sofia), who was queen mother
of Mehmed III, corresponded with Queen Elizabeth I. In one letter,
Nurbanu Sultan petitions for the release of a Muslim who had fallen
into the hands of the prince of Palermo, probably at the battle of
Lepanto in 1571. The following excerpt is from a letter from Catherine
to Nurbanu. Among other things, she requests Nurbanu's help in the
renewal of the Capitulations, trading privileges first granted to France
in 1535.

The very exalted, the very excellent and magnanimous Princess, the Sultana Queen mother of the very exalted, very excellent Seigneur, and our very dear and perfect friend, may God increase your grandeur with a very happy conclusion. Knowing the lofty place Your Highness holds next to His Highness the great Emperor your son because of your rare and excellent virtues, and [knowing] that [Your Highness] will always judge wisely and surely the extent to which it is necessary that the inviolable friendship which has long existed between [His Highness's] predecessors and this crown be maintained and conserved for the common good and contentment of the two Princes, we have thought to write you to request, with the greatest possible affection, that you might use all good and appropriate offices in such a commendable work; and that you might also, to the extent possible, assist in the immediate renewal of the existing Capitulations, which have formerly been established between the predecessors of His Highness your aforementioned son and this afore-mentioned Crown, as things very necessary for the security of the traffic between our subjects and the lands under the authority [of your son]; in which, apart from the fact that [Your Highness] will be demonstrating that love and maternal affection that you bear for your afore-mentioned son, for whom you always seek the things that can most add to his contentment, we will forever bear you gratitude, and will by means of all praiseworthy efforts cause our sincere and cordial good will to become manifest when the opportunity arises.

From Leslie Peirce, The Imperial Harem: Women and Sovereignty in the Ottoman Empire (Oxford: Oxford University Press, 1993), 227. Reprinted by permission of the publisher.

Marine Merchant
William Shakespeare (1596)

William Shakespeare (1564–1616) based *The Merchant of Venice* on Giovanni Fiorentino's novel *Il Pecarone* (1558). The reader can also detect strains of Boccaccio, who influenced the English bard's other comedies. Set in the vibrant, cosmopolitan trading city of Venice just after the victory at Lepanto, the play reveals the rampant anti-Semitism of the time. The wealthy merchant Antonio borrows from the usurer Shylock money that he will repay when his ships, scattered around the Sea, return. Yet ships were often wrecked and economic success was closely tied to the moods of the Sea. When Antonio's ships are thought lost, he must find a way to repay the Jew the debt he owes him. Complicated negotiations turn the creditor into the debtor and end with the Duke of Venice dividing Shylock's fortunes between the state and Antonio. The latter surrenders his claim when the Jew agrees to convert to Christianity. Conversion, a motivating factor in civilizing missions, had become part of European trade. At the opening of the play, Antonio talks with friends about the anxieties of sea trade.

ACT 1, SCENE 1—VENICE, A STREET

Enter Antonio, Salarino, and Solanio.
Ant. In sooth, I know not why I am so sad:
It wearies me; you say it wearies you;
But how I caught it, found it, or came by it,
What stuff 'tis made of, whereof it is born,
I am to learn,
And such a want-wit sadness makes of me
That I have much ado to know myself.
Salar. Your mind is tossing on the ocean;
There where your argosies, with portly sail,
Like signiors and rich burghers of the flood,
Or, as it were, the pageants of the sea,
Do overpeer the petty traffickers
That curt'sy to them, do them reverence,
As they fly by them with their woven wings.
Solan. My wind, cooling my broth,
Would blow me to an ague when I thought
What harm a wind too great might do at sea.
I should not see the sandy hour-glass run
But I should think of shallows and of flats,
And see my wealthy Andrew dock'd in sand,
Vailing her high-top lower than her ribs,
To kiss her burial. Should I go to church,
And see the holy edifice of stone,
And not bethink me straight of dangerous rocks,
Which, touching but my gentle vessel's side,
Would scatter all her spices on the stream,
Enrobe the roaring waters with my silks,
And, in a word, but even now worth this,
And now worth nothing? Shall I have the thought
To think on this; and shall I lack the thought
That such a thing bechanc'd would make me sad?

But tell not me; I know Antonio
Is sad to think upon his merchandize.
Ant. Believe me, no; I thank my fortune for it,
My ventures are not in one bottom trusted,
Nor to one place; nor is my whole estate
Upon the fortune of this present year:
Therefore my merchandize makes me not sad.

William Shakespeare, The Merchant of Venice (1596).

The Captive's Tale
Miguel de Cervantes Saavedra (1605)

Cervantes (1547–1616) was a novelist, dramatist, and poet best
known for *Don Quixote de la Mancha*, a novel he published in 1605
that was to have a lasting influence on the European novel. He fought
at the battle of Lepanto, where his left arm was crippled. On his return
to Spain in 1575 he was captured by Barbary pirates and sold into
slavery. The viceroy of Algiers ransomed him in 1580. The following
excerpt is taken from *Don Quixote*. Cervantes was slave to a Muslim
and then to a Christian. His experience can be read allegorically in
that it mirrors the fate of cities like Tunis that kept changing hands
between the Christian Spanish and the Muslim Ottomans.

I embarked at Alicant, and had a good passage to Genoa: from thence I
went to Milan, where I furnished myself with arms, and some military
finery; and from thence determined to go into the service in Piedmont:
and being upon the road to Alexandria de la Paglia, I was informed that
the great duke D'Alva was passing into Flanders with an army. Hereupon I changed my mind, went with him, and served under him in all
his engagements. I was present at the death of the counts D'Egmont
and Horn. I got an ensign's commission in the company of a famous
captain of Guadalajara, called Diego de Urbina. And, soon after my arrival in Flanders, news came of the league concluded between Pope
Pius V. of happy memory, and Spain, against the common enemy the
Turk; who, about the same time, had taken with his fleet the famous
island of Cyprus, which was before subject to the Venetians; a sad and
unfortunate loss! It was known for certain, that the most serene Don
John of Austria, natural brother of our good king Philip, was appointed
generalissimo of this league, and great preparations for war were every
where talked of. All of which incited a vehement desire in me to be

present in the battle that was expected; and though I had reason to be-lieve, and had some promises, and almost assurances, that, on the first occasion that offered, I should be promoted to the rank of a captain, I resolved to quit all, and go, as I did, into Italy. And my good fortune would have it, that Don John of Austria was just then come to Genoa, and was going to Naples to join the Venetian fleet, as he afterwards did at Messina. In short, I was present at that glorious action, being already made a captain of foot, to which honourable post I was advanced, rather by my good fortune, than by my deserts. But that day, which was so fortunate to Christendom (for all nations were then undeceived of their error, in believing that the Turks were invincible by sea); on that day, I say, on which the Ottoman pride and haughtiness were broken; among so many happy persons as were there (for sure the Christians, who died there, had better fortune than the survivors and conquerors) I alone remained unfortunate, since, instead of what I might have expected, had it been in the times of the Romans, some naval crown, I found my-self, the night following that famous day, with chains on my feet, and manacles on my hands. Which happened thus:

Uchali, king of Algiers, a bold and successful corsair, having boarded and taken the captain-galley of John Andrea D'Oria came up to her re-lief, on board of which I was with my company; and, doing my duty upon this occasion, I leaped into the enemy's galley, which getting off suddenly form ours, my soldiers could not follow me; and so I was left alone among my enemies, whom I could not resist, being so many: in short, I was carried off prisoner, and sorely wounded. And, as you must have heard, gentlemen, that Uchali escaped with his whole squadron, by that means I remained a captive in his power, being the only sad per-son, when so many were joyful; and a slave, when so many were freed: for fifteen thousand Christians, who were at the oar in the Turkish gal-leys, did that day recover their long-wished-for liberty. They carried me to Constantinople, where the Grand Signor Selim made my master general of the sea, for having done his duty in the fight, and having brought off, as a proof of his valour, the flag of the order of Malta. The year following, which was Seventy-two, I was a Navarino, rowing in the captain-galley of the Three Lanthorns; and there I saw and observed the opportunity that was then lost of taking the whole Turkish navy in port. For all the Levantines and Janizaries on board took it for granted they should be attacked in the very harbour, and had their baggage and their passamaques (or shoes) in readiness for running away immediately by land, without staying for an engagement: such terror had our navy

struck into them. But heaven ordered it otherwise, not through any fault or neglect of the general, who commanded our men, but for the sins of Christendom, and because God permits and ordains that there should always be some scourges to chastise us. In short, Uchali got into Modon, an island near Navarino, and, putting his men on shore, he fortified the entrance of the port, and lay still until the season of the year forced Don John to return home. In this campaign, the galley, called the Prize, whose captain was a son of the famous corsair Barbarossa, was taken by the captain-galley of Naples, called the She-wolf, commanded by that thunderbolt of war, that father of the soldiers, that fortunate and invincible captain, Don Alvaro de Basan, marquis of Santa Cruz. And I cannot forbear relating what happened at the taking of the Prize.

The son of Barbarossa was so cruel, and treated his slaves so ill, that, as soon as they, who were at the oar, saw that the She-wolf was ready to board and take them, they all at once let fall their oars, and, laying hold on their captain, who stood near the poop, calling out to them to row hard, and passing him along from bank to bank, and from the poop to the prow, they gave him such blows, that he had passed but little beyond the mast, before his soul was passed to hell: such was the cruelty wherewith he treated them, and the hatred they bore to him.

We returned to Constantinople, and, the year following, which was Seventy-three, it was known there, that Don John had taken Tunis, and that kingdom from the Turks, and put Muley Hamet in possession thereof, cutting off the hopes that Muley Hamida had of reigning again there, who was one of the cruelest, and yet bravest Moors, that ever was in the world. The grand Turk felt this loss very sensibly, and putting in practice that sagacity, which is inherent in the Ottoman family, he clapped up a peace with the Venetians, who desired it more than he: and, the year following, being that of Seventy-four, he attacked the fortress of Goleta, and the fort which Don John had left half finished near Tunis. During all these transactions, I was still at the oar, without any hope of redemption: at least I did not expect to be ransomed; for I was determined not to write an account of my misfortune to my father. In short, the Goleta was lost, and the fort also; before which places the Turks had seventy-five thousand men in pay, besides above four hundred thousand Moors and Arabs from all parts of Africa: and this vast multitude was furnished with such quantities of ammunition, and such large warlike stores, together with so many pioneers, that, each man bringing only a handful of earth, they might therewith have covered both the Goleta and the fort. The Goleta, until then thought impregnable, was first taken, not through default of the besieged, who did all that men could do, but because experience had now shewn, how easily trenches might be raised in that desert land; for though the water used to be within two spans of the surface, the Turks now met with none within two yards and so by the help of a great number of sacks of sand, they raised their works so high, as to overlook and command the fortifications: and so leveling from a cavalier, they put it out of the power of the besieged to make any defence. It was the general opinion, that our troops ought not to have shut themselves up in the Goleta, but have met the enemy in the open field, at the place of debarkment: but they, who talk thus, speak at random, and like men little experienced in affairs of this kind. For if there were scarce seven thousand soldiers in the Goleta and in the fort, how could so small a number, though ever so resolute, both take the field and garrison the forts, against such a multitude as that of the enemy? And how can a place be maintained, which is not relieved, and especially when besieged by an army, that is both numerous and obstinate, and besides in their own country? But many were of opinion, and I was of the number, that heaven did a particular grace and favour to Spain, in suffering the destruction of that forge and refuge of all iniquity, that devourer, that sponge, and that moth of infinite sums of money, idly spent there, to no other purpose, than to preserve the memory of its having been a conquest of the invincible emperor "Charles the fifth;" as if it were necessary to the making that memory eternal, as it will be, that those stones should keep it up. The fort also was taken at last: but the Turks were forced to purchase it inch by inch; for the soldiers, who defended it, fought with such bravery and resolution, that they killed above twenty five thousand of the enemy in two-and-twenty general assaults. And of three hundred that were left alive, not one was taken prisoner unwounded; an evident proof of their courage and bravery, and of the vigorous defence they had made. A little fort also, or tower, in the middle of the lake, commanded by Don John Zanoguera, a cavalier of Valencia, and a famous soldier, surrendered upon terms. They took prisoner Don Pedro Portocarrero, general of Goleta, who did all that was possible for the defence of his fortress, and took the loss of it so much to heart, that he died for grief on the way to Constantinople, whither they were carrying him prisoner. They took also the commander of the fort, called Gabrio Cerbellon, a Milanese gentleman, a great engineer, and a most valiant soldier. Several persons of distinction lost their lives in these two garrisons; among whom was Pagan D'Oria, knight of Malta, a gentleman of great generosity, as appeared by his exceeding liberality to his brother, the famous John Andrea D'Oria: and what made his death the more lamented was, his

dying by the hands of some African Arabs, who, upon seeing that the fort was lost, offered to convey him, disguised as a Moor, to Tabarca, a small haven or settlement, which the Genoese have on that coast for the coral-fishing. These Arabs cut off his head, and carried it to the general of the Turkish fleet, who made good upon them our Castilian proverb, that, "though we love the treason, we hate the traitor:" For it is said, the general ordered, that those who brought him the present should be instantly hanged, because they had not brought him alive. Among the Christians, who were taken in the fort, was one Don Pedro d'Aguilar, a native of some town in Andalusia, who had been an ensign in the garrison, a good soldier, and a man of excellent parts: in particular he had a happy talent in poetry. I mention this, because his fortune brought him to be slave to the same patron with me, and we served in the same galley, and at the same oar: and before we parted from that port, this cavalier made two sonnets, by way of epitaphs, one upon Goleta, and the other upon the fort. And indeed I have a mind to repeat them; for I have them by heart, and I believe they will rather be entertaining than disagreeable to you. [. . .]

When he mentioned the sonnets, one of them said: Pray, Sir, before you go any further, I beseech you to tell me what became of that Don Pedro d'Aguilar you talk of? All I know, answered the captive, is, that, after he had been two years at Constantinople, he escaped in the habit of an Arnaut, with a Greek spy, and I cannot tell whether he recovered his liberty: though I believe he did; for, about a year after, I saw the Greek in Constantinople but had not an opportunity of asking him the success of that journey. He returned to Spain, said the gentleman; for that Don Pedro is my brother, and is now in our town, in health, and rich; is married, and has three children. Thanks be to God, said the captive, for the blessings bestowed on him; for, in my opinion, there is not on earth a satisfaction equal to that of recovering one's liberty. Besides, replied the gentleman, I have by heart the sonnets my brother made. Then, pray, Sir, repeat them, said the captive; for you will be able to do it better than I can. With all my heart, answered the gentleman: that upon Goleta was thus. Goleta and the fort being delivered up, the Turks gave orders to dismantle Goleta: as for the fort, it was in such a condition, that there was nothing left to be demolished. And to do the work more speedily, and with less labour, they undermined it in three places: it is true, they could not blow up what seemed to be least strong, the old walls; but whatever remained of the new fortification, made by the engineer Fratin, came very easily down. In short, the fleet returned to Constantinople victorious and triumphant; and, within a few months, died my master the famous Uchali, whom people called Uchali Fartax, that is to say in the Turkish language, "the scabby renegado:" for he was so; and it is customary among the Turks to nick-name people from some good quality belonging to them. And the reason is, because there are but four sirnames of families, which contend for nobility with the Ottoman; and the rest, as I have said, take names and sirnames either from the blemishes of the body, or the virtues of the mind. This leper had been at the oar fourteen years, being a slave of the grand Signor's; and, at about thirty-four years of age, being enraged at a blow given him by a Turk while he was at the oar, to have it in his power to be revenged on him, he renounced his religion. And so great was his valour, that, without rising by those base methods, by which the minions of the grand Signor usually rise, he came to be king of Algiers, and afterwards general of the sea, which is the third command in that empire. He was born in Calabria, and was a good moral man, and treated his slaves with great humanity. He had three thousand of them, and they were divided after his death, as he had ordered by his last will, one half to the grand Signor, who is every man's heir in part, sharing equally with the children of the deceased, and the other among his renegadoes. I fell to the lot of a Venetian renegado who, having been cabin-boy in a ship, was taken by Uchali, and was so beloved by him, that he became one of his most favourite boys. He was one of the cruellest renegadoes that ever was seen: his name was Azanaga. He grew very rich, and became king of Algiers; and with him I came from Constantinople, a little comforted by being so near Spain: not that I intended to write an account to any body of my unfortunate circumstances, but in hopes fortune would be more favourable to me in Algiers, than it had been in Constantinople, where I had tried a thousand ways of making my escape, but none rightly timed nor successful: and in Algiers I purposed to try other means of compassing what I desired: for the hope of recovering my liberty never entirely abandoned me; and whenever what I devised, contrived, and put in execution, did not answer my design, I presently, without desponding, searched out and formed to myself fresh hopes to sustain me, though they were slight and inconsiderable.

Thus I made a shift to support life, shut up in a prison, or house, which the Turks call a Bath, where they keep their Christian captives locked up, as well those who belong to the king, as some of those belonging to private persons, and those also whom they call of the Almazen, that is to say, "captives of the council," who serve the city in its public works, and in other offices. This kind of captives find it very difficult to recover their liberty; for as they belong to the publick, and have

no particular master, there is nobody for them to treat with about their ransom, though they should have it ready. To these baths, as I have said, private persons sometimes carry their slaves, especially when their ransom is agreed upon; for there they keep them without work, and in safety, until their ransom comes. The king's slaves also, who are to be ransomed, do not go out to work with the rest of the crew, unless it be when their ransom is long in coming: for then, to make them write for it with greater importunity, they are made to work, and go for wood with the rest; which is no small toil and pains. As they knew I had been a captain, I was one upon ransom; and, though I assured them I wanted both interest and money, it did not hinder me from being put among the gentleman, and those who were to be ransomed. They put a chain on me, rather as a sign of ransom, than to secure me; and so I passed my life in that bath, with many other gentlemen and persons of condition, distinguished and accounted as ransomable. And though hunger and nakedness often, and indeed generally, afflicted us, nothing troubled us so much as to see, at every turn, the unparalleled and excessive cruelties, with which our master used the Christians. Each day he hanged one, impaled another, and cut off the ears of a third; and that upon the least provocation, and sometimes none at all, insomuch that the very Turks were sensible he did it for the mere pleasure of doing it, and to gratify his murderous and inhuman disposition. One Spanish soldier only, called such an one de Saavedra, happened to be in his good graces; and though he did things, which will remain in the memory of those people for many years, and all towards obtaining his liberty, yet he never gave him a blow, nor ordered one to be given him, nor ever gave him so much as a hard word: and for the least of many things he did, we all feared he would be impaled alive, and he feared it himself more than once: and, were it not that the time will not allow me, I would now tell you of some things done by this soldier, which would be more entertaining, and more surprising, than the relation of my story.

Miguel Cervantes de Saavedra, The Life and Exploits of the Ingenious Gentleman Don Quixote de la Mancha, *5th ed., vol. 2, trans. Charles Jarvis (London: Dodsley, 1788).*

An Ottoman Tourist
Evliya Çelebi Efendi (ca. 1670)

Evliya Çelebi (1611–82) was a dervish, muezzin, man of letters, and renowned traveler of the eastern Mediterranean. For forty years he journeyed throughout the Ottoman Empire and the neighboring lands. After initially taking notes on the buildings, markets, customs, and culture of Istanbul, he started his first journey outside the city in 1640. His collection of travel writing formed a ten-volume work called the *Seyahatname* (*Book of Travels*) that describes Istanbul, Anatolia, Persia, Ottoman Europe, North Africa, Austria, and Cairo. In a tone that varies from the descriptive to the argumentative and the ironic, Evliya Çelebi reveals Ottoman perceptions of the world in geography, topography, administration, urban institutions, socioeconomic systems, religion, folklore, sexual relations, and dream interpretation. Treating Istanbul and Cairo as the two capital cities of the Ottoman world, the work is a valuable source on Ottoman culture, the lands on which he reports, and seventeenth-century daily life. The following excerpt describes Evliya's divine call to travel.

In the name of God, the All-clement, the All-merciful!

To God, who ennobles exalted minds by travels, and has enabled me to visit the holy places; to Him who laid the foundations of the fortresses of legislation, and established them on the groundwork of prophecy and revelation, all praise be given: and may the richest blessings and most excellent benedictions be offered to the most noble and perfect of all creatures, the pattern of prayer, who said, "Pray as you see me pray;" to the infallible guide, Mohammed; because it is in his favour that God, the Lord of empires and Creator of the heavens, made the earth an agreeable residence for the sons of Adam, and created man the most noble of all his creatures. Praise to Him, who directs all events according to His will, without injustice or incongruity! And, after having offered all adoration to God, let every pious aspiration be expressed for the prosperity of his shadow upon earth, the ruler of terrestrial things, the Sultán son of a Sultán, the victorious Prince Murád Khán, fourth son of Sultán Ahmed Khán, and eighth in descent from Sultán Mohammed Khán, the Conqueror, the mercy of God rest upon them all! But most especially on Sultán Murád Ghází, the conqueror of Baghdád, the great Monarch with whose service I was blessed when I began to write an account of my travels.

It was in the time of his illustrious reign, in the year A.H. 1041 (A.D. 1631), that by making excursions on foot in the villages and gardens near Islámbúl (Constantinople), I began to think of extensive travels, and to escape from the power of my father, mother, and brethren. Forming a design of traveling over the whole earth, I entreated God to give me health for my body and faith for my soul; I sought the conversation of dervíshes, and when I had heard a description of the seven climates and of the four quarters of the earth, I became still more anxious to see the world, to visit the Holy Land, Cairo, Damascus, Mecca and Medina, and to prostrate myself on the purified soil of the places where the prophet, the glory of all creatures, was born, and died.

I, a poor, destitute traveler, but a friend of mankind, Evliya, son of the dervísh Mohammed, being continually engaged in prayer and petitions for divine guidance, meditating upon the holy chapters and mighty verses of the Korán, and looking out for assistance from above, was blessed in the night 'Ashúrá, in the month of *Moharrem*, while sleeping in my father's house at Islámbúl, with the following vision: I dreamt that I was in the mosque of Akhí chelebí, near the Yemish iskeleh-sí (fruit-stairs or scale), a mosque built with money lawfully gotten, from which prayers therefore ascend to heaven. The gates were thrown open at once, and the mosque filled with a brilliant crowd who were saying the morning prayers. I was concealed behind the pulpit, and was lost in astonishment on beholding that brilliant assembly. I looked on my neighbour, and said, "May I ask, my lord, who you are, and what is your illustrious name?" He answered, "I am one of the ten evangelists, Sa'd Vakkás, the patron of archers." I kissed his hands, and asked further: "Who are the refulgent multitude on my right hand?" He said, "They are all blessed saints and pure spirits, the spirits of the followers of the Prophet, the Muhájirín, who followed him in his flight from Mecca, and the Ansárí who assisted him on his arrival at Medína, the companions of Saffah and the martyrs of Kerbelá. On the right of the *mihráb* (altar) stand Abú Bekr and 'Omar, and on the left 'Osmán and 'Ali; before it stand Veis; and close to the left wall of the mosque, the first Muezzin, Belál the Habeshí. The man who regulates and ranks the whole assembly is Amru. Observe the host in red garments now advancing with a standard; that is the host of martyrs who fell in the holy wars, with the hero Hamzah at their head." Thus did he point out to me the different companies of that blessed assembly, and each time I looked on one of them, I laid my hand on my breast, and felt my soul refreshed by the sight. "My lord," said I, "what is the reason of the appearance of this assembly in this mosque?" He answered, "The faithful Tártárs being in great danger at Azák (Azof), we are marching to their assistance. The Prophet himself, with his two grandsons Hasan and Hosaïn, the twelve *Imáms* and the ten disciples, will immediately come hither to perform the appointed morning service (*sabáh-namáz*). They will give you a sign to perform your duty as Muezzin, which you must do accordingly. You must begin to cry out with a loud voice '*Allah Ekber*' (God is great!) and then repeat the verses of the Throne (Súrah II. 259). Belál will repeat the 'Subhánullah' (Glory to God!), and you must answer 'Elhamdu-li-llah' (God be praised!) Belál will answer, 'Allah ekber,' and you must say 'Amín' (Amen), while we all join in the tevhíd (i.e. declaration of the divine unity). You shall then, after saying 'Blessed be all the prophets, and praise to God the Lord of both worlds,' get up, and kiss the hand of the prophet, saying 'Yá resúlu-llah' (O Apostle of God!)."

When Sa'd Vakkás had given me these instructions, I saw flashes of lightning burst from the door of the mosque, and the whole building was filled with a refulgent crowd of saints and martyrs all standing up at once. It was the prophet overshadowed by his green banner, covered with his green veil, carrying his staff in his right hand, and the Imám Hoseïn on his left. As he placed his right foot on the threshold, he cried out "Bismillah," and throwing off his veil, said, "Es-selám aleik yá ommetí" (health unto thee, O my people). The whole assembly answered: "Unto thee be health, O prophet of God, lord of the nations!" The prophet advanced towards the mihráb and offered up a morning prayer of two inflexions (rik'ah). I trembled in every limb; but observed, however, the whole of his sacred figure, and found it exactly agreeing with the description given in the Hallyehi khákání. The veil on his face was a white shawl, and his turban was formed of a white sash with twelve folds; his mantle was of camel's hair, in colour inclining to yellow; on his neck he wore a yellow woolen shawl. His boots were yellow, and in his turban was stuck a toothpick. After giving the salutation he looked upon me, and having struck his knees with his right hand, commanded me to stand up and take the lead in the prayer. I began immediately, according to the instruction of Belál, by saying: "The blessing of God be upon our lord Mohammed and his family, and may He grant them peace!" afterwards adding, "Allah ekber." The prophet followed by saying the fátihah (the 1st chapter of the Korán), and some other verses. I then recited that of the throne. Belál pronounced the Subhánullah, I the El-hamdulillah, and Belál the Allah ekber. The whole service was closed by a general cry of "Allah" which very nearly awoke me from my sleep. After the prophet had repeated some verses, from the Suráh yás, and other chapters of the Korán, Sa'd Vakkás took me by the hand and carried me before him, saying: "Thy loving and faithful servant Evliyà entreats thy intercession." I kissed his hand, pouring forth tears, and instead of crying "shifá'at" (intercession), I said, from my confusion, "siyáhat (traveling) O apostle of God!" The prophet smiled, and said, "shifá'at and siyáhat (i.e. intercession and traveling) be granted to thee, with health and peace!" He then again repeated the fátihah, in which he was followed by the whole assembly, and I afterwards went round, kissed the hands, and received the blessings of each. Their hands were perfumed with musk, ambergris, spikenard, sweet-basil, violets, and carnations; but that of the prophet himself smelt of nothing but saffron and roses, felt when touched as if it had no bones, and was as soft as cotton. The hands of the other prophets had the odor of quinces; that of Abú-bekr had the fragrance of melons, 'Omar's smelt like ambergris, 'Osmán's like violets, Alí's like Jessamine, Hasán's like carnations, and Hoseïn's like white roses. When I had kissed the hands of each, the prophet had again recited the *fátihah*, and all his chosen companions had repeated aloud the seven verses of the exordium to the Korán, *saba'u-l mesání*; and the prophet himself had pronounced the parting salutation (*es-selám aleïkom eyyá ikhwánún*) from the *mihráb*; he advanced towards the door, and the whole illustrious assembly giving me various greetings and blessings, went out of the mosque. Sa'd Vakkás at the same time, taking his quiver from his own belt and putting it into mine, said: "Go, be victorious with thy bow and arrow; be in God's keeping, and receive from me the good tidings that thou shalt visit the tombs of all the prophets and holy men whose hands thou hast now kissed. Thou shalt travel through the whole world, and be a marvel among men. Of the countries through which thou shalt pass, of their castles, strong-holds, wonderful antiquities, products, eatables and drinkables, arts and manufacturers, the extent of their provinces, and the length of the days there, draw up a description, which shall be a monument worthy of thee. Use my arms, and never depart, my son, from the ways of God. Be free from fraud and malice, thankful for bread and salt (hospitality), a faithful friend to the good, but no friend to the bad." Having finished his sermon, he kissed my hand, and went out of the mosque. When I awoke, I was in great doubt whether what I had seen were a dream or a reality; and I enjoyed for some time the beatific contemplations which filled my soul. Having afterwards performed my ablutions, and offered up the morning prayer I crossed over from Constantinople to the suburb of Kásim-páshá, and consulted the interpreter of dreams, Ibráhím Efendi, about my vision. From him I received the comfortable news that I should become a great traveler, and after making my way through the world, by the intercession of the prophet, should close my career by being admitted into Paradise. I next went to Abdu-llah Dedeh, Sheïkh of the convent of Mevleví dervishes in the same suburb (Kásim-páshá), and having kissed his hand, related my vision to him. He interpreted it in the same satisfactory manner, and presenting to me seven historical works, and recommending me to follow Sa'd Vakkás's counsels, dismissed me with prayers for my success. I then retired to my humble abode, applied myself to the study of history, and began a description of my birth-place, Islámbúl, that envy of kings, the celestial haven, and strong-hold of Mákedún (Macedonia, i.e. Constantinople).

From the preface to Narrative of Travels in Europe, Asia and Africa in the Seventeenth Century, trans. Joseph von Hammer (London: Oriental Translation Fund, 1846–50), 2–5.

The Conversion of Sabbatai Sevi
Samuel Brett, Sir Paul Rycaut, and Richard Kidder (1666)

Acclaimed messiah, kabbalist, and founder of the *Dönmes*, Sabbatai Sevi (1626–76) was born in Izmir (Smyrna). Dönmes, crypto-Jews, flourished in the Ottoman Empire, drawing from Judaism, Christianity, and Islam. Sevi descended from the Greek-speaking Jews of the Ottoman Empire who were neither Sephardi nor Ashkenazi but belonged to a distinctive group known as Romaniotes. In 1666, Sabbatai left Izmir for Istanbul, either because he was compelled to by authorities or because of a hope in a miracle to fulfill the prophecy of Nathan Ghazzati that Sabbatai would wear the sultan's crown. As soon as he arrived, however, he was arrested and cast into prison. At the command of Ottoman Sultan Mehmed IV, Sabbatai was taken to Edirne, where the sultan's physician, a Jewish convert to Islam, advised him to convert as well. Sabbatai, realizing his life was at risk, took the physician's advice. On the following day, before the sultan, he cast off his Jewish garb and donned a turban to symbolize his conversion. The sultan rewarded Sabbatai by conferring on him the title (Mehmed) Effendi, and appointing him a salary. The following excerpt describes Sabbatai's travels between Izmir, Thessolonika, and Istanbul.

According to the Predictions of several *Christian* Writers, especially of such who comment on the *Apocalyps*, or *Revelations*, this Year of 1666 was to prove a Year of Wonders, of strange Revolutions of the World, and particularly of Blessing to the *Jews*; either in respect of their Conversion to the *Christian* Faith, or of their Restoration to their Temporal Kingdom. This Opinion was so widely spread, and fixt in the Countries of the Reformed Religion, and in the Heads of Fanatical Enthusiasts, who dreamed of a Fifth Monarchy, the downfal of the Pope and Antichrist, and the Greatness of the *Jews*, that this subtil People judged the Year present the proper time to stir, and to fit their Motion according

228

to the Season of the modern Prophecies. Hereupon strange Reports flew from Place to Place, of the March of Multitudes of People from unknown Parts into the remote Desarts of *Arabia*, supposed to be the *Ten Tribes and Half*, lost for so many Ages: That a Ship was arrived in the northern Parts of *Scotland* with her Sails and Cordage of Silk, navigated by Mariners who spake nothing but *Hebrew*; with this Motto on their Sails, *The Twelve Tribes of Israel*. These Reports agreeing thus near to former Predictions, put the wild Sort of the World into an Expectation of strange Events, which this Year was to produce, in reference to the *Jewish* Monarchy.

In this Manner Millions of People were possessed, when *Sabatay Sevi* first appeared at *Smyrna*, and published himself to the *Jews* for their *Messiah*, relating the Greatness of their approaching Kingdom, and with how strong a Hand God was about to deliver them from Bondage, and gather them from all Parts of the World. It was strange to see how the Fancy took, and how fast the Report of *Sabatay* and his Doctrine flew through all Parts, where *Turks* and *Jews* inhabited; the latter of whom were so deeply possessed with a Belief of their new Kingdom and Riches, and many of them with Promotion to Offices of Government, Renown, and Greatness, that in all Parts, from *Constantinople* to *Buda*, (which Road it was my Fortune that Year to travel) I perceived a strange Transport in the *Jews*, none of them attending to any Business, unless to wind up former Negotiations, and prepare themselves and Families for a Journey to *Jerusalem*: All their Discourses, their Dreams, and Disposal of their Affairs tended to no other Design but a Re-establishment in the *Land of Promise*, to the Greatness, Glory, Wisdom, and Doctrine of the *Messiah*, whose Original, Birth, and Education are first to be recounted.

Sabatay Sevi was Son of *Mordecai Sevi*, an Inhabitant and Native of *Smyrna*, who gained his Livelihood by being Broker to an *English* Merchant in that Place: This Person, before his Death, grew very decrepit in his Body, being full of the Gout, and other Infirmities, but his son *Sabatay Sevi*, addicting himself to Study, became a notable Proficient in *Hebrew* and Metaphysics; in which and Divinity he arrived to such a Pitch, that he developed a new Doctrine in their Law, drawing to the Profession of it many Disciples, as raised one Day a Tumult in the Synagogue; for which afterwards he was by a Censure of the *Khokbams* (who are Expounders of the *Tora*) banished from the City.

During the time of his Exile, he traveled to *Thessalonika*, now called *Salonika*, where he married a very handsome Woman; but either not having that Part of Occonomy proper to govern a Wife, or being impotent towards Women, as was pretended, or that she found not Favour in his Eyes, she was divorced from him: Again, he took a second Wife, more beautiful than the former, but the same Causes of Discontent raising a Difference between them, he obtained another Divorce from her also. Being now free from the Incumbrances of a Family, his wandering Head moved him to travel through the *Morea*, thence to *Tripoli* in *Syria*, *Gaza*, and *Jerusalem*; by the Way picked up a *Ligonese* Lady, whom he made his third Wife, the Daughter of some *Polonian* or *German*, her origin and parentage not being very well known. During his Stay at *Jerusalem* he began to reform the Law of the *Jews*, and abolish the Fast of *Tamuz*, (which they keep in the Month of *June*) and there meeting with one of his own Nation, called *Nathan*, a proper Instrument to promote his Design, he communicated to him his Condition, his Course of Life, and Intentions to proclaim himself the *Messiah* of the World, so long expected and desired by the *Jews*. This Project took wonderfully with *Nathan*; and because it was thought necessary, according to *Scripture* and ancient Prophecies, that *Elias* should Precede the *Messiah*, as *John the Baptist* had been the Forerunner of *Christ*, *Nathan* thought no man so proper to act the Part of the Prophet as himself; no sooner had *Sabatay* declared himself the *Messiah*, but *Nathan* discovers himself to be his Harbinger, forbidding all the Fasts of the *Jews* in *Jerusalem*; and declaring, that the Bridegroom being come, nothing but Joy and Triumph ought to dwell in their Habitations; he likewise wrote to all the Assemblies of the *Jews*, to persuade them to the same Belief.

And now the Schism being begun, and many *Jews* really believing what they so much desired, *Nathan* took the Courage and Boldness to Prophesy, that one Year from the 27th of *Kisleu* (which is the Month of *June*) the *Messiah* should appear before the Grand Signior, and, taking from him his Crown, lead him in Chains like a Captive.

Sabatay also, at *Gaza*, preached Repentance to the *Jews*, and Obedience to Himself and Doctrine, for that the Coming of the *Messiah* was at hand: Which Novelties so affected the *Jewish* Inhabitants of those Parts, that they gave up themselves wholly to their Prayers, Alms, and Devotions; and, to confirm this Belief the more, it happened that at the same Time News hereof, with all the Particulars, were dispatched from *Gaza*, to acquaint the Brethren in foreign Parts. The Rumour of the *Messiah* had flown so swiftly, and gained such Reception, that Intelligence came from all Quarters and Countries where the *Jews* inhabited, by Letters to *Gaza* and *Jerusalem*, congratulating the Happinesss of their Deliverance, and Expiration of the Time of their Servitude, but the Appearance of the *Messiah*. These Rumors were accompanied with

Prophecies, relating to that Dominion which the *Messiah* was to have over all the World; as that after his Coming he was to disappear for nine Month, during which Time the *Jews* were to suffer, and many of them to undergo Martyrdom; but then returning again, mounted on a Celestial Lion, with his Bridle made of Serpents with seven Heads, accompanied with his Brethren the *Jews*, who inhabited on the other Side of the River *Sabation*, he should be acknowledged for sole Monarch of the Universe; and then the Holy Temple should descend from Heaven, ready built, framed, and beautified, wherein they should offer Sacrifice for ever.

And here I leave you to consider, says our Author, how strangely this deceived People were amused, when these confident and vain Reports, and Dreams of Power and Kingdoms, had wholly diverted them from the ordinary Course of their Trade, Occupations and Interest.

This Noise and Rumour of the *Messiah* having begun to fill all Places, *Sabatay Sevi* resolved to travel towards *Smyrna*, the Country of his Nativity; and thence to *Constantinople*, the capital City, where the principal Work of Preaching was to have been performed: *Nathan* thought it not fit to be long after him, and therefore travels by the Way of *Damascus*; where resolving to continue some Time, for better Propagation of their new Doctrine, he in the mean while writes this Letter to *Sabatay Sevi*, as followeth:

22nd Kesvan *of this Year.*

To the King, our King, Lord of our Lords, who gathers the dispersed of *Israel*, who redeems our Captivity, the Man elevated to the Height of all Sublimity, the *Messiah* of the *God* of *Jacob*, the true *Messiah*, the *Celestial Lion, Sabatay Sevi*, whose Honour be exhalted, and his Dominion raised in a short Time, and for ever, *Amen.* After having kissed your Hands, and swept the Dust from your Feet, as my Duty is to the King of Kings (whose Majesty be exalted, and his Empire enlarged) these are to make known to the supreme Excellency of that Place, which is adorned with the Beauty of your Sanctity, that the Word of the King, and his Law, hath enlightened our Faces. That Day hath been a solemn Day unto *Israel*, and a Day of Light unto our Rulers, for immediately we applied ourselves to perform your Commands, as our Duty is. And although we have heard of many strange Things, yet we are couragious, and our Heart is as the Heart of a Lion; nor ought we to enquire a Reason of your Doings, for your Works are marvelous, and past finding out; and we are confirmed in our Fidelity, without all Exception, resigning up our very Souls for the Holiness of your name: And now we are come as far as *Damascus*, intending shortly to proceed in our Journey to *Skanderone*, according as you have commanded us; that so we may ascend, and see

231

the Face of God in Light, as the Light of the Face of the King of Life: And we, Servants of your Servants, shall cleanse the Dust from your Feet, beseeching the Majesty of your Excellency and Glory to vouchsafe from your Habitation to have a care of us, and help us with the Force of your Right-hand of Strength, and shorten our Way which is before us: And we have our Eyes towards *Jab, Jab*, who will make haste to help us, and save us, that the Children of Iniquity shall not hurt us; and towards whom our Hearts pant, and are consumed within us; who shall give us Tallons of Iron to be worthy to stand under the Shadow of your Ass. These are the Words of the Servant of your Servants, who prostrates himself to be troden on by the Soles of your Feet,
Nathan Benjamin.

From A Looking-Glass for the Jews, *published in 1753 (London), a volume assembled from writings by Samuel Brett, Sir Paul Rycaut, and Richard Kidder.*

A New World
Lady Mary Wortley Montagu (1717)

The *Turkish Embassy Letters* of Lady Mary Wortley Montagu (1689–1762) chronicle their author's impressions of the strange new world in which she found herself. A feminist, she wrote about the liberties Turkish women enjoyed, including ironically the veils that rendered a woman incognita in the street (the better, she thought, to conduct secret love affairs). She was struck by the unpretentious behavior of women in the Turkish baths. She had a keen sense of the literary value of her letters, which are held up as lively models of the epistolary genre. The *Turkish Embassy Letters* were written while Montagu traveled with her husband, Edward Wortley Montagu, who had been appointed Ambassador Extraordinary to the Court of Turkey. Edward Montagu was also a representative of the London-based Levant Company, which traded in this region for items such as tulips, coffee, and silk.

To Lady ———, *Adrianople, April 1, 1717*

I am now got into a new World where every thing I see appears to me a change of scene, and I write to your ladyship with some content of mind, hoping at least that you will find the charm of novelty in my letters and no longer reproach me that I tell you nothing extraordinary. I won't trouble you with a relation of our tedious journey, but I must not omit what I saw remarkable at Sophia, one of the most beautiful towns in the Turkish Empire and famous for its hot baths that are resorted to both for diversion and health. I stop'd here one day on purpose to see them. Designing to go incognito, I hir'd a Turkish Coach. These voitures are not at all like ours, but much more convenient for the country, the heat being so great that glasses would be very troublesome. They are made a good deal in the manner of the Dutch stage coaches, having wooden lattices painted and gilded, the inside being also painted with baskets and nosegays of flowers, intermix'd commonly with little poetical motto's. They are cover'd all over with scarlet cloth, lined with silk and very often richly embroidered and fringed. This covering entirely hides the persons in them, but may be thrown back at pleasure, and thus permit the ladies to peep through the lattices. They hold four people very conveniently, seated on cushions, but not raised.

In one of these covered waggons I went to the Bagnio about ten a clock. It was already full of women. It is built of stone in the shape of a dome with no windows but in the roof, which gives light enough. There were five of these domes joined together, the outmost being less than the rest and serving only as a hall where the portress stood at the door. Ladies of quality generally give this woman a crown or ten shillings, and I did not forget that ceremony. The next room is a very large one, paved with marble, and all round it are two raised sofas of marble, one above another. There were four fountains of cold water in this room, falling first into marble basins and then running on the floor in little channels made for that purpose, which carried the streams into the next room, something less than this, with the same sort of marble sofas, but so hot with steams of sulphur proceeding from the baths joining to it, 'twas impossible to stay there with one's cloaths on. The two other domes were the hot baths, one of which had cocks of cold water turning into it to temper it to what degree of warmth the bathers pleased to have.

I was in my travelling Habit, which is a riding dress, and certainly appeared very extraordinary to them, yet there was not one of them that shewed the least surprize or impertinent curiosity, but received me with all the obliging civility possible. I know no European court where the ladies would have behaved them selves in so polite a manner to such a stranger. I believe in the whole there were two hundred women and yet none of those disdainful smiles and satyric whispers that never fail in our assemblies when any body appears that is not dressed exactly in fashion. They repeated over and over to me, "*Uzelle, pek uzelle,*" which is nothing but "Charming, very charming." The first sofas were covered with cushions and rich carpets, on which sat the ladies, and on the second their slaves behind them, but without any distinction of rank by their dress, all being in the state of nature, that is, in plain English, stark naked, without any beauty or defect concealed. Yet there was not the least wanton smile or immodest gesture amongst them. They walked and moved with the same majestic grace which Milton describes our General Mother with. There were many amongst them as exactly proportioned as ever any goddess was drawn by the pencil of a Guido or Titian, and most of their skins shiningly white, only adorned by their beautiful hair divided into many tresses hanging on their shoulders, braided either with pearl or ribbon, perfectly representing the figures of the Graces. I was here convinced of the truth of a reflection that I had often made, that if it were the fashion to go naked, the face would be hardly observed. I perceived that the ladies of the most delicate shapes and the finest skins had the greatest share of my admiration, though their faces were sometimes less beautiful than those of their companions. To tell you the truth, I had wickedness enough to wish secretly that Mr Gervais could have been there invisible. I fancy it would have very much improved his art to see so many fine women naked, in different postures, some in conversation, some working, others drinking coffee or sherbet, and many negligently lying on their cushions while their slaves (generally pretty girls of seventeen or eighteen) were employ'd in braiding their hair in several pretty fancies. In short, 'tis the women's coffee house, where all the news of the town is told, scandal invented, etc. They generally take this diversion once a week, and stay there at least four or five hours without getting cold by immediately coming out of the hot bath into the cool room, which was very surprizing to me. The Lady that seemed the most considerable amongst them entreated me to sit by her and would fain have undress'd me for the bath. I excused myself with some difficulty. They being all so earnest in persuading me, I was at last forced to open my shirt and shew them my stays, which satisfied them very well, for I saw they believed I was so locked up in that machine that it was not in my own power to open it, which contrivance they attributed to my husband. I was charmed with their civility and beauty and should have been very glad to pass more time with them, but Mr W[ortley] resolving to pursue his journey next morning early, I was in haste to see the ruins of Justinian's church, which did not afford me so agreeable a prospect as I had left, being little more than a heap of stones.

Adieu, Madam. I am sure I have now entertained you with an account of such a sight as you never saw in your life and what no book of travels could inform you of, as 'tis no less than death for a man to be found in one of these places.

Letters of the Right Honourable Lady M[ary] W[ortle]y M[ontagu]e, Written during her Travels in Europe, Asia and Africa, *3 vols. in one (London: Becket and de Hondt, 1763), 1:157–65.*

From Rome to Naples
William Beckford (1780)

During the eighteenth century, the Grand Tour to Europe was an essential part of wealthy young Englishmen's education. The Mediterranean section of the tour generally took in classical sites, especially in Italy and Greece. Such journeys could have different motivations; for example, William Beckford (1760–1844) was evading a sexual scandal at home. A novelist, art critic, travel writer, politician, and son of the lord mayor of London, Beckford wrote the following letters in Rome in November 1780. His classical learning is reflected in his notion that Homer's Odysseus and Virgil's Aeneas visited the same locations on and around the Bay of Naples. The landscape through which Beckford traveled is suffused with classical pasts — unexpectedly disrupted in this case by a storm. Circe is the sorceress of *The Odyssey*, and Picus is her former lover who had been turned into a woodpecker for spurning her; the port of Caieta had been named by Aeneas for his wet-nurse in the *Aeneid*.

November 2, 1780

I arose at daybreak, and, forgetting fevers and mortalities, ran into a level meadow without the town, whilst the horses were putting to the carriage. Why should I calumniate the pearly transparent air? I seemed at least purer than any I had before inhaled. Being perfectly alone, and not discovering any trace of the neighbouring city, I fancied myself existing in the ancient days of Hesperia, and hoped to meet Picus in his woods before the evening. But, instead of those shrull clamours which used to echo through the thickets when Pan joined with mortals in the chase, I heard the rumbling of our carriage, and the cursing of postilions. Mounting a horse I flew before them, and seemed to catch inspiration from the breezes. Now turned my eyes to the ridge of precipices, in whose grots and caverns Saturn and his people passed their life; then to the distant ocean. Afar off rose the cliff, so famous for Circe's incantations, and the whole line of coasts, which was once covered with her forests.

Whilst I was advancing with full speed, the sunbeams began to shoot athwart the mountains, the plains to light up by degrees, and their shrubberies of myrtle to glisten with dew-drops. The sea brightened, and the Circean promontory soon glowed with purple. All day we kept winding through this enchanged country. Towards evening Terracina appeared before us, in a bold romantic scite; house above house, and turret looking over turret, on the steeps of a mountain, enclosed with mouldering walls, and crowned by the ruined terraces of a palace; one of those, perhaps, which the luxurious Romans inhabited during the summer, when so free and lofty an exposition (the sea below, with its gales and murmurs) must have been delightful. Groves of orange and citron hang on the declivity, rough with the Indian fig, whose bright red flowers, illuminated by the sun, had a magic splendour. A palm-tree, growing on the highest crag, adds not a little to its singular appearance. Being the largest I had yet seen, and clustered with fruit, I climbed up the rocks to take a sketch of it; and looking down upon the beach and glassy plains of ocean, exclaimed with Martial:

> O nemus! O fontes! solidumque madentis arenae
> Litus, et aequoreis splendidus Anxur aquis!
> [*O grove, o fountains, unbroken sea-shore of moist sand, and Anxur*
> *(i.e., Terracina), magnificent with its watery waves!:*
> Martial, Epigrams, 10.51]

Glancing my eyes athwart the sea, I fixed them on the rock of Circe, which lies right opposite to Terracina, joined to the continent by a very narrow strip of land, and appearing like an island. The roar of the waves lashing the base of the precipices, might still be thought the howl of savage monsters; but where are those woods which shaded the dome of the goddess? Scarce a tree appears. A few thickets, and but a few, are the sole remains of this once impenetrable vegetation; yet even these I longed to visit, such was my predilection for the spot.

Descending the cliff, and pursuing our route to Mola along the shore, by a grand road formed on the ruins of the Appian Way, we drove under an enormous perpendicular rock, standing detached, like a watch tower, and cut into arsenals and magazines. Day closed just as we got beyond it, and new moon gleamed faintly on the waters. We saw fires afar off in the bay, some twinkling on the coast, others upon the waves, and heard the murmur of voices; for the night was still and solemn, like that of Cajetas's funeral. I looked anxiously on a sea, where the heroes of the Odyssey and Aeneid had sailed to fulfil destinies.

Nine struck and we arrived at Mola di Gaeta. The boats were just coming in (whose lights we had seen out upon the main), and brought such fish as Neptune, I dare say, would have grudged Aeneas and Ulysses.

November 3, 1780

The morning was soft, but hazy. I walked in a grove of orange trees, white with blossoms, and at the same time glowing with fruit. The spot sloped pleasantly toward the sea, and here I loitered till the horses were ready, then set off on the Appian Way, between hedges of myrtle and aloes. We observed a variety of towns, with battlemented walls and ancient turrets, crowning the pinnacles of rocky steeps, surrounded by wilds, and rude uncultivated mountains. The Liris, now Garigliano, winds its peaceful course through wide extensive meadows, scattered over with the remains of aqueducts, and waters the base of the rocks I have just mentioned. Such a prospect could not fail of bringing Virgil's panegyric of Italy into my mind:

Tot congesta manu praeruptis oppida saxis
Fluminaque antiquos subterlabentia muros.
[*So many towns piled upon steep hills, and rivers flowing beneath
ancient walls: Virgil*, Georgics, *2.156–57*]

As soon as we arrived in sight of Capua, the sky darkened, clouds covered the horizone, and presently poured down such deluges of rain as floated the whole country. The gloom was general; Vesuvius disappeared just after we had discovered it. At four o'clock darkness universally prevailed, except when a livid glare of lightning presented momentary glimpses of the bay and mountains. We lighted torches, and forded several torrents almost at the hazard of our lives. The plains of Aversa were filled with herds, lowing most piteously, and yet not half so much scared as their masters, who ran about raving and ranting like Indians during the eclipse of the moon. I knew Vesuvius had often put their courage to proof, but little thought of an inundation occasioning such commotions.

For three hours the storm increased in violence, and instead of entering Naples on a calm evening, and viewing its delightful shores by moonlight—instead of finding the squares and terraces thronged with people and animated by music, we advanced with fear and terror through dark streets totally deserted, every creature being shut up in their houses, and we heard nothing by driving rain, rushing torrents, and the fall of fragments beaten down by their violence. Our inn, like every other habitation, was in great disorder, and we waited a long while before we could settle in our apartments with any comfort. All night long the waves roared round the rocky foundations of a fortress beneath my windows, and the lightning played clear in my eyes.

William Beckford, Italy, with Sketches of Spain and Portugal, *2nd ed., 2 vols. (London: Bentley, 1834), 1:230–36.*

From Naples to Palermo
Johann Wolfgang von Goethe (1787)

In 1786, poet, dramatist, and novelist Goethe (1749–1832) went to Italy, where he spent two years and was inspired by its classical heritage. He wrote several volumes while under the impact of this trip. He drew particular inspiration from the city of Rome's antiquities and its wealth of contemporary visual art. His response to the physical environment of the Mediterranean was profound—to an extent that not even seasickness could dampen, as the following excerpt reveals. The many letters he wrote in this time were not published until 1816–17, to some degree edited, as his *Italian Journey*. Subsequent letters from Palermo (April 1787) reveal his botanical interests and especially his desire to find the supposed "archetypal plant" (*Urpflanze*). Further afield, the collection *East-West Divan* (1819) reflects the influence of the East on Goethe's writing, notably the divan of the fourteenth-century Persian poet Hafiz.

At sea, Thursday, March 29th
Unlike the most recent departure of the mailboat, when a favorable, fresh northeaster blew, this time there was unfortunately a mild southwester from the opposite direction, the least favorable wind. We realized then to what degree the sailor depends on the vicissitudes of wind and weather. Impatiently we spent the morning, by turns, at the harbor and at a café. Finally we could board the ship at midday and relished the gorgeous view in the most beautiful weather. Not far from the Molo the corvette lay at anchor. A hazy atmosphere with clear sunlight, so that the cliffs of Sorrento were covered in beautiful blue shade. Lively Naples glistened with color. The boat did not move from its berth until sunset,

and then only slowly. The contrary wind pushed us toward Posillipo and its promontory. The ship proceeded calmly the entire night. It was built in America, capable of high speeds, and equipped with exquisite little cabins and individual sleeping quarters. The passengers were cheerful but well behaved: opera singers and dancers on their way to perform in Palermo.

Friday, March 30th

At daybreak we found ourselves between Ischia and Capri, roughly one mile from the latter. The sun rose magnificently from behind the mountains of Capri and Capo Minerva. Diligently, Kniep sketched the outlines of the coasts and islands and their various views; the slow pace of the voyage aided his efforts. We continued on a weak and half-strength wind. Around four o'clock Vesuvius disappeared from view, though Capo Minerva and Ischia were still visible, but these too disappeared by evening. The sun sank into the sea, accompanied by clouds and a long band of purple light stretching for a mile. Kniep sketched this sight too. Now there was no more land in view, the entire horizon a circle of water, the night clear and the moonlight beautiful.

I was able to relish this magnificent view for only a few moments before seasickness overcame me. I retired to my cabin, lay down, abstained from all food and drink apart from white bread and red wine, and felt quite comfortable. Cut off from the outside world I let myself take control of the inner, and since a slow voyage was expected I took on a challenging task in order to keep myself occupied. From all my manuscripts I had brought only the first two acts of Tasso, in poetic prose. These two acts, roughly the same as the current version with regard to conception and plot, though written ten years earlier, had a weak, nebulous quality, which it lost as soon as I added metre and let the form prevail.

Saturday, March 31st

The sun was clear as it rose from the sea. At seven o'clock we reached a French ship, which had left two days ahead of us; our progress seemed all the better, and still the end of our voyage was not yet in view. We derived some consolation from the island of Ustica, but unfortunately on the left rather than (like Capri) on the right side. Around midday the wind was directly contrary and we could not move forward. The waves began to rise, and on board nearly everybody was sick.

I remained in my reclining position, able to rethink the entire work through and through. Hours passed, and I noticed the time of day only because the mischievous Kniep, whose appetite was unaffected by the waves, from time to time brought wine and bread, gloating over his own fine meal as well as the bonhomie and charm of the able young captain, who regretted that I was not able to take part. The behavior of the passengers, as jest and good humor gave way to discomfort and illness, provided him with rich material for malicious description.

At four in the afternoon the captain set the ship on a different course. The large sail was raised and our path directed straight at the island of Ustica, behind which, to our enormous pleasure, we caught sight of the mountains of Sicily. The wind picked up, we sailed more quickly toward Sicily, and some other islands came into view. Sunset was bleak, the sun hidden behind clouds. The entire evening a fairly favorable wind blew. Around midnight the sea started becoming very choppy.

Sunday, April 1st

Around three in the morning a huge storm broke. Between sleep and wakefulness I continued planning my play, while on the deck there was commotion. The sail had to be furled, and the ship was rocked on the high waves. At daybreak the storm subsided, and the atmosphere cleared. Now the island of Ustica lay to our left. Someone pointed out a large turtle at some distance, and our telescopes confirmed that it was a living object. By midday we were closer to the shore. The west coast, from the foothills of Lilibeo to Capo Gallo, were clearly visible in fine weather and bright sunshine.

A school of dolphins accompanied the ship on both sides of the prow, constantly shooting ahead. It was delightful to see how, now covered by the clearly transparent waves, they would swim ahead, sometimes jumping clean out of the water with their spinal and dorsal fins, their sides glistening green and gold.

Since we were at the mercy of the wind, the captain headed straight for a bay beyond Capo Gallo. Kniep did not lose the opportunity of sketching the most various vistas in considerable detail. At sunset the captain directed the ship again to the open sea and turned northward so as to reach the latitude of Palermo. Occasionally I ventured onto the deck, but I did not leave my aims as author and I more or less envisaged the entire work. In the vague heavens was bright moonlight, and the reflection on the sea unbelievably beautiful. Painters seeking effect would have us believe that the reflection of heavenly lights in the water is widest where it is strongest, that is, closest to the viewer. But here

I saw the reflection widest at the horizon, which ended in the playful waves, tapering like a pyramid as it reached the ship. Several times during the night the captain repeated the maneuver.

Johann Wolfgang von Goethe, Italienische Reise, *vol. 1 (Project Gutenberg, <www.gutenberg.org/etext/2404>), trans. Grant Parker.*

May the Mamluks Be Cursed
Napoleon Bonaparte (1798)

Napoleon Bonaparte (1769–1821) was born in Corsica in the year that the French bought the island from the Genoese. He entered the French army as a young man and quickly rose through the ranks, being appointed general in 1793. His aim ultimately was to seize Egypt from what he calls the Mamluks, local rulers who may have been descendants of the soldier-slave dynasty that had ruled between the thirteenth and sixteenth centuries. His three-year Egyptian campaign, replete with scientists and artists, produced a twenty-two-volume encyclopedia called the *Description de l'Égypte*. The 1799 discovery of the Rosetta Stone, with its Greek translation of the hieroglyphs, gave new life to the science of Egyptology. The campaign is taken as a historical starting point for a Mediterranean era of modern colonialism that would last until the mid-twentieth century. Literary theorist Edward W. Said situates his political and cultural critique of Orientalism with "Napoleon in Egypt" and traces its persistence through present-day American military involvement in the region.

Bonaparte, member of the National Institute, General-in-Chief:

For a long time, the beys governing Egypt have insulted the French nation and its traders: the hour of their punishment has come.

For too long, this assortment of slaves bought in Georgia and the Caucasus have tyrannized the most beautiful part of the world; but God, on whom all depends, has ordained that their empire is finished.

Peoples of Egypt, you will be told that I have come to destroy your religion; do not believe it! Reply that I have come to restore your rights, to punish the usurpers, and that I respect, more than the Mamluks, God, his Prophet and the Quran.

Tell them that all men are equal before God; that wisdom, talents and virtues alone make them different from one another.

But, what wisdom, what talents, what virtues distinguish the Mamluks, that they should possess exclusively that which makes life pleasant and sweet?

Is there a good piece of land? It belongs to the Mamluks. Is there a pretty slave, a fine horse, a beautiful house? They belong to the Mamluks.

If Egypt is their farm, let them show the lease which God has granted them. But God is just and merciful to the people.

All Egyptians will be called to administer all places; the wisest, the best educated and the most virtuous will govern, and the people will be happy.

Of old, there used to exist here, in your midst, big cities, big canals, a thriving commerce. What has destroyed all this, but Mamluk avarice, injustice and tyranny?

Qadis, shaykhs, imams, çorbacis, tell the people that we are friends of the true Mussulmans.

Did we not destroy the Pope, who said that war should be waged against the Mussulmans? Did we not destroy the Knights of Malta, because those insane people thought that God wanted them to wage war against the Mussulmans? Have we not been for centuries the friends of the Grand Seigneur (may God fulfill his wishes!) and the enemies of his enemies? Have not the Mamluks, on the contrary, always revolted against the authority of the Grand Seigneur, whom they still ignore? They do nothing but satisfy their own whims.

Thrice happy are those who join us! They shall prosper in wealth and rank. Happy are those who remain neutral! They will have time to know us and they will take our side.

But unhappiness, threefold unhappiness to those who arm themselves against us! There shall be no hope for them; they shall perish.

From J. C. Hurewitz, Diplomacy in the Near and Middle East: A Documentary Record: 1535–1914 *(Princeton: Van Rostand, 1956), 63–64.*

Base Ignorance and Disbelief
'Abd al-Rahman al-Jabarti (1798)

In 'Aja'ib al-athar fi al-tarajim wa al-akhbar, his chronicle of Napoleon Bonaparte's invasion of Egypt in 1798, the historian al-Jabarti (1756–1825) records the first sighting of the French ships in Alexandria. His text provides an eyewitness account of Napoleon's

invasion and local resistance. His description of the uncouth
Frenchmen recalls Usama ibn Munqidh's bemused reaction to Franks
he met on their way to Jerusalem. He is outraged with Napoleon's
Proclamation, delivered in Arabic, in which the emperor posed as
a defender of Muslims and a liberator of the Egyptians from the
tyrannical rule of the Mamluks. Mocking the terrible Arabic, he
curses the foolish, deranged, and hypocritical Napoleon for his claim
to bring Egyptians the liberty, fraternity, and equality of the French
Revolution. This epic encounter launched an era of French and British
competition for control of the south and east of the Mediterranean,
and the spread of ideas of sovereignty, modernization, and education.

IN THE NAME OF GOD THE COMPASSIONATE THE MERCIFUL! THE YEAR 1213 (JUNE 15, 1798–JUNE 4, 1799)

This was the first year of the fierce fights and important incidents; of
the momentous mishaps and appalling afflictions of the multiplication
of malice and the acceleration of affairs; of successive sufferings and
turning times; of the inversion of the innate and the elimination of the
established; of horrors upon horrors and contradicting conditions; of
the perversion of all precepts and the onset of annihilation; of the dominance of destruction and the occurrence of occasions: "Yet thy Lord
would never destroy the cities unjustly, while as yet their people were
putting things right."

On Sunday, the 10th of Muharram of this year (June 24th, 1798), letters came by messengers from the port of Alexandria reporting that on
Thursday, the eighth, 10 English ships came to the port. They anchored
in the distance so that the people of the port could see them. Soon
another 15 ships came. The people of the port waited to see what they
wanted. Suddenly a little boat came forth from them with 10 people in
it. They landed and met with the dignitaries of the city and the governor,
who at that time wielded full power in it, Sayyid Muhammad Kurayyim,
about whom more will be said below. The latter talked with them and
asked them about their intentions. They said that they were English and
had come in search of the French, who had set sail with a powerful fleet
bound for an unknown destination: "We are not aware of their purpose;
perhaps they will attack you, and you will be unable to repel them and
incapable of stopping them." Sayyid Muhammad Kurayyim did not be-

lieve what they said. Suspecting that it was a trick, he answered them rudely. The English emissaries replied: "We shall stay on our ships at sea, guarding the harbor. We need nothing from you except provisions of water and supplies and food for which we shall pay." Their request, however, was not granted, and they were told: "This is the sultan's land. Neither the French nor anyone else has access to it. So leave us alone!" The English emissaries then went away and set sail to obtain supplies from somewhere other than Alexandria—"That God might determine a matter that was done."

Thereupon, the people of the harbor sent to the *kashif* of Buhayra (Province) to gather bedouins and come with them to guard the port. When these communications were read in Cairo, the people raised a great uproar and talked about it among themselves. There were many discussions and rumors.

Three days after the arrival of the first letters, others arrived reporting that the ships which had come to the port had left again. The people then became calm and the rumor-mongering ceased. The amirs took no interest in the entire affair and did not worry about it, rather, they relied on their strength and their belief that even if all the French came, they would not hesitate to confront them and trample them underfoot with their horses.

Wednesday, the 20th of the month (July 4, 1798), letters arrived from Alexandria, Rosetta, and Damanhur announcing that on Monday, the 18th, many French ships and vessels had come to anchor off the coast, and that they had dispatched a party to ask for the consul and some people of the city. When the latter went to them they were detained. At nightfall, some of their ships withdrew toward al-Ajami, where they landed military equipment and troops. By the time the inhabitants of the port sensed the dawn, the French were already spread over the town like locusts. At that point, the inhabitants of the port, together with the assembled bedouins who had joined them, and the *kashif* of Buhayra, came out; but they could not repel or stop the French and did not hold their ground fighting them. The *kashif* and the bedouins with him were defeated. The inhabitants returned to barricade themselves in the houses and behind the walls. The French entered the city and a great many of them spread throughout it—all this while the inhabitants took to shooting, defending themselves and their families, and putting up resistance. When, however, circumstances had thwarted all their efforts, and they realized that they were trapped in any case, and were not prepared to fight because the towers were empty of weapons and powder, and that the enemy was great in number and overpowering, the inhabitants sued for peace. The French granted them safe conduct, put an end to the fight, and made them come down from the fortifications. The French proclaimed a safe conduct and raised their flag over the town. They asked for the dignitaries of the port and the latter appeared before them and were forced to collect the weapons and surrender them. The French also made them attach the cockade on their chests over their clothes. This cockade consists of three round pieces of broadcloth, silk, or other material, the size of a *riyal*, black [*sic*], red, and white, one on top of the other, arranged so that each circle is smaller than the one below it, so that the three colors appear like circles, one surrounding the other.

When this news reached Cairo, people became troubled. Most resolved to flee and leave quickly. As for the amirs in Cairo, Ibrahim Bey rode to al-'Ayni Palace. Murad Bey came to him from Giza, where he resided. The rest of the amirs convened with the 'ulama' and the qadi and discussed this recent event. They agreed to send a letter reporting it to Istanbul, and that Murad Bey should equip the troops and go forth to join the battle with the French. With that, the meeting adjourned. They wrote the letter, and Bakr Pasha sent it with his envoy overland in order to bring "the antidote from Iraq."

They started to make preparations for the port and to provide necessities and equipment over the course of five days. They began to make exactions from the people and took most of what they needed without payment. Murad Bey set out after the Friday prayer. He pitched his tents and pavillions at al-Jisr al-Aswad, where he stayed two days until the troops and units reached full strength. With him were 'Ali Pasha and al-Tarabulusi al-Nasif Pasha, his intimate friends living with him in Giza. He took with him many guns and much gunpowder and traveled overland with the cavalry. The infantry, however, consisting of marines, and al-ildashat, Greeks, and Maghribis, traveled on the Nile on the small galleons which the aforementioned amir had constructed. Upon leaving al-Jisr al-Aswad, (Murad Bey) sent orders to Cairo to forge an iron chain of the utmost thickness and strength, 130 cubit in length, such that it would fit across the straits at Burj Mughayzil from one bank of the river to the other to prevent the French Pasha to construct a bridge of ships there and to position barricades and guns on them. It was assumed that the French would be unable to fight the mamluks on land and would move with ships to engage them in a naval battle, but that the latter would persevere and outlast them in the battle until reinforcements were brought in.

The facts, however, were otherwise. Having taken possession of   245

Alexandria, the French marched along the western bank without encountering resistance.

While Murad Bey moved out with all commotion, gloom settled over the markets. Confusion and rumors spread among the people; the roads were cut off, bandits began to reach the outskirts of the city every night. Pedestrians ceased passing through the roads and markets after dusk. The agha and the *wali*, therefore, ordered the markets and coffeehouses to be opened at night and the houses and shops to be lit with lamps. There were two reasons for this: first, dispelling the mood of gloom and creating an atmosphere of confidences second; fearing infiltrators in the city.

On Monday news arrived that the French had reached Damanhur and Rosetta. The majority of the people of these cities departed on their own and went to Fuwwa and its districts. Some sued for peace and stayed in their city—those were the judicious ones.

When the French took over Alexandria, they drew up a declaration, printed it, and sent copies of it to each city toward which they were advancing, reassuring the people. This text arrived with a group of captives whom the French had picked up in Malta and who had come with them. A few of them reached Bulaq a day or two before the arrival of the French, and they had a number of copies with them. Some of them were Maghribis; among them were spies. In their appearance they were infidels from Malta familiar with several languages. The text reads:

> "In the name of God, the Merciful, the Compassionate. There is no God but God. He has no son and no companion in his sovereignty. On behalf of France, which was built on the foundations of freedom and equality—the commander in chief of the French armies, Bonaparte, informs the inhabitants of Egypt that the *sancaks*, who hold sway over the land of Egypt, have for a long time treated the rights of the French nation with disgrace and contempt. They have oppressed her merchants with all sorts of injury and offense. Now, the hour of their punishment has come. How sad that for centuries this band of mamluks, procured from Georgia and Circassia, has spread corruption in a most beautiful country, one whose equal is not to be found on the whole globe. However, the Lord of this world and the hereafter, the Almighty, has already decreed the end of their rule. Egyptians! They may tell you I came here solely to abolish your religion, but this is a patent lie: do not believe it. Tell these slanderers that I came to you only to restore your rights from the hand of the oppressors, and that I

am more of a servant of God—may He be praised and exulted—
than the mamluks, and that I venerate His Prophet and the great
Koran. Tell them also that all men are equal before God, and that
what differentiates them from each other is intellect, virtues,
and knowledge alone. But the mamluks are the very opposite of
intellect and virtue. What distinguishes them from others that they
should deserve to rule over Egypt by themselves, and that they
should take exclusive possession of the best of everything: beautiful
slave girls, noble horses, and delightful residences? If Egypt is the
monopoly of the mamluks, let them show us the authorization that
God wrote out for them. But the Lord of the universe is merciful,
just, and compassionate. With His sublime help, henceforth no
inhabitant of Egypt shall despair of obtaining high offices and
achieving exalted stations; for the learned, the virtuous, and the
intelligent among them will direct affairs, and thus the welfare
of the whole nation will be improved. Previously there were in
Egypt great cities, wide canals, and extensive commerce. Only the
oppression and the greed of the mamluks put an end to all this.
Shaykhs, *qadis*, *imams*, *çorbacis*, and notables of the land! Tell your
nation that the French, too, are sincere Muslims: proof of it is
that they descended upon the great Rome and destroyed the Papal
See which had always urged the Christians to fight Islam. Then
they turned to Malta and expelled the Knights, who claimed that
God—may He be exalted—demanded that they fight the Muslims.
Furthermore, the French have always been sincere friends of his
Majesty the Ottoman sultan and enemies of his enemies—may
God perpetuate his rule! But the mamluks have refused to obey
the sultan, never complying with his orders. They have obeyed, in
fact, only their own greed. How blessed are those Egyptians who
agree with us without delay! Their situation will improve and their
position will rise. Blessed also are those who stay in their houses
without leaning toward either of the two warring factions. If they
knew us better, they would hasten toward us wholeheartedly. But,
woe unto those who rely on the mamluks to fight us. Afterwards
they shall not find a way to salvation, and no trace will remain of
them.

All villages which lie within three hours' distance of the
positions along which the French army passes are obliged to send
to the commander in chief representatives in order that he may
know that they are obedient and have raised the French flag, which
is white, blue, and red.

All villages resisting the French army will be burned.

All villages obeying the French are also to raise the standard of the Ottoman sultan, our friend—long may he live!

The shaykhs in each town are to seal off immediately all wealth, houses, and properties belonging to the mamluks. They must make a full effort so that not the least item is lost.

It is a duty of the shaykhs, the *'ulama'*, the *qadis*, and the *imams* to remain in their functions. Each inhabitant of the country must remain calmly in his house. Likewise, the prayers in the mosques shall be held as usual. It behooves the Egyptians altogether to thank God—may he be praised and exulted—for the termination of mamluk rule, saying aloud: May God perpetuate the glory of the Ottoman sultan. May God perpetuate the glory of the French army. May he curse the mamluks and improve the condition of the Egyptian nation."

Written at the camp of Alexandria, on the 13th of Messidor, in the sixth year of the establishment of the French Republic, i.e. at the end of Muharram, 1213 A.H. (middle of July, 1798) (A word for word copy)

Here is an explanation of the incoherent words and vulgar constructions which he put into this miserable letter:

His statement: "In the name of God, the Merciful, the Compassionate. There is no God but God. He has no son, nor has He an associate in His Dominion." In mentioning these three sentences there is an indication the French agree with the three religions, but at the same time they do not agree with them, nor with any religion. They are consistent with the Muslims in stating the formula "In the name of God," in denying that He has a son or an associate. They disagree with the Muslims in not mentioning the two Articles of Faith, in rejecting the mission of Muhammad, and the legal words and deeds which are necessarily recognized by religion. They agree with the Christians in most of their words and deeds, but disagree with them by not mentioning the Trinity, and denying the mission and furthermore in rejecting their beliefs, killing the priests, and destroying the churches. They agree with the Jews on the unity of God, which the Jews do not call trinity. Yet they clearly disagree with them on their religion. What becomes clear from their principles is that they are not interested in religion and do not agree upon the community. Each of them follows a religion which he contrives by the improvement of his mind. There are also those among them who continue to adhere to their Christian faith, hiding it. Among them is also a group of true Jews. But each person of faith comes to insist on it, corresponding to the public in their error upon which they insist.

[. . .]

His saying *qad hattama* etc. ("has decreed") shows that they are appointing themselves controllers of God's secrets, but there is no disgrace worse than disbelief. Saying "I have not come to you except for the purpose of restoring your rights from the hands of the oppressors," is the first lie he uttered and a falsehood which he invented. Then he proceeds to something even worse than that, may God cast him into perdition, with his words: "I more than the Mamluks serve God . . ." There is no doubt that this is a derangement of his mind, and an excess of foolishness. Whatever worship he is speaking about, however great its intensity, disbelief had dulled his heart, and prevented him from reaching the way of salvation. There is inversion in the words which should read *innani a'budu Allah akthar min al-mamalik* ("I serve God more than the mamluks do"). However, it is possible that there is no inversion, and that the meaning is "I have more troops than the mamluks," and that the accusative of specification has been omitted. So his words "I serve God" are a new sentence and a new lie.

His statement "(I) revere His Prophet" is conjoined to what goes before, as one lie joined to another, because if he respected him he would believe in him, accept his truth, and respect his nation. His statement al-Qur'an al-'azim ("the glorious Koran") is joined to "His Prophet," that is, "I respect the glorious Koran," and this too is a lie, because to respect the Koran means to glorify it, and one glorifies it by believing in what it contains. The Koran is one of the miracles of the Prophet which proves his truth, and that he is the Prophet to the end of time, and that his nation is the most noble of all nations. These people deny all that and lie in every thing they enumerate. "How many a sign there is in heavens and in earth that they pass by, turning away from it." But the palpable glorification is ordained as is stated in His sublime saying "None but the purified shall touch." It is forbidden for the defecating and impure to touch the verses of the Koran. But those people have often been witnessed to defecate and to wipe themselves with sheets from books and to throw them soiled on the way and into filthy places. They never wash with water. High and low use whatever paper they find. Somebody went to one of their houses and found the door of the toilet supported by a big book. He took it and opening it he found it to be an authorized recitation of the Koran. He was seized by shock and demanded to ransom it for money from the owner of the house. He refused to sell it but for a certain sum. The visitor negotiated until he satisfied his mind and rescued the recitation. During all this the people laughed and considered the man to be a fool. Where is—may God help you—the honor which this slanderer claims.

[. . .]

His statement *fa 'l-yuwarruna* ("let them then produce"), this is a colloquial word which is not in accordance with Arabic style. His saying "the title-deed, which God conferred upon them": this is base ignorance and disbelief, because God does not give men possession of anything by writing a title-deed. What he means is that the people pass the country from hand to hand from their masters as these mamluks did, or from their masters' successors, or by conquest and compulsion.

[. . .]

As for his statement "and destroyed there the Papal See," by this deed they have gone against the Christians as has already been pointed out. So those people are opposed to both Christians and Muslims, and do not hold fast to any religion. You see that they are materialists, who deny all God's attributes, the Hereafter and resurrection, and who reject prophethood and messengership. They believe that the world was not created, and that the heavenly bodies and the occurrences of the Universe are influenced by the movement of the stars, and that nations appear and states decline, according to the nature of the conjunctions and the aspects to the moon. Some believe in transmigration of souls, or other fantasies, nonsense and erroneous belief like that.

The creed they follow is to make human reason supreme and what people will approve in accord with their whims. They do not care whether they uncover their private parts, though it is repulsive to reason and tradition. If anyone feels a call of nature he does it wherever he happens to be—even in full view of people. Then he goes away as he is, without washing or embarrassment. Sometimes wiping the spot with whatever he finds—even paper with writing on it. They have intercourse with any woman who pleases them. They shave both their beard and mustache. Some of them leave hair on their cheeks only. They do not shave their head or pubic hair. They mix their foods and drinks. They never take their shoes off and settle with them on precious carpets. They blow their noses and spit on the carpets and wipe their feet on them.

[. . .]

May God hurry misfortune and punishment upon them, may He strike their tongues with dumbness, may He scatter their hosts, and disperse them, confound their intelligence, and cause their breath to cease. He was the power to do that, and it is up to Him to answer.

On Thursday, the 28th of the month (July 12th, 1798) news arrived that the French had reached the area of Fuwwa and then al-Rahmaniya.

The month of Safar 1213 began.

(JULY 15TH–AUGUST 12TH, 1798)

On Sunday, the first of Safar, news arrived that on Friday, the 29th of Muharram, the Egyptian army had encountered the French. Barely an hour had passed before Murad Bey and those with him were defeated. There occurred not even a real battle, but rather a skirmish between the vanguard of the two armies so that only a few on either side were killed. Murad Bey's ships, with the ammunition and weapons on them, burned and with them the commander of the artillery, Khalil al-Kurdli, was also burned. He had fought a remarkable battle on the river. It was God's will that the sails went up in flames and the fire jumped from them onto the gunpowder and everything broke into flames. The ship burned, with all the soldiers and their commander on it, and they were blown into the air. When Murad Bey saw this sight, he was terrified and turned back defeated. He left the baggage and the guns behind and his troops followed him. The infantry embarked on the ships trying to return to Cairo.

'Abd al-Rahman al-Jabarti, History of Egypt, *3 vols., trans. and ed. Thomas Philipp and Moshe Perlmann (Stuttgart: Franz Steiner, 1994), 2:1–9. Reprinted by permission of the publisher.*

Epic Encounters

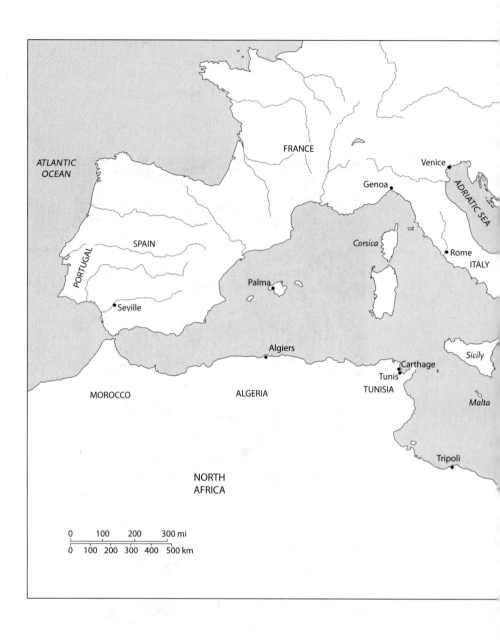

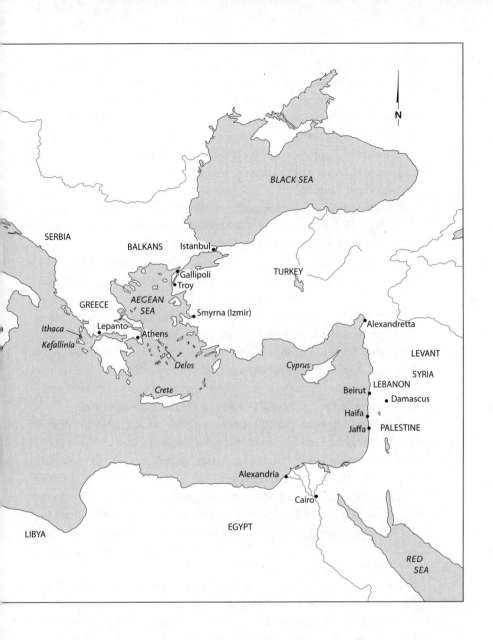

"Grand Tours" instigated struggles over Mediterranean land, history, and identity. In the nineteenth century, modern colonial projects gave rise to struggles between tradition and modernity, colonizer and colonized, and self and other, and over the rights of women. The Egyptian chronicler al-Jabarti's withering rejoinder to Napolean that concludes Chapter 4 foreshadows epic encounters that would follow.

The Grand Tour rooted the classics in the Romantic imagination and spurred archaeological discoveries that turned myths into history. Writers from Lord Byron and Thomas Mann to Constantine Cavafy and Erich Auerbach felt impelled to cite Homer, Virgil, Aeschylus, and Aristotle in their reflections on the Mediterranean. However, their nostalgic conception of a harmonious history and civilization was at odds with the continuing violence ignited by Napoleon's invasion of Egypt. The work of these writers and artists, conflating classical allusions with crises of modernity, reveals the clash between idealism and the stark realities of the industrial-colonial age. Ethnic and religious nationalism, the disintegration of the Austro-Hungarian and Ottoman Empires at the beginning of the twentieth century, and then the rise of fascism in Europe caused dispersion of populations so massive that, ironically, the stateless refugee became not only the tragic subtext of Mediterranean nationalism but also the central figure of the modern nation-state.

Communities from the Balkans through the Levant to North Africa fought for independence from European colonial rule. Imperialist precedents set by the "Scramble for Africa" spilled over into the eastern Mediterranean, culminating in World War I and the division of the region among colonial powers. Suppressed perhaps because of its sympathy for alternatives to European hegemony or because of self-interest, the American King-Crane Commission Report articulated local desires for social justice and national autonomy and called for American protection against French and the British rivalries in this region. Nevertheless, bloody struggles between external and internal forces resulted in the remapping of the Mediterranean.

The stories of Romantics like Lord Byron, Heinrich Schliemann, and Lawrence of Arabia can be read as vestiges of the Grand Tour. Armed with a classical education, each author tried to revive a golden age in his time using evidence from the new sciences of archaeology and racial ethnography. These Romantic narratives provided models for the construction of new nations that both resisted and relied on European precedents.

From the 1830s on, due in part to colonial processes, in part to local perceptions of European scientific and technological superiority, Mediterranean citizens began to travel in unprecedented numbers. The French occupation of the city of Algiers, triggered by nothing more than the slap of a fly whisk, launched the process. While Frenchmen like the famous historian of American democracy Alexis de Tocqueville visited Algiers to observe the changes, most of those who went there were subsistence migrants from Europe's impoverished south or from overpopulated islands. The movement of peoples to the north included Algerian rebels shipped across the Sea to prisons in France, Corsica, and the French West Indies and also local elites who were beginning to study in European universities. The scientific missions from Egypt to France and England brought back reports about life in cosmopolitan Europe. By the turn of the century it was quite common for students from the eastern and southern shores of the Mediterranean to spend some time in European universities, training to become doctors, lawyers, or civil servants. Some wrote about their experiences of cultural shock and their fascination with the differences they found. All struggled to reconcile the norms and values of both cultures. Yahya Haqqi's 1940s story of an Egyptian ophthalmology student's seven years of medical study in England was upheld as a model of how to harmonize tradition and modernity, East and West, Islam and secularism.

A Mediterranean aesthetic emerged out of the encounter between locals and travelers like the poet Alphonse-Marie-Louis de Prat de Lamartine and the Orientalist Eugene Delacroix. The latter's three-day stopover in Algiers transformed his aesthetic vision and subsequently influenced impressionist and early abstract painters. He later wrote that "men and things appear to me in a new light." His iconic painting of Algerian women was echoed later by others like the French short story writer Guy de Maupassant in his ecstatic discovery of the *Thousand and One Nights* world of a Tunisian brothel. Artistic "beauty" in the guise of the forbidden and exotic was the hallmark of Orientalism.

While Orientalists were depicting southern and eastern Mediterranean women as odalisques languishing in harems, the women themselves were becoming politicized. In the 1920s feminist activists like the Turkish Halide Edip and the Egyptian Huda Shaarawi demanded attention to women's rights. Shaarawi's public removal of her veil after returning from an international conference in Rome has become an emblem of Muslim women's liberation.

In the modern era, with the rise of alternative histories, the notions of time and space were fragmented so that master narratives, like colo-

nialism and the Enlightenment, began to lose their hold. Outsider attempts to understand the local situation caused by the establishment
of new national borders revealed not only how great was the suffering
but also how determined was the resistance. By the time Americans like
Hemingway and the King-Crane Commission had arrived on the scene,
the romance of nationalism revealed its costs: mass exile and death.

Epic encounters recast local history as universal histories. Biblical,
crusader, and imperial myths were nationalized and used to justify new
conquests and ideas. Christian communities in the Balkans expelling
their Muslim and Jewish compatriots in the early twentieth century
echoed the Spanish Inquisition in the fifteenth. The battles at Gallipoli
(1915), near the shores of Troy, reenacted the Trojan War. Mussolini, on
coming to power, announced the recreation of the Roman Empire; at
the same time, the Greek *megali idea* envisaged the resurrection of the
Byzantine Empire with its capital in Istanbul/Constantinople. Zionists
mapped the new Israeli state onto the Old Testament. In each case,
new nation-states derived their legitimacy from religious and mytho-
historical precedents.

Archaeology bolstered the new rulers' bombast; excavations produced evidence for the epic foundations of Western civilization. Objects
in newly established museums throughout the region provided arguments for various contested identities. Heinrich Schliemann, seduced
by the challenge of proving the reality of ancient epics through excavation, claimed he had laid open Homeric Troy and "proved the *Iliad* to be
based upon real facts." Greatly influenced by Schliemann's discovery of
Troy, Freud described the modern psyche with reference to the eternal
city of Rome, where "nothing that has once come into existence will
have passed away." From legends and epics to the Torah, the Bible, and
the Qur'an, from philosophy to literature to travelogue, the cycle of
"exile and return" caused by the epic encounters of the late nineteenth
and early twentieth centuries defined modern identities.

The end of direct European colonialism began with World War II,
even though European influence in the region was to persist for the
rest of the century. During the early 1940s, the British and the French
sent forces to their Mediterranean colonies to fight on one of the major
fronts. Their military ships sometimes passed others ferrying thousands
of Jewish refugees out of the hecatomb of fascist Europe to the eastern
Mediterranean. Some, like the American journalist I. F. Stone, were
bound for Haifa in Palestine, while others, like the German scholar
Erich Auerbach were headed to Turkey. The utter misery of those jour-

neys was mitigated only by the horrified memory of Hitler's Holocaust, which each had been lucky enough to escape.

Where Sappho Loved
Lord Byron (1819)

One of the first modern Romantic tourists in the Mediterranean was Lord Byron (1788–1824). In 1823, while living in Genoa with one of his many mistresses, the Countess Guiccioli, Byron became bored with his quiet existence. News of the Greek revolt that had aroused public sympathy and financial support in Europe reached him, and when representatives of the Greek independence movement requested his backing, he immediately threw his reputation and wealth into the cause. In July of 1823 Byron went to Kefallinía in the Ionian Islands, where he joined Prince Mavrokordatos, leader of the rebels. Byron had composed his poem "The Isles of Greece" celebrating Greek independence in 1819, presaging the outbreak of the rebellion. Among its many classical allusions, the reference to the "Persians' grave" alludes to the Persian Wars. The military plan of attack worked out by Lord Byron and the Greek rebels included besieging the Turkish fortress of Lepanto, situated at the entry to the Gulf of Corinth. However, before the plan could be executed, Byron fell ill and died in 1824. His memory would long live on among writers and artists as the Byronic hero.

THE isles of Greece! the isles of Greece
    Where burning Sappho loved and sung,
Where grew the arts of war and peace,
    Where Delos rose, and Phoebus sprung!
Eternal summer gilds them yet,
· But all, except their sun, is set.

The Scian and the Teian muse,
    The hero's harp, the lover's lute,
Have found the fame your shores refuse:
    · Their place of birth alone is mute
To sounds which echo further west
Than your sires' "Islands of the Blest."

The mountains look on Marathon—
    And Marathon looks on the sea;

And musing there an hour alone,
    I dream'd that Greece might still be free;
For standing on the Persians' grave,
I could not deem myself a slave.

A king sate on the rocky brow
    Which looks o'er sea-born Salamis;
And ships, by thousands, lay below,
    And men in nations;—all were his!
He counted them at break of day—
And when the sun set, where were they?

And where are they? and where art thou,
    My country? On thy voiceless shore
The heroic lay is tuneless now—
    The heroic bosom beats no more!
And must thy lyre, so long divine,
Degenerate into hands like mine?
[. . .]
Place me on Sunium's marbled steep,
    Where nothing, save the waves and I,
May hear our mutual murmurs sweep;
    There, swan-like, let me sing and die:
A land of slaves shall ne'er be mine—
Dash down yon cup of Samian wine!

Don Juan, *vol. 1 of* The Works of Lord Byron *(Leipzig: Tauchnitz, 1842), 138–48.*

The Bejeweled Fly Whisk
Pierre Deval (1827)

After their failure in Egypt, the French turned to Algeria. In 1830, they seized religious buildings, looted homes, pillaged the state treasury, burned the state archives, and usurped much of the country's arable land. The Ottoman-Islamic city of Algiers was destroyed and replaced by European buildings and monumental spaces. Muslim cemeteries were made into roads, and the Hawwatim Mosque into a cathedral. The pretext for the French military adventure in Algiers was a crisis unleashed when Husayn Dey struck Pierre Deval, the French consul, in the face with a bejeweled fly whisk during an altercation in April of 1827. ("Dey" was the title used by Ottoman rulers of Algeria.)

The origins of the dispute lie in the Napoleonic Wars (1804–15) when the French refused to pay for Algerian grains for the revolutionary army.

THE DEVAL REPORT, APRIL 30, 1827

The privilege granted to Consuls of France in this town, of complimenting the Dey in private audience on the eve of the feats of *bayram*, led me to ask at what hour His Highness wished to receive me. The Dey sent word that he would receive me one hour after noon but that he wished to see Your Excellency's latest dispatch which the King's schooner, destined for the coral-fishing station, had brought to me. I sent an immediate reply with the Turkish dragoman of the Consulate that I had received no letter from Your Excellency on that occasion, and that I had received no other than that from His Excellency the Minister of the Navy relating to fishing. I was, however, not a little surprised at the Dey's pretension of personal knowledge about dispatches that Your Excellency has done the honor of addressing to me, and I could not imagine what end he had in mind. Nevertheless, I went to the palace at the appointed hour. The Dey asked me, as soon as I was introduced into his audience, if it were true that England had declared war on France. I told him that this was only a false rumor, arising from troubles stirred up in Portugal, in which the Government of the King in its dignity and loyalty had not wished to meddle. "Thus," said the Dey, "France grants England whatever it wishes, and nothing at all to me!" "It seems to me, Lord, that the King's Government has always granted you what it could." "Why has your Minister not replied to the letter I wrote him?" "I had the honor to bring you the reply as soon as I received it." "Why did he not reply directly? Am I a clodhopper, a man of mud, a barefoot tramp? You are a wicked man, an infidel, an idolater!" Then, rising from his seat, with the handle of his fly whisk, he gave me three violent blows about the body and told me to retire. If your Excellency does not wish to give this affair the severe and well-publicized attention that it merits, he should at least be willing to grant me permission to retire with leave.

REPORT OF THE DEY HÜSEYIN PASA, TO THE OTTOMAN GRAND VEZIR, DECEMBER 19, 1827

His Lordship, my master, my very powerful Sultan, benefactor, merciful and magnificent disperser of favors, and master of the graces, my very humble letter is the following:

Although on my humble behalf three friendly letters were written to the King of France requesting that the sums which the French owe the victorious Ocak [*garrison*] be sent to the Muslim public treasury, these letters were ignored and I have received no reply. I therefore raised the matter with the French Consul who resides in our country, in courteous terms and with a deliberately friendly attitude, stating that, if the long friendship between the government of his country and the imperial Ocak is to continue in accordance with the terms of the letters addressed to the pasas, my predecessors, and preserved in my archives, I am no less obliged by my office as delegated vezir to uphold the interests of the victorious Ocak of our master, the Padisah, fortunate, generous [*and*] powerful asylum of the world, of whom I am the servant. "Why did no reply come to my letters written and sent to your [*French*] Government?" The Consul, in stubbornness and arrogance, replied in offensive terms that "the King and state of France may not send replies to letters which you have addressed to them." He dared to blaspheme the Muslim religion and showed contempt for the honor of His Majesty, protector of the world. Unable to endure this insult, which exceeded all bearable limits, and having recourse to the courage natural only to Muslims, I hit him two or three times with light blows of the fly whisk which I held in my humble hand.

From "Reports on the Fly Whisk Incident of 1827," in The Middle East and North Africa in World Politics: A Documentary Record, *2nd ed., 2 vols., ed. J. C. Hurewitz (New Haven: Yale University Press, 1975), 1.*

From Palma to Malta
Alphonse-Marie-Louis de Prat de Lamartine (1832)

French poet, novelist, and statesman de Lamartine (1790–1869) is considered to be the first French Romantic poet and a major influence on symbolist literature. In the 1820s he was appointed to the French embassy in Rome. After the February Revolution of 1848 that overthrew the monarchy of Louis Philippe and established the Second French Republic, he briefly headed the provisional government. Among his many works are the famous *Voyages en Orient* (1838) and *Histoire de la Turquie* (1854). In this selection he recounts the early part of his journey to the Holy Land in the early 1830s.

July 20, 1832

We departed from the bay of Palma over a smooth and tranquil sea, and with a light breeze from the West, scarcely sufficient to dry up the night dews that still sparkled on the entwined branches of the mastich trees, the only verdure of these arid coasts, which already assume an African aspect. While at sea we have had a calm day, a pleasant breeze that drove us six or seven knots an hour—a beautiful evening—a starlight night—and a sea sleeping as quietly as ourselves.

July 21, 1832

We awoke at about twenty-five leagues' distance from the coast of Africa. I am reading the history of St. Louis, to bring to my recollection the circumstances attending his death on the coast of Tunis, near Cape Carthage, which we shall see this evening or to-morrow.

I was ignorant, when young, why some communities inspired me with an antipathy against them that might be called innate, while the history of others attracted and detained my attention by an unaccountable fascination. I experienced the same feelings towards those empty shadows of the past, those lifeless memorials of nations that I now experience with an irresistible impulse either in favour of, or against the features of individuals with whom I live or have intercourse. I love or abhor, in the literal acceptation of the words; at first sight, at a glance, I judge of a man or woman for ever. Reason, reflection, or even violence, which have been often tried by me, prevail nothing against these first impressions. When the metal has once taken the impress of the die, no turning of it over and over in the hand will alter it; it still retains it. Thus it is with my feelings and affections. This is peculiar to beings with whom instinct is prompt, strong, instantaneous, and inflexible. If it be asked—what is instinct? It will be found that it is the highest kind of reason; but yet innate and not inductive; reason as God forms it, not as man finds it. It strikes on the view like lightning, without the effort of the eye to search for it, and illumines every thing with its first burst of light. Sagacity in all the arts, and on the field of battle, is also this instinct, this foreknown reasoning. Genius also is instinct, and not ratiocination and labour.

[. . .]

These were my thoughts while listening to the sound of the prow, on which I was sitting, as it hissed through the waves of the African sea, and looking out continually, through the red mists in the horizon, for the first view of Cape Carthage.

The breeze abated; the sea grew calmer, and the day passed away in fruitless gazing on the cloudy coasts of Africa. In the evening a strong gale arose, the vessel rolling from one side to the other, and oppressed by the weight of the sails, which resembled the broken wings of a wounded sea fowl, shook us within its sides with a terrible noise, like that of a falling house. I passed the evening upon deck, with my arm clinging round a cable. Dusky clouds, collected like a great mountain in the deep bay of Tunis, darted out lightning and emitted claps of distant thunder. Africa appeared to me, as I always imagined it, with its coasts torn by the fires of heaven, and its scorched mountain-tops hidden by clouds. As we approached, Cape Bysertus, and afterwards Cape Carthage, broke through the obscurity, and appeared to come close to us. All the great characters that have appeared, and all the fabulous or heroic names that have resounded on that shore, came also into my memory, and recalled to my mind the poetical and historical transactions of which these places have successively been the scene. Virgil, like all poets who endeavour to outdo truth, nature, and history, has rather spoiled than embellished the character of Dido. The historical Dido, the widow of Sichaeus, faithful to the manes of her first husband, erects her funeral pile on Cape Carthage, and ascends it as a sublime and voluntary victim of a pure love, and fidelity even unto death. This has *a little more* beauty, sanctity, and pathos, than the silly amours the Roman poet has ascribed to her with his ridiculous and pious Aeneas, and her love-lorn despair, in which the reader cannot sympathize. But the "*Anna, soror,*" with the magnificent adieu and immortal imprecation that follow, will always procure Virgil's pardon [Aeneid, 4.9].

The historical annals of Carthage possess more poetry than the poetical. The heavenly death and the funeral of St. Louis,—blind Belisarius,—Marius, a savage beast himself, expiating among the fierce animals of Carthage, his crimes against Rome; the woeful day, when, like a scorpion surrounded by fire, and piercing itself with its own envenomed sting, Carthage surrounded by Scipio and Massinissa set fire herself to her buildings and riches;—the wife of Hasdrubal, shut up with her children in the temple of Jupiter, reproaching her husband for not having known how to die, and lighting with her own hand the torch which was to consume herself, her children, and all the remains of her country, in order that only the ashes might remain to the Romans;—Cato Uticensis;—the two Scipios;—Hannibal;—all these great names and events still stand on the deserted shore like erect columns before a ruined temple. Nothing appears to the eye but a naked promontory rising over a deserted sea, some cisterns, either empty or filled with their own fragments, some ruined aqueducts, piers destroyed by the waves and overflowed by the billows, and a barbarian town where even the names now mentioned are entirely unknown;—like men who live too long and become strangers in their own country. But the recollections of the past are sufficient, when they shine with so much splendour. How do I know, indeed, that I do not like them better, thus solitary and isolated amid their own ruins, than if profaned and disturbed by the noise and crowd of new generations? It is with ruins as with tombs; amidst the tumult of a great city and the filth of the streets, they grieve and afflict the sight, and are blots upon the bustle and agitation of life; but in solitude, on sea-coasts, on a desolate cape, or an inhospitable strand, two or three stones, discoloured by time and shattered by lightning, give rise to thought, reflection, musing, or tears.

The ideas of solitude, death, and the past (which is the grave of events) are necessarily connected with each other, and their agreement forms a mysterious harmony. I prefer the naked promontory of Carthage, the melancholy cape of Sunium, or the dreary pestilential strand of Paestum, as the scenes of by-gone times, than the temples, arches, and coliseums of Rome deceased, trodden under foot by Rome still living, with the indifference of familiarity, and the profanation of forgetfulness.

The same day

At ten o'clock the wind lulls; we are all able to come on deck, and running seven knots an hour, we soon find ourselves opposite the lofty, solitary island of Pantelleria, the ancient isle of Calypso, still pleasant with its African verdure and its cool refreshing valleys and streams. It was there that the emperors used to send their political prisoners condemned to exile. It appears to us only as a cone standing up out of the sea, and covered, two-thirds of its height, by a white mist flung around it by the night wind. No ship can obtain access to it; it has no ports to receive any thing by the small boats that convey the Neapolitan and Sicilian exiles, who languish there for ten years, as a punishment for having indulged in premature dreams of liberty.

Unhappy are those men who advance before their times in every thing; their times destroy them. This is the lot of us impartial and rational political men in France. France is as yet a century and a half behind *our* ideas; she is determined to have in every thing sectarian views and party men. What matters to her about patriotism and reason?—hatred, rancour, and alternate persecution, are what she in her ignorance desires. And these she will have, till, wounded by the mortal weapons that she would obstinately make use of, she falls; or else casts them far from her, to turn to the only grounds for hope of political amelioration: these are God, his law, and reason, which is his law inwardly imprinted.

July 22, 1832

The sea, at my awaking, after a stormy night, seems to be sporting with the remains of yesterday's wind; the foam still covers it, like the froth clinging to the sides of a horse wearied by a severe run, or shook from his bit as he tosses his head impatiently for a fresh start. The waves move rapidly and irregularly, but are light, small, and transparent, and the sea resembles a field of fine oats waving in the breezes of a spring morning after a tempestuous night. We see the islands of Gozzo and Malta rising beneath the mists in the horizon at six or seven leagues' distance.

The same day, arrival at Malta

As we approach Malta, the low coast seems to grow higher and more distinct, but appears barren and dull. We soon distinguish the fortifications and the bays that form the harbours; and soon, an umber of little boats, each manned by two rowers, issue out of these bays and approach the bows of our vessel. The sea runs high, and the swell sometimes throws them into the deep furrow left behind us in the sea; they seem to be swallowed up in it, but the next wave brings them up again, and they follow in our wake; and while tossed up and down by the side of the brig, they throw out ropes to us to tow us into the road. The pilots announce to us a quarantine of ten days, and conduct us to a separate harbour under the fortifications of the city of Valetta. The French consul, M. Miége, informs the governor, Sir Frederick Ponsonby, of our arrival, who assembles the board of health, and reduces our quarantine to three days. We obtain leave to take a boat, and to walk this evening along the canals that extend from the quarantine port.

It is Sunday—the scorching mid-day sun has set, at the extremity of a peaceful and narrow inlet of the bay that lies behind the prow of our ship. The sea, smooth and dazzling, shines with the metallic lustre of the untarnished surface of tin. The sky above is of an orange colour, with a tinge of pink; it becomes less brilliant as it lies higher overhead, and farther from the west, and in the east is of a pale greyish blue, resembling no longer the bright azure above the bay of Naples, or even the deep black sky over the Alps of Savoy. The colour of African skies corresponds with the fiery atmosphere and scorching heat of that land. The radiation from the naked mountains causes the sky to be dry and hot;

and the burning dust of the barren sandy deserts is raised into the air, and tarnished the vaulted firmament suspended over that continent.

Our rowers take us a few fathoms from the land. The low shore, bordered by a beach that extends a few inches above high-water mark, is covered for the length of half a mile, with a range of houses joining one another, which seem to come as near as possible to the sea, to breathe its fresh breezes, and listen to its murmurs. The following is a description of one of the houses and scenes that are seen repeated on every threshold, balcony, and terrace: and multiplying this house and scene into five or six hundred all similar, an exact representation will be obtained of a landscape unique to Europeans, if unacquainted with Seville, Cordova, or Grenada; it is a representation which should be delineated entire, and with all its details of manners, in order to call it once more to mind amidst the dull and somber uniformity of our western cities. These recollections, recalled by memory during our days and months of snow, fogs, and rain, resemble a view of a portion of the serene, blue sky, in the midst of a protracted tempest. Sunshine is to the eye what love is to the heart and faith and truth are to the soul, nor can I exist without a portion of each of these three comforts of my earthly exile. My eyes belong to the East, my heart to love, and my soul to those who bear within them a luminous instinct, a self-evident perception, that is not capable of proof, yet never deceives, and is always consolatory.

Here then is the sketch:—a sweetly serene golden light, like that radiating from the eyes and features of a young maiden, ere love hath imprinted a wrinkle on her forehead, or cast a shade over her eye,—this light spreads uniformly over sea, earth, and sky, strikes on the white and yellow stones of which the houses are built, and leaves the carvings of the cornices, the points of the gables, the balustrades of the terraces, and the sculpture of the balconies, clearly and distinctly delineated against the blue horizon, which has that aerial trembling, that irregular and vapoury vibration, which our western countries, in despair of obtaining in their own climate, have constituted a principal beauty in their productions of art. This property of the air, with the brilliant, golden-yellow colour of the stone, and great depth of outline, confers on the smallest house a magnificence and solidity that strike strongly and agreeably on the view. Every house appears, not to have been built stone after stone, with plaster and mortar; but to have been carved entire and erect in solid rock, and then placed on the earth, like a block drawn from its bosom, and lasting as the ground on which it stands. Two large and elegant pilasters occupy the angles of every front;—they rise half-way up the second story; where an elegant cornice, sculptured in shining stone, surmounts them, and serves as a base for a splendid and massive balustrade, which extends the whole length of the parapet, and surpersedes the flat, irregular, pointed, or grotesque roofs, which disgrace every style of architecture, and destroy every outline that harmonized with the horizon, in the collections of misshapen buildings that we call *cities* in Germany, England, and France. Between these pilasters, which stand out to a depth of some inches from the front, the architect marks out only three openings, one door and two windows. The door, arched, lofty, and wide, has not its threshold on the level of the street, but opens on a broad terrace outside, that advances forward on the pavement to the extent of seven or eight feet. This terrace, being surrounded by a balustrade of sculptured stone, serves as a sort of exterior apartment, as well as an entrance to the house. In describing the scene exhibited by one of these terraces, we describe them all. One or two men in white garments, having dusky features, African eyes, and long pipes in their hands, are lying carelessly on a bench, made of rushes, by the side of a door; before them, three young women, gracefully leaning over the balustrades in different gowns, which reach halfway down the leg, white corsets with capacious plaited sleeves, and their dark hair is braided and covered with a mantle made of black silk like the gown, covering the half of the figure, and the shoulder of the arm that holds it in its place;—this mantle, formed of a thin material, and blown about by the breeze, takes the form of the sail of a skiff, and in its capricious flutterings sometimes conceals, and sometimes discloses, the mysterious figure it envelopes, and which appears to disengage itself at pleasure. Some of them now gracefully raise their heads to chat with other young girls, who are leaning over a balcony above, and throwing down pomegranates and oranges;—others are conversing with young men, wearing long mustachios, black knotted hair, short narrow jackets, white trousers, and red belts. Seated on the parapet surrounding the terrace, are two young *abbés*, in black gowns and silver shoe-buckles, conversing familiarly together, and playfully handling large green fans; whilst at the bottom of the flight of steps is a fine looking mendicant monk, who, barefoot and pale, with white shaven crown, and having his body wrapped in the heavy folds of his brown cassock, stands like a statue of mendacity, placed on the threshold of some rich and fortunate man, and looks carelessly and vacantly on this scene of happiness, ease, and gaiety. On the higher story, in a wide balcony, supported by elegant Caryatides, and covered by an Indian verandah, adorned with curtains and fringes, is seen a family of English, those fortunate and invincible conquerors of modern Malta. There, some Moorish nurses, with sparkling eyes, and shining black complexions, are holding in their arms some of those beautiful British children, whose braided flaxen hair, and fair rosy skins, resist the effects of the sun at Calcutta, as well as at Corfu or Malta. To see these children under the black mantles and fiery looks of these semi-African females, is like beholding pretty, white lambs hanging at the teats of the tigresses of the desert. The terraced roof presents another scene; the English and Maltese share it between them. On one side are seen some native girls, holding a guitar under the arm, and striking a few notes of an old national air, wild as the aspect of the country; on the other is a beautiful young English lady, leaning sorrowfully on her elbow, and looking with indifference at the lively scene passing before her eyes, or turning over the pages of the immortal poets of her country.

Add to this view, the Arabian horses, ridden by the English officers, galloping with flowing hair on the sand of the beach; the Maltese carriages (a kind of chaise on two wheels, drawn by one Barbary horse,) at full gallop, followed by the driver on foot, with his loins girt by a red, long-fringed sash, and his forehead covered by the *résille*, or the reed cap hanging down to the girdle, worn by the Spanish muleteers; then the wild cries of the naked children, as they throw themselves into the sea, and swim round our boat; the songs of the Greeks and Sicilians anchored in the adjoining harbour, and answering each other in choruses from the deck of one ship to another; the monotonous twanging of the guitar, constituting a pleasant bass to all these trebles of the evening concert: and then you have a tolerable idea of the quay of the Empsida on a Sunday evening.

July 24, 1832

Free entrance obtained into the harbour of Valetta:—the governor, Sir Frederick Ponsonby, receives us at two o'clock at the Grand Master's palace. An excellent model of the English gentleman; integrity is the expression of these men's features; magnanimity, gravity, and dignity characterize the real English nobleman. We admire the palace;—its magnificent and becoming simplicity;—its massive beauty, and freedom from all tasteless decorations, within and without;—its large saloons;—long corridors;—deep coloured paintings;—wide, elegant, echoing staircase;—the armoury, two hundred feet long, containing arms of every period of the existence of the order of St. John of Jerusalem;—the library, containing 40,000 volumes, where we were received by the librarian, the Abbé Bollanti, a young Maltese ecclesiastic, exactly resembling the Romish abbes of the old school; his eye mild and piercing, his mouth thoughtful and smiling, his forehead clear and pale, his language elegant and harmonious, and his address, simple, natural, refined, and polite. We chatted together for a long time, for he is just the sort of man most proper for a long, deep, and interesting conversation. He has, like all the eminent ecclesiastics that I have met with in Italy, an air of sadness, indifference, and resignation, which speaks of the noble and dignified abdication of lost power. Educated amidst ruins, the ruins of shattered magnificence, they have thence contracted habits of melancholy and carelessness about the present. "How," said I to him, "can a man like you, bear the intellectual exile and seclusion in which you live in this deserted palace, and amidst the dust of these books?" "It is true," replied he, "that I live in sorrow and solitude; the horizon of this island is very limited; any noise I might make here by my writings would not resound very far, and the fame of other men in distant places scarcely reaches us; but my mind sees, beyond this, a more vast and unbounded horizon, to which my thoughts love to transport themselves: we have a fine sky overhead, a mild atmosphere around us, and a wide blue sea within our view; these are sufficient for the gratification of the senses: and as to the life of the spirit, that is nowhere more intense than in silence and solitude; there the soul re-ascends directly to God, the source from whence she emanated, without let or hindrance from the cares and things of the world. When St. Paul, traveling to carry the precious communication of Christianity to the Gentiles, was shipwrecked at Malta, and remained there three months, to sow the grain of mustard-seed, he murmured not at his shipwreck and exile, as they were the means of bringing to this island the early knowledge of the divine word and doctrine;—and shall I complain—I who was born on these barren rocks, if the Lord detains me here to preserve his Christian truth in hearts where so many truths are in danger of death? This life is poetical as well," added he; "and when I am at last at liberty from my classifications and catalogues, I too, may perhaps commit to writing the poetry of solitude and prayer." I left him with regret, and longing to see him again.

The church of St. John, the cathedral of the island, has all that solemnity of character, all that grandeur, dignity, and magnificence, that might be looked for in such an edifice erected in such a place. The keys of Rhodes, carried there by the knights after their defeat, hang on both sides of the altar as memorials of perpetual regrets, or of hopes still destined to be disappointed. The superb roof is painted all over by Le Calabrese, a production worthy of modern Rome's best days of art. One picture particularly strikes me in the chapel of the election; it is by Michael Angelo Caravaggio, whom the knights of that time had invited into the island to paint the roof of St. John. He undertook it, but the impatience and irritability of his fierce temper got the better of him; he was frightened at the length of time it required, and departed, leaving his masterpiece at Malta,—the Beheading of St. John. If our modern painters who hunt romantics by system, instead of finding them in nature, were to look at this magnificent picture, they would find their pretended inventions already invented. This is fruit from its native tree, not fruit moulded in wax and painted with artificial colours; picturesque attitudes, energy of expression, depth of thought, truth and majesty blended, strength of contrast and harmony united, horror and beauty mingled together; these constitute the picture. It is one of the most beautiful I ever saw in my life. It is such a picture as all the painters of the modern school are striving after. Here it is—it is found; let them seek no longer. Thus there is nothing new either in nature or art; all that is doing, has been done; all that is saying, has been said; all that is meditating, has been meditated. Every age is the copyist of a former; for all of us, whoever we are, whether artists or philosophers, being frail and transitory, copy in different styles the same immutable and eternal original—Nature, that single and diversified idea of the creative Mind.

Malta, July 28, 29, and 30, 1832

Our stay at Malta was inevitably protracted, on account of the indisposition of Julia. She has recovered, and we have determined on going to Smyrna, touching at Athens in the way. There I shall leave my wife and children, and go forward alone, across Asia Minor, to visit the other parts of the East. We weigh anchor, and are about to depart out of port, when a ship arrives from Archipelago; she brings news of the capture of several vessels by the Greek pirates, and the massacre of their crews. The French consul, M. Miége, advises us to wait a few days. Captain Lyons, of the English frigate *Madagascar*, offers to convoy us to Nauplia in the Morea, and even to take us in tow, should our brig prove to be a heavier sailer than the frigate. He has accompanied his offer with all the obliging marks of politeness that can enhance its value.

De Lamartine, Visit to the Holy Land: or, Recollections of the East, accompanied with Interesting Descriptions and Engravings of the Principal Scenes of Our Saviour's Ministry, *trans. Thomas Phipson (London: George Virtue, 1878).*

Voyage to Algeria
Alexis de Tocqueville (1841)

When political scientist Alexis de Tocqueville (1805–59) visited Algeria in 1841, he condemned French colonial methods, especially the destruction of old Algiers. Like the society he had observed in America, Algiers was in the midst of upheaval as the French rearranged everything. During the Second Empire (1852–70), Baron Georges Haussmann, mayor of Paris, embarked on an ambitious plan to restructure the city physically and socially through demolitions inspired by the example of Algiers. The modernization of Paris served as a model for similar urban renewal programs in Istanbul, Vienna, and elsewhere in Europe. So, one can see in the situation that de Tocqueville was observing here a prototype for the construction of cities in Europe over the following century.

May 7, 1841

Arrived in Algiers from the direction of Oran, having gone too far west. Cape Caxine, a very green and furrowed mountain that plunges right into the sea. The sky is hazy. The whole scene is like that one that the Hague's coastline presents from the sea. As we approach, we perceive a multitude of small white houses garnishing the mountain's furrows. As we round Cape Caxine, Algiers appears: an immense quarry of white rock sparkling in the sun.

First appearance of the town: I have never seen anything like it. Prodigious mix of races and costumes, Arab, Kabyle, Moor, Negro, Mahonais [*Balearic Islanders, from Port Mahon on Minorca*], French. Each of these races, tossed together in a space much too tight to contain them, speaks its language, wears its attire, displays different mores. This whole world moves about with an activity that seems feverish. The entire lower town seems in a state of destruction and reconstruction. On all sides, one sees nothing but recent ruins, buildings going up; one hears nothing but the noise of the hammer. It is Cincinnati transported onto the soil of Africa.

The French are substituting broad arcaded streets for the Moors' tortuous little alleys. This is a necessity of our civilization. But they are also substituting their architecture for that of the Moors, and this is wrong; for the latter is very appropriate to the needs of the country, and besides, it is charming. The most beautiful Moorish house shows, on the outside, only a wall with no opening other than an arched door. This door leads into a vestibule supported by columns. From this vestibule a staircase leads to a square courtyard surrounded by galleries, which are supported by arcades and columns. It is the same on each floor. All the rooms open onto this courtyard, whose appearance is fresher and more elegant than I can say. In all the better houses, the columns are of curiously sculpted white marble, as are the edges of the arcades, and festooned as if with lace. The whole very much presents the appearance of life turned inward. Architecture depicts needs and mores: the architecture here does not merely result from the heat of the climate, it also marvelously depicts the social and political state of the Muslim and oriental populations: polygamy, the sequestration of women, the absence of any public life, a tyrannical and suspicious government that forces one to conceal one's life and keep all affections within the family.

Saturday 8th

Visit to the environs of Algiers, at Couba. Superb road that seems as though it must lead to the provinces of a vast empire, and that one cannot follow more than three leagues without being beheaded. Delicious country, Sicily with the industry of France. Prodigious vegetation, the land dense with vegetation. A promised land, if one didn't have to farm with gun in hand. From the height of Couba we see the Metidja [*usually Mitidja*]: magnificent plain, five leagues wide and thirty long, and entire province. Looks like Alsace. Green, but not a house, not a tree, not a man. Astonishing contrast: the Sahel the image of nature cultivated by industry and the most advanced civilization; the plain: *wilderness*.

Visit the bishop's. An intelligent man, very intelligent. But a tint of charlatanism. Evening, a trip to the Casaubah [*Casbah, or Qasba*]. Old Algiers seemed an immense fox burrow: narrow, dark, smoky. The population, at this hour, seems idle and dissolute. Indigenous cabaret where Moorish public girls sing and people drink wine. Mix the vices of both civilizations. Such is the external appearance.

Alexis de Tocqueville, Writings on Empire and Slavery, *ed. and trans. Jennifer Pitts (Baltimore: Johns Hopkins University Press, 2001), 36–37. Reprinted by permission of the publisher.*

Treasures of Troy
Heinrich Schliemann (1873)

The discovery of ancient Troy at Hisarlık in Ottoman Anatolia in 1873 is commonly attributed to the German businessman-turned-archaeologist Heinrich Schliemann (1822–90). Homer's poems, which had fascinated him since childhood, were his incentive and guide. He became obsessed with the goal of proving their historical accuracy. At one point he gave his young Greek wife, Sophia, gold jewelry that he claimed was from King Priam's treasure. The sensation he created popularized the new science of archaeology, though he never escaped accusations of amateurishness and even charlatanry. Yet in his memoirs, excerpted below, he writes: "I value truth above everything, and I rejoice that my three years' excavations have laid open the Homeric Troy, even though on a diminished scale, and that I have proved the *Iliad* to be based upon real facts." But was Schliemann engaged in scientific discovery or living a delusion? Scholars, indeed, have questioned the validity of Schliemann's claim, identifying Englishman Frank Calvert (1828–1908) as the man who deserves the credit for locating Troy. Schliemann seems to have promoted Calvert's ideas as his own and reaped the fame. As for Priam's treasure, evidence suggests that it, too, was faked.

I now perceive that the cutting which I made in April 1870 was exactly at the proper point, and that if I had only continued it, I should in a few weeks have uncovered the most remarkable buildings in Troy, namely, the Palace of King Priam, the Scaean Gate, the Great Surrounding Wall, and the Great Tower of Ilium; whereas, in consequence of abandoning this cutting, I had to make colossal excavations from east to west and from north to south through the entire hill in order to find those most interesting buildings. [. . .]

But Troy was not large. I have altogether made twenty borings down to the rock, on the west, southwest, south, southeast, and east of the Pergamus, directly at its foot or at some distance from it, on the plateau of the Ilium of the Greek colony. As I find in these borings no trace either of fragments of Trojan pottery or of Trojan house-walls, and nothing but fragments of Hellenic pottery and Hellenic house-walls, and as, moreover, the hill of the Pergamus has a very steep slope towards the north, the northeast, and the northwest, facing the Hellespont, and is also very steep towards the plain, the city could not possibly have extended in any one of these directions. I now most emphatically declare that the city of Priam cannot have extended on any one side beyond the primeval plateau of this fortress, the circumference of which is indicated to the south and southwest by the Great Tower and the Scaean Gate, and to the northwest, northeast, and east by the surrounding wall of Troy. The city was so strongly fortified by nature on the north side, that the wall there consisted only of those large blocks of stone, loosely piled one upon another in the form of a wall, which last year gave me such immense trouble to remove. This wall can be recognized at once, immediately to the right in the northern entrance of my large cutting, which runs through the entire hill.

I am extremely disappointed at being obliged to give so small a plan of Troy; nay, I had wished to be able to make it a thousand times larger, but I value truth above everything, and I rejoice that my three years' excavations have laid open the Homeric Troy, even though on a diminished scale, and that I have proved the *Iliad* to be based upon real facts.

Homer is an epic poet, and not an historian: so it is quite natural that he should have exaggerated everything with poetic licence. Moreover, the events which he describes are so marvellous, that many scholars have long doubted the very existence of Troy, and have considered the city to be a mere invention of the poet's fancy. I venture to hope that the civilized world will not only be disappointed that the city of Priam has shown itself to be scarcely a twentieth part as large as was to be expected from the statements of the *Iliad*, but that, on the contrary, it will accept with delight and enthusiasm the certainty that Ilium did really exist, that a large portion of it has now been brought to light, and that Homer, even although he exaggerates, nevertheless sings of events that actually happened. Besides, it ought to be remembered that the area of Troy, now reduced to this small hill, is still as large as, or even larger than, the royal city of Athens, which was confined to the Acropolis. [. . .]

But this little Troy was immensely rich for the circumstances of those times, since I find here a treasure of gold and silver articles, such as is now scarcely to be found in an emperor's palace; and as the town was wealthy, so was it also powerful, and ruled over a large territory.

The houses of Troy were all very high and had several storeys, as is obvious from the thickness of the walls and the colossal heaps of *débris*. But even if we assume the houses to have been of three storeys, and standing close by the side of one another, the town can nevertheless not have contained more than 5,000 inhabitants, and cannot have mustered more than 500 soldiers; but it could always raise a considerable army from among its subjects, and as it was rich and powerful, it could obtain mercenaries from all quarters. [. . .]

Homer can *never* have seen Ilium's Great Tower, the surrounding wall of Poseidon and Apollo, the Scaean Gate or the Palace of King Priam, for all these monuments lay buried deep in heaps of rubbish, and he made no excavations to bring them to light. He knew of these monuments of immortal fame only from hearsay, for the tragic fate of ancient Troy was then still in fresh remembrance, and had already been for centuries in the mouth of all minstrels.

Homer rarely mentions temples, and although he speaks of the temple of Athena, yet, considering the smallness of the city, it is very doubtful whether it actually existed. [. . .]

I formerly believed that the most ancient people who inhabited this site were the Trojans [*of Homer*], because I fancied that among their ruins I had found the *depas amphikupellon* [*two-handled cup*], but I now perceive that Priam's people were the succeeding nation. [. . .]

In consequence of my former mistaken idea, that Troy was to be found on the primary soil or close above it, I unfortunately, in 1871 and 1872, destroyed a large portion of the city, for I at the time broke down all the house-walls in the higher strata which obstructed my way. This year, however, as soon as I had come by clear proofs to the firm conviction that Troy was not to be found upon the primary soil, but at a depth of from 23 to 33 feet, I ceased to break down any house-wall in these strata, so that in my excavations of this year a number of Trojan houses have been brought to light. They will still stand for centuries, and visitors to the Troad may convince themselves that the stones of the Trojan buildings can *never* have been used for building other towns, for the greater part of them are still *in situ.* Moreover, they are small, and millions of such stones are to be found upon all the fields of this district.

Valuable stones, such as those large flags which cover the road leading from the Scaean Gate to the plain, as well as the stones of the enclosing wall and of the Great Tower, have been left untouched, and not a single stone of the Scaean Gate is wanting. [. . .]

In closing the excavations at Ilium for ever, I cannot but fervently thank God for His great mercy, in that, notwithstanding the terrible danger to which we have been exposed owing to the continual hurricanes, during the last three years' gigantic excavations, no misfortune had happened, no one has been killed, and no one has ever been seriously hurt. [. . .]

In December of the same year [*1873*] the Turkish authorities of Kum-Kaleh seized many gold ornaments which two of my workmen had found in three different places in the preceding March, whilst working for me in the trenches of Hissarlik, at a depth of nearly thirty feet below the surface of the hill. Most of these jewels were contained in a vase with an owl's head. [. . .] But as the statements of the labourers differ as to the particular objects contained in each treasure, I can only describe them here conjointly. The two workmen had stolen and divided the three treasures between themselves, and probably I should never have had any knowledge of it, had it not been for the lucky circumstance that the wife of the workman of Yeni Shehr, who had got his share of the plunder, besides two more pendants, had the boldness to parade one Sunday with the earrings and pendants. This excited the envy of her companions; she was denounced to the Turkish authorities of Kum-Kaleh, who put her and her husband in prison; and, having been threatened that her husband would be hanged if they did not give up the jewels, she betrayed the hiding-place, and thus this part of the treasure was at once recovered and is now exhibited in the Imperial Museum of Constantinople. The pair also denounced their accomplice at Kalifatli, but here the authorities came too late, because he had already had his part of the spoil melted down by a goldsmith in Ben Kioi, who, at his desire, had made of it a very large, broad, and heavy necklace, with clumsy flowery ornaments in the Turkish fashion. Thus this part of the treasure is for ever lost to science [. . .] as both thieves declared separately on oath before the authorities of Kum-Kaleh that the owl-vase, with part of the gold, was found by them immediately to the west of the wall, and that the two other treasures were found close by, and indicated the exact spot of the discovery, there can be no doubt as to its accuracy. [. . .]

All these gold ornaments, both genuine and re-made, are now in the Imperial Museum at Constantinople. The genuine ones [. . .] are nearly all of the same type as those contained in the great treasure discovered by me, though similar types had never before been found elsewhere. [. . .]

This treasure of the supposed mythical king Priam, of the mythical heroic age, which I discovered at a great depth in the ruins of the supposed mythical Troy, is at all events a discovery which stands alone in archaeology, revealing great wealth, great civilization and a great taste for art, in an age preceding the discovery of bronze, when weapons and implements of pure copper were employed contemporaneously with enormous quantities of stone weapons and implements. This treasure further leaves no doubt that Homer must have actually seen gold and silver articles, such as he continually describes; it is, in every respect, of inestimable value to science, and will for centuries remain the object of careful investigation. [. . .]

From Leo Deuel, Memoirs of Heinrich Schliemann: A Documentary Portrait Drawn from his Autobiographical Writings (New York: Harper and Row, 1977), 108–12. Reprinted by permission of HarperCollins Publishers.

Exquisite Whores

Guy de Maupassant (1890)

Born in Normandy into an aristocratic family, Guy de Maupassant (1850–92) is considered the most important French short story writer of the psychological realist school. He published about 300 stories, six novels, three travel books, and a poetry anthology. He was part of the Paris literary circle that included Gustave Flaubert, Émile Zola, and Henry James. In 1880 he published his most famous story, "Boule de Suif" (Ball of Fat). The next year he went to Tunisia, where he reported on the French campaign under way in that country. In 1889 he traveled to great Tunisian sites and cities and wrote about his experiences in *La vie errante* (1890), from which the following selection is taken. His mixing of sex and religion, ugliness and beauty in this ecstatic description of a fifteen-year-old prostitute is emblematic of the Orientalist fascination of nineteenth-century Europeans with the exotic, forbidden Arab Mediterranean.

In Algiers the Arab town is full of movement at night, but as soon as the night falls in Tunis everything is dead. The small, narrow streets, winding and irregular, look like the corridors of a deserted city where no one has remembered to turn off the gas.

We have come deep into this maze of white walls to see the Jewesses performing the "belly dance." This dance is ugly and ungraceful, of interest only for the manner in which it is executed by the artist. Three sisters, all heavily adorned, were performing their indecent contortions under the protective eye of their mother, an enormous ball of fat wearing a headdress of gold paper. She went around begging for the expenses of the establishment whenever her daughters' bellies had achieved a par-oxysm of quivering. Around the room three half-open doors revealed low beds. I opened a fourth door and saw a woman who seemed very beautiful lying on a bed. Immediately, the mother, the dancers, two negro servants, and a man hidden behind a curtain all hurled them-selves upon me. I was about to enter the room of his lawful wife, the daughter-in-law, the sister-in-law of the three hussies who tried, but in vain, to mingle us in with the family, if only for one evening. That I might forgive them for not allowing me to go in they showed me the woman's first child, a little girl of three or four years who could already give a sketchy performance of the belly dance.

I left extremely disgusted.

I was now taken with great precaution to the house of some famous

Arab courtesans. We had to look around carefully at the end of the streets, enter into long discussions and even make threats for, if the natives discovered that a Christian had entered, the women would be abandoned, disgraced, and ruined. Once inside I saw some dark, stout girls of mediocre beauty, in hovels full of mirror wardrobes.

We were thinking of returning to the hotel when the native policeman offered, quite openly, to take us to a brothel, a place of sex, which he would get us into by using his authority.

Once again we are following him, groping about in the unforgettable, dark, narrow streets, lighting matches to see our way but still stumbling into holes, banging our hands and shoulders against houses. Sometimes we hear muffled voices, strains of music, the murmurs of wild festivities coming through the walls as from far away, a terrifying feeling of deadened sound and mystery. We are right in the middle of the area of debauchery.

We stop in front of a door and conceal ourselves on all sides while the police officer bangs on the door with his fists, shouting an order in Arabic.

From behind the door a frail, old voice replies, and now we notice the sound of instruments and the high-pitched singing of Arab women coming from the depths within.

They don't want to open and the officer becomes angry and shouts out some raucous, violent words. Finally the door is half-opened, the man pushes it and marches in like a conqueror gesturing us to follow.

We follow him down three steps leading into a low room where four Arab children belonging to the house are sleeping on carpets along the walls. An old woman—one of these old native women who look like a bundle of rags tied around something that moves, with an unbelievable head sticking out from the top, tattooed like a witch—tries to stop us going any further. But the door has been closed, so we go on into the first room where some men who have not been able to get into the second one are standing blocking the entrance and listening with a rapt air to the strange, shrill music being played inside. The officer makes his way on into the first room, pushes aside the regular clients and leads us into a long, narrow room where piles of Arabs are crouching on benches along the white walls to the far end.

There, on a large French bed as wide as the room, a pyramid of more Arabs rises up in tiers, amazingly piled up and jumbled together, a heap of burnouses with five turbanned heads sticking up.

In front of them, at the foot of the bed on a bench facing us, and behind a mahogany pedestal table covered with glasses, bottles of beer, coffee cups and small pewter spoons, four women are sitting singing an interminable and drawling song from the south, accompanied by some Jewish musicians.

They are decked out in fairy-tale costumes, like the princesses in the *Thousand and One Nights*, and one of them aged about fifteen is of a beauty so surprising, so perfect, so rare, that she illuminates the strange place transforming it into something unexpected, symbolic and quite unforgettable.

Her hair is held back by a golden scarf which cuts across the forehead from one temple to the other. Underneath this straight, metallic stripe two enormous eyes open in a fixed stare, indifferent, incomparable — two elongated black eyes, somehow distant, separated by a nose like that of an idol, dropping to a small child-like mouth which opens to sing and seems to be the only part of the face that is alive. It is a face without expression, quite unexpectedly regular, primitive and superb, composed of lines so simple that they seemed to be the natural and unique forms of this human face.

Consider any face and I am sure that you could replace one feature, one detail by something taken from another person. There is nothing you could change on the head of this Arab woman since the design is quite perfect and true to type. This smooth forehead, this nose, these cheeks so delicately moulded, ending in the fine point of the chin, the only nose and the only mouth that could possibly be there. This is the ideal of a conception of absolute beauty which delights our eyes — and it is only in our dreams that we could feel less than completely satisfied.

Beside her is another girl, also charming but not exceptional, with one of those white, sweet faces that seem to have been made from milk pastry. On either side of these two stars two other women are sitting. They are of the bestial type, with short heads and prominent cheekbones, prostitutes from the nomadic people, lost souls whom the tribes discard along the wayside, gather up again only to lose once more, then finally one day they leave them trailing behind a group of soldiers who take them to town.

They are singing and tapping on the darbouka with their henna-coloured hands, and some Jewish musicians accompany them on small guitars, tambourines and flutes.

There is no talking, no laughter, everyone listens with an air of majestic seriousness.

Where are we? In a temple of some barbaric religion, or in a brothel?

A brothel? Yes indeed we are in a brothel, and never before have I experienced a sensation so unexpected, so new, so full of colour, as I did when I came into this long low room where these girls, decked out as though for a sacred cult, waiting for the whim of one of these grave men who seem to be murmuring the Koran in the middle of the debauchery.

One of these men is pointed out to me, sitting with a miniscule cup of coffee in front of him, his eyes lifted up in a state of meditation. It is he who has engaged the idol, and nearly all the others are his guests. He offers them refreshments and music, and the chance to look at this beautiful girl until such time as he asks them to go home. And then they will go, greeting him with majestic gestures. He is handsome this man of taste, young, tall, with the transparent complexion of the Arab of the town, enhanced by a silky, glossy, black beard and sparse hair on his cheeks. [. . .]

Nobody talked to the women, who sat as still as statues, and I began to chat to my two Algerian neighbours with the help of the native policemen.

I learned that they were shepherds and landowners from near Bougie, and that in the folds of their burnous they carried a flute from the country to play in the evenings and amuse themselves. Of course they wanted someone to admire their talent and showed me two thin reeds with holes in them, genuine reeds which they had cut from the edge of a river.

I begged that they be allowed to play and everyone immediately stopped talking with a perfect politeness.

Oh, the astonishing and delicious sensation which stole into my heart with those first notes—so light, so strange, so unknown, so unexpected, the two small voices of these two little tubes which had grown in the water. It was so delicate, so sweet, disconnected and jerky; the sounds flew up, fluttered around in the air one after the other, but never caught up with each other, never found each other, never came together. It was a song that constantly faded away, then started up again, weaving its way and floating around us like a breath of the spirit of the leaves, the spirit of the woods, the spirit of the rivers and the wind which these two shepherds from the Kabyle mountains had brought with them into this brothel in the suburbs of Tunis.

From Veiled Half-Truths: Western Travelers' Perceptions of Middle Eastern Women, *ed. Judy Mabro (London: I. B. Tauris, 1991), 236–40. Reprinted by permission of the publisher.*

Pray for a Long Journey
Constantine Cavafy (1911)

A member of the Greek community of Alexandria, Egypt, Constantine Cavafy (1863–1933) elaborated a pagan Greco-Roman vision of the Mediterranean through his poetry. The following poems reflect on the meanings of travel across time and space. Narratives of the ancient and the modern meet in his work to deepen themes of exile and community. In terms of imperial conquest, nationalism, and identity, the violent return of ancient history is an ironic trope of the twentieth century. Poems such as "Ithaca" and "To the Harbor" convey the pathos of exile while valorizing the journey and questioning the finality and closure of return.

ITHACA

When you set out on the ship for Ithaca
Pray for a long journey
Rich in adventures, full of experience.
Do not fear the Cyclops or Lastrygonians
Or the anger of Poseidon
You will not find such dangers on your way
If your thoughts stay high
And high feeling moves your body and soul
You will not meet the Lastrygonians or the Cyclops
Nor fierce Poseidon
Unless you transport them within your soul,
Unless your soul sets them in your path

Pray for a long journey
For many a summer's morning
When—with what pleasure and joy—
You will enter ports you have never seen before
Pray to stop at the markets of the Phoenicians
And acquire the lovely things they sell,
Nacre, coral, amber, ebony,
And fragrant spices and perfumes of every kind
And buy perfume, as many as you can
Pray to visit the cities of Egypt,
To gain knowledge there, and learn from the wise.

Keep Ithaca forever before you in your mind,
And let your goal be your arrival there,
But by no means hurry on in your journey there.
Better that it stretch over many years,
That you drop anchor there an older man,
Wealthy from all you have gained on the way,
With no hope that Ithaca will give you wealth.

Ithaca gave you your good voyage;
Without her you would not have set out.
There is nothing more she can give you.

And if you find her poor, Ithaca has not cheated you.
As wise as you have become with all of your experience,
You will have already understood
The meaning of islands like Ithaca.

Trans. Diskin Clay, "The Poetry of Greece," The Charioteer: A Review of Modern Greek Culture *39, no. 40 (2000–2002): 98–99.*

TO THE HARBOR

Young, aged twenty-eight, Emis
reached this Syrian port on a ship from Tenos.
He wanted to master the incense trade.
Yet he fell sick at sea
and, as soon as he disembarked, he died.
His is a pauper's grave. He is buried here.
A few hours before he died he whispered
something about "a home" and "aged parents."
But no one knows who these parents are
or where his country is in this vast Greek world.
So much the better. He is buried in this port
and his parents can hope that he is still alive.

Trans. Diskin Clay

The Corrupting Sea

Thomas Mann (1911)

The modernist novella *Death in Venice* by Thomas Mann (1875–1955) reveals how the sea transforms and sensualizes. Mann's protagonist, the writer Aschenbach, visiting Venice from Munich, is consumed by passion for Tadzio. Tadzio is a beautiful boy who is described in the excerpt below in mythical terms and compared to Greek sculpture, to the god of love, to Hyacinth and Narcissus, and to Plato's character Phaedrus. Aschenbach's trip across the lagoon into the canal city of Venice is portrayed in terms that suggest the legendary journey across the River Styx into the underworld. The protagonist's death at the end of the work is both literal and figurative, revealing the consuming power and passion of the sea to corrupt the reason and routine of the modern world.

Who would not have to suppress a fleeting shudder, a vague timidity and uneasiness, if it were a matter of boarding a Venetian gondola for the first time or after several years? The strange craft, an entirely un-altered survival from the times of balladry, with that peculiar blackness which is found elsewhere only in coffins—it suggests silent, criminal adventures in the rippling night, it suggests even more strongly death itself, the bier and the mournful funeral, and the last silent journey. And has it been observed that the seat of such a barque, this arm-chair of coffin-black veneer and dull black upholstery, is the softest most luxu-riant, most lulling seat in the world? Aschenbach noted this when he had relaxed at the feet of the gondolier, opposite his luggage, which lay neatly assembled on the prow. The rowers were still wrangling, harshly, incomprehensibly, with threatening gestures. But the strange silence of this canal city seemed to soften their voices, to disembody them, and dissipate them over the water. It was warm here in the harbour. Touched faintly by the warm breeze of the sirocco, leaning back against the limber portions of the cushions, the traveler closed his eyes in the enjoyment of a lassitude which was as unusual with him as it was sweet. The trip would be short, he thought; if only it went on for ever! He felt himself glide with a gentle motion away from the crowd and the con-fusion of voices.

[. . .]

So they arrived, tossed in the wake of a steamer plying towards the city. Two municipal officers, their hands behind their backs, their faces turned in the direction of the lagoon, were walking back and forth on the bank. Aschenbach left the gondola at the dock, supported by that old man who is stationed with his grappling-hook at each one of Venice's landing places. And since he had no small money, he crossed over to the hotel by the steamer wharf to get change and pay the rower what was due him. He got what he wanted in the lobby, he returned and found his traveling-bags in a cart on the dock, and gondola and gondolier had vanished.

"He got out in a hurry," said the old man with the grappling-hook. "A bad man, a man without a licence, sir. He is the only gondolier who doesn't have a licence. The others telephoned here."

Aschenbach shrugged his shoulders.

"The gentleman rode for nothing," the old man said, and held out his hat. Aschenbach tossed in a coin. He gave instructions to have his luggage taken to the beach hotel, and followed the cart through the avenue, the white-blossomed avenue which, lined on both sides with taverns, shops, and boarding-houses, runs across the island to the shore.

He entered the spacious hotel from the rear, by the terrace garden, and passed through the vestibule and the lobby until he reached the desk. Since he had been announced, he was received with obliging promptness. A manager, a small, frail, flatteringly polite man with a blank moustache and a French style frock-coat, accompanied him to the third floor in the lift, and showed him his room, an agreeable place furnished in cherry wood. It was decorated with strong-smelling flowers, and its high windows afforded a view out across the open sea. He stepped up to one of them after the employee had left; and while his luggage was being brought up and placed in the room behind him, he looked down on the beach (it was comparatively deserted in the afternoon) and on the sunless ocean which was at floodtide and was sending long low waves against the bank in a calm regular rhythm.

The experiences of a man who lives alone and in silence are both vaguer and more penetrating than those of people in society; his thoughts are heavier, more odd, and touched always with melancholy. Images and observations which could easily be disposed of by a glance, a smile, an exchange of opinion, will occupy him unbearably, sink deep into the silence, become full of meaning, become life, adventure, emotion. Loneliness ripens the eccentric, the daringly and estrangingly beautiful, the poetic. But loneliness also ripens the perverse, the disproportionate, the absurd, and the illicit. — So, the things he had met with on the trip, the ugly fop with his twaddle about sweethearts, the lawbreaking gondolier who was cheated of his pay, still left the traveler uneasy. Without really providing any resistance to the mind, without offering any solid stuff to think over, they were nevertheless profoundly strange, as it seemed to him, and disturbing precisely because of this contradiction. In the meanwhile, he greeted the sea with his eyes, and felt pleasure at the knowledge that Venice was so conveniently near. Finally he turned away, bathed his face, left orders to the chambermaid for a few things he still needed done to make his comfort complete, and let himself be taken to the ground floor by the green-uniformed Swiss who operated the lift.

He took his tea on the terrace facing the ocean, then descended and followed the boardwalk for quite a way in the direction of the Hotel Excelsior. When he returned it seemed time to dress for dinner. He did this with his usual care and slowness, since he was accustomed to working over his toilet. And yet he came down a little early to the lobby, where he found a great many of the hotel guests assembled, mixing distantly and with a show of mutual indifference to one another, but all waiting for meal-time. He took a paper from the table, dropped into a leather chair, and observed the company; they differed agreeably from the guests where he had first stopped.

A wide and tolerantly inclusive horizon was spread out before him. Sounds of all the principal languages formed a subdued murmur. The accepted evening dress, a uniform of good manners, brought all human varieties into a fitting unity. There were Americans with their long wry features, large Russian families, English ladies, German children with French nurses. The Slavic element seemed to predominate. Polish was being spoken near by.

It was a group of children gathered around a little wicker table, under the protection of a teacher or governess: three young girls, apparently fifteen to seventeen, and a long-haired boy about fourteen years old. With astonishment Aschenbach noted that the boy was absolutely beautiful. His face, pale and reserved, framed with honey-coloured hair, the straight sloping nose, the lovely mouth, the expression of sweet and godlike seriousness, recalled Greek sculpture of the noblest period; and the complete purity of the forms was accompanied by such a rare personal charm that, as he watched, he felt that he had never met with anything equally felicitous in nature or the plastic arts. He was further struck by the obviously intentional contrast with the principles of upbringing which showed in the sisters' attire and bearing. The three girls, the eldest of whom could be considered grown up, were dressed with a chasteness and severity bordering on disfigurement. Uniformly cloister-like costumes, of medium length, slate-coloured, sober, and deliberately unbecoming in cut, with white turned-down collars as the only relief, suppressed every possible appeal of shapeliness. Their hair, brushed down flat and tight against the head, gave their faces a nun-like emptiness and lack of character. Surely this was a mother's influence, and it had not even occurred to her to apply the pedagogical strictness to the boy which she seemed to find necessary for the girls.

286

It was clear that in his existence the first factors were gentleness and tenderness. The shears had been resolutely kept from his beautiful hair; like a Prince Charming's, it fell in curls over his forehead, his ears, and still deeper, across his neck. The English sailor suit, with its braids, stitchings, and embroideries, its puffy sleeves narrowing at the ends and fitting snugly about the fine wrists of his still childish but slender hands, gave the delicate figure something rich and luxurious. He was sitting, half profile to the observer, one foot in its black patent-leather shoe placed before the other, an elbow resting on the arm of his wicker chair, a cheek pressed against his first, in a position of negligent good manners, entirely free of the almost subservient stiffness to which his sisters seemed accustomed. Did he have some illness? For his skin stood out as white as ivory against the golden darkness of the surrounding curls. Or was he simply a pampered favourite child, made this way by a doting and moody love? Aschenbach inclined to believe the latter. Almost every artist is born with a rich and treacherous tendency to recognize injustices which have created beauty, and to meet aristocratic distinction with sympathy and reverence.

A waiter passed through and announced in English that the meal was ready. Gradually the guests disappeared through the glass door into the dining-hall. Stragglers crossed, coming from the entrance, or the lifts. Inside, they had already begun serving, but the young Poles were still waiting around the little wicker table; and Aschenbach, comfortably propped in his deep chair, and with this beauty before his eyes, stayed with them.

[. . .]

The weather did not improve any the following day. A land breeze was blowing. Under a cloudy ashen sky, the sea lay in dull peacefulness; it seemed shriveled up, with a close dreary horizon, and it had retreated from the beach, baring the long ribs of several sandbanks. As Aschenbach opened his window, he thought that he could detect the foul smell of the lagoon.

He felt depressed. He thought already of leaving. Once, years ago, after several weeks of spring here, this same weather had afflicted him, and impaired his health so seriously that he had to abandon Venice like a fugitive. Was not this old feverish unrest again setting in, the pressure in the temples, the heaviness of the eyelids? It would be annoying to change his residence still another time; but if the wind did not turn, he could not stay here. To be safe, he did not unpack completely. He breakfasted at nine in the buffet-room provided for this purpose between the lobby and dining-room.

That formal silence reigned here which is the ambition of large hotels. The waiters who were serving walked about on soft soles. Nothing was audible but the tinkling of the tea-things, a word half whispered. In one corner, obliquely across from the door, and two tables removed from his own, Aschenbach observed the Polish girls with their governess. Erect and red-eyed, their ash-blond hair freshly smoothed down, dressed in stiff blue linen with little white cuffs and turned-down collars—they were sitting there, handing around a glass of marmalade. They had almost finished their breakfast. They boy was missing.

Aschenbach smiled. "Well, little Phaeacian!" he thought. "You seem to be enjoying the pleasant privilege of having your sleep out." And, suddenly exhilarated, he recited to himself the line: "A frequent change of dress; warm baths, and rest."

He breakfasted without haste. From the porter, who entered the hall holding his braided cap in his hand, he received some forwarded mail; and while he smoked a cigarette he opened a few letters. In this way it happened that he was present at the entrance of the late sleeper who was being waited for over yonder.

He came through the glass door and crossed the room in silence to his sisters' table. His approach—the way he held the upper part of his body, and bent his knees, the movement of his white-shod feet—had an extraordinary charm; he walked very lightly, at once timid and proud, and this became still more lovely through the childish embarrassment with which, twice as he proceeded, he turned his face towards the centre of the room, raising and lowering his eyes. Smiling, with something half-muttered in his soft vague tongue, he took his place; and now, as he turned his full profile to the observer, Aschenbach was again astonished, terrified even, by the really godlike beauty of this human child. Today the boy was wearing a light blouse of blue and white striped cotton goods, with a red silk tie in front, and closed at the neck by a plain white high collar. This collar lacked the distinctiveness of the blouse, but above it the flowering head was poised with an incomparable seductiveness—the head of an Eros, in blended yellows of Parian marble, with fine serious brows, the temples and ears covered softly by the abrupt encroachment of his curls.

"Good, good!" Aschenbach thought, with that deliberate expert appraisal which artists sometimes employ as a subterfuge when they have been carried away with delight before a masterwork. And he thought further: "Really, if the sea and the beach weren't waiting for me, I should stay here as long as you stayed!" But he went then, passed through the lobby under the inspection of the servants, down the wide terrace, and straight across the boardwalk to the section of the beach reserved for the hotel guests. The barefoot old man in dungarees and straw hat who was functioning here as bathing-master assigned him to the bath-house he had rented; a table and a seat were placed on the sandy board platform, and he made himself comfortable in the lounge chair which he had drawn closer to the sea, out into the waxen yellow sand.

More than ever before, he was entertained and amused by the sights on the beach, this spectacle of carefree, civilized people getting sensuous enjoyment at the very edge of the elements. The grey flat sea was already alive with wading children, swimmers, a motley crowd of figures lying on the sand-banks with arms bent behind their heads. Others were rowing about in little red and blue striped boats without keels; they were continually upsetting, amid laughter. Before the long stretches of bathing-houses, where people were sitting on the platforms as though on small verandas, there was a play of movement against the line of rest and inertness behind—visits and chatter, fastidious morning elegance alongside the nakedness which, boldly at ease, was enjoying the freedom which the place afforded. Farther in front, on the damp firm sand, people were parading about in white bathing-cloaks, in ample, brilliantly coloured wrappers. An elaborate sand pile to the right, erected by children, had flags in the colours of all nations planted around it. Venders of shells, cakes, and fruit spread out their wares, kneeling. To the left, before one of the bathing-houses which stood at right angles to the others and to the sea, a Russian family was encamped: men with beards and large teeth, slow delicate women, a Baltic girl sitting by an easel and painting the sea amidst exclamations of despair, two ugly good-natured children, an old maid servant who wore a kerchief on her head and had the alert scraping manners of a slave. Delighted and appreciative, they were living there, patiently calling the names of the two rowdy disobedient children, using their scanty Italian to joke with the humorous old man from whom they were buying candy, kissing one another on the cheek, and not in the least concerned with anyone who might be observing their community.

"Yes, I shall stay," Aschenbach thought. "Where would things be better?" And, his hands folded in his lap, he let his eyes lose themselves in the expanses of the sea, his gaze gliding, swimming, and failing in the monotone mist of the wilderness of space. He loved the ocean for deep-seated reasons: because of that yearning for rest, when the hard-pressed artist hungers to shut out the exacting multiplicities of experience and hide himself on the breast of the simple, the vast; and because of a forbidden hankering—seductive, by virtue of its being directly opposed to his obligation—after the incommunicable, the incommensurate, the eternal, the non-existent. To be at rest in the face of perfection is the hunger of everyone who is aiming at excellence; and what is the non-existent but a form of perfection? But now, just as his dreams were so far out in vacancy, suddenly the horizontal fringe of the sea was broken by a human figure; and as he brought his eyes back from the unbounded, and focused them, it was the lovely boy who was there, coming from the left and passing him on the sand. He was barefooted, ready for wading, his slender legs exposed above the knees; he walked slowly, but as lightly and proudly as though it were the customary thing for him to move about without shoes; and he was looking around him towards the line of bathing-houses opposite. But as soon as he had noticed the Russian family, occupied with their own harmony and contentment, a cloud of scorn and detestation passed over his face. His brow darkened, his mouth was compressed, he gave his lips an embittered twist to one side so that the cheek was distorted and the forehead became so heavily furrowed that the eyes seemed sunken beneath its pressure: malicious and glowering, they spoke the language of hate. He looked down, looked back once more threateningly, then with his shoulder made an abrupt gesture of disdain and dismissal, and left the enemy behind him.

A kind of prudence or confusion, something like respect and shyness, caused Aschenbach to turn away as though he had seen nothing. For the earnest-minded who have been casual observers of some passion, struggle against making use, even to themselves, of what they have seen. But he was both cheered and unstrung—which is to say, he was happy. This childish fanaticism, directed against the most good-natured possible aspect of life—it brought the divinely arbitrary into human relationships; it made a delightful natural picture which had appealed only to the eye now seem worthy of a deeper sympathy; and it gave the figure of this half-grown boy, who had already been important enough by his sheer beauty, something to offset him still further, and to make one take him more seriously than his years justified. Still looking away, Aschenbach could hear the boy's voice, the shrill, somewhat weak voice with which, in the distance now, he was trying to call hello to his playfellows busied around the sand pile. They answered him, shouting back his name, or some affectionate nickname; and Aschenbach listened with a certain curiosity, without being able to catch anything more definite than two melodic syllables like "Adgio," or still more frequently "Adgiu," with a ringing u-sound prolonged at the end. He was pleased with the resonance of this; he found it adequate to the subject. He repeated it silently and, satisfied, turned to his letters and manuscripts.

His small portable writing-desk on his knees, he began writing with his fountain pen an answer to this or that bit of correspondence. But after the first fifteen minutes he found it a pity to abandon the situation—the most enjoyable he could think of—in this manner and waste it in activities which did not interest him. He tossed the writing-materials to one side, and he faced the ocean again; soon afterwards, diverted by the childish voices around the sand heap, he revolved his head comfortably along the back of the chair towards the right, to discover where that excellent little Adgio might be and what he was doing.

He was found at a glance; the red tie on his breast was not to be overlooked. Busied with the others in laying an old plank across the damp moat of the sand castle, he was nodding, and shouting instructions for this work. There were about ten companions with him, boys and girls of his age, and a few younger ones who were chattering with one another in Polish, French, and in several Balkan tongues. But it was his name which rang out most often. He was openly in demand, sought after, admired. One boy especially, like him a Pole, a stocky fellow who was called something like "Jaschu," with sleek black hair and a belted linen coat, seemed to be his closest vassal and friend. When the work on the sand structure was finished for the time being, they walked arm-in-arm along the beach, and the boy who was called "Jaschu" kissed the beauty.

Aschenbach was half-minded to raise a warning finger. "I advise you, Critobulus," he thought, smiling, "to travel for a year! For you need that much time at least to get over it." And then he breakfasted on large ripe strawberries which he got from a pedlar. It had become very warm, although the sun could no longer penetrate the blanket of mist in the sky. Laziness clogged his brain, even while his senses delighted in the numbing, drugging distractions of the ocean's stillness. To guess, to puzzle out just what name it was that sounded something like "Adgio," seemed to the sober man an appropriate ambition, a thoroughly comprehensive pursuit. And with the aid of a few scrappy recollections of Polish he decided that they must mean "Tadzio," the shortened form of "Tadeusz," and sounding like "Tadziu" when it is called.

Tadzio was bathing. Aschenbach, who had lost sight of him, spied his head and the arm with which he was propelling himself, far out in the water; for the sea must have been smooth for a long distance out. But already people seemed worried about him; women's voices were calling after him from the bathing-houses, uttering this name again and again. It almost dominated the beach like a battle cry, and with its soft consonants, its long-drawn u-note at the end, it had something at once sweet and wild about it: "Tadziu! Tadziu!" He turned back; beating the resistant water into a foam with his legs, he hurried, his head bent down over the waves. And to see how this living figure, graceful and clean-cut in its advance, with dripping curls, and lovely as some frail god, came up out of the depths of the sky and sea, rose and separated from the ele-ments—this spectacle aroused a sense of myth, it was like some poet's recovery of time at its beginning, of the origin of forms and the birth of gods. Aschenbach listened with closed eyes to this song ringing within him, and he thought again that it was pleasant here, and that he would like to remain.

Thomas Mann, Death in Venice, *trans. Kenneth Burke (New York: Knopf, 1925), 45, 48–60. Reprinted by permission of the publisher.*

Remapping the Mediterranean
The King-Crane Commission (1919)

The American King-Crane Commission toured the eastern Mediterranean during the Paris Peace Conference (1919–20) to help determine who should rightly govern the communities of the Levant after the demise of the Ottoman state. The itinerary of the commission took them first by train from Paris to Istanbul, then by boat to Jaffa, Beirut, and Alexandretta. In June and July 1919, the commission toured Palestine, Syria, and the southern Anatolian coast. Disagreements arose out of conflicting secret agreements between Allied powers and local representatives made during the war. This attempt at reconciliation between "outsiders" and "insiders" ended in open disregard of local sentiments. The report issued by the King-Crane Commission on August 28, 1919, was meant to ascertain "the opinions and desires of the whole people." However, the report was suppressed and was not made public until 1922. It was controversial in that it strongly advocated American mandates over Asia Minor, Syria, and Mesopotamia, and it opposed the Zionist program in Palestine. America withdrew from the Peace Conference in 1920. The following excerpt summarizes the arguments of various local communities that the commission encountered during the Mediterranean tour. The excerpt forecasts a cold war U.S. imperial role in the region after the withdrawal of Britain and France.

1. FOR AND AGAINST ZIONISM

The arguments in favor of Zionism as presented by its supporters have often been stated and need not now be presented in detail. The chief elements are that Palestine belonged once to the Jews, and they were driven out by force; for two thousand years they have been longing and praying to come back; while the Jews of the world are now far too numerous to be collected in Palestine, they are entitled to have some-where a state which can be a refuge to the oppressed among them, and an expression of their continuance and unity; despite proposals at Paris there is persecution of the Jews in Poland at the present moment, there is a prospect of a disintegration of the Jews in western civilization and their coalescence with the nations where they reside; they should have an opportunity to restore their ancient language and culture and preserve them in the old environment; there is no need of displacing the present population, for with the afforestation, modern methods of agriculture, utilization of water-power, reclamation of waste lands, sci-entific irrigation and the like, the land can contain several times its present number of inhabitants; if some of the present population desire to sell their lands they will receive a good price and there is plenty of room for them in other Arab countries; the Jewish colonies have been a great benefit to the native Arabs by teaching methods of agriculture, improving sanitation and the like; the unfolding of the Zionistic plan would bring great prosperity to all in the land, both present population and immigrants.

The native Arabs and Christians, who so unitedly oppose Zionism, urged the following principal considerations: The land is owned and occupied by them; Arabs were there before the Jews came; the Jews were immigrants, who treated the former inhabitants with the greatest cruelty (This alludes to the wars by the Children of Israel when they "possessed" the Land of Promise) and who remained a comparatively short time; they were unable to maintain control over the whole land or even union among themselves; they were expelled by the Romans and formed permanent residence elsewhere 2,000 years ago; the Arabs con-quered the land 1,300 years ago, and have remained ever since; it is their actual home, and not merely a residence of long ago; as Christians and

Moslems, they can honor all the holy places, whereas the Jews can honor only their own; the Jews are a religion and not a nation; they will, if given control, forbid the use of the Arabic language, the measure which caused the break between the Young Turks and the Arabs; the Jewish colonies have shown no benevolence to the Arabs in their neighborhood; it is denied that their activities have influenced the Arabs toward progress; the Jews have much money, education and shrewdness, and will soon buy out and manoeuvre away the present inhabitants; the Arabs are friendly toward the Jews long resident in the land who use the Arabic language; they will resist to the uttermost the immigration of foreign Jews and the establishment of a Jewish government.

2. ARAB FEELING TOWARD THE FRENCH

While the Commission was prepared beforehand for some disinclination toward France in Syria, the strength, universality and persistency of anti-French feeling among practically all Moslems and non-Catholic Christians (except a division of the Greek Orthodox), came as a distinct surprise. [. . .] Apart from the questions of process and recency, the anti-French feeling does seem to be deep-rooted in a large proportion of the Syrian population. This appears in an examination of the principal reasons given by the Syrians for their opposition to all French interference in their affairs. They say:

i. The French are enemies of religion, having none at home, and supporting Roman Catholics abroad for purely political motives.

ii. They disapprove of the French attitude toward women.

iii. The French education is superficial and inferior in character-building to the Anglo-Saxon. It leads to familiarity with that kind of French literature which is irreligious and immoral. The Moslems recognize that the time has come for the education of their women, and they say that those who receive French education tend to become uncontrollable.

iv. The French have not treated the natives as equals in Algeria and Tunisia but have imposed differences in office holding and in various civil rights. This argument was presented very often and developed in some detail.

v. The French have shown a marked tendency to give an undue proportion of offices, concessions, and the like, to the Christians of Syria. Non-Catholics complain that the same discrimination is shown in favor of Catholics and Maronites.

vi. By this discrimination, and by various intrigues since the occupation, the French have increased the religious divisions in Syria, which had been reduced greatly during the war. They thus endanger the possibility of Syrian nationalism on a non-religious basis. [. . .]

x. The French are inclined toward financial exploitation of subject areas, and would govern Syria not for its own development, but for the profit of Frenchmen. [. . .]

Much feeling persists in connection with the execution of Arabs by Jemal Pasha, and this acts against the French. Despite the fact that France was intriguing with the Arabs against the Turks before the Great War, the knowledge that M. Picot, upon leaving his position as Consul in 1914, failed to secure his correspondence, so that fatal evidence fell into Turkish hands, has played into position so that France is held responsible for the hangings. Every reference to the "Arab Martyrs," by subscriptions for their orphans, exhibitions of these children, meetings of the relatives—the "Unfortunate Syrians," now not only strengthens the sentiment for Arab independence, but stirs feeling against France.

3. THE REQUEST FOR AN AMERICAN MANDATE

Four possibilities were seriously contemplated by the supporters of a United Syria: Absolute independence, the mandate of Britain, the mandate of France and the mandate of America. The only considerable groups that favored division were those who supported a separate Palestine for Zionism under Britain, and a separate Lebanon, whether or not enlarged, under France in case the rest of Syria is under another mandatary.

Only Jews supported the Zionistic scheme, except that a few Christians were willing to entrust the question to the mandatary power. The Jews are distinctly for Britain as mandatory power, because of the Balfour declaration though many think if the scheme goes ahead, American Jews will become its chief promoters. France is felt to be against it, and America indifferent.

As regards the Lebanon the official Maronites and Catholics who support a separation scheme are undoubtedly sincere. Not only have they many sentimental ties toward France, but they realize that no other Power than France will support them in their privileged situation. [. . .]

Practically all of the Moslems, who number about four-fifths of the

295

population of Syria, are for America as their first choice. It is true that there was little direct expression of this in Palestine, since after their first declarations at Jaffa, the question of choice of mandate was held up and referred to Damascus. Possibly this was done under instructions from the Emir Feisal, who may have been trying to hold the field for Britain. If so, the evidence of sincere declaration for America is all the stronger, since the Congress reached unanimity for America. [. . .] It was furthermore always possible to ask why a group or individual objected to France or England, but not to ask why a group failed to declare for the United States. It is of course, also a fact that France, and only less openly England, were making bids for the mandate, while the United States was not.

The principal reasons advanced for desiring an American mandate were as follows:

> i. Confidence in President Wilson as mainly responsible for the freedom of Syria, and as championing the rights of small and oppressed peoples.
>
> ii. Gratitude to America for relief of the starving and naked. Thanks to President Wilson and America was expressed in a thousand forms and with the greatest emotion, independently of the desire as regards a mandate.
>
> iii. The feeling that America came into the war for no selfish reason, and could be trusted to take care of a small people in an unselfish way.
>
> iv. The knowledge that America is not a colonizing power, seeking to govern for the advantage of its own people, and to exploit the governed. The examples of Cuba and the Philippines were frequently cited.
>
> v. The feeling that America can be relied upon to withdraw from the country when her work is done, which is the case with no other power. The experience of Cuba was contrasted with that of Egypt and Algeria.
>
> vi. The feeling that America is rich, and abundantly able to advance the means for the desirable speedy development of the country economically.
>
> vii. A hearty approval of and desire for the extension of American education in the country. England has done little educationally for Syria. While France has done much, she seeks to denationalize the native peoples and make Frenchmen of them. America, especially through the Syrian Protestant College, has

taught Syrian nationalism. The American training and the Anglo-Saxon literature and civilization, are regarded as morally superior to the French.

viii. A conviction that America will be absolutely fair and just as between the different religions and sects. France would be expected to favor Christians especially Roman Catholics, and England to favor Moslems.

ix. America is abundantly supplied with trained men, from whom experts can be supplied in "various branches of science, industry, administration, and, above all, education."

x. The Americans are "lovers of humanity."

Many British officials, not excepting General Allenby, think the best solution to be an American mandate over the whole of Syria. England might be very glad to get out of the difficulties of the situation in this way. As for France, she cannot desire to take the whole of Syria, when so much of it is utterly averse to her. She also may ultimately conclude that the best way out is complete withdrawal. This would, perhaps not hurt her pride seriously if at the same time England were to withdraw and if her special pre-war relationships be scrupulously continued.

Confidential Appendix of King-Crane Commission Report, originally printed in Editor and Publisher *55.27, 2nd Section (December 2, 1922).*

Remember the Harbor
Ernest Hemingway (1922)

During the interwar years, U.S. interest in the geopolitics of the Mediterranean gradually increased. Later, during the cold war, U.S. foreign policy treated the eastern Mediterranean as an ideological and geopolitical battleground. In the wake of World War I, a young Ernest Hemingway (1899–1961) was sent to the Aegean region as foreign correspondent for the *Toronto Star*. In fifteen terse dispatches from Istanbul, he addressed the refugee situation in Istanbul and Thrace, competing Greek and Turkish nationalisms, and, generally, the horrors and displacements of regional conflicts that persisted after World War I. Describing one of the early catastrophes stemming from the Paris Peace Conference, he used historical metaphors to make the Anatolian War (1919–22) between Greece and the Turkish nationalists accessible to his readership. Hemingway compared the defeat of the Greeks to the Trojan War. In an early dispatch to the *Toronto Star*, he wrote, "They are the last of the glory that was Greece. This is the end of their second siege of Troy." His experiences in and around the region were also partially reflected in his collection *In Our Time*, whose "introduction," excerpted below, was the haunting vignette "On the Quai at Smyrna," a meditation on the confrontation of imperial British and national (i.e., Greek and Turkish) logics.

The strange thing was, he said, how they screamed every night at midnight. I do not know why they screamed at that time. We were in the harbor and they were all on the pier and at midnight they started screaming. We used to turn the searchlight on them to quiet them. That always did the trick. We'd run the searchlight up and down over them two or three times and they stopped it. One time I was senior officer on the pier and a Turkish officer came up to me in a frightful rage because one of our sailors had been most insulting to him. So I told him the fellow would be sent on ship and be most severely punished. I asked him to point him out. So he pointed out a gunner's mate, most inoffensive chap. Said he'd been most frightfully and repeatedly insulting; talking to me through an interpreter. I couldn't imagine how the gunner's mate knew enough Turkish to be insulting. I called him over and said, "And just in case you should have spoken to any Turkish officers."

"I haven't spoken to any of them, sir."

"I'm quite sure of it," I said, "but you'd best go on board ship and not come ashore again for the rest of the day."

Then I told the Turk the man was being sent on board ship and would be most severely dealt with. Oh most rigorously. He felt topping about it. Great friends we were.

The worst, he said, were the women with dead babies. You couldn't get the women to give up their dead babies. They'd have babies dead for six days. Wouldn't give them up. Nothing you could do about it. Had to take them away finally. Then there was an old lady, most extraordinary case. I told it to a doctor and he said I was lying. We were clearing them off the pier, had to clear off the dead ones, and this old woman was lying on a sort of litter. They said, "Will you have a look at her, sir?" So I had a look at her and just then she died and went absolutely stiff. Her legs drew up and she drew up from the waist and went quite rigid. Exactly as though she had been dead over night. She was quite dead and absolutely rigid. I told a medical chap about it and he told me it was impossible.

They were all out there on the pier and it wasn't at all like an earthquake or that sort of thing because they never knew about the Turk.

They never knew what the old Turk would do. You remember when they ordered us not to come in to take off any more? I had the wind up when we came in that morning. He had any amount of batteries and could have blown us clean out of the water. We were going to come in, run close to the pier, let go the front and rear anchors and then shell the Turkish quarter of the town. They would have blown us out of the water but we would have blown the town simply to hell. They just fired a few blank charges at us as we came in. Kemal came down and sacked the Turkish commander. For exceeding his authority or some such thing. He got a bit above himself. It would have been the hell of a mess.

You remember the harbor. There were plenty of nice things floating around in it. That was the only time in my life I got so I dreamed about things. You didn't mind the women who were having babies as you did those with the dead ones. They had them all right. Surprising how few of them died. You just covered them over with something and let them go to it. They'd always pick out the darkest place in the hold to have them. None of them minded anything once they got off the pier.

The Greeks were nice chaps too. When they evacuated they had all their baggage animals they couldn't take off with them so they just broke their forelegs and dumped them into the shallow water. All those mules with their forelegs broken pushed over into the shallow water. It was all a pleasant business. My word yes a pleasant business.

Ernest Hemingway, In Our Time *(New York: Scribner, 1930), 11–12. Reprinted by permission of the publisher.*

Women Unveil
Huda Shaarawi (1923)

Huda Shaarawi (1879–1947) was a pioneer Egyptian feminist leader and nationalist. She was tutored in Arabic, Persian, Turkish, and Islamic subjects by Muslim women in Cairo. She helped to organize a women's social service organization, the Union of Educated Egyptian Women, and in March 1923 formed the Egyptian Feminist Union (EFU). Two months later, she went with Nabawiya Musa, pioneer in girls' education, and Ceza Nabarawi, later editor-in-chief of the EFU monthly journal, to Rome to participate in the ninth congress of the International Woman Suffrage Alliance. Delegates came from forty-three countries. On her return from Rome, Shaarawi performed an act that has come to symbolize her life: she removed her face-veil upon arrival at the Cairo train station. Her autobiography, from which the following excerpt comes, includes several pictures of herself, wearing a scarf without any face-covering. She continued to lead the EFU and to represent Egypt at women's congresses in Europe until her death. She was instrumental in convening the first Arab Feminist Conference (1944) and in forming the Arab Feminist Union (1945), which called for solidarity with the Arabs of Palestine.

The intellectual awakening of upper-class women that had been under-way over the past years, stimulated and shaped in part by the women's salon and the lecture series, convinced me of the need for an association to bring women together for further intellectual, social and recreational pursuits. I mentioned the idea to some of the princesses and asked for support, which they willingly agreed to give. We met in my house to conclude plans. Princess Amina Halim presided over the gathering of princesses, Egyptians and foreign women. Thus in April 1914 the Intel-lectual Association of Egyptian Women was born. Among the members were Mai Ziyada, the gifted writer, then at the beginning of her liter-ary career, and Labiba Hashim, the founder and editor of the magazine *Fatat al-Sharq* (*The Young Woman of the East*, established in 1906) who also served as the Arabic secretary.

In my correspondence with Marguerite Clement, continuing since her visit to Egypt, I had revealed my hopes for creating an intellectual society for women. She promised, if it happened, she would come to Egypt to take part in our programme and offered to give lectures on themes of our choice. I wrote a formal request for her to present to offi-cials in France to facilitate her travel. She came to Cairo and delivered a series of lectures held in my house and at the Egyptian university. She also became a corresponding member of the society.

Before long, I began to search for a headquarters for our society which we had dared not call a club (*nadi*), as our traditions would not allow it. At that time it was still not acceptable for women to have a place of their own outside private houses. With the approach of summer many of the princesses departed for Europe, as usual. They expected the final arrangements for the headquarters to be made by the time they returned.

Huda Shaarawi, Harem Years: The Memoirs of an Egyptian Feminist, *trans. Margot Badran (New York: Feminist Press, 1986), 98–100. Reprinted by permission of the publisher.*

City and Psyche
Sigmund Freud (1930)

Mediterranean antiquities fascinated Sigmund Freud (1856–1939): for him, psychoanalysis was a kind of archaeology. References to archaeology and ancient culture popularized his work and helped provide a working model of the modern psyche. Like Schliemann's discovery of Troy and Sir Arthur Evans's excavation of Knossos (Crete) that uncovered relics and ruins to demonstrate the truth of legend and uncover lost worlds, psychoanalysis would reveal forgotten memories and repressed trauma to heal the psyche. In the following passage on Rome, Freud reveals the importance of the archaeological metaphor and of excavation in understanding the spatial and temporal workings of the mind. Just as Rome was built and rebuilt, with the past lasting into the present, so too were the structures of the psyche. Understanding the buried past was vital to understanding present motivations of individuals and communities in the modern world; the modern mind and the ancient Mediterranean were bound together. History could be mined for the determinants of present-day events, and to Freud it seemed that the Mediterranean past held possible answers to various crises of modernity. Freud had a large collection of artifacts from the ancient Near East, Egypt, Greece, and Rome.

We will choose as an example the history of the Eternal City. Historians tell us that the oldest Rome was the *Roma Quadrata*, a fenced settlement on the Palatine. Then followed the phase of the *Septimontium*, a federation of the settlements on the different hills; after that came the city bounded by the Servian wall; and later still, after all the transformations during the periods of the republic and the early Caesars, the city which the Emperor Aurelian surrounded with his walls. We will not follow the changes which the city went through any further, but we will ask ourselves how much a visitor, whom we will suppose to be equipped with the most complete historical and topographical knowledge, may still find left of these early stages in the Rome of today. Except for a few gaps, he will see the wall of Aurelian almost unchanged. In some places he will be able to find sections of the Servian wall where they have been excavated and brought to light. If he knows enough—more than present-day archaeology does—he may perhaps be able to trace out in the plan of the city the whole course of that wall and the outline of *Roma Quadrata*. Of the buildings which once occupied this ancient area he will find nothing, or only scanty remains, for they exist no longer. The best information about Rome in the republican era would only enable him at the most to point out the sites where the temples and public buildings stood. Their place is now taken by ruins, but not by ruins of themselves but of later restorations made after fires or destruction. It is hardly necessary to remark that all these remains of ancient Rome are found dovetailed into the jumble of a great metropolis which has grown up in the last few centuries since the Renaissance. There is not a little that is ancient still buried in the soil of the city or beneath its modern buildings. This is the manner in which the past is presented in historical sites like Rome.

Now let us, by a flight of imagination, suppose that Rome is not a human habitation but a psychical entity with a similarly long and copious past—an entity, that is to say, in which nothing that has once come into existence will have passed away and all the earlier phases of development continue to exist alongside the latest one. This would mean that in Rome the palaces of the Caesars and the septizonium of Septimus Severus would still be rising to their old height on the Palatine and that the castle of San Angelo would still be carrying on its battlements the beautiful statues which graced it until the siege by the Goths, and so on.

Sigmund Freud, Civilization and Its Discontents, trans. James Strachey (New York: Norton, 1961), 17–19. Reprinted by permission of the publisher.

Reconciling Tradition and Modernity
Yahya Haqqi (1944)

Called the "goldsmith of the Arabic language," the Egyptian essayist and short story writer Yahya Haqqi (1905–92) wrote his famous novella "The Lamp of Umm Hashim" during the Second World War. It tells the story of a young man who studies ophthalmology in England for a period of seven years and returns home a changed man. The idealized Egypt of his dreams in the cold north quickly separates from the reality of the people that he sees as though for the first time. He can see nothing but their faults and their need for the talents he brings from the lands of modernity. Initial failure to cure his cousin's blindness makes him realize that he must combine his Western science with local traditional and Islamic medicine—the oil from the lamp in the shrine of Umm Hashim. This time he succeeds.

It was not only the Egyptians' blind traditionalism that Haqqi was criticizing; he was also pointing to the weaknesses at the source of the colonial system that had dominated his country for over sixty years. The scientific prowess that lay at the heart of European claims to civilizational superiority was inadequate: "There is no sight without insight." The play on blindness, sight, and insight runs through the novella that was hailed as a modern parable reconciling Islam and modernity. The following selection narrates the docking of the ship in Alexandria.

Seven years passed and the ship returned.

Who was this tall, elegant young man jumping down the gangway with his head held high and his face shining? By God, it's Isma'il! It's Dr. Isma'il, the eye specialist whom English universities recognized as having a rare talent and extraordinary skills. His professor would joke with him, saying: "I bet that the soul of a Pharaonic priest-doctor has transmigrated into you, Mr. Isma'il. Your country is in urgent need of you because it is the land of the blind."

He saw in him a knowledge as though it were inspired and a clarity that went back long generations and an elegant dexterity inherited from hands that had chiseled out of solid stone statues that were almost alive.

Come, Isma'il, we long for you. We haven't seen you for seven years that felt like ages. Your letters were frequent and then few and were unable to quench our thirst. Come, bring us health and succor. Take your place in the family and you will see that like a machine it had not only stopped but also rusted because its motor had been removed. Ah! How much this family spent on you! Do you have any idea?

Isma'il slept fitfully the eve of his arrival. He rushed up on to the deck at dawn anxious not to miss the first sighting of the coast of Alexandria. He saw nothing on the horizon, but he smelt in the breeze an unfamiliar scent. The first being to meet him from his native land was a pure white bird hovering high and alone above the ship. Why do ships take such a long time to reach shore and rush so quickly away from it? It advanced slowly, uncaring of the passengers and their feelings. Isma'il had not told his family when he was arriving to spare his old father the difficulty of the trip to Alexandria. Instead he would send a telegram to them with the time of the train's arrival in Cairo. Here was the lighthouse in the sea; here was the yellow shore almost even with the water. Egypt, you are a hand stretched out to the sea.

Yahya Haqqi, Qindil Umm Hashim [The lamp of Umm Hashim] (Cairo: Madbouli, 1944), 23–30. Trans. miriam cooke.

Ship of Misery
I. F. Stone (1946)

Isidor Feinstein Stone (1907–89) was an American journalist who published a political newsletter titled *I. F. Stone's Weekly*. In 1939 he became associate editor of *The Nation*. In 1946, he decided to cover the story of Jews escaping fascist Europe and Hitler's gas chambers. His account of a harrowing sea journey from the Adriatic to Palestine in *Underground to Palestine* documents the Jews' burning desire for a modern promised land (or nation-state) and also underscores the diversity of the people to be nationalized as citizens of Israel, "old-new land." The following excerpt describes passages of surrender to the inscrutable will of the sea, where origin and destination, exile and return, are confused.

XI

We were about eighty miles farther from our goal than we had been at the point of transfer.

We didn't know what the attitude of the British would be. We hoped that the destroyer had come in answer to our sos, that they would take a few of our sick on board their ship, perhaps give us some food and water and tow us into Haifa. Perhaps we had too high an opinion of British gallantry.

The British moved closer and we read that the number of this destroyer was R-75 and its name the *Virago*. When it came alongside one of the *shomrim* handed me a megaphone and asked me to talk to the British.

"Hullo, hullo! We're in a bad way. Can you give us a tow to Haifa?" I shouted across the water.

Sailors on the deck of the destroyer pulled the covers off a lifeboat and lowered it into the sea. Six sailors and an ensign got into the boat and began to row toward our ship. Aboard they made their way gingerly to the wheelhouse. Many people lay underfoot, too sick or exhausted to move. The British sailors stepped over them carefully. They wore white shorts. Their officer, a fledgling ensign, tried hard to look imperturbable.

"Who's spokesman for these people?" The officer asked me.

"*Ich kenn nit reden English* (I can't speak English)," I answered in Yiddish.

I was taking no chances on being taken off that boat by the British before I could reach Palestine. I waved my hand to my German friend. He spoke a rather awkward English with a strong Dutch accent. He had learned English in Holland before the war.

I have never seen a more complicated bit of linguistics than the interrogation of our Turkish captain by the British ensign. The ensign spoke English with that calm assurance Englishmen seem to have abroad that they will of course be understood. It took a chain of translators, however, to make this possible.

The ensign spoke to my German friend in English. The German translated this into Hebrew. One of our Greeks stood by and interpreted the Hebrew into broken Russian for one of the Turkish sailors, who, in turn, translated for the Turkish captain.

One of the British sailors stood at the top of the wheelhouse with two signal flags. In his white shorts, bare knees and brown, heavy socks he looked like an enlarged Boy Scout. His name, satisfyingly enough, turned out to be Popham.

Another sailor with a message pad stood beside the ensign. They were surrounded by an unwashed horde of refugees, your correspondent included.

The ensign, flustered by the stares of the women, some of whom didn't look too unattractive even on that dreadful morning, handed a knife to the sailor with which to sharpen a stub of a pencil. He proceeded to dictate the results of his interrogation.

The sailor wrote it all down respectfully, rereading it aloud for the benefit of Popham, who signaled it across the water to the destroyer. The ensign dictated, much like a businessman in an office, pausing nervously over his choice of words. At one point his youthful upper class dignity broke down completely and he shouted to the sailor on the wheelhouse:

"Did you get that, Pop?"

But otherwise he addressed him as "Pop'm."

The most important question asked by the ensign was whether we were willing voluntarily to be towed into Haifa. There was a good reason for this question. We were outside Palestinian territorial waters. Under international law the British have no right to seize a boat on the high seas, even if they know for a certainty that it is carrying unauthorized immigrants to Palestine. On two occasions the British have been ordered by their own courts in Palestine to return Jewish ships captured on the high seas. On the other hand, if an illegal boat voluntarily submits to British jurisdiction on the high seas the seizure is of course a legal one.

We told the ensign that we were willing to submit to British authority and asked him to tow us to Haifa.

The ensign dictated to the destroyer, "Severe engine trouble, plus overcrowding, make it impossible to proceed," and that we would place ourselves voluntarily under British authority to be towed in. A big signal lamp on the destroyer twinkled back a question:

"Is there enough food and water on board?"

The ensign answered that we were out of both, and stood nervously twiddling his pencil against his pants under the stares of the numb and savage horde surrounding him. He was thin, blond, of somewhat more than medium height. He looked the picture of a well-bred English boy of good family. He was obviously distressed by our plight. My friends and I liked him.

The ensign asked whether we had a towline aboard. We hadn't. Then he asked if we could clear the foredeck so that a towline could be attached to our boat. *Shomrim* made their way slowly and painfully to the foredeck to clear a path, but with little success.

The foredeck was packed tight with girls and women, they had slept leaning against each other. The lucky ones had sat all night at the railing, their feet hanging over the water. They were dazed, sleepy, tired, and resentful. Each was afraid to move lest she lose her precious space.

I megaphoned an appeal to them in my rather inadequate Yiddish.

"Comrades," I pleaded, "the British officer on board is a kind man and he is offering to tow us into Haifa. That means we can be in *Eretz* this evening. You must clear the foredeck so that a towline can be attached to the British destroyer. Please move and make place so that when the British sailors come back on board they will have room."

A few began to move off the upper deck and down the rail. Some of those on the deck below should have moved into the cargo hold and made room for the women from the upper deck, and some did. But the hold itself was jammed with men clamoring for a chance to get up into the light and air.

In the meantime the ensign and his six sailors climbed back into the lifeboat in which they had come and started back to the destroyer. We watched them hopefully. We were hungry and thirsty and hoped for food and water.

306   The *shomrim* were busy on both decks, forcing men into the hold

and bringing women down from the foredeck. It looked as though the English would save us after all.

We were in for an unpleasant surprise. We saw the ensign and the six sailors go aboard the destroyer. Then we saw tiny figures hoisting the lifeboat on board. We wondered why, since a boat would be needed to bring us food and water.

The destroyer began to move and for one relieved moment we thought it was maneuvering into position to attach a towline to our cargo boat. But the distance between us widened. The destroyer sailed off to the east.

This destruction of our hopes was so unexpected that our reaction was one of dulled amazement rather than indignation. No one shouted or cursed or shook a fist at the vanishing British destroyer. We just watched it in silence. The destroyer grew smaller and smaller and finally vanished over the horizon.

"It will be a miracle if we ever get to *Eretz*," the doctor said.

XII

The second day and night on the Turkish cargo boat were the worst I ever spent. The British destroyer steamed off shortly after 7 A.M. without giving us food and water or the tow into Haifa for which we had asked. We were to the south of Cyprus, about 180 miles from Palestine. The sky was cloudless and the sea calm but the day was brutally hot.

The boat from which we had transferred on the seas early the previous morning had given us water and provisions for but one day. Had our Turkish captain sailed straight for Palestine we would have reached there that night. Either he had lost his way or his nerve and headed north instead of east. We were eighty miles further away from Palestine than we had been at our transfer point.

Some people on board still had the remains of the lunch bag given us the day before but there was very little water; all we had were a few precious and closely guarded regulation cans of water, the kind packed on lifeboats in case of a shipwreck, and it was over water that our first crisis that day was to arise.

The heat was sickening. There were a score or more of people on board, including four pregnant women and a cardiac case who had to be given injections at regular intervals. The doctor was on the upper deck amidships with a small store of medicines. He was ill himself, and our *Red Mogen Dovid* (Jewish Red Cross) workers would come to him during the day for medicines and instructions.

307

On the lower deck one of the *shomrim* had attached a rope to a bucket and given showers to those who wanted them. The men would strip to the waist and lean far over the side. A *shomrim* would pull up a bucket of water and throw it over them. I had one every hour or so during the day. The shock of the cold water was very refreshing.

I got another bucket and tied a rope to it and had one of the *shomrim* fill it and hand it up to the top deck amidships, where there were many men and women sick with the heat and thirst. I went around with the bucket sprinkling water over the need and wetting handkerchiefs so people could put them on their foreheads. The women didn't like the shock of the water; the men did, even one sick old man I called *zeida* (grandpa) but who told me he had neither children nor grandchildren.

The men stretched blankets as awnings against the sun. People lay down under the lifeboats and there was a bit of shade and even around the hot smokestack. Most of them were too miserable to think of anyone but themselves.

Tempers wore very thin on the boat. It was difficult to keep a way open to the wheelhouse and to make people take turns in the hot hold. One *shomer* said to me in exasperation, "*Juden und pferd seinen die selbe sach—beide muss men treiben.*" ("Jews and horses are the same thing—you have to drive both of them.") I'm afraid I lost my temper several times and I apologize to those of my comrades whose feelings I may have hurt.

At one point I was trying to make room on the starboard side amidships for a sick woman. A boy of about twelve was sitting there. I asked him to give up his place. He refused, and a woman near him whom I took to be his mother looked indignantly at me. I yanked him to his feet, shouting:

"What do you mean you won't give your place to a sick woman. If you don't want to be a *mensch* (man) don't go to *Eretz*."

The word *mensch* is richer in Yiddish than in English and has a richer connotation of manliness.

The boy moved away resentfully, but later I saw him helping to put up a blanket as an awning and shouting to another boy:

"Come on, help! If you want to go to *Eretz* you must be a *mensch*."

"Now you're acting like a real *Chalutz*," I said, patting him on the back.

In my water-soaked notebook for that day there is this notation:

"I feel sick. No water yet today. I found a piece of hardtack under the boom. Someone else had eaten part of it. I chewed on the rest with relish. I had an odd experience I have read about in stories of shipwreck.

The hardtack did not dissolve or even grow wet in my mouth. I had no saliva. It pulverized, and I swallowed it dry."

The one cool spot on the boat was the wheelhouse. I had a nap there in the afternoon, and found an opened tin of concentrated lifeboat rations. I ate a biscuit and a chocolate tablet and had a tiny mouthful of brackish water from a very dirty glass. I rinsed my mouth with the water before swallowing. It might have been nectar, it tasted so delicious.

Four sick women were lying on the floor around the wheelhouse.

The shortage of water precipitated a crisis in the afternoon. There was a terrific fight on the lower deck and a lot of shouting. Rudy jumped on the stairs leading to the afterdeck and yelled:

"I take over all power on this boat and order the *shomrim* to distribute the rest of the water."

He was finally calmed down, but not until he was promised that one of our last remaining cans of water would be passed around.

I felt guilty that evening because of a special treat. I was near the wheelhouse and looked in to see the Turkish captain in his pajamas eating his dinner and drinking tea. The crew had a small store of food and a spirit lamp with which they prepared tea. I looked at the tea so longingly that he invited me to have a cup. It was hot and sweet and I have never tasted anything quite so good. I insisted on giving him one of my last packs of Camels in return.

That night there was a panic. The barometer began to fall. There was a dead calm on the sea, as if before a storm. About eleven o'clock the captain became alarmed. He was afraid the boat would capsize in a storm. His fear spread to the *shomrim* who began to herd people off the decks and into the holds. Fights broke out and women became hysterical. Word spread that a storm was coming and that the boat might sink. Even some of the best of the women *Chalutzim* lost their nerve.

We sent out an sos. About two in the morning a British destroyer came alongside. It turned floodlights on us and we saw the number R-75 on its sides, the same number as the boat which had refused us aid the previous morning.

I handled the megaphone:

"Is that the *Virago?*"

I repeated the question, but again got no answer.

We asked how far we were from Haifa.

"Thirty-five miles," was the reply.

"The barometer's falling," I shouted, "and our captain is afraid that we may go under in a storm. We're terribly overloaded. Can you take some of our sick people on board and give us a tow to Haifa?"

We waited but got no answer.

"Won't you please answer?"

There was no reply this time either.

The captain had shut off our engines and the whole ship waited anxiously for some response.

"Won't you please answer?" I asked for the third time.

But they remained silent.

One of the *shomrim* standing near me said:

"The hell with the bastards."

We waited about fifteen minutes. I picked up the megaphone and shouted derisively,

"Thank you."

We started up our engines to a full six or seven knots and started off for Haifa.

In spite of our fears and a rough sea, we avoided a storm. Shortly before dawn I slept for a while on top of the wheelhouse. I woke to see the dim outlines of a mountain toward the southeast.

As the light increased and the sun rose, a cry ran over the ship.

"It's *Eretz Israel*."

We saw Mount Carmel ahead of us, and the town of Haifa sleeping in the morning sun below us. In the harbor as we came in we saw what seemed to be a whole British fleet waiting for us.

The refugees cheered and began to sing *Hatikvah*, the Jewish national anthem. We pulled down the Turkish flag at our helm and raised the *Mogen Dovid* and the Union Jack side by side. People jumped for joy, kissed and hugged each other on the deck.

So singing we moved into the arms of the waiting British, in *Eretz* at last.

I. F. Stone, Underground to Palestine *(New York: Pantheon, 1978), 209–20.*

© *1978 by I. F. Stone; reprinted by permission of The Wylie Agency.*

Odysseus's Scar

Erich Auerbach (1945)

While I. F. Stone was crossing the Mediterranean in his ship of misery, Erich Auerbach (1892–1957) was in Istanbul writing his study of realism in literature, *Mimesis*. A scholar of Romance philology and a soldier who was decorated with the Iron Cross for his service on the front in World War I, he had taught in the University of Marburg. In 1935 the Nazis dismissed him from his teaching post because he was a Jew. A year later, he fled to Turkey, where he taught at the Istanbul University, along with other scholar-exiles escaping the Nazis. In a letter to literary critic Walter Benjamin he writes that in Turkey "they have thrown all tradition overboard here, and they want to build a thoroughly rationalized—extreme Turkish nationalist—state of the European sort." Between 1942 and 1945, he wrote *Mimesis* in the Dominican monastery of San Pietro di Galata. The work opens with the ironic discussion of Odysseus's return to Ithaca from exile and war as related in Homer's *Odyssey*. He is identified by the scar on his thigh. The healed wound is like a completed, or healed, journey. The condition of exile represented here foregrounds the Sea as a medium of separation, conveyance, and connection in a cycle that produces myth and history. The circumstances under which Auerbach wrote in the 1940s are reflected in his selection and analysis of Odysseus's return home.

Readers of the *Odyssey* will remember the well-prepared and touching scene in Book 19, when Odysseus has at last come home, the scene in which the old housekeeper Euryclea, who had been his nurse, recognizes him by a scar on his thigh. The stranger has won Penelope's good will; at his request she tells the housekeeper to wash his feet, which, in all old stories, is the first duty of hospitality toward a tired traveler. Euryclea busies herself fetching water and mixing cold with hot, meanwhile speaking sadly of her absent master, who is probably of the same age as the guest, and who perhaps, like the guest, is even now wandering somewhere, a stranger; and she remarks how astonishingly like him the guest looks. Meanwhile Odysseus, remembering his scar, moves back out of the light; he knows that, despite his efforts to hide his identity, Euryclea will now recognize him, but he wants at least to keep Penelope in ignorance. No sooner has the old woman touched the scar than, in her joyous surprise, she lets Odysseus' foot drop into the basin; the water spills over, she is about to cry out her joy; Odysseus restrains her with whispered threats and endearments; she recovers herself and conceals her emotion. Penelope, whose attention Athena's foresight had diverted from the incident, has observed nothing.

All this is scrupulously externalized and narrated in leisurely fashion. The two women express their feelings in copious direct discourse. Feelings though they are, with only a slight admixture of the most general considerations upon human destiny, the syntactical connection between part and part is perfectly clear, no contour is blurred. There is also room and time for orderly, perfectly well-articulated, uniformly illuminated descriptions of implements, ministrations, and gestures; even in the dramatic moment of recognition, Homer does not omit to tell the reader that it is with his right hand that Odysseus takes the old woman by the throat to keep her from speaking, at the same time that he draws her closer to him with his left. Clearly outlined, brightly and uniformly illuminated, men and things stand out in a realm where everything is visible; and not less clear—wholly expressed, orderly even in their ardor—are the feelings and thoughts of the persons involved.

In my account of the incident I have so far passed over a whole series of verses which interrupt it in the middle. There are more than seventy of these verses—while to the incident itself some forty are devoted before the interruption and some forty after it. The interruption, which comes just at the point when the housekeeper recognizes the scar—that is, at the moment of crisis—describes the origin of the scar, a hunting accident which occurred in Odysseus' boyhood, at a boar hunt, during the time of his visit to his grandfather Autolycus. This first affords an opportunity to inform the reader about Autolycus, his house, the precise degree of the kinship, his character, and, no less exhaustively than touchingly, his behavior after the birth of his grandson; then follows the visit of Odysseus, now grown to be a youth; the exchange of greetings, the banquet with which he is welcomed, sleep and waking, the early start for the hunt, the tracking of the beast, the struggle, Odysseus' being wounded by the boar's tusk, his recovery, his return to Ithaca, his parents' anxious questions—all is narrated, again with such a complete externalization of all the elements of the story and of their interconnections as to leave nothing in obscurity. Not until then does the narrator return to Penelope's chamber, not until then, the digression having run its course, does Euryclea, who had recognized the scar before the digression began, let Odysseus' foot fall back into the basin.

The first thought of a modern reader—that this is a device to increase suspense—is, if not wholly wrong, at least not the essential explanation of this Homeric procedure. For the element of suspense is very slight in the Homeric poems; nothing in their entire style is calculated to keep the reader or hearer breathless. The digressions are not meant to keep the reader in suspense, but rather to relax the tension. And this frequently occurs, as in the passage before us. The broadly narrated, charming, and subtly fashioned story of the hunt, with all its elegance and self-sufficiency, its wealth of idyllic pictures, seeks to win the reader over wholly to itself as long as he is hearing it, to make him forget what had just taken place during the foot-washing. But an episode that will increase suspense by retarding the action must be so constructed that

it will not fill the present entirely, will not put the crisis, whose resolution is being awaited, entirely out of the reader's mind, and thereby
destroy the mood of suspense; the crisis and the suspense must continue, must remain vibrant in the background. But Homer — and to this
we shall have to return later — knows no background. What he narrates
is for the time being the only present, and fills both the stage and the
reader's mind completely. So it is with the passage before us. When the
young Euryclea sets the infant Odysseus on his grandfather Autolycus'
lap after the banquet, the aged Euryclea, who a few lines earlier had
touched the wanderer's foot, has entirely vanished from the stage and
from the reader's mind.

Goethe and Schiller, who, though not referring to this particular episode, exchanged letters in April 1797 on the subject of "the retarding
element" in the Homeric poems in general, put it in direct opposition
to the element of suspense — the latter word is not used, but is clearly
implied when the "retarding" procedure is opposed, as something
proper to epic, to tragic procedure (letters of April 19, 21, and 22). The
"retarding element," the "going back and forth" by means of episodes,
seems to me, too, in the Homeric poems, to be opposed to any tensional
and suspensive striving toward a goal, and doubtless Schiller is right in
regard to Homer when he says that what he gives us is "simply the quiet
existence and operation of things in accordance with their natures";
Homer's goal is "already present in every point of his progress." But
both Schiller and Goethe raise Homer's procedure to the level of a law
for epic poetry in general, and Schiller's words quoted above are meant
to be universally binding upon the epic poet, in contradistinction from
the tragic. Yet in both modern and ancient times, there are important
epic works which are composed throughout with no "retarding element"
in this sense but, on the contrary, with suspense throughout, and which
perpetually "rob us of our emotional freedom" — which power Schiller
will grant only to the tragic poet. And besides it seems to me unde-
monstrable and improbable that this procedure of Homeric poetry was
directed by aesthetic considerations or even by an aesthetic feeling of
the sort postulated by Goethe and Schiller. The effect, to be sure, is precisely that which they describe, and is, furthermore, the actual source
of the conception of epic which they themselves hold, and with them all
writers decisively influenced by classical antiquity. But the true cause of
the impression of "retardation" appears to me to lie elsewhere — namely,
in the need of the Homeric style to leave nothing which it mentions half
in darkness and unexternalized.

The excursus upon the origin of Odysseus' scar is not basically different from the many passages in which a newly introduced character, or even a newly appearing object or implement, though it be in the thick of a battle, is described as to its nature and origin; or in which, upon the appearance of a god, we are told where he last was, what he was doing there, and by what road he reached the scene; indeed, even the Homeric epithets seem to me in the final analysis to be traceable to the same need for an externalization of phenomena in terms perceptible to the senses. Here is the scar, which comes up in the course of the narrative; and Homer's feeling simply will not permit him to see it appear out of the darkness of an unilluminated past; it must be set in full light, and with it a portion of the hero's boyhood—just as, in the *Iliad*, when the first ship is already burning and the Myrmidons finally arm that they may hasten to help, there is still time not only for the wonderful simile of the wolf, not only for the order of the Myrmidon host, but also for a detailed account of the ancestry of several subordinate leaders (16.155ff.). To be sure, the aesthetic effect thus produced was soon noticed and thereafter consciously sought; but the more original cause must have lain in the basic impulse of the Homeric style: to represent phenomena in a fully externalized form, visible and palpable in all their parts, and completely fixed in their spatial and temporal relations. Nor do psychological processes receive any other treatment: here too nothing must remain hidden and unexpressed. With the utmost fullness, with an orderliness which even passion does not disturb, Homer's personages vent their inmost hearts in speech; what they do not say to others, they speak in their own minds, so that the reader is informed of it. Much that is terrible takes place in the Homeric poems, but it seldom takes place wordlessly: Polyphemus talks to Odysseus; Odysseus talks to the suitors when he begins to kill them; Hector and Achilles talk at length, before battle and after; and no speech is so filled with anger or scorn that the particles which express logical and grammatical connections are lacking or out of place. This last observation is true, of course, not only of speeches but of the presentation in general. The separate elements of a phenomenon are most clearly placed in relation to one another; a large number of conjunctions, adverbs, particles, and other syntactical tools, all clearly circumscribed and delicately differentiated in meaning, delimit persons, things, and portions of incidents in respect to one another, and at the same time bring them together in a continuous and ever flexible connection; like the separate phenomena themselves, their relationships—their temporal, local, causal, final, consecutive, comparative, concessive, antithetical, and conditional limitations—are brought to light in perfect fullness; so that a continuous rhythmic procession of phenomena passes by, and never is there a form left fragmentary or half-illuminated, never a lacuna, never a gap, never a glimpse of unplumbed depths.

And this procession of phenomena takes place in the foreground—that is, in a local and temporal present which is absolute. One might think that the many interpolations, the frequent moving back and forth, would create a sort of perspective in time and place; but the Homeric style never gives any such impression. The way in which any impression of perspective is avoided can be clearly observed in the procedure for introducing episodes, a syntactical construction with which every reader of Homer is familiar; it is used in the passage we are considering, but can also be found in cases when the episodes are much shorter. To the word scar (19.393) there is first attached a relative clause ("which once long ago a boar . . ."), which enlarges into a voluminous syntactical parenthesis; into this an independent sentence unexpectedly intrudes (19.396: "A god himself gave him . . ."), which quietly disentangles itself from syntactical subordination, until, with verse 399, an equally free syntactical treatment of the new content begins a new present which continues unchallenged until, with verse 467 ("The old woman now touched it . . ."), the scene which had been broken off is resumed. To be sure, in the case of such long episodes as the one we are considering, a purely syntactical connection with the principal theme would hardly have been possible; but a connection with it through perspective would have been all the easier had the content been arranged with that end in view; if, that is, the entire story of the scar had been presented as a recollection which awakens in Odysseus' mind at this particular moment. It would have been perfectly easy to do; the story of the scar had only to be inserted two verses earlier, at the first mention of the word scar, where the motifs "Odysseus" and "recollection" were already at hand. But any such subjectivistic-perspectivistic procedure, creating a foreground and background, resulting in the present lying open to the depths of the past, is entirely foreign to the Homeric style; the Homeric style knows only a foreground, only a uniformly illuminated, uniformly objective present. And so the excursus does not begin until two lines later, when Euryclea has discovered the scar—the possibility for a perspectivistic connection no longer exists, and the story of the wound becomes an independent and exclusive present.

Erich Auerbach, Mimesis: The Representation of Reality in Western Literature, *trans. Willard R. Trask (1946; Princeton: Princeton University Press, 1953), 3–7. Reprinted by permission of the publisher.*

CHAPTER 6

A Global Pond

ATLANTIC
OCEAN

ALSACE

FRANCE

Venice

ADRIATIC SEA

PROVENCE

Marseilles
Toulon

SPAIN

Madrid

Barcelona

Rome

ITALY

Naples

PORTUGAL

Minorca

Mallorca

Ischia

Seville

Granada

Palermo   Messin

Tangiers

Algiers

Sicily

Constantine

Volubilis

TUNISIA

MOROCCO

ALGERIA

NORTH
AFRICA

Leptis
Magna

0		100		200		300 mi
0	100	200	300	400	500 km	

This chapter documents the material, cultural, political, and philosophical developments during the latest stage of Mediterranean history. Technological innovations in travel have decreased the time necessary to cross from one shore to another even while some travelers continue to use oars or sails to reach their destinations. Cartography has moved beyond cosmological and navigational charts and Ptolemaic world maps to the virtual world of the Global Positioning System, or GPS. Newly independent nation-states are claiming rights to be included on an equal basis in the community of nations. Below the surface of such radical shifts, however, the Mediterranean continues to enchant and to inspire poets and philosophers with myths and heroes from antiquity.

The middle of the twentieth century was witness to increasing conflict and tension in the region. In the Spanish Civil War (1936–39) and World War II (1939–45), fascists played the lead role: after winning in Spain, they lost elsewhere. When Franco's forces claimed victory, many Republicans, among them a certain Américo Castro, left Spain. In exile, this historian reviewed his nation's past and suggested that the catastrophe was due to the fundamentalization of Catholicism. Spain was heir to a vibrant, multicultural, and religiously pluralist civilization that should form the basis of a new and more inclusive understanding of what it meant to be Spanish. Others also were rethinking their pasts, as the Mediterranean was split ideologically along cold war and then cultural fronts.

European refugees in Palestine established the new state of Israel. Despite the guarantee of freedom of religion announced in Israeli prime minister David Ben-Gurion's declaration of independence, the explicitly Jewish nature of the new nation-state rendered precarious the lives of the indigenous residents. Carrying with them nothing other than memory maps, Palestinian exiles became nodes in the international network that the Palestinian Diaspora formed over the following sixty years. Poet Mahmud Darwish mourned the 500-year anniversary of the Spanish Reconquista, and recalling the Muslims driven in 1492 from the paradise of Granada, he vowed that modern Palestinians would hold on to the keys of their usurped homes. The double exodus of Jews and Palestinians was mapped on to past experiences of Mediterranean exile.

The Second World War drained the British, Italians, and French of their energy and resources, and one by one North African and West Asian nations seized their liberty and sent the European colonizers back across the Mediterranean. Yet their influence persists today. Writers, like the Turkish Orhan Pamuk and the Algerian Assia Djebar, began to rewrite national history from the margins. Pamuk reflected on the parallel constructions of Mediterranean identity through the seventeenth-century confrontation between an Ottoman scholar and his European slave. Djebar narrated the 1830 French invasion of Algeria through the eyes of women who had surely witnessed the arrival of the first gunboats into the bay of Algiers, even if women had been erased from history. When the French occupation of Algeria ended in the summer of 1962, thousands of Europeans re-crossed the Mediterranean.

Despite such violence, romantics flocked to the eastern and southern shores, where they extolled the beauty of the region, in Lawrence Durrell's case distilled in the allure of its women. Other travelers, like the Greek Margarita Karapanou, recalled the malaise of Aschenbach in Venice.

The Mediterranean has shrunk into a pond in the global village. Travel has lost in glamour what it has gained in speed, efficiency, and availability as mass tourism reaches even the most remote places. Today Japanese competes with Russian and Dutch as the wonders of Minoan culture sparkle with the flashes of disposable cameras. The ruins of multiple civilizations layered one on top of the other have become a commodity for impatient tourists. For those unable to spare the time or money to travel, or to obtain a visa, the information revolution has provided a convenient alternative: virtual tourism. A favorite Grand Tour site such as Athens can be visited via <www.athensvirtualtour.com>. Lesser-known sites are equally accessible from the comfort of home, for example Pula in Croatia (<www.aroundcroatia.com>). The complexity of historical sites that read like palimpsests takes on a plastic sameness when visited from the antiseptic comfort of international hotels, cruise ships, and computer screens.

The underbelly of such slick travel is the illegal movement of people and goods. In the postindependence period, the formerly colonized board small boats and escape poverty by heading north. Once there, many end up in ghettos where they have created their own hybrid languages and music such as *ray*, cultures that braid together North African, French, and American influences.

By the end of the century, one of the more assimilated migrants, the Algerian-born philosopher Jacques Derrida, could reflect on his life's trajectory and how it resembled or differed from that of his less fortunate compatriots. Derrida's French in this context gestures toward Verlan, a secret language of the ghettos that combines French and Arabic and then reverses the combinations. He declares himself to be an alien, one who might be presumed to share the condition of the disenfranchised immigrants, the Beurs (this word itself being the Verlan translation of Arab). Born a Jew, he situated himself on the border separating and bringing together the European self and the African other, the Christian and the Muslim. Maghrebians such as Fadila al-Faruq who return home to North Africa may find that there is no place to call home.

Around this time, politicians met in Barcelona to forge a "Euro-Mediterranean Partnership." Their stated goal was to strengthen the peace, stability, and development of the region through dialogue, exchange, and cooperation. They were trying to turn the Mediterranean into a global pond. In fact, however, they divided the northern/ "European" from the southern/"Mediterranean" littorals, reaffirming the age-old gap between the Africans and their European partners. The Barcelona Declaration calls for control of migration flows, like the clandestine boat people, and urges the adoption of practical measures "to improve cooperation among police, judicial, customs, administrative and other authorities in order to combat illegal immigration." The echoes from nineteenth-century epic encounters ring loud and clear. Likewise, the disintegration of Yugoslavia resulted in a remapping of the Balkans.

Within a few years, some Maghrebians were denouncing the Barcelona Declaration as a ruse for northerners to regain a footing in the region while others continued to sing the pride, even if faded, of the millennial Sea. Speaking of the palimpsestic history of his native port city and comparing it with Prometheus, the Moroccan poet Mohammed Serifi Villar said in a 1996 speech, "Tangier, this insomniac city of ours, loved, hated, banished, forgotten by God and the Gods, prefers to remain riveted by chains to the rock, rather than to kneel before the messenger of the Gods, Hermes. Perhaps the salvation of Tangier lies in this intransigence, in this rebel beauty, in its universal character." Tangier is, *mutatis mutandis*, the Mediterranean.

Occluding the violence of forced migrations, the rivalries of the cold war that fragmented the Sea, and the U.S. war on terror that now threatens the region, the Italian Franco Cassano closes the book with a meditation on Mediterranean thinking, a lyrical paean to the transformative qualities of life in the Sea.

Mediterraneanizing Identity

Américo Castro (1948)

Américo Castro (1885–1972) is a major figure in twentieth-century
Spanish philology and historiography. After the Spanish Civil War,
Castro, like other intellectuals committed to the socialist project of
the Spanish Republic, went into exile. At Princeton University, he
wrote his major work, *Spain in Her History* (*España en su historia*,
1948). This new look at the role of Spain in Mediterranean history
immediately became the subject of a fierce polemic. Revising his
earlier Europeanist view of Spanish culture, Castro located the
origin of Spanish national identity in the centuries of coexistence
and tension among Jews, Muslims, and Christians in the Iberian
Peninsula. In sharp contrast to the Francoist official discourse of 1948
Spain that equated Spanishness with fundamentalist Catholicism,
Castro celebrated the contributions of Judaism and Islam to Spanish
culture. He asserted that the peculiar form Catholicism took in Spain
could be traced back to the influence of Islam.

In no Catholic country does religion displace a greater social volume
than in Spain and in the Hispano-Portuguese nations; and the truth is
that religious belief has never been replaced by anything that is equivalent to it in extension and force. This is not to say that the majority of
Hispanic people think that they must live according to Christian norms,
or that literature and culture as a whole are affected now by religion as
they were in 1700. The domes of transcendence under which everyone
felt that he had his place and was protected, have disappeared; and with
this transcendence has also been lost the pure prestige of the values
incarnate in it. But in spite of all this, but with all this, the religion
of the Spaniard, the Portuguese, and the Ibero-American is something
which is everpresent, as a permanent and infrangible reality, although
it may become noticeable and although we may realize the tremendous
dimensions of its existence only when someone tries to suppress it.
[. . .]

Spain lived her religion with all its consequences, knowing at every
moment that she was risking in such a gamble with destiny, and playing
this game with a greater seriousness than some of the Roman Popes
showed at times. Some Popes were willing to go to war to defend their
temporal interests, and they did not ruin or depopulate their states by
fighting against heretics and infidels, as Spain did. [. . .] Rome fought

323

at Lepanto (1571) under the leadership of a Spanish prince, Don Juan of Austria. But in 1611, the Duke of Osuna, Spanish viceroy in Sicily, heaped reproaches upon the Pope, whose galleys would come to load silk at Messina but would refuse to fight the Turk at the same time that the Spanish fleet was rushing into battle. That man of genius, Machiavelli, had already written that "the closer people are to the Roman Church, which is the head of our religion, the less religion they have." The Reformation deflected religious interest toward the social conduct and efficacy of man; and with this, the way was eventually closed to the emotional soliloquy of the soul with God.

[. . .]

Spanish religion, we may then conclude, is based on a Catholicism very different from that of Rome and France—not to mention the Catholicism of the United States. It is a form of belief characteristic of Spain, intelligible only within the peculiar structure of her history. Spanish religion—like her language, her institutions, her very limited capacity for objective science, her prodigality of expressiveness, and her integral personalism—must be referred to the 900 years of Christian-Islamic-Jewish interaction. The Hispanic theocracy, the impossibility of organizing Spain or Hispanic-America as a purely civil state founded on objective interests and not on the magical power of individuals, are just an expression of the possibilities and limitations of their living disposition.

As a social institution, the Spanish Church is something that nobody and nothing have succeeded in suppressing or replacing. This failure is, after all, probably quite normal: other religions likewise continue to exist in other countries, and there is no point in regretting it. But the peculiar thing in Spain is not this, but rather that the Church continues to be a power there set up against the State, in a form which is not known to either France or Italy, the other great Catholic countries. As a nation included in the circle of occidental culture, Spain has possessed a State; this State, however, has existed even in recent times as a co-power alongside the Church, which still preserves the memory of the time when Spain was governed Inquisitorially. The efforts to dispense with ecclesiastic power have had only a passing and superficial effect. Deprived of her properties in 1836, the Church succeeded, through the religious orders, in acquiring again in considerable economic power and in exercising a very broad influence through her educational centers. It is useless to resort to explanations of an external kind to account for a fact of such scope. What happens in reality is that the masses continue to find inspiration in a static and immutable belief, and not in objective realities governed by the play of human actions and interests. Spanish capitalists very often preferred to keep their money in bank accounts or to invest it in government bonds instead of risking it in industrial enterprises. The great industries, the richest mines, and many railroads belonged to foreign concerns. In 1935 there were 17,000 foreign technicians in Spain. Attitudes of quietistic apathy have been frequent there. Earlier, I cited the expression of Islamic origin "if God wills" (*si Dios quiere*), to which should be added at this point, "it is the will of God, it was the will of God" (*está de Dios, estaba de Dios*), rooted in the bowels of the people, and used at every turn.

Over against the quietistic apathy—old and deeply rooted—of the ruling classes rose up the Messianic hope of the mass of the people, founded on a belief opposite in sign but analogous in root. Among the popular beliefs, anarchism, as great an enemy of the State as religious fanaticism in its own way, has been the most widespread. Several old forms of anarchism, under the disguise of foreign ideologues, have recently rent the soul of Spain in the atrocious conflict that went on from 1936 to 1939. The Spaniard does not think that he is a member of the national collectivity, or that the march and destiny of this collectivity, which he is in but not of, depend on the actions of the people in concert and as individuals; he waits for things to happen, or for some leader with thaumaturgic gifts to rise up. The people who fought against fascism thought, and in good faith in many cases, that they were offering their lives for a sublime and universal cause, and that the sacrifice of the poor Spanish masses would bring about a change in the course of history. This is not new: at the end of the fifteenth century the Spanish masses believed that Ferdinand and Isabella had been sent by God to establish happiness on the earth and to put an end to the tyranny of all the powerful. A few Renaissance thinkers *wrote* utopias, but the Spaniards *have shed their blood* for such dreams on more than one occasion, thus erasing the boundary between the possible and the impossible, the real and the imagined.

It will be said that something similar has happened in every human society; but the chief difference between the Iberic world and the other western peoples is that the history of the latter is integrated not only by persons who fire with their ideals and disenchant with their failures (Cromwell, Napoleon, etc.), but also by extra-personal realities (economics, original political concepts, scientific and industrial changes, etc.). Phenomena of this kind are scarce in Hispanic history, and when they have been present—always as an importation from the outside, not as an innovation emergent from within—their influence has been slight. The "personal" in Spanish history is more important that any objective cultural achievement. History thus turns into an alternating process of illusíons and disenchantments, the products of faith or dis- illusion with reference to the leaders of the nation, of the Messianic hope and "anti-Christism," of the exaltation of an idol or of the vitu- peration of the guilty. From the depths of the Middle Ages till the nine- teenth century, literature continued to occupy itself with Rodrigo, the last king of the Goths, and with the traitor Julián, who opened the gates of Spain to Islam to avenge the outrage of his daughter by the lewd king. Both were the "culprits" in the ruination of Spain, and the legend of the wicked king was expanded with exquisite stories of revenge. Some cen- turies later another "personal" cause was forged to alter the course of history. In 1497 the crown prince Don Juan died, the only male child of Ferdinand and Isabella, and to this misfortune has been traditionally at- tributed the tortuous course of subsequent history, a course for which, it is said, the House of Austria is responsible. In another sense, an ex- ample of transcendent personalism can be found in the enthusiasm of the Spanish people for King Ferdinand VII, who was called nothing less that "the longed for," albeit out of pleasure of Messiah-seeking, since he was the most villainous and perverse monarch conceivable. Yet in spite of this, Ferdinand VII served as an incentive for the Spanish masses to throw out the armies of Napoleon (1808–14). The cultural splendor of Spain during the eighteenth century is attributed to Charles III, whose only merit was that he did not disturb the constructive work of a group of aristocrats won to the cause of intellectualism.

In what Catholic country is there anything like the processions in Seville during Holy Week? The images vie with one another in luxury and splendor, and the rival confraternities in charge of the different ones carry on psychological and sentimental warfare with each other. Among those who carry the images in such spectacular and dramatic processions there are men of the people who, as people, may very well be anarchists (indeed, sometime they are) who dream of razing the so- cial structure and with it the Church; they are capable of killing each other in defense of the honor and supremacy of "their" image, the image (such as the "Jesús del Gran Poder," the "Virgen de la Macarena," etc.), of which they are the bearers. It is customary to explain such behavior frivolously by referring to the "superstition" of the people, an explana- tion which clarifies nothing, for there is as much superstition in En- gland (belief in ghosts), in southern Italy, and in Poland as there is in Spain, and there may be more, yet nothing comparable takes place in those countries. A person is superstitious when he is motivated by the harm or good that may come to him through unknowable and indomitable forces; the man who helps to carry a religious image in Seville becomes one with his "superstition," converting it into the substance of his own existence and suffering trials and tribulations for it. I do not think, needless to say, that many of the "Catholics" who participate in the processions in Seville believe in and approve of everything that the Church commands to be believed—among other reasons, because they do not even know what these things are. What is important is that the person includes himself in a halo, in something that is "his" but which, being his, transcends him. He lives trusting in something that is located outside him and that operates outside what he himself does. He lives off what the earth, like a generous "alma mater," gives him. When her fruits are not easily produced, he has recourse to foreign capital and technology. Therefore in the Hispanic countries the mines and oil wells are usually in foreign hands. Or, he lives off the magical munificence of the State, which distributes jobs in abundance, also like a generous "almus pater," without too much concern over the efficiency of the functions that are performed. He floats on the belief in the State, just as he does on the previously mentioned religious belief. In either case he remains shut up within himself—which has little to do with what popular, superficial thinkers have called individualism. Shut up in himself, with his eyes on each of these transcendent objects (Church and State), he lives by expressing himself, presenting and representing his existence, like a theater of his own life, in gestures, in words, in attitudes—at times in prodigious works of art, or in acts of beautiful and unselfish morality. That part of his life which is not this—I repeat—is or has been imported from other peoples, which is not to say that the Spaniards may not occasionally excel in one or another of these imported activities. But the permanent, the basic, is the other.

A way of life with this kind of structure is bound to defend its special form of religious transcendence with tooth and nail, and is bound to oppose every effort to create political forms to be imposed on it as an objective and extra-personal thing. This is why the Hispanic states are shot through with inefficiency and immorality, and it has been impossible for them to be penetrated by an objectified religious consciousness that is the same for everyone. The Hispanic religion is a personalized belief, not a guide for conduct. But the Hispanic man is capable of killing and of being killed in the defense of "his" religion, of that world of his in which reign his will, his dream, and his caprice. He would feel lost in a world governed by norms which he could not inflect according to his will. To keep such a world from eventuating, he can commit the

most horrendous crimes and atrocities, incompatible with the most elemental Christianity. Seen in this light, the Civil War (1936–39) was a
struggle between the old Hispanic religiosity, petrified by the centuries,
and an effort towards a new religiosity, towards the creation of another
transcendent orbit, vague and misty, in which the Spanish "I want to"
(*me da la gana*) was to be combined with a utopian project for universal
happiness. The rest—fascism, communism—amount to frivolous side-
shows, in servile imitation of foreign models.

I suspect that Spaniards engendered and developed such a way of
confronting life in the conquest of the Islamic people, and in having
to let themselves be conquered through the Islamic people, as it were,
by a way of life based on submission to one belief which in turn begat
others. Even though in orthodox Mohammedanism Mohammed was
the last prophet inspired by God, it is known that since shortly after his
death and up to the present time, the Moslem has quickened his vital
quietism with the hopeful dream of a Messiah, a Mahdi. If we add to
this the actual presence of the Hispanic Jews and the Jewish converts
to Christianity in the upper classes of society, we will be on our way to
understanding important aspects of Spanish religion and its dramatic
impact on Spanish history.

It is, of course, very difficult to present in a visible and comprehen-
sible form the process by which the quality of Islamic religion penetrated into the Spanish-Christian religiosity, because we are not ma-
nipulating "things" but considering vital points of view, the feelings
of a people as they faced the world around them. These ways of facing
the world, as they came to predominate over others, came to constitute a habit, and finally a manner of existing. To be sure, the wide and
deep presence of all these manifestations of Islamism in Hispanic life,
reflected in the language and customs, was an unconscious effect of
the prestige always radiated by a powerful enemy. Islamic life imposed
itself on the life of its neighbors, on a life which it opposed; wherefore
the neighbors took over whatever attracted them and was materially
and spiritually necessary to them, from cosmetics to forms of miracles,
as we shall see later. But if we limited ourselves to cataloguing "influences," the result would be a presentation of the Spanish Christians as
colonists of the Moors, and there would be no possibility of understanding how they succeeded in leaving behind their colonial condition, nor
of articulating the history of Spain. The only way to write this history
that would adapt itself to my theme must take as its starting point the
following assumption: The Saracens imposed themselves on and op-

posed themselves to the Christians. The Christians imitated the enemy and at the same time defended themselves, using the same approach to life which the Moors had imposed on them, that is, from within a "belief," a belief in extra-rational power. The Christians opposed and finally conquered the Moslems, thanks to their own faith in the efficacy of an anti-Mohammed in warfare, who not only won battles but also provided the first expression of the singular form of Hispanic life. The Spaniards did not live their beliefs after the fashion of the Italians, the French, or the Germans, and therefore the Spanish religion was very different from that of the others; outside of Spain there was an "other world" (*más allá*) and also a "this world" (*más aca*). The stimulus for the Italian life structure has been essentially this-worldly—commerce, luxury, naval science, inquiring thought, heroism of mind (Campanella, Giordano Bruno), scant enthusiasm for war, sensuality, absence of national spirit and, consequently, of epic poetry, etc.; religion was not an essential ingredient for her history, which was often a theater of war for foreigners covetous of the fine fruits of Italian intelligence and art. France's structure grew out of the centripetal force of the capital city of her kings, whose dynasty (injected with divine powers, as we shall presently see) served as the country's spinal column. England, Germany, and the other nations of Western Europe, in one way or another built their existence on earthly foundations; but Spain rests on "godly" foundations, as we have heard Don Alonso de Cartagena put it so well when he distinguished motives behind the Castilian wars from those "other interests" which impelled the English to make war. The history of Spain is indeed *godly*, and only by accepting this evidence without reservation will we attain to an understanding of it.

Américo Castro, The Structure of Spanish History, *trans.* Edmund L. King (Princeton: Princeton University Press, 1954), 120, 121, 122–28.

Oldnewland

David Ben-Gurion (1948)

Together with Theodor Herzl and Chaim Weizmann, David Ben-Gurion (1886–1973) is considered to be one of the foremost leaders of the Zionist movement. His lifelong efforts toward the creation of a Jewish state in Palestine culminated when he proclaimed the establishment of the state of Israel on May 14, 1948, and became its first prime minister. A few hours before the expiration of the British mandate, Ben-Gurion read the declaration of independence to the members of the national council in the Tel Aviv Museum that was surrounded by ecstatic Jewish crowds who heard the declaration, made in Hebrew, on loudspeakers. Invoking the Orientalist fantasy of a land without people for a people without land, the foundational document of the State of Israel drew upon ancient Jewish pasts to claim legitimacy, and to set up the basic structure of the future state. Ben-Gurion's use of Jewish dates fixes the uninterrupted millennial history of the Jews on the land of Israel. With the establishment of this new sovereign state, Israel opened its doors to immigrants from the Mediterranean and beyond.

Eretz-Israel [*the Land of Israel*] was the birthplace of the Jewish people. Here their spiritual, religious and political identity was shaped. Here they first attained to statehood, created cultural values of national and universal significance and gave to the world the eternal Book of Books.

After being forcibly exiled from their land, the people kept faith with it throughout their Dispersion and never ceased to pray and hope for their return to it and for the restoration in it of their political freedom.

Impelled by this historic and traditional attachment, Jews strove in every successive generation to re-establish themselves in their ancient homeland. In recent decades they returned in their masses. Pioneers, *ma'pilim [immigrants coming to Eretz-Israel in defiance of restrictive legislation]* and defenders, they made deserts bloom, revived the Hebrew language, built villages and towns, and created a thriving community controlling its own economy and culture, loving peace but knowing how to defend itself, bringing the blessings of progress to all the country's inhabitants, and aspiring towards independent nationhood.

In the year 5657 (1897), at the summons of the spiritual father of the Jewish State, Theodore Herzl, the First Zionist Congress convened and proclaimed the right of the Jewish people to national rebirth in its own country.

This right was recognized in the Balfour Declaration of the 2nd November, 1917, and re-affirmed in the Mandate of the League of Nations which, in particular, gave international sanction to the historic connection between the Jewish people and Eretz-Israel and to the right of the Jewish people to rebuild its National Home.

The catastrophe which recently befell the Jewish people—the massacre of millions of Jews in Europe—was another clear demonstration of the urgency of solving the problem of its homelessness by re-establishing in Eretz-Israel the Jewish State, which would open the gates of the homeland wide to every Jew and confer upon the Jewish people the status of a fully privileged member of the commity of nations.

Survivors of the Nazi holocaust in Europe, as well as Jews from other parts of the world, continued to migrate to Eretz-Israel, undaunted by difficulties, restrictions and dangers, and never ceased to assert their right to a life of dignity, freedom and honest toil in their national homeland.

In the Second World War, the Jewish community of this country contributed its full share to the struggle of the freedom- and peace-loving nations against the forces of Nazi wickedness and, by the blood of its soldiers and its war effort, gained the right to be reckoned among the peoples who founded the United Nations.

On the 29th November, 1947, the United Nations General Assembly passed a resolution calling for the establishment of a Jewish State in Eretz-Israel; the General Assembly required the inhabitants of Eretz-Israel to take such steps as were necessary on their part for the implementation of that resolution. This recognition by the United Nations of the right of the Jewish people to establish their State is irrevocable.

This right is the natural right of the Jewish people to be masters of their own fate, like all other nations, in their own sovereign State.

Accordingly we, members of the people's council, representatives of the Jewish community of Eretz-Israel and of the Zionist movement, are here assembled on the day of the termination of the British mandate over Eretz-Israel and, by virtue of our natural and historic right and on the strength of the resolution of the United Nations General Assembly, hereby declare the establishment of a Jewish state in Eretz-Israel, to be known as the State of Israel.

We declare that, with effect from the moment of the termination of the Mandate being tonight, the eve of Sabbath, the 6th Iyar, 5708 (15th May, 1948), until the establishment of the elected, regular authorities of the State in accordance with the Constitution which shall be adopted by the Elected Constituent Assembly not later than the 1st October, 1948, the People's Council shall act as a Provisional Council of State, and its executive organ, the People's Administration, shall be the Provisional Government of the Jewish State, to be called "Israel."

The State of Israel will be open for Jewish immigration and for the Ingathering of the Exiles; it will foster the development of the country for the benefit of all its inhabitants; it will be based on freedom, justice and peace as envisaged by the prophets of Israel; it will ensure complete equality of social and political rights to all its inhabitants irrespective of religion, race or sex; it will guarantee freedom of religion, conscience, language, education and culture; it will safeguard the Holy Places of all religions; and it will be faithful to the principles of the Charter of the United Nations.

The State of Israel is prepared to cooperate with the agencies and representatives of the United Nations in implementing the resolution of the General Assembly of the 29th November, 1947, and will take steps to bring about the economic union of the whole of Eretz-Israel.

We appeal to the United Nations to assist the Jewish people in the building-up of its State and to receive the State of Israel into the comity of nations.

We appeal—in the very midst of the onslaught launched against us now for months—to the Arab inhabitants of the State of Israel to preserve peace and participate in the upbuilding of the State on the basis of full and equal citizenship and due representation in all its provisional and permanent institutions.

We extend our hand to all neighbouring states and their peoples in an offer of peace and good neighbourliness, and appeal to them to establish bonds of cooperation and mutual help with the sovereign Jewish people settled in its own land. The State of Israel is prepared to do its share in a common effort for the advancement of the entire Middle East.

We appeal to the Jewish people throughout the Diaspora to rally round the Jews of Eretz-Israel in the tasks of immigration and upbuilding and to stand by them in the great struggle for the realization of the age-old dream—the redemption of Israel.

Placing our trust in the Almighty, we affix our signatures to this proclamation at this session of the provisional Council of State, on the soil of the homeland, in the city of Tel-Aviv, on this Sabbath eve, the 5th day of Iyar, 5708 (14th May, 1948).

David Ben-Gurion (with many signatories)

Daughters of Aphrodite
Lawrence Durrell (1961)

Born and educated in British India, Lawrence Durrell (1912–90) served in the British foreign service and he spent much of his life traveling and writing about his travels in a variety of genres. He wrote many letters about his trips; of special interest are the ones from 1949 to 1952 when he was posted to Belgrade. It was there that he began his love affair with the Mediterranean, and it is there that he set his famous *Alexandria Quartet* (comprising *Justine, Balthazar, Mountolive,* and *Clea*), published between 1957 and 1960. A year after the publication of the fourth volume, *Clea*, this essay on Mediterranean women came out. It is an example of the kind of Romantic essentialism that marks many lyrical writings on the Mediterranean. As the title of the book from which this essay is taken suggests, *Spirit of Place*, the Mediterranean is indeed a place with a spirit. For Durrell, the huge variety in terms of geography, societies, cultures, and languages is reduced to a single essence, a mysterious something that can be instinctively sensed. This is the place that has produced such women. Time changes little from this perspective.

WOMEN OF THE MEDITERRANEAN

A suggestive title, a phrase full of echoes and associations—although at first it is a little difficult to say why. Perhaps it is due to the qualifying of a mysterious known by an even more mysterious adjective [. . .] are they really any different from other women in other places, and if so, how? Certainly you could not alter the adjective without damaging the rich mental image conjured up by the phrase. (Try to say "British Women" or "Swiss Women"—and all at once you feel that you are talking about a different genus.)

The Mediterranean woman has never subconsciously forgotten that, by origin, she is descended from her foam-born prototype Aphrodite. If the Nordics ever had a type-goddess of the same epoch she must have been a goddess of fertility, of marriage, of domesticity, and not one who raised woman's independence into a cult which combined freedom and sensuality in equal parts. As for the actual historic specimens of Mediterranean womanhood, a poet could get drunk simply by making a rosary of the great names they have bequeathed us. ("When Mausolus died, his wife Artemisia pounded his bones in wine and drank the potion that she might get his skill in battle . . .") Metanira, Cleopatra, Hypatia, Theodora, Beatrice, Laura, Catherine Cornaro, Sappho, Agrippina, Lucrezia Borgia, Clytemnestra, Thaïs, Penelope, Bouboulina [. . .] the list could be prolonged almost indefinitely. They are all children of this mysterious sea, occupying its landscapes in human forms which seem as unvaryingly eternal as the olive, the asphodel, the cypress, the laurel, and above all the sacred vine.

I would be right, I think, in suggesting that the word "Mediterranean" should be applied to all the wine-drinking countries around the basin; and that the character of their women emerges as distinctly as the

333

odour of thyme bruised by the hoofs of the sheep on these sun-drunk hills and dales. I must remind the reader that the vine was first discovered in Egypt.

In this context, then, as a creature of landscape one sees her very clearly. She is to be distinguished from other women by the violent coherence of a character which is composed of fierce extremes. The poetry and the vehemence of her feelings are both proverbial; but they combine happily with a certain innocence, a purity of mind. You will easily see what I mean if you reflect upon the Nordic version of her—if you think of Catherine the Great or Queen Elizabeth. The contrast is instructive, for in the North something had had to be sacrificed in order that these women might become as great as they undoubtedly were. The something is *femininity*. In order to perform their great deeds they had to become, in a sense, mannish women. What characterizes the southerner is that she can do just as great deeds without once sacrificing the female side of her character. (Theodora, Semiramis, Cleopatra.) There is a constant in the character which does not change however various different women were. This difference of character seems all the more marked when we reflect upon the long battle which women in the North have fought for equal rights. In the South, no such battle has been necessary, for women do not envy men at all. Why should they ask for equality with the feebler sex—man? They know that nothing is stronger than the mother and the cult of the mother—and they have been content with their role as procreators, the handers-on of the man-children.

She is as various as the history of the Mediterranean itself, the Mediterranean woman, whether she is skirting the dark labyrinths of Crete, whether she walks knife in hand along the blood-soaked corridors of Tiryns or Mycenae, whether she poisons with a Renaissance smile or accepts with beating heart the blood-spattered trophy from the toreador's crimson hand. But we dare not imagine that she has no weaknesses—for her overpowering sensuality and single-heartedness, the pride and naivety of her feelings have more than once driven great poets to open their veins, or great soldiers to start unjust wars in her name like Helen did. Yet we would not wish her otherwise than she is. Even the Moslems who say that women have no souls are unable to imagine a Paradise which is not perfected by her presence: their afterworld is peopled by the fluttering shapes of the *hanoumi*, brilliant and soulless as fireflies on an autumn night.

Her struggle, it seems to me, has always been the same one: to break through the pattern of sexual greed and self-indulgence in order to discover herself, to find a magical identification with the earth-rhythms whose slow pulses beat in her blood. (I am thinking of the abstracted faces of Greek women as they join in the age-old dances and beat up the red dust with their bare soles. Faces purged of everything except the sensual concentration on the music's throb and swing. They burn inwardly like altar candles. I am thinking of the Spanish dancers with their proud-shrill parrot-voices and the maddening rataplan of their castanets upon the watchers' heartstrings. I am thinking of the peasant dancers in Italy who pause as the first flights of fireworks stain the dark velvet sky in honour of a patron saint (as in Ischia), only once more to resume the grave poignant measures which have been handed down to them through the generations and which were first intended, perhaps, to copy the motions of the stars.)

But the Mediterranean is older than history and stronger than religion; one of the reasons why we love it so much is this unfailing sense of continuity in which it invests the present. If you go to an Easter service in a Catholic church at Marseilles, Naples or Madrid, you feel very certainly that the Christian mysteries were evolved out of the Eleusinian mysteries and that invisibly the worshippers are linking hands with their ancestors through the communion of the saints. This feeling is even stronger in an Orthodox church, because the Greek language of the service vibrates like the wind in the Aeolian harp of the mind. What do these faces tell one except that nothing Mediterranean can change for it is landscape-dominated; its people are simply the landscape-wishes of the earth sharing their particularities with the wine and the food, the sunlight and the sea.

And the woman of this landscape? At certain times she has been better-loved and understood than at others; though she has always been feared. I think the Greeks got nearest to treating her as such a rare animal deserves to be treated. Pythagoras included her among his pupils as did Apollonius. Epicurus built up a philosophy to share with her which is perhaps the most perfect ever made—a philosophy of poetry which excluded her from nothing. She was granted the importance and the affection which today she finds only in Paris. Indeed, it is not simply a whim to see that France, even today, is as near to modern man has got to Ancient Greece.

The two worlds, northern and southern, have maintained a curious dialogue in art and culture. They hate much about each other, but they envy more. Perhaps, unconsciously, they feel that each is complementary to the other. But the axis (the spiritual axis) which passes through them crosses the centre of France, from Alsace to Provence, from beer to wine, from Gothic to Romance. It passes, like white light, through the brilliant, discordantly radiant prism of Paris which will always remain the mediatrix between these two aspects of European temperament. What gives the French temperament its balance and form is precisely the uneasy polarity between these two influences. What gives France the enormous range and span and force of its art is, quite literally, that the French artist has the best of both worlds. He can choose, so to speak the mixture he needs for his work. The spark of French genius leaps between the two poles, northern and southern, Puritan and Pagan. Where else can you span the two worlds so effectively— that of Rabelais and Pascal, that of Stendhal and Chateaubriand, that of Camus and Genet? It was through France that the Mediterranean woman projected her power and influence northward to inflame the imagination of the slow and ox-like northerners. In the time of Shakespeare, the Elizabethan heroine was really a Mediterranean. Stendhal, who discovered Shakespeare in middle age, was delighted to find that his heroines shared many of the qualities of energy and passion that he admired among his beloved Italians. "How he *Italianizes*!" he writes with delight. In the Elizabethan age, the power of the Italian tradition in feeling was a marked one on the stage—and it alarmed the Puritans who were always attacking this southern infatuation.

The Englishman Italianate
Is the Devil incarnate.

With the political and religious broils which severed the British from Europe and inflicted on them the deep psychic wound which has not healed today, this vein of feeling became exhausted. Nowadays, the British artist is still vainly trying to join the Common Market in arts and letters.

Here an anecdote comes to mind which will perhaps describe the Mediterranean woman better than a dozen historical generalizations which the reader might find arguable. During the last war an Italian lady of Alexandria who sympathized with the Allies gave a weekly tea-party for the troops stationed in town. To this little party she always invited a dozen or so of the prettiest and most eligible Italian ladies of the town thinking that their beauty and their conversation would be some compensation to the allied soldiers and sailors for the harsh life of danger which was theirs. On one of these occasions a young American was present, very shy, extremely polite, and undoubtedly inhibited by the beauty of the ladies and the magnificence of the house in which he found himself. A young lady approached him and began to converse. In order to show himself anxious to make a good impression, the young man, after racking his brains for a subject, took out his fountain-pen (a very modern one) and demonstrated some of its gadgets to her. They discussed it. The subject once exhausted, he showed her some even more modern gadgets on his expensive wrist-watch and chronometer combined. They discussed it. Finally he passed to his cigarette-lighter which was also a marvel. The young woman put up with him for some time, but finally she leaned forward, touched his wrist gently with her forefinger, and smiling beatifically at the Anglo-Saxon said: "yes—but *what do you feel?*" at the same time placing one hand upon her heart. There was no answer to this artless question. Stendhal would have been ravished, but the youth choked on his tea and took himself off as fast as he could.

It is the sacredness of emotion, the uncritical enjoyment of feeling for its own sake that is one of the keys to the Mediterranean woman's character.

"In Italy," writes Stendhal, "a country totally devoid of the vanity of France and England, every man laughs at his neighbour and even despises and detests him. His judgment of the arts is founded solely upon his own feelings. The Italians [. . .] form a total contrast, it is clear, to the inhabitants of France and England who are better off politically, but who have been deprived of all individual character by their ambition to become, in every sense of the terms, a fashionable and well-bred copy of a certain conventional pattern. Unlike the Englishman and the Frenchman, the Italian listens only to the promptings of his own heart, employing all the energy of his character to give predominance to his own peculiar mode of feeling." Our author, who divined the Italian character so clearly, remains in my opinion somewhat unfair to his own country. (The symbol of Marianne is still quite recognizably Mediterranean, but not that of Boadica.) Stendhal, who came of what we might call puritan inheritance, simply longed to free himself from it and espouse the pagan side of the national character. He never quite succeeded. He hated all that was cold, vain and calculating and loved everything that was energetic, passionate, simple, and generous. The mystery to me is why his sojourn in Marseilles did not teach him that the spirit he so admired was the very lifeblood of the French Midi.

But if this direct abandonment to her feelings is one of the great strengths of the Mediterranean woman, it is also one of her signal weaknesses. It has given her great powers but it has also enfeebled her political and social position. Men have not been slow to take advantage of this factor; she is extremely male-dominated in the countries of the Mediterranean where cheerful use is made of her as a beast of burden and a money-raiser. In Greece, in Egypt, it is she who does the rough work, carrying and fetching, while the male is content to sit under a tree and fan himself or talk politics. He seems to be quite content with his role — why should he not be? He has the pleasure of begetting the children, she the trouble of bringing them up. Indeed, perhaps her bondage is a willing and self-created one. Who else is responsible for all the truly Mediterranean fetishes which have grown up about the idea of a male child? We confidently assert that the Anglo-Saxon males are mother-fixated, but whoever had watched the way Mediterranean mothers bring up their male offspring would hesitate to be so dogmatic. Before her son can walk or talk the Mediterranean mother has crowned him the king of her life. He can do no wrong, and his sisters soon learn an appropriate female attitude of inferiority before his young god whose word is law. In some ways the bondage of the Mediterranean female may be said to begin in the nursery; she can thereafter only recover her independence by the creation of a male child of her own. Her self-respect as a woman is deeply bound up with the question of whether she can bear sons or not. This mother-son link seems to me every bit as strong as that described by the psychologists in the North, and in some ways even such a great novel of the Oedipus complex as *Sons and Lovers* could be translated into Mediterranean terms and remain true to its thesis. (I have noticed over and over again that seasick Greeks and Italians and Spaniards are apt to call upon their mothers when *in extremis* — often in the accents of five-year-old children.)

But if the Mediterranean woman spoils her male child the balance is often restored by the pattern and rhythm of her family life which is unvarying in its respect for certain basic values. The importance of the family as a tribe is perhaps the most important aspect of the matter. The family holds together as a living unit and provides a frame inside which there is room for every generation. Granny, for example, whether you find her in Naples or Madrid, in Marseilles or Piraeus, is the dominating member of the Latin household. She is not only loved and admired but also deeply respected; more important than this, she keeps on working right to the end. In England today, when a couple marries the old people are relegated to the scrap-heap, so to speak; to the furnished hotel on the South Coast. They are no longer useful or productive. In the North, the idea of a family (look at our advertisements) has come to mean only mother, father and the children. In the Mediterranean it is a whole tribe, shading away on all sides to the most remote corners of cousin-ship or aunthood. So complicated does this cobweb become that some nations (I am thinking especially of the Greeks) have a full vocabulary to express the fine distinctions of relationship. I once heard a man say to another: "Please go to the hotel in Athens and give this letter to my brother's second cousin's aunt Loula—the one by marriage and not the divorced one." It is possible that this notion of family pattern has been helped and engendered by Catholicism as some people have said; but I think this explanation does not go far enough, for it exists in Orthodox countries as well. It existed among the ancient Greeks.

The Mediterranean woman, then, while from many points of view she may seem enslaved, is nevertheless the queen bee of the family hive. She is the beloved tyrant of her grandchildren.

Is she herself religious? Not in the strictest meaning of the word. An anthropologist would say that she was more superstitious than reli-gious. This is because in her passion she is wholly uncritical. She loves her church as she loves her man or her son—with a completely un-rationalized self-surrender. She refuses to make a theology out of her passions. Moral questions, questions of principle or judgment, do not sway her. Her life has no critical apparatus so to speak. She has never bothered to worry herself with all the paradoxes of existence. Life for her is as simple as a glass of wine—and she drinks her wine without water. This is what makes me suspect that all the changes of politics and history are, from her point of view, illusory; she has always remained a pagan, devoutly and unconsciously pagan. This is so apparent to any-one who watches her at prayer in a church of Marseilles of Naples! Even if you go further south and watch her Orthodox counterpart praying at the miracle-working shrine of the Virgin on the island of Tinos on the 15th of August every year. See how she attacks the shrine with her prayers, as if she would wrench, by the irresistible force of her prayer, the required miracle from it. No, she does not "pray," for the very word smacks of self-conscious intercessions with forces which she fears; she besieges her God as she does her lover. She is importuning an earth-force, something elemental which existed long before the Gods were condensed into conceptual forms.

Fundamentally she enjoys everything, even her own despair, with a vibrating innocence [. . .], if you like, we could consider this a sort of passionate blindness—a limitation. Yet, if it is one, it effectively blinds her to many things which bedevil us northerners, and which we would gladly shed. I recall that in many years of lecturing about literature to boys and girls I never succeeded in making Mediterranean students fully grasp the literary notions which have grown up about two northern concepts: namely "Spleen" and "Ennui." As for "Angst" I did not even dare to try.

This portrait, I know, lacks much fine detail: it is too black and white. Nevertheless, it is the best that one can do in words. Luckier men have painted her in other media more successfully, more truthfully. In the Ponoma of Mailol, for example, you see the young earth Goddess that she is, fruitful and heavy-breasted. She is a spirit of place and not simply "a woman." She defeats words, as all true goddesses must.

Finally, let us talk a little about her as a lover. I do not use the word "wife" for that to her is a duty she performs perfectly and unselfconsciously. She is destined to be a wife and she knows it and accepts. She is *born* to be a lover. And when she is in love she shows her Mediterranean character at its highest potential. We know the phrase of Shakespeare about Cleopatra: "age shall not wither her nor custom stale her infinite variety." This phrase which echoes in the European subconscious and which may be thought by some to be only a piece of poetic license is in fact a factual statement, and as true as a stock report. The infinite variety comes out of her innocence. Whether she wears a pistol and chooses her own lovers by force (as Bouboulina of the Greek Independence days) or whether she will have no lovers because she is in love with someone whom she cannot have—the pattern is the same: a totality. She can die for love as easily as a bird leaves a branch. In the North we have not begun to live for it. She can let her sensuality overturn a whole world if it is given in free rein, but on the other hand she can become an anchorite because no other men (except the one she loves) seem worth loving. It is this comprehensiveness of her passion which can inspire great poets, can inspire men to become eunuchs for her sake. (That is why she is dangerous to the ordinary run of men.) In fact, she was born to sire poets, and she will continue to try to do so as long as olive-trees and asphodels exist, and as long as the blue waves of the Mediterranean roll upon these deserted beaches. Who would want her otherwise?

Lawrence Durrell, Spirit of Place *(New York: Marlowe, 1969), 369–77.*

The Sixth Continent

Halikarnas Balıkçısı (1971)

Author, popular historian, and travel writer Cevat Şakir Kabaağçlı (1886–1973) took the pen name the "Halikarnas Balıkçısı" (or, the Fisherman of Halicarnassus) after he was exiled to the then small Aegean town of Bodrum in the late 1920s for a story critical of the Turkish military. In novels such as *Anchors Aweigh* (1945) and *Sea Exiles* (1969), he describes the daily lives of common people who lived and died by the sea. In popular histories like *Blue Exile* (1961) and *The Voice of Anatolia* (1971), he resituates Turkish and Mediterranean identities around the Ionian coast. The underlying dilemma that the author struggles with throughout his work centers on the following question: "How is Mediterranean identity possible in the age of the nation-state?" Often moonlighting as a tour guide, the author is also responsible for popularizing the famous "Blue Cruise" tour along the Anatolian coasts of the Mediterranean. In the following selection, the "Fisherman" links Mediterranean and Anatolian identities as having emerged from an unprecedented layering of civilizations.

The Mediterranean, from ethnic and other perspectives, could be considered the world's sixth continent. Geographers have arbitrarily designated extensive landmasses as being Europe or Asia, etc. Thereby, there are three continents that border the Mediterranean Sea. But the shores of the Mediterranean are neither Europe, nor Asia, nor Africa; they are the Mediterranean. Essentially, Africa begins south of the great Sahara Desert. Greece, France, and Italy are not just European they are all Mediterranean. Take people from the remotest corners of the world, sprinkle them along the Mediterranean coast, and before long, through the alchemy of the sixth continent, they will become Mediterranean to the bone. Like its very waters, the Mediterranean embodies a fluent and cerulean history of humanity. [. . .] And the eastern littoral is where the Mediterranean is quintessentially Mediterranean. This is not literary flourish or poetry, but the truth. Other regions of the world might boast of a single civilization, if that; but the eastern Mediterranean and its surroundings can lay claim to the Sumerian, Akkadian, Babylonian, Assyrian, Egyptian, Hittite, Persian, Minoan, Ionian, and Greek civilizations. . . . For civilization is such a phenomenon that its seed cannot be sown by one or another people alone. Civilization, which is humanist, has never been the monopoly of one pure line of descent. It has always taken hold through the intermingling of diverse strains. [. . .]

The location of the Anatolian peninsula between the three continents of Europe, Asia, and Africa, its orientation on an east-west axis, rather than vertically north-south like the other Mediterranean peninsulas (Greece, Italy, Spain), has served to make it a land-bridge for waves of human migration; not to mention that its location at the juncture of the continents serves to link them all. Additionally, Anatolia has a coastline 2,000 miles long opening to warm seas which shimmer fiery and blue and containing portals for the throngs of people who have come and gone. These characteristics of Anatolia have facilitated the mixing of races and ethnicities there more than elsewhere. [. . .]

The Aegean coast of Anatolia is a complex of inlets and isthmuses. Large, high-ridged promontories jump into and emerge out of the sea, creating islands. Thereby, as the process continues between land and sea, chains of islands are strung in the deep blue like pearls. Migratory masses encountering the sea could not withstand the call of its vastness, and leaping from island to island, ended up creating Cretan civilization, the first sea civilization of Anatolia and the world. Why? Norms and traditions condemn societies to stasis and the status quo, whereas the intermingling of peoples, their grinding contact, smoothes and softens the sharp points and jagged edges that various traditions harbor toward one another; through this process, people come to adapt to others.

Intermarriage among foreign groups ends up doing away with foreignness itself. The exchange of goods coming from the East furthers the trade of ideas. Thus, each wave of migration and the exchange of goods it fostered, moved the structure of society toward humanism and civilization. [. . .]

About seventy years ago, no one knew a thing about the spectacular Minos or Aegean Sea civilization of the Island of Crete, nor about the Hittite civilization of Anatolia; both had been lost to oblivion, buried beneath the earth of thousands of years. Histories of that era went directly from the Phoenicians to the Greeks. [. . .]

Aside from research in Egyptology, Western specialists had two principle aims: One was to shed further light onto Hellenism and the other was religious. That is, to document the biblical Hebrew culture of Christianity. Anatolia had little importance in their eyes. Even Turks themselves were not interested in Anatolia as their own true homeland, and considered it to be nothing but unfamiliar.

Halikarnas Balıkçısı, Andolu'nun Sesi *[The Voice of Anatolia] (Ankara: Bilgi, 1971), 17–24. Trans. Erdağ Göknar.*

Mirror of the Self

Orhan Pamuk (1985)

The plot of *The White Castle*, Nobel laureate Orhan Pamuk's historical novel set in the 1670s, focuses on the relationship between a Venetian slave captured on the Sea and the Ottoman Hoja, his captor. The Italian scholar is sailing from Venice to Naples, and ends up being taken to Istanbul. In the winter 1997/1998 issue of *Mediterraneans*, Pamuk writes, "In *The White Castle* it is not coincidence that the Italian hero is captured by the Turks on the Mediterranean. Nor is it a coincidence that in the opening pages of the novel I refer to the Mediterranean simply as 'the sea,' not the White Sea or the Mediterranean. It's as if, in Turkish, the Mediterranean was merely a place where 'the others' were confronted." But the master/slave relationship is not as simple as it might seem. In one vital scene, the two protagonists, symbolizing "self" and "other," venture to look at their reflections. What they see foreshadows the novel's climax, wherein the narrative voice unites the shores of the Mediterranean by emerging from Venice and Istanbul at once.

When Hoja once again fell silent, we were no longer close. He'd risen from the table, and out of the corner of my eye, I could follow his shadow roaming about the room; next, he took up the lamp in the midst of the table and passed behind me, and I could see neither shadow nor Hoja; I desired to turn and look, but I couldn't bring myself to do so, for I dreaded some impending mischief. Before long, I did turn fearfully, having heard the rustle of garments being removed. He was bare from the waist up, had stepped before the mirror, and was carefully examining his chest and stomach, which were illuminated by the light cast by the lamp. "Allah!" he said, "What kind of pustule might this be?" I was dumbfounded. "Do come have a look at this." I was petrified; he shouted: "Approach, I say to you!" I did so apprehensively, like a truant about to receive his punishment.

I'd never before been so close to his exposed body, and this proximity did not in the least please me. At first I wanted to believe that this was the very reason I was unable to approach him, but I knew I feared the pustule. He, too, understood this despite the fact that I'd lowered my head close to his corpus, posturing like a physician so he wouldn't realize my torment, and stared at that protrusion, that redness, as I muttered some nonsense or other. "You are afraid, are you not?" said Hoja

343

at last. In order to prove that I wasn't, I brought my head down even closer. "You're afraid this is a plague bubo." I pretended not to comprehend that word; I verged on telling him that an insect had bitten him, and that it must by needs have been a strange bug that had previously once bitten me somewhere, but the name of the pest escaped me. "Why don't you touch it?" said Hoja. "Indeed, how can you be certain, if you don't touch it? Why do you not touch me?"

When he saw that I wouldn't touch it, he became overjoyed. He brought the fingers that he'd drawn over the protrusion close to my visage. When he saw me shudder in disgust, he made a cackle and mocked me because I feared a mere insect bite, but his joy did not last long. "I am afraid of death," he blurted. It was as if he were talking about various and sundry things; more than shame, he displayed anger, the wrath of one who has been wronged. "Don't you have one of these pustules? Are you certain? Take off your shirt, why don't you?" When he insisted, I removed my shirt like a child who loathes being washed. The room was hot, the window shut, but from somewhere a cooling breeze blew; I cannot be for certain, maybe it was the coldness of the mirror that disturbed me. Because I was ashamed of my appearance, I took a step and moved out of the frame. Next, in the mirror, I saw Hoja's face in profile and he was lowering his head toward my body; that enormous head that everyone said resembled mine had leaned down to my body. "In order to poison my soul," I thought unexpectedly; whereas I had been doing the exact opposite, and because I'd been mentoring him, I'd been proud for years. That it even came to mind was comical, but I momentarily thought the bearded head grown brazen in the light of the lamp was on the verge of sucking my lifeblood! So, apparently, I did enjoy those tales of horror that I'd heard in my youth. Thinking this, I sensed his fingers on my stomach; I wanted to escape, I wanted to strike his head with something. "You don't have one," he said. He'd passed behind me to examine my underarms, neck, and the backs of my ears. "Nothing here either, the bug hasn't bitten you."

Placing his hand on my shoulder, he stood beside me. I was like a childhood friend with whom he commiserated. He squeezed the nape of my neck with his fingers and drew me toward him. "Come, let's gaze into the mirror together." I looked, and beneath the naked light of the lamp, I saw, once again, how much we resembled each other. I recalled how I'd been overwhelmed by this feeling upon first seeing him while waiting at Sadık Pasha's door. Back then, I'd seen somebody whom I must become; whereas now, I thought that he must become someone like me. I realized that the two of us were *one*! Presently, this seemed to be an obvious truth. It seemed as if I'd been bound hand-and-arm, fixed in my spot. I made a gesture to flee, as if to verify that I was who I was: I hastily drew my hand through my forelocks. But, he mimicked me, moreover, masterfully, without in the least disturbing our symmetry within the mirror. He was also imitating the manner of my glance, aping the position of my head and my horror, which I could not bring myself to watch in the mirror yet from which I could not look away, overcome by the curiosity of fear: afterward, he became jubilant like a child who pestered his friend by mimicking his words and gestures. He howled! He said we were to die together! "How ridiculous," thought I. But I was agitated nonetheless. It was the most unsettling of the nights that I'd passed in his company.

In course of time, he insisted that he'd suspected the plague from the beginning and that he was doing it all in order to test me. Supposedly, this was also the case when Sadık Pasha's executioners had taken me away in order to kill me, and when others said that we resembled each other; next, he said that he'd taken possession of my soul; just like he'd done while aping my movements previously, he now said he knew what I thought, and what I knew, he was thinking! Next, he asked me what I was contemplating at that instant, and I said there was nothing in my thoughts beside him, and I said that I wasn't thinking about anything, but he wasn't listening, because he was conversing not in order to learn, but only to strike terror into me, for the sake of toying with his own fear, so that I might receive my due portion of that fear. I sensed that as he realized his own loneliness he wanted to retaliate with acts of evil; while he caressed our faces with his hand, while he desired to terrify me through the magick of that peculiar resemblance, and while he, more than I, became agitated and animated, I thought that he wanted to make mischief: and because his heart couldn't manage to resign itself to that evil all at once, I told myself, he kept me before the mirror, squeezing the back of my neck, though I found him to be completely stupid and desperate: He was correct, the things that he said, I too, wanted to say and do, and I was jealous of him because he was able to act before I did and frolic in the fear of the plague and the mirror.

I couldn't manage to escape the feeling of a ruse, despite being so frightened, despite thinking that I'd realized things about myself that I'd not considered before. He'd loosened his grip on my neck, but I did not step away from the mirror. "I have become like you," he said next. "I now know how you feel fear. I have become you!" I tried to dismiss his saying "I know" and this prophecy as being idiotic and puerile—though today I have no doubt about half its truth. He maintained that he could see the world the way I did; he said "they" again, and now he apparently understood finally how "they" thought and felt. Making his gaze wander beyond the confines of the mirror, he looked at the table, glasses, chairs, and objects in the half-light cast by the lamp, and spoke sparingly. Next, he claimed that he could now explain things that he couldn't explain earlier because he hadn't been able to see them before, but I thought he was in error: Both words and objects were the same. The only thing that was different was his fear; not that either, his way of experiencing fear; nevertheless, I thought that this manner, what it was I cannot now clearly record—was something that he'd assumed before the mirror, a new ruse. As if beyond his own will, his mind, casting aside this ruse as well, churned and churned to fixate back upon that red pustule, which he pondered and debated—was it a bug or the plague?

For a time, he declared he wanted to continue with everything from where I'd left off. We were still half-naked, and we hadn't stepped away from the mirror. He informed me that he would take my place, and I his, and that exchanging our clothes and he letting his beard grow while I sheared off mine was sufficient to the task. This idea made our resemblance in the mirror even more terrifying, and my nerves grew tense and I listened: At that juncture he said I would be the one to make a freedman of him: He described with glee everything he who usurped my place in the world would do when he returned to my country. I was astonished to discover that everything I'd described to him about my childhood and youth, down to the smallest detail, he had committed to memory, and I was further surprised to see that from those details, according to him, he'd fabricated an odd and unreal, imaginary home-land. My life was out of my control, and in his hands, being dragged elsewhere, and I was helpless to do anything but watch from a distance all that would happen to me as in a dream. However, the voyage that he would undertake to my country and the life that he would live there had a comic peculiarity and innocence that prevented me from believing him completely. On the other hand, I was astounded by the consistency of the imaginary details: I felt like saying that all this was seemingly possible, and I could live like this. It was then that I realized that I'd learned for the first time something about Hoja's life, but I wasn't able to say what that was. Simply listening, in a state of shock, to what I would do in my former world, which I'd contemplated with longing for years, made me forget about phobia of the plague.

But this didn't last long. Hoja, now, wanted me to say what I would do when I took his place. Trying to convince myself that we didn't resemble each other and that the pustule was really an insect bite, and being put eerily on the spot, had strained my nerves to such a degree that nothing came to mind. When he insisted, I recollected that at one time I had planned to pen my memoirs when I returned to my country, and I told him so: And then, when I said that I would perhaps one day make a good tale out of his thoughts and write it down, he belittled me in disgust. Apparently, I wasn't at all acquainted with him at all as he was with me! Pushing me away, he stepped in front of the mirror alone: He said that when he took my place he would be the one to describe my fate! First, he declared that the pustule was a plague bubo; he informed me that I would die. Next, he described to me how I would writhe in agony before death; the fear, for which I was unprepared because I was not aware of it until then, was a fate worse than death. As he explained how I would struggle with the torments of the disease, Hoja had moved away from the mirror; shortly, when I looked again, he had stretched out on top of the disheveled bed laid onto the floor, detailing the aches and pains I would suffer. His hand was over his stomach, and I thought the cramp he described was actually afflicting him. At that moment, he called to me, and I approached him with trepidation and immediately regretted having done so; he'd again tried to brush his hand onto me. For whatever reason, I now thought that it was merely an insect bite, but I was afraid, nevertheless.

The entire night passed this way. As he tried to communicate his disease and the fear of it to me, he repeated again and again that I was he and he was I.

Orhan Pamuk, Beyaz Kale [*The White Castle*] (Istanbul: İletişim, 1985), 89–94. Trans. Erdağ Göknar.

Thousands of Watchful Eyes
Assia Djebar (1985)

After the war of independence was won in 1962, Algerians turned to the business of nation building and statecraft. A new government was formed, new laws were promulgated, and a new struggle was engaged to define and shape an authentic Algerian identity. Male combatants were rewarded with posts; female combatants were forgotten. This erasure of women's role during the war became a cause célèbre for intellectuals in Algeria and in France. The historian and novelist Assia Djebar became one of the most outspoken defendants of women's right to recognition for their contributions not only to the war of independence but also to the resistance from the moment the French troops first landed on Algerian soil. In her 1985 novel *L'amour la fantasia*, she paints the canvas of nineteenth-century Algeria. In the following selection, she imagines women back into the history that has eliminated their presence and has their eyes plant the French ships on to the waters of the port of Algiers.

Dawn on this thirteenth day of June 1830, at the exact moment when the sun suddenly blazes forth above the fathomless bowl of the bay. It is fine in the morning. As the majestic fleet rends the horizon the Impregnable City sheds her veils and emerges, a wraith-like apparition, through the blue-grey haze. A distant triangle aslant, glinting in the last shreds of nocturnal mist and then settling softly, like a figure sprawling on a carpet of muted greens. The mountain shuts out the background, dark against the blue wash of the sky.

The first confrontation. The city, a vista of crenelated roofs and pastel hues, makes her first appearance in the rôle of "Oriental Woman," motionless, mysterious. At first light the French Armada starts its slow glide past, continuing its stately ballet until noon spills its spangled radiance over the scene. No sound accompanies this transformation—this solemn moment of anticipation, breathless with suspense, the moment before the overture strikes up. But who are to be the performers? On which side shall we find the audience? Five in the morning. A Sunday; and what is more, it is the Feast of Corpus Christi in the Christian calendar. The first lookout, wearing the uniform of a frigate captain, stands on the poop of one of the craft of the reserve fleet which will sail past ahead of the battle squadron, preceding a hundred or so men-o'-war. The name of the lookout man is Amable Matterer. He keeps watch and that same day will write, "I was the first to catch sight of the city of Algiers, a tiny triangle on a mountain slope."

Half past five in the morning. The immense flotilla of frigates, brigs and schooners, bedecked with multicoloured pennons, streams endlessly, three by three, into the entrance to the bay, from which all traces of night and threats of storm have vanished. It has been decided that the decks of the *Provence*, the admiral's flagship, shall be cleared for action.

Units of able-seamen and soldiers clatter up in their thousands on to the decks and swarm on forecastle and poop. The scene is suddenly blanketed in silence, as if the intense silken light, squandered so lavishly in dazzling pools, were about to be rent with a strident screech.

Nothing stirs in the Barbary city. Not a quiver disturbs the milky dazzle of the terraced houses that can gradually be distinguished on the slopes of the mountain whose mass is now clearly silhouetted in a series of gentle emerald-green undulations.

Officers and men are drawn up in tight formation close to the rails and stanchions, taking care that their swords do not rattle at their sides; silence save for an occasional interjection, a muffled oath, a throat being cleared, an expectoration. The host of men waiting to invade, stand and watch amidst the jumble of hammocks, in between pieces of artillery and big guns drawn up in their firing position, like circus animals waiting under the spotlights, ready to perform. The city faces them in the unchanging light which absorbs the sounds.

Amable Matterer, first officer, of the *Ville de Marseille*, does not stir, nor do his companions. The Impregnable City confronts them with its many invisible eyes. Although they had been prepared for its skyline—here a dome reflected in the water, there the silhouette of a fortress or the tip of a minaret—nevertheless the dazzling white panorama freezes before them in its disturbing proximity.

Thousands of watchful eyes there are doubtless estimating the number of vessels. Who will pass on the number? Who will write of it? Which of all these silent spectators will live to tell the tale when the encounter is over? Amable Matterer is at his post in the first squadron which glides slowly westward; he gazes at the city which returns his gaze. The same day he writes of the confrontation, dispassionately, objectively.

I, in my turn, write, using his language, but more than one hundred and fifty years later. I wonder, just as the general staff of the fleet must have done, whether the Dey Hussein has gone up on to the terrace of his Kasbah, telescope in hand. Is he personally watching the foreign armada approach? Does he consider this threat beneath contempt? So many foes have sailed away after a token bombardment or two, just as Charles V of Spain did in the sixteenth century! [. . .] Is the Dey at a loss? Is he unmoved? Or is he giving vent to one of his dramatic rages, such as he recently displayed when the King of France sent his envoy with a demand for unreasonable apologies: the Dey's reply is enshrined in legend: "The King of France may as well demand my wife!"

I can imagine Hussein's wife neglecting her dawn prayer to climb up too on to the terrace. How many other women, who normally only retreated to their terraces at the end of the day, must also have gathered there to catch a glimpse of the dazzling French fleet.

When the squadron left Toulon, there were four painters, five draughtsmen and about a dozen engravers on board. [. . .] The battle is not yet joined, they are not yet even in sight of their prey, but they are already anxious to ensure a pictorial record of the campaign. As if the imminent war were to be considered as some sort of festivity.

As this day dawns when the two sides will come face to face, what are the women of the town saying to each other? What dreams of romance are lit in their hearts or are extinguished for ever, as they gaze on the proud fleet tracing the figures of a mysterious ballet? [. . .] I muse on this brief respite; I slip into the antechamber of this recent past, like an importunate visitor, removing my sandals according to the accustomed ritual, holding my breath in an attempt to overhear everything. [. . .]

On this the thirteenth day of June 1830, the confrontation continues for two, three hours, well into the glare of the afternoon. As if the invaders were coming as lovers! The vessels sail so slowly, so quietly westward, that they might well have been planted there above the glassy surface of the water, by the eyes of the Impregnable City, blinded by mutual love at first sight.

And the silence of this majestic morning is but the prelude to the cavalcade of screams and carnage which will fill the ensuing decades.

Assia Djebar, Fantasia: An Algerian Cavalcade, *trans. Dorothy S. Blair (Portsmouth, N.H.: Heinemann, 1993), 6–8.*

Last Evening in this Land
Mahmud Darwish (1992)

A voice of Palestinian resistance, poet Mahmud Darwish was born in 1945. The village of his birth was El Bireh, and it was razed to the ground during the Israeli war of independence. In his epic poem "The Adam of Two Edens," he crosses the 500 years that have elapsed since the Muslims were driven out of Granada and were scattered around the shores of the Mediterranean. While defiant, he sounds a note of despair when he calls himself "the last gasp of the Arabs." This last gasp refers to Boabdil, last ruler of Granada, whose mother had taunted him for what has come to be called "the Moor's last sigh," he being that Moor. She was berating him for weeping like a woman for what he could not defend as a man. The hope in this poem is that the exile is destined to return however far she has wandered and however long the absence.

THE ADAM OF TWO EDENS

(1) The Last Evening in This Land

On our last evening in this land
we tear our days down from the trellises,
tally the ribs we carry away with us
and the ribs we leave behind.

On the last evening
we bid farewell to nothing,
we've no time to finish,
everything's left as it is,
places change dreams the way they
change casts of characters.

Suddenly we can no longer be lighthearted,
this place is about to play host to nothing.

On the last evening
we contemplate mountains surrounding the clouds,
Invasion and counter-invasion,
the ancient era handing our door keys over to a new age.
Enter, O invaders, come, enter our houses,
drink the sweet wine of our Andalusian songs!
We are the night at midnight,
no horsemen galloping toward us
from the safety of the last call to prayer
to deliver the dawn
Our tea is hot and green—so drink!
Our pistachios are ripe and fresh—so drink!
The beds are green with new cedarwood—give in to your
    drowsiness!
After such a long siege, sleep on the soft down of our dreams!
Fresh sheets, scents at the door, and many mirrors.
Enter our mirrors so we can vacate the premises
completely!

Later we'll look up what was recorded in our history
about yours in faraway lands.

Then we'll ask ourselves,
"*Was Andalusia
here or there? On earth,
or only in poems?*"

351

(2) How Can I Write Above the Clouds?

How can I write my peoples' testament above the clouds?
They leave time behind
The way people leave their overcoats at home.
They erect a citadel, tear it down to raise a tent on its foundations
nostalgic for a first glimpse of palm trees.

My people betray my people
in wars defending salt.
But Granada is gold,
silken words embroidered with almonds,
tears of silvery glitter on lute strings.

Granada is a law unto herself,
proudly becomes whatever she wishes,
yearns for anything
past or passing.

If a swallow's wing brushes a woman's breast in bed,
she screams, "Granada is my body!"
If someone loses a gazelle in green meadows
he screams, *"Granada is my land. That's where I'm from!"*
Sing so goldfinches can build
stairways to heaven from my ribs!
Sing the chivalry of men meeting death, moon by moon, in the
    beloved's alleyway.
Sing garden birds stone by stone!
O how I love you, who
cut me down sinew by sinew
on the road to her hot night.
Sing, *"No smells of freshly brewed coffee in the morning after you've
    gone."*
Sing my migration
from the cooing of mourning doves on your knee,
from my spirit's rest
in the letters of your liquid name.

Granada belongs to song.
So sing!

(3) A sky Beyond sky for Me

There's a sky beyond sky for my return.
But I polish the metal of this place into a sheen
and live for an hour gazing into the Unseen.

I know time can't be my ally twice.

I'll emerge from my flag in the form of a bird
never landing on the trees of the garden.

I'll shed my skin and from my language
words of love
will filter down through the poetry of Garcia Lorca
who'll dwell in my bedroom
and see what I've seen of the bedouin moon.

I'll emerge from almond trees as
cotton fluff floating on sea foam.

A stranger passed by
bearing seven hundred years of raw horsepower.

A stranger passed by here
so a stranger could pass by there.
I'll emerge from the wrinkles of my own time for awhile,
a stranger to Syria as well as Andalusia.

This earth is not my heaven, yet this evening
is my evening.

The keys belong to me, as well as the minarets and lamps.
I even belong to myself.

I'm the Adam of two Edens lost to me twice.
Expel me slowly. Kill me slowly

With Garcia Lorca
under my olive tree.

Mahmud Darwish, The Adam of Two Edens: Selected Poems, *ed. Munir Akash and Daniel Moore (1992; Syracuse: Syracuse University Press, 2000), 149–54. Reprinted by permission of Jusoor.*

Guarding the Coasts

Euro-Mediterranean Partnership (1995)

In November 1995, twenty-seven ministers for foreign affairs from countries surrounding the Mediterranean, fifteen from the European Union and twelve from the "pays tiers méditerranéens," met in Barcelona to negotiate a shared future that they named the "Euro-Mediterranean Partnership." They stressed that the goal of this partnership initiative was to strengthen the peace, stability, and development of the region through dialogue, exchange, and cooperation at the political, economic, social, and cultural levels. The establishment of a free-trade zone would be underwritten by "a substantial increase in the European Union's financial assistance to its partners and [. . .] promoting programmes for the benefit of the neediest populations." But they also expressed concern about illegal migrations and terrorism, presumably from the southern and eastern shores of the Mediterranean. This selection is the third section, titled: *Partnership in Social, Cultural and Human Affairs.*

MIGRATION

Given the importance of the issue of migration for Euro-Mediterranean relations, meetings will be encouraged in order to make proposals concerning migration flows and pressures. These meetings will take account of experience acquired, inter alia, under the MED-Migration programme, particularly as regards improving the living conditions of migrants legally established in the Union.

TERRORISM, DRUG TRAFFICKING, AND ORGANISED CRIME

Fighting terrorism will have to be a priority for all the parties. To that end, officials will meet periodically with the aim of strengthening cooperation among police, judicial and other authorities. In this context, consideration will be given, in particular, to stepping up exchanges of information and improving extradition procedures.

Officials will meet periodically to discuss practical measures which can be taken to improve cooperation among police, judicial, customs, administrative and other authorities in order to combat, in particular, drug trafficking and organised crime, including smuggling. All these meetings will be organised with due regard for the need for a differen-

tiated approach that takes into account the diversity of the situation in each country.

Island Melancholy
Margarita Karapanou (1997)

Born in Athens in 1946 and raised between Greece and France, Karapanou studied cinema in Paris before returning to Athens, where she is a nursery school teacher. In 1988 her novel *The Sleepwalker*, which is mentioned below, won the French Prix National du Meilleur Livre Étranger. In this story, the narrator visits the melancholy island of Kalymnos, whose major income was sponge diving. She describes her boat trip there and her contradictory feelings about this alienating and sometimes terrifying place.

Kalymnos is a melancholic island, strange and mysterious. In the streets you see old men and women with black scarves and sad faces, sad looks, tired gaits, bent backs. They have lost their sons to the spongeries, to the dives that bring death along with those priceless sponges or, even worse, leaving them paralyzed. Now, fortunately, this tragedy is over. The diving equipment has improved. Sponge diving today is much safer. Accidents don't happen anymore. The young men can go down to the depths to gather sponges without the same dangers.

I remember, many years ago, the first time I went to Kalymnos. There was a rough sea and I couldn't take the regular boat that goes from Piraeus to Kalymnos. I had to take an airplane to Kos—I am terrified of planes. [. . .] In Kos there was a horrible wind, and after a flight when I was sure the airplane would crash I arrived in Kos, with the wind sweeping everything to and fro. They put me up in a disgusting hotel, in a room with a mattress full of fleas. In the next bed a very polite policeman was sleeping—it reminded me of my novel *The Sleepwalker*.

At around three in the morning the boat finally arrived, and they told us to embark. It would take us to Kalymnos. The winds must have reached almost hurricane conditions. Usually with such winds it is forbidden to sail. The captain shouted some nautical terms that I didn't understand. He kept shouting "shit" and "fuck" until, with great difficulty, the ship moored at the pier. We boarded by a ladder that consisted of a few planks and two ropes to hold on to. "Get in quickly, folks, we're going to sink!" the captain shouted. We stepped onto the sparsely arranged planks, which shook from the stormy sea splashing us up to our waists. I was trembling with fear. It was three in the morning, February, the coldest month of the year. It was raining waterfalls. Night. We couldn't see a thing out of the portholes. All we heard was the terrible sound of the rain pitilessly pelting the ship. We felt the prow of the ship dive deep into the huge waves and then finally emerge, like a drunk, like Rimbaud's "Drunken Boat."

An old lady jumped into my arms and clung to my neck. "I'll never see my son again, the one who went to Australia. I'll never see him again. He's coming back tomorrow to Kalymnos, and we, my child, will be swallowed up by the sea tonight in this rotten wreck. Maybe it's Saturday of the Souls? Oh, God, at least my soul will see my son and welcome him. And then our souls will be reunited after death."

"What's your name?" I asked her.

"Mrs. Aryiro. I am a pastry maker. Kalymnos makes the best *galaktoboureka* in the world, my child, and mine will drive you crazy: lots of butter, lots of cream; our *galaktoboureka* swim in butter. Come tomorrow to the harbor to our store and eat a whole pan."

And though I felt terribly nauseous from the unbelievable swaying of the boat, my mouth got all watery in anticipation. I am a total glutton. The nausea got mixed up with my appetite for a whole pan of *galaktoboureka*. The old lady and I fell asleep in each other's arms.

When we arrived in Kalymnos, my friend was waiting for me. I didn't see any of the island, just like when I crossed New York City in a truck with my eyes shut because I was afraid of the heights and the skyscrapers. It was the same with Kalymnos: I didn't see a thing that first night, such a long time ago now. I went to my friend's house, fell into bed, and slept for twenty-four hours.

The next morning I went for my first walk. It was drizzling. The island was melancholic, remote, as if it had been forgotten by the rest of the world. A mist hung over the sea, which was now calm as oil. It looked like a lake. I went down to the harbor. It was full of cafés and bakeries. I went to Mrs. Aryiro's shop and ate a few pieces of *galaktoboureka*. I drank a glass of cold water. Motorcycles were racing around giddily. Even before I had gotten to the harbor I had seen them racing through the back alleys doing wheelies. I heard an old fisherman near me say that many kids had been killed from such stupidity and carelessness. My desire to leave Kalymnos had become harder to control.

I caught a cab and said, "take me to see a view, if there are any." We left the harbor, passing by incredible beaches with deep black stones eaten away by the sea, beaches that looked like volcanoes. The sea was deep green. The sun had come out. All at once I fell in love with Kalymnos. We drove up into the mountains. We saw the sea from up high sparkling in the sun. We passed by countless beaches.

In the afternoon we went back to the port. Again the same melancholy, the sad wrinkled faces of the women. Again the strong desire to leave Kalymnos, to leave now, immediately. The sea had gotten rough again. There were no boats, not even the little ones that take you to Kos. My relation with Kalymnos was and remains even now strange, like a love affair. Contradictory and paradoxical, at once hate and attraction. All the time I was there, one minute I wanted to leave, the next I wanted to stay forever. When I think of all the places in Greece, only Kalymnos brings on such emotions. Greek landscapes are transparent, clean. They inspire peace or awe or happiness. Epidauros arouses a sense of awe, the Cyclades unbelievable joy; they are prosperous islands. But Kalymnos is a melancholic island. It is the island of sponge divers and poverty. The young people, back then, went diving in the deepest waters to find the biggest, most valuable sponges. Often they either died or came out paralyzed. It is the island of terror. Their mothers wore black clothes, black scarves on their head, and grew old before their time. It is and remains the island of departure and separation: the young boys leave with the ships to seek their fortunes elsewhere, to come back to the island rich, to help their family. They'll make fortunes. But at what a cost. They drown growing older like Odysseus on his never-ending wanderings. [. . .]

The fifth day I left as if I were being chased. Such an irresistible urge to leave. I didn't even wait for the big boat that came later. I took the small one to Kos and felt that I had been rescued from a terrible fate.

From Greece: A Traveler's Literary Companion, *ed. Artemis Leontis (San Francisco: Whereabouts Press, 1997), 239–42. Reprinted by permission of the publisher.*

Blind Dreams
Fadila al-Faruq (1997)

An Algerian writer and journalist who worked for Algerian radio, al-Faruq published her first collection, *A Moment for Love in Beirut*, in 1997. In her story "Homecoming" from that collection, a woman returns from her "exile" in France. Her joy at finally being able to leave the humiliating life of the Arab migrant in Europe gives way to despair when she realizes that she no longer fits in the place that she had considered home.

At last, I was returning from my long journey, liberated from my exile. More accurately, soon I would be liberated from it, and be certain that I had left the foreign country which I had previously chosen out of love, conviction, and "blindness" as my future. I wondered whether I would be overcome by a fit of maddening joy that would make me bend down and kiss the ground at the airport, or was such eccentric behavior reserved for leaders and celebrities? Would I dash toward the taxi stand and hire the most expensive driver who would take me in the shortest time to my small neighborhood? There, I would rid myself of all the ugly images that used to surround me. I would surely not see an Arab woman sitting on the sidewalk and exposing her body to whomever would pay her more because she could not afford the bus fare home, despite all the purchases that she had stashed somewhere. I would then breathe my full share of clean air, unlike the air that I had breathed furtively and shamefully from mouths that deeply offended my dignity.

During my daily routine at work, I often encountered unpleasant tourists—fellow Arabs—who disgraced the streets with their behavior. I would wither in a moment of grief at the sights, swallow my bitterness, and silence my raging protest. After all, I was not one of those reformers. I was not a prophet. I didn't possess King Solomon's magic ring. I had barely enough strength to stand all day in Monsieur Pernand's shop.

"I'm going back to my country, Monsieur Pernand." That was what I had told him, so he would give me my salary before the end of the week. He smiled and said in a sarcastic voice in French, "I will miss you, Brunette." The wicked man had never called me by my name since the day I had come to work for him, although he knew very well that my name was Fatima.

Strands of memory and the vicissitudes of life seemed to overwhelm me. I felt that the plane was suspended in midair, unwilling to advance toward my homeland. I could no longer bear the throbbing heartbeats of yearning and joy when the flight attendant leaned toward me and said, "Madam, please fasten your seat belt. The plane is going to land in a few minutes."

In a few minutes, I would throw myself into the arms of this rough country, and the pleasure of descending would remind me of the swings that I played on in my childhood.

The past was always with me, as if my experiences away from home were testing my love for my country. Here I was now, tired of having been tested and fearing the result.

"Have you come to spend your holiday here?" asked the taxi driver, interrupting my reverie.

"No. I've come back for good," I said.

He laughed, then fell silent for a while. I imagined that he had forgotten me or found it difficult to continue the conversation with me. But he surprised me again.

"Go back to where you came from. This country is not meant for human beings."

"God protect me from you!" I replied and frowned. Then I grumbled to silence him. He surely could not understand the residual fear that paralyzed my steps at the first indication of disapproval for my presence here.

He didn't notice my frown, and my grumbling meant nothing to him. He continued to chatter as I broke into tears when my old neighborhood appeared in the distance. Familiar scenes embraced me, welcoming me, despite the many changes that had taken place. And all those children! How reckless my people were! They bred like rabbits, perhaps because their hours of sleep greatly exceeded their hours of wakefulness. People crammed the streets, as I threaded my way among them. I climbed the old staircase leading to our house, and opened the door, which had no lock. Suddenly my mother stood before me, as if she had anticipated my arrival, and was waiting to embrace me.

Until that moment, I had not known the taste of a mother's tears, but here I was now, sharing her tears and melting away on her scented chest. Then I vanished among the children of my brothers and their wives. I felt as if the sweat dripping from my body was dark, poisonous, reeking of repression, exile, longing, pain, and joy all at once. Resting on my mother's bed, I surrendered again to her scent, and childhood memories came flooding back to me when she squeezed my hand and spoke words that were music to my ears: "I forgive you, my little girl."

As I was falling asleep for the first time in many long years, I heard a voice saying, "Is she going to stay with us despite our cramped living conditions?"

"You're happy with her presents, but not with her being here?"

"I don't mean that Auntie. She has lived most of her life in France, and her nature and way of thinking must have changed. How will she endure the human misery here?"

Then the discussion became angry, throwing me into utter confusion. A chill began to creep slowly into my body. My mother's scent filled my lungs. Her voice argued on my behalf. I was dazed, and my heart fluttered, for my dream was cracking. Voices interrupted each other, rising higher. My dream was collapsing. A child's cry rang out. My dream was shattered. Monsieur Pernand, with his small round glasses, smiled wickedly, then laughed, then burst into guffaws. My dream turned to rubble. Sleep escaped me. Weariness overwhelmed me. My mother's scent wafted against my skin as she bent over me, removed a piece of gum from her mouth, and stuffed it into my ears.

"Homecoming," in Arab Women Writers: An Anthology of Short Stories, *ed. Dalya Cohen-Mor (Albany: SUNY Press, 2005), 214–16.*

The Language of the Other
Jacques Derrida (1996)

In his autobiographical essay about leaving Algeria for France, the philosopher Jacques Derrida (1930–2004) announced that French was not his language, even though he had no other. In a profoundly alienating gesture, he called himself a Franco-Maghrebian who had only one language and it was not his. This linguistic alienation began in 1870 with the Crémieux Decree, which privileged Jews above Muslims of Algeria by making them French citizens. As such they had to speak French, thereby losing linguistic connection to their Arabic or Berber-speaking compatriots. It was the first time that the "French" philosopher had spoken openly and directly about his personal relationship to language. Despite his thirty years dissecting French and making it distinctively his own and strange to others, he here disavows any inherent connection to this language. As a Franco-Maghrebian Jew, his linguistic hybridity was marked by lack: no French, no Arabic, no Hebrew, and no Ladino. The hyphen connecting the Franco (colonizer) and the Maghrebian in him cannot "conceal protests, cries of anger or suffering, the noise of weapons, airplanes and bombs." This is the hyphen that marks all Jews and Muslims who have repeated the 711 crossing of Tariq Ibn Ziyad and the 1492 return through the Pillars of Hercules.

Perhaps we have just described a first circle of generality. Between the model called academic, grammatical, or literary, on the one hand, and spoken language, on the other, *the sea* was there: symbolically an infinite space for all the students of the French school in Algeria, a chasm, an abyss. I did not cross it, body and soul, or body without soul (but will I ever have crossed it, crossed it otherwise?), until, for the first time, sailing across on a boat, on the *Ville d'Alger*, at the age of nineteen. First journey, first crossing of my life, twenty hours of sea-sickness and vomiting—before a week of distress and a child's tears in the sinister boarding house of the "Baz'Grand" (in the *khâgne* of the Louis-le-Grand lycée, in a district I have practically never left since that time).

As some people have already begun to do here and there, we could also "recount" infinitely what was being "recounted" to us about, precisely, the "history of France;" understanding by that what was taught in school under the name of the "history of France:" an incredible discipline, a fable and bible, yet a doctrine of indoctrination almost uneffaceable for children of my generation. Without speaking of geography: not a word about Algeria, not a single one concerning its history and its geography, whereas we could draw the coast of Brittany and the Gironde estuary with our eyes closed. And we had to be familiar with them in depth, in bulk, and in detail; indeed, we used to recite by rote the names of the major towns of all the French departments, the smallest tributaries of the Seine, the Rhône, the Loire, or the Garonne, their sources and their mouths. Those four invisible rivers had nearly the allegorical power of the Parisian statues which represent them, and which I discovered much later with great hilarity: I was confronting the truth of my geography lessons. But let that be. I shall content myself with a few allusions to literature. It is the first thing I received from French education in Algeria, the only thing, in any event, that I enjoyed receiving. The discovery of French literature, the access to this so unique mode of writing that is called "French-literature" was the experience of a world without any tangible continuity with the one in which we lived, with almost nothing in common with our natural or social landscapes.

But this discontinuity was forging another one. And it was becoming, as a result, *doubly* revealing. It undoubtedly exhibited the haughtiness that always separates literary culture—"literariness" as a certain treatment of language, meaning, and reference—from non-literary culture, even if this separation is never reducible to the "pure and simple." But outside this essential heterogeneity, outside this universal hierarchy, a brutal severance was, in this particular case, fostering a more acute partition: the one that separates French literature—its history, its works, its models, its cult of the dead, its modes of transmission and celebration, its "posh districts," its name of authors and editors—from the culture "proper" to "French Algerians." One entered French literature only by using one's accent. I think I have not lost my accent; not everything in my "French Algerian" accent is lost. Its intonation is more apparent in certain "pragmatic" situations (anger or exclamation in familial or familiar surroundings, more often in private than in public, which is quite a reliable criterion for the experience of this strange and precarious distinction). But I would like to hope, I would very much prefer, that no publication permit my "French Algerian" to appear. In the meantime, and until the contrary is proven, I do not believe that anyone can detect *by reading*, if I do not myself declare it, that I am a "French Algerian." I retain, no doubt, a sort of acquired reflex from the necessity of this vigilant transformation. I am not proud of it, I make no doctrine of it, but so it is: an accent—any French accent, but above all a strong southern accent—seems incompatible to me with the intellectual dignity of public speech. (Inadmissible, isn't it? Well, I admit it.) Incompatible, a fortiori, with the vocation of a poetic speech: for example, when I heard René Char read his sententious aphorisms with an accent that struck me as at once comical and obscene, as the betrayal of a truth, it ruined, in no small measure, an admiration of my youth.

The accent indicates a hand-to-hand combat with language in general; it says more than accentuation. Its symptomatology invades writing. That is unjust, but it is so. Throughout the story I am relating, despite everything I sometimes appear to profess, I concede that I have contracted a shameful but intractable intolerance: at least in French, insofar as the language is concerned, I cannot bear or admire anything other than pure French. As I do in all fields, I have never ceased calling into question the motif of "purity" in all its forms (the first impulse of what is called "deconstruction" carries it toward this "critique" of the phantasm or the axiom of purity, or toward the analytical decomposition of a purification that would lead back to the indecomposable simplicity of the origin), I still do not dare admit this compulsive demand for a purity of language except within boundaries of which I can be sure: this demand is neither ethical, political, nor social. It does not inspire any judgment in me. It simply exposes me to suffering when someone, who can be myself, happens to fall short of it. I suffer even further when I catch myself or am caught "red-handed" in the act. (There I go again, speaking about offenses in spite of what I have just disclaimed.) [. . .]

I therefore admit to a purity which is not very pure. Anything but purism. It is, at least, the only impure "purity" for which I dare confess a taste. It is a pronounced taste for a certain pronunciation. I have never ceased learning, especially when teaching, to speak softly, a difficult task for a "pied noir," and especially from within my family, but to ensure that this soft spokenness reveal the reserve of what is thus held in reserve, with difficulty, and with great difficulty, contained by the floodgate, a precarious floodgate that allows one to apprehend the catastrophe. The worst can happen at every turn.

I say "floodgate," a floodgate of the verb and of the voice. I have spoken a great deal about this elsewhere, as if a clever maneuverer, a cybernetics expert of the tone, still kept the illusion of governing a mechanism and of watching over a gauge for the time of a turn. I could have spoken of a boom for waters that are not very navigable. This boom is always threatening to give way. I was the first to be afraid of my own voice, as if it were not mine, and to contest it, even to detest it.

If I have always trembled before what I could say, it was fundamentally [au fond] because of the tone, and not the substance [non du fond]. And what, obscurely, I seek to impart as if in spite of myself, to give or lend to others as well as to myself, to myself as well as to the other, is perhaps a tone. Everything is summoned from an intonation. [. . .]

In the middle of the war, just after landing of the Allied forces in North Africa in November 1942, we witnessed the constitution of a sort of literary capital of France in exile at Algiers: a cultural effervescence, the presence of "famous" writers, the proliferation of journals and editorial initiatives. This also bestows a more theatrical visibility upon Algerian literature of—as they call it—French Expression, whether one is dealing with writers of European origin (such as Camus and many others) or with writers of Algerian origin, who constitute a very different mutation. [. . .]

Within this group, itself deprived of easily accessible models of identification, it is possible to distinguish one of the subgroups to which I belonged to a certain degree. Only to a certain degree, for as soon as one is dealing with questions of culture, language, or writing, the concept of group or class can no longer give rise to a simple topic of exclusion, inclusion, or belonging. This quasi-subgroup will then be that of "indigenous Jews," as they were then called. Being French citizens from 1870 until the laws of exclusion of 1940, they could not properly *identify themselves*, in the double sense of "identifying oneself" and "identifying oneself with" the other. They could not identify themselves in the terms of models, norms, or values whose development was to them alien because French, metropolitan, Christian, and Catholic. In the milieu where I lived, we used to say "the Catholics"; we called all the non-Jewish people "Catholics," even if they were sometimes Protestants, or perhaps even Orthodox: "Catholic" meant anyone who was neither a

Jew, a Berber, nor an Arab. At that time, these young indigenous Jews could easily identify neither with the "Catholics," the Arabs, nor the Berbers, whose language they did not generally speak in that generation. Two generations before them, some of their grandparents still spoke Arabic, at least a certain form of Arabic.

But being already strangers to the roots of French culture, even if that was their only acquired culture, their only educational instruction, and especially, their only language, being strangers, still more radically, for the most part, to Arab or Berber cultures, the greater majority of these young "indigenous Jews" remained, in addition, strangers to Jewish culture: a strangely bottomless alienation of the soul: a catastrophe; others will also say a paradoxical opportunity. Such, in any event, would have been the radical lack of culture [*inculture*] from which I undoubtedly never completely emerged. From which I emerge without emerging from it, by emerging from it completely without my having ever emerged from it. [. . .]

As for language in the strict sense, we could not even resort to some familiar substitute, to some idiom internal to the Jewish community, to any sort of language of refuge that, like Yiddish, would have ensured an element of intimacy, the protection of a "home-of-one's-own" (*un "chez-soi"*) against the language of official culture, a second auxiliary in different socio-semiotic situations. "Ladino" was not spoken in the Algeria I knew, especially not in the big cities like Algiers, where the Jewish population happened to be concentrated.

In a word, here was a disintegrated "community," cut up and cut off. One can imagine the desire to efface such an event or, at the very least, to attenuate it, to make up for it, and also to disclaim it. But whether the desire is fulfilled or not, the traumatism will have taken place, with its indefinite consequences, at once destructuring and structuring. This "community" will have been three times dissociated by what, a little hastily, we are calling interdicts. (1) First of all, it was cut off from both Arabic or Berber (more properly Maghrebian) language and culture. (2) It was also cut off from French, and even European language and culture, which from its viewpoint, only constituted a distanced pole or metropole, heterogeneous to its history. (3) It was cut off, finally, or to begin with, from Jewish memory, and from the history and language that one must presume to be their own, but which, at a certain point, no longer was. [. . .]

My attachment to the French language takes forms that I sometimes consider "neurotic." I feel lost outside the French language. The other languages which, more or less clumsily, I read, decode, or sometimes speak, are languages I shall never inhabit. Where "inhabiting" begins to mean something to me. And dwelling [*demeurer*]. Not only am I lost, fallen, and condemned outside the French language, I have the feeling of honoring or serving all idioms, in a word, of writing the "most" and the "best" when I sharpen the resistance of *my* French, the secret "purity" of my French, the one I was speaking about earlier on, hence its resistance, its *relentless* resistance to translation; translation into *all* languages, including another such French.

Not that I am cultivating the untranslatable. Nothing is untranslatable, however little time is given to the expenditure or expansion of a competent discourse that measures itself against the power of the original. But the "untranslatable" remains—should remain, as my law tells me—the poetic economy of the idiom, the one that is important to me, for I would die even more quickly without it, and which is important to me, myself to myself, where a given formal "quantity" always fails to restore the singular event of the original, that is, to let it be forgotten once recorded, to carry away its number, the prosodic shadow of its quantum. Word for word, if you like, syllable by syllable. From the moment the economic equivalence—strictly impossible, by the way—is renounced, everything can be translated, but in a loose translation, in the loose sense of the word "translation." I am not even talking about poetry, only about prosody, about metrics (accent and quantity of the time in pronunciation). In a sense, nothing is untranslatable; but *in another sense*, everything is untranslatable; translation is another name for the impossible. In another sense of the word "translation," of course, and from one sense to the other—it is easy for me always to hold firm between these two hyperboles which are fundamentally the same, and always translate each other. [. . .]

But above all, and here is the most fatal question: how is it possible that this language, the only language that this monolingual speaks, and is destined to speak, forever and ever, is not his? How can one believe that it remains always mute for the one who inhabits it, and whom it inhabits most intimately, that it remains *distant, heterogeneous, uninhabitable, deserted?* Deserted like a desert in which one must grow, makes things grow, build, and project up to the idea of a route, and the trace of a return, *yet another language?* [. . .]

To inhabit: this is a value that is quite *disconcerting* and equivocal; one never inhabits what one is in the habit of calling inhabiting. There is no possible habitat without the difference of this exile and this nostalgia.

Most certainly. That is all too well known. But it does not follow that all exiles are equivalent. From this shore, yes, *from this* shore or this common drift, all expatriations remain singular.

Jacques Derrida, Monolingualism of the Other, or, The Prosthesis of Origin, *trans. Patrick Mensah (Stanford: Stanford University Press, 1996), 44–48, 50, 52–58. Reprinted by permission of the publisher.*

Partners Adrift
Fawzi Mellah (2000)

In 1997 the Tunisian journalist Fawzi Mellah joined five Africans on a perilous boat trip to Europe. They were part of a growing number of clandestines, what might be termed Mediterranean boat people, escaping destitution with dreams of streets paved with gold. Like I. F. Stone over fifty years earlier, he wanted to know firsthand what these economic fugitives experienced from the moment they left Tunis for Sicily and then on to their final destinations.

My neighbor (let's call him Jeff) told me that he came from Constantine. He had tried to matriculate in a French university but had not been given a visa. So he was going to France by way of Italy to join friends who had preceded him. He was hoping to see them in Rome.

He started to ask me questions, but I didn't have time to respond. We had to be quiet because a trembling light coming right at us seemed to make the captain nervous. He slowed down, not because we were going fast but in order to reduce the sound of the motor.

The lights danced a bit and then receded into the distance. [. . .]

Fishermen? Coast guard? Another ferry going south? We'll never know.

We picked up the thread of the conversation and were joined by a Tunisian. Solid and serious he was just going to Palermo. He knew the city well but wasn't planning to stay there or to go north. He was just interested in Palermo.

[. . .]

We shared snacks we had just bought (what felt like an eternity). We ate oranges and smoked. The Libyan offered us some chocolate, saying that there was no way he was staying in Sicily. He was planning to go to Rome because, he assured us, things were easier in Rome than anywhere else in Europe. He said he could have obtained a visa but the

Italian consulate had taken its time to respond because Rome systematically investigated Libyan citizens.

From afar some twinkling lights surprised us again and forced us to be silent. This time, however, the captain did not reduce speed. He was just concerned to identify the source of the anxiety.

Its size and the number of its lights indicated that it must be a cargo boat or a liner going in the same direction as we were, just a little to the north.

A liner?

In my other life, I often traveled by liner.

Memories of that time; I began to imagine what the passengers were doing. Some of them must be at the bar listening to music or drinking. Others must be on the bridge looking at the stars, and some must be in their cabins reading the newspaper or caressing a woman or perhaps sleeping. In a few hours, they would arrive fresh and fit, in a bright harbor. Rich among the rich; nobles among nobles. Fortified with visas, addresses of people they know and money they openly declare at customs, they can afford to look the world in the eye, will not have to hide behind a borrowed name, will not have to struggle against sleep, will not have to make up some story about losing a passport, will have absolutely no worries about cops. [. . .]

Could they even only imagine that at the distance of voices from their cabins six clandestine travelers, wracked by fear and cold, were going in the same direction as them [. . .] but probably not in the same world?

I dozed on these memories and images of another planet, the human one that I had just left a few hours ago.

Fawzi Mellah, Clandestins en Mediterranée *(Tunis: Cérès Editions, 2000), 29, 31–33. Trans. miriam cooke.*

Mediterranean Thinking
Franco Cassano (2001)

This is a poetic meditation on the role of the south and particularly of the Mediterranean in connected thinking. The Italian sociologist Franco Cassano (b. 1943) imagines a geographically determined project that allows for the juxtaposition of contradictions without need for resolution. Cassano radically opposes all forms of fundamentalist thinking.

1. THINKING SOUTHERN

As time goes by, the identification seems irreversible: in the public opinion of western countries, the word "south" has become synonymous with backwardness, hunger, ethnic atrocities, refugees, and mass exodus—images of pain and poverty. The south is the disease of the world, the part without hope which will be able to smile again only when (and if) it becomes north itself; a quiet province of the northwestern world, an overdue and failed replica of the western form of life. The pain that the developed world feels for the south, its television participation in the problems of the south and its philanthropic campaigns, do little else but perpetuate a sentiment of superiority. These noble emotions produce limited practical results; instead, they reaffirm the most unsympathetic fundamentalist tendencies of the world's northwest: they confirm its belief that the west is the incarnation of perfection and therefore the universal remedy. The south itself often shares this sentiment of frustration and thinks of itself as an error, a fault, a hell to be escaped, an unhappy prison from which the strongest and the bravest have to break away in order to save themselves.

And yet this is not the right road, and now is the time to say it, even though stating it runs contrary to the predominant opinion. The south must re-conquer its own outlook: it has to learn to view itself independently and not through northwestern eyes, which see the south as an anomaly, an anachronism, an accumulation of pathologies that will disappear only if and when the south becomes something other than itself—if and when it becomes northwest. *Southern thought is first and foremost this movement, this epistemological motion through which the south begins to think about itself on its own, re-conquering the ancient dignity of the subject of thought. Southern thought is primarily a way to think southern while succinctly criticizing the pretense of northwestern thinking that presents itself as a universal and, therefore, the only way of thinking.* The first act of southern thinking is to unmask this false neutrality, to dismantle the western pretense that proposes itself and its own way of life as a model to be exported to the entire world. Without this initial friction, without this discontinuity, not only will the south lose all autonomy, but its thinking will also be impoverished and it will remain prisoner of the single form of thinking elaborated by the northwest for the entire world. The freedom of thought and the cultural autonomy of the south have a common interest, and a long road ahead to travel together.

The south is not, in fact, an error, an obstacle to development, a paralysing past that never goes away. Instead it is an extraordinary resource for the future. The rhythms of the south, its slowness—what leading brand-name watches, newspaper hacks and intellectuals of *"la pensée unique"* view as its sins—are only an idea of time radically different from the Faustian one dominating and suffocating western life. These rhythms represent a scandal only for the clerics of our social order, for those fanatical, calloused (and well-paid) modernizers who travel the world preaching development as the mandatory form of salvation. Their tiresome litany is called thought, but in reality it is an instrument of production, little more than a lubricant. Our way of life is, in fact, like a vehicle that is being continuously perfected and is becoming faster and faster, equipped with all the comforts (from air conditioning to telephone and radio), but utterly lacking brakes. Everything is based on the elimination of brakes. This unfortunate thought is born when we surrender ownership of our own time; it is based on the foolish premise that progress coincides with the continuous acceleration of life, that to slow down, or to get off last, is impossible, a sort of suicide. For this parody of thought, slowness is only the ancient history, the not yet attained velocity of our way of life; it is something to overcome, something to be discarded as soon as possible.

Southern thought starts from the opposite direction: for the south slowness is the highest form of any experience, it is the time of the wise ones and the kings, of those who are not owned by time but are capable of controlling it; it is the time of a profound agreement between the body and the world, of wisdom that must be awaited, that is attainable only with patience, maybe even by walking down the street or stopping to do something else. Slowness is this lateral wisdom, this exposing oneself to unexpected encounters, to curved trajectories; it is the love of side streets. Without slowness not only is it impossible to obtain true education (unless one confuses education with those intensive and exhausting courses, the corporate brainwashing so popular today), but meditation, authentic knowledge of another person and relationships also become impossible. Without slowness, democracy is likely to be impossible (for it requires not only discussion, but also enjoyment in the same). Contemplation of beauty is impossible. Love is impossible (for it requires ambush, trepidation, deceit, prolonged fantasizing, and the slow pleasure of conquest). Even faith, at which one arrives only following a crisis and time in the desert, is impossible.

Civilizations that we term undeveloped are, on the contrary, more developed in other spheres of life. They hold knowledge and capacity that we are unable to recognize or appreciate. They have a different language, a different idea of the relationship between people, a different relationship with time and space. To flatten other cultures' tri-dimensional geometry to the level geometry of our yardstick is not only a sign of limitation similar to the one mocked by Edwin Abbott in his *Flatland*, but is also an act of true cultural genocide.

[. . .]

2. THE MEDITERRANEAN: A SEA AGAINST ALL FUNDAMENTALISMS

This is the point that allows us to understand the roots of southern thinking in the Mediterranean: as its name suggests, the Mediterranean is a sea *between* lands, a sea that separates and links at the same time, a sea that never becomes an abyss that knows the pleasure of leaving, but also that of returning. It is therefore very far from fundamentalism of either land or sea.

Fundamentalism of the land is what chains men and women, immures them with their belongings, shreds their individualization, and prevents them from taking the road of the sea, from leaving, from encountering other worlds. Freedom cannot be conceived without this rift between fundamentalism of the land and the desire to leave, without those sailors whom Plato distrusts for obvious reasons. A land surrounded by land without the sea does not know freedom, or is afraid of it because it was never able to see itself from afar or from the outside. It does not know the adventure and the romance of the individual, the intoxication of departure and the desire of return. Fundamentalism of the land knows only fidelity, and sacrifices every other value to it, impaling those who try to escape. It does not know shades and complexities; it divides humanity into faithful ones and traitors. In every freedom it sees the roots of looseness and abuse. It lives between prohibitions and revenge.

There are fundamentalisms other than this telluric one, however, with its abhorrence of mobility and restlessness. From the opposite direction, there is the fundamentalism of the sea, born when the sea obliterates the beauty and the sweetness of the land, the call of anchoring and return. Here the sea becomes absolute as it eliminates shorelines and borders. It becomes an ocean: the vast uneasy expanse where people live their own eradication, having deserted an anchor, a mooring, a refuge, a home. This sea without land, this unstoppable liquidity distorts human freedom and transforms it into allegory of any kind of bondage, on the one hand, and an incurable dependence on the prosthetics of unleashed technology, on the other. In a completely liquid world, the only solid dwelling is given by technical structures: people live aboard technological devices, with human power directly proportional to bewilderment.

[. . .]

While the fundamentalism of the land sacrifices everything to fidelity, the fundamentalism of the sea makes the individual unfaithful even to himself.

The Mediterranean has always been a frontier sea stretching between three continents, a sea which knows three religions of the book and their internal variants, and which has known many before this sea brought philosophy and democracy to the world. It knows the equilibrium of land and sea: not of land alone, or belonging, group, ethnicity, state, language: nor of sea alone, the individuals wrapped up in themselves, irresponsible, the ridiculous isolation of the individual caused by utilitarianism, the silent and frigid fundamentalism of economy. The Mediterranean, which is at the same time departure and return, guards a complex consciousness, the desire to leave in those who remain, and the desire to return in those who depart. Its hero is Ulysses, the hero of voyage and return, and not Captain Ahab, absolute metaphysical surge without borders and ties, who goes down taking Starbuck, a courageous man who, nevertheless, wanted to return to the land, with him to the bottom of the ocean. Ahab wants to kill the white whale, but in the end it is the ocean that wins.

This ancient sense of measure, this consciousness forced into complexity by geography and history, bestows upon the Mediterranean a great epistemological force: it is at the same time a place of division and connection. Those who sail off are not leaving for suicidal metaphysical adventures, but to reach lands, which, on some clear mornings, they can see, to their trepidation and surprise, from the shore of departure. The Mediterranean is the sea where, precisely because one encounters the others there, the real game begins, the one that can lead to hostility and confrontation, or to the road to peace. However, peace in the Mediterranean is not born from domination, annihilation and silencing of others, but from a balance, from mutual recognition, from respect for the dignity of others, from translations, from curiosity and knowledge. The sea that stands *between* the lands knows very well that the frontier is a place where the richest and the most complex personalities are gathered, precisely because the old worn-out litany of identity is absent, and one can experience diversity.

Those who stand on the frontier know that there are many ways to speak, pray, eat, love and die, and surely once in their life have thought that each civilization has its own wisdom and dignity. The Mediterranean is a sea of this difficult but essential mutual recognition, of building the difficult harmony among people who, even though they cherish their own identity, are still capable of understanding that contact with others expands the spirit, that it does not represent danger but enrichment.

3. THE MULTI-DIRECTIONAL MEDITERRANEAN

The Mediterranean exposes the limits of any uni-versalism; it clearly shows that the unity of the human race depends on the plurality of directions, instead of their *reductio ad unum*, reduction to the strongest one who dominates communication and dictates the pace of life. It clearly demonstrates that peace will not come from overpowering, not even an overpowering carried out by free-trading modernization, the hurricane that will engulf the entire planet, spreading an oceanic uprooting of economy and the domination of Monsieur le Capital's whims. These days everyone bows to the will of the markets and dismantles their instruments of social protection in order to attract investments. Even states, like prostitutes, make themselves pretty to catch Monsieur le Capital who, free and unfaithful, passes by, asks the price, then chooses, and stays until he has extracted the maximum amount of pleasure and profit from his investment. The fundamentalism of the west has its shrines in the Cities of the world; its clerics are the priests of finance, its breviaries the quotation lists, its fanatical impulses the disastrous (oceanic) and unpredictable convulsions of the stock market.

It is not my intention to demonize an extraordinary culture, its miracles and victories; they are before the world, displayed with pride in a thousand colorful images, coveted by everyone. The pathology is the epistemological violence that is being committed, in the fact that a way of life in one part of the world aspires to become the way of life of the entire planet. This all-encompassing ambition, this violation of limits and of measure, is the big problem. When a civilization overwhelms its riverbanks and floods the surrounding area like a swelling river, it ends up washing away other cultures, as it imposes on them its own rules of the game. Other cultures, being more dedicated to their own games, are obviously less apt to play. The conquering civilization, even though it claims to be secular, eventually demands a cold conversion to the religion of competition and pursuit, nourishes the flames of fundamental-ism again, increases the resentment of the losers, and fully multiplies the martyrs of faith who are trying to take revenge on Satan with the ferocious desperation of terrorism.

The road cannot be the aggressive and destructive spiral, the mutual affirmation of auto-referential closure, the harmful infinity between McWorld and Jihad that [*political scientist*] Benjamin Barber talks about. The Mediterranean stands there reminding us that between fundamen-talism of the land or the sea there is a balance of measure. There exists a form of life capable of reconciling freedom and protection, a civilization that knows the beauty of belonging, but also of leaving, a civilization ac-customed to a multi-dimensional geometry, a civilization that is never puzzled by the complexity of life.

This role of the Mediterranean must also be reinforced against the skeptics, against those who think that reference to the Mediterranean is only a suggestive anachronism, a prisoner of nostalgia. The Medi-terranean, they say, was a great cultural center. This is true, but only in antiquity, they add. Modernism is born from the overcoming of the Mediterranean and the yielding to the spirit of a world that is proceed-ing toward the west, as Hegel puts it, and has long left behind a sea, which seems like a small lake compared to vast oceanic spaces. The era of technology flies above the Mediterranean with its satellites and looks at it with tenderness from the heights of its power. The Mediterranean is a magnificent infancy, the return to which is obviously not possible.

These critical observations are joined by another one, which is based on a consideration that claims to be realistic. The Mediterranean is, it is said, a sea marked by conflicts, where ties are impossible to build, because it is a place on the line of conflict between civilizations that [*political scientist*] Samuel Huntington speaks about, in the telluric zone which for centuries has been the place of encounter and confrontation between Islam and Christianity. It is precisely this image of the Medi-terranean as a periphery and a southeastern frontier of the west that allows us to discern the heart of the problem and to respond to the ob-jections cited.

In the first place, the fact that the Mediterranean is a sea of conflicts attests to its contemporary quality. Anything but the sea of the past! If the Mediterranean belonged only to memory it would not be guarded by the Fifth Fleet. The presence of conflicts shows that some of the most pressing issues of the planet are found in their highest concentration on this sea, that the most important game is played there and not some-where else. In short, the second observation invalidates the first one, because it shows in the most convincing way that the Mediterranean is not a delicate dream-like nostalgia but belongs to the present.

Secondly, it is precisely the existence of these conflicts that makes us understand the problem that the Mediterranean puts before the entire planet. It places us mercilessly before the following alternative: we could decide to make a ditch out of it, as Huntington seems to suggest, where the fundamentalism of turbans and of the stock market confront each other. In that case the Mediterranean would become a mere trench, the frontline interests that have their heart and brain somewhere else, intent on reproducing only its marginality and subordination.

Or we could try to reverse this scenario by re-attributing to the Mediterranean the role of a new center, a paradoxical center, because it is situated on the borderline. To do this would be to wager a global bet on the possibility of all cultures coexisting even though they emerge with a head start on their shores. Instead of war grounds for others, the Mediterranean could try to bring to its surface the ancient knowledge embedded in its geography; it could give form to criticism of all fundamentalisms, deconstruct hostility between the principal points, and launch another page of history, in which land and sea, belonging and freedom, slowness and speed, are no longer at war with each other but, respectful of balance and measure, together collaborate to bring about a higher form of life.

As we have seen, fundamentalism is not a phenomenon related to a particular religion, rather it grows where one culture sees the other cultures as pathological, and offers itself as a remedy; where it loses sight of its own limits and particularities and strives to become universal therapy. No culture is immune to this risk, unless endowed with a strong and continuous awareness of its own limits. It is for this reason that the contemporary quality of the Mediterranean is not, as some simple mind might suggest, an idea born from nostalgia and the past. This sea between the lands continuously sends to each of those lands the awareness of their own limits and the necessity of encounters with other lands; it continuously re-elaborates the awareness of plurality of languages, it reminds them that there is no uni-versal language which is sacred and equidistant to all human beings.

The idea that God spoke in one language alone (be it Greek, Aramaic, Latin, Arabic or English) is first of all blasphemous, because it limits God's power and knowledge. The only sacred language is that of translation, the motion that leads us to depart from our language to encounter and get to know another, the incessant effort that presumes the inescapable existence of several languages. Surely the plurality of languages, which forces us to resort to translation, wastes time, but this waste of time prevents us from reducing others to ourselves; it reminds us that humanity is multiple; it is a spiritual exercise against loss of measure. That is why, in its way, the act of translation (*trans-ducere*: to bring to the other side) is a secular form of prayer, a crossing that breaks through every closure. Peace is made of many verbs that begin with a prefix *trans*, of the gathering of practices that, while bordering continually on one another, build unknown and transversal ties.

4. THE MEDITERRANEAN PLANET

The Mediterranean also embodies the idea of rebalancing the human race, of rebalancing its capacity to have a multiple voice. It is not only, as often is believed, a place of convergence of all the colors and all the music contained in a sole rich and affluent model of life, but it also manages to preserve the multiplicity of vital rhythms of this planet, the richness of its stories, the plurality of its shrines. It is about something much more ambitious than an invitation to participate in an appealing and inviting version of the northeast extended to all humanity; it is about *reformulating the idea of richness*.

The friction in the Mediterranean thus unexpectedly becomes a resource, the premise necessary to understand the idea that quality of life requires multi-dimensionality, it needs to consist of several indicators and not only those that register the quantity of merchandise purchased. This idea of a quality of life depends, above all, on the quality of relationships and the quality of goods (public goods), the enjoyment of which does not require the exclusion of others. It requires the capacity to allow the speed of real time and prayer time to coexist side by side. It consists in the freedom of an individual and the feeling of dignity and honor. It is made of coexistence of times, and it is inhabited by pilgrims and tourists, by people of doubt as well as people of faith, by people of the sea and those of the desert. It favors the uncomfortable but vital coexistence of various experiences. It is not a quiet, bourgeois inner setting, far away from the pushing and screaming of the world; it is not a hypocritical sleepy order; it is not an Austrian garden or a Swiss silence; instead it is the quality that is not considered far removed from the unpredictable creativity of life, from commotions and arrivals. It is the quality known by all those who put their houses on the borderline, and who build transits and passages untroubled by telluric quakes.

Certainly the need for a quality of life that cannot be reduced to economic indicators, the need to understand deserving behaviors as "well-meaning actions" rather than quotations of profit sharing goes well beyond the boundaries of the Mediterranean. It is not by chance that books by Peter Handke, Milan Kundera, Sten Nadolny as well as the best films by Wim Wenders, Werner Herzog, Theo Angelopolous, Abbas Kiarostami, and the last film by David Lynch entitled *The Straight Story* (1999) speak about slowness. The protagonist of the latter film, an older man from the Midwest, upon learning that his estranged brother is about to die, decides to visit him. He sets out on a long journey on a lawn mower, the only vehicle he can drive at his age. The journey thus becomes a long pilgrimage, the rediscovery of the course of his life, a necessary purification for the encounter with the one who has become distant, even though he was born from the same parents. Slowness succeeds where speed would have failed; it reconciles because it allows for the display of the intense desire to meet again, and favors a transformation that would not have happened had the protagonist traveled at a different speed.

This need for a multiplicity of times, for an experience that can relativize modernism and unmask instead of attacking its rhetoric, comes from people of most diverse origins; it does not belong to a particular ideology, but comes from a re-emergent need for measure and balance. When this measure appears, a culture can thematize its contingency and accept a higher degree of reflection, from which height it can see itself side by side with others, *between* others, while it also remains faithful to itself. Through its situated, reflective placement, it can become a citizen of the world. In this sense the Mediterranean is everywhere, wherever there is curiosity for that part of well-being that cannot be bought, but has to be won with great effort; curiosity for all those things that we have thrown away, and which today we are trying to dig up from the garbage like dogs. Besides, if it is true that today technology allows us to see the Mediterranean as a big lake, it is also true that this same technology, by shortening distances, makes the oceans small and similar to the Mediterranean, so they can be crossed in a smaller amount of time than used to be required to go from Venice to Algiers. Far from belonging to the past, the Mediterranean speaks to us of the future, of coexistence and quality to be pursued.

The Mediterranean exists, therefore, wherever people respect others, wherever they greet each other, wherever they sit down for the pleasure of conversation and telling stories, wherever they eat and drink together, wherever they become friends and spend time together until late at night, wherever they waste time because this is the only way to gain time. The Mediterranean exists wherever people speculate that perfection can have several faces, that it can come from work, from angels, from fantasy, but also from the tactile pleasure of the possibility of coexistence, from the highest, indolent agreement with the world. Finally, the fact that these meeting points faced the same old sea is not really important. It could be Rio or Tokyo, San Francisco or Athens: *the Mediterranean is wherever one strives to bridge the distance between lands.* It is wherever the idea of the individual manages to emerge, expanding the oppressive straits of social bonds, but also where freedom, instead of recoiling into an autistic spiral, knows how to accept the responsibilities toward all men and women, toward all human beings and toward that fragile balance on which we all depend. Until recently all of that was called "Creation" or "God's abundance." Today, even those who lost their faith somewhere along the road could decide that those words are worth preserving, not for bigoted regurgitation, but because they help us remember that this infinite mystery that surrounds us is much more than a mere resource at the disposal of the insatiable metabolism of human beings.

Franco Cassano, "Southern Thought," trans. Sandra Palaich, Thesis Eleven 67, no. 1 (November 2001): 1–4, 5–10. Reprinted by permission of Sage Publications Ltd.

Further Readings

Abulafia, David, ed. *The Mediterranean in History*. Los Angeles: Getty, 2003.

Abu-Lughod, J. L. *Before European Hegemony: The World System AD 1250–1350*. New York: Oxford University Press, 1989.

Alcalay, Ammiel. *After Jews and Arabs: Remaking Levantine Culture*. Minneapolis: University of Minnesota Press, 1993.

Balta, Paul, ed. *La Méditerranée réinventée. Réalités et espoirs de la coopération*. Paris: la Découverte, 1992.

Black, Jeremy. *Italy and the Grand Tour*. New Haven: Yale University Press, 2003.

Boorstin, Daniel J. *The Discoverers: A History of Man's Search to Know his World and Himself*. New York: Random House, 1983.

Braudel, Fernand. *The Mediterranean and the Mediterranean World in the Age of Philip II*. 2 vols. Trans. Siân Reynolds. New York: Harper and Row, 1972 (orig. French edition, 1949).

Brown, Carl L., ed. *Imperial Legacy: The Ottoman Imprint on the Balkans and the Middle East*. New York: Columbia University Press, 1996.

Brummet, Palmira. *Ottoman Seapower and Levantine Diplomacy in the Age of Discovery*. Albany: SUNY Press, 1994.

Fabre, Thierry, ed. *Rencontres d'Averroès. La Méditerranée entre la raison et la foi*. Marseilles: Babel, 1994.

Goffman, Daniel. *The Ottoman Empire and Early Modern Europe*. Cambridge: Cambridge University Press, 2002.

Goitein, Shlomo D. *A Mediterranean Society: The Jewish Communities of the Arab World as Portrayed in the Documents of the Geniza*. 6 vols. Berkeley: University of California Press, 1967–93.

Gutas, Dimitri. *Greek Thought, Arabic Culture: The Graeco-Arabic Translation Movement in Baghdad and Early ʿAbbāsid Society (2nd–4th/8th–10th centuries)*. New York: Routledge, 1998.

Harris, William V., ed. *Rethinking the Mediterranean*. New York: Oxford University Press, 2005.

Hillenbrand, Carole. *The Crusades: Islamic Perspectives*. New York: Routledge, 1999.

Horden, Peregrine, and Nicholas Purcell. *The Corrupting Sea: A Study of Mediterranean History*. Malden, Ma.: Blackwell, 2000.

Lewis, Martin W., and Karen E. Wigen. *The Myth of Continents: A Critique of Metageography*. Berkeley: University of California Press, 1997.

Matvejevic, P. *Mediterranean: A Cultural Landscape*. Berkeley: University of California Press, 1999.

McAlister, Melani. *Epic Encounters: Culture, Media and U.S. Interests in the Middle East since 1945*. Berkeley: University of California Press, 2001.

Menocal, María Rosa. *Ornament of the World: How Muslims, Jews, and Christians Created a Culture of Tolerance in Medieval Spain*. Boston: Little, Brown, 2002.

Norwich, John Julius. *The Middle Sea: A History of the Mediterranean*. New York: Doubleday, 2006.

Pratt, Mary Louise. *Imperial Eyes: Travel Writing and Transculturation*. New York: Routledge, 1992.

Raven, Susan. *Rome in Africa*. 3rd ed. New York: Routledge, 1993.

Sparto, A. *Mediterraneo. L'utopia possibile*. Palermo: Ila Palma, 1999.

Talbert, Richard J. A., ed. *Barrington Atlas of the Greek and Roman World*. Princeton, N.J.: Princeton University Press, 2000.

Index

Page numbers in italics indicate illustrations.